From Language to Multimodality

Functional Linguistics
Series Editor: Robin Fawcett, Cardiff University

This series publishes monographs that seek to understand the nature of language by exploring one or other of various cognitive models or in terms of the communicative use of language. It concentrates on studies that are in, or on the borders of, various functional theories of language.

Published:

Functional Dimensions of Ape-Human Discourse
Edited by James D. Benson and William S. Greaves

System and Corpus: Exploring Connections
Edited by Geoff Thompson and Susan Hunston

Text Type and Texture
Edited by Geoff Thompson and Gail Forey

Meaningful Arrangement: Exploring the Syntactic Description of Texts
Edward McDonald

Explorations in Stylistics
Andrew Goatly

Systemic Functional Perspectives of Japanese: Descriptions and Applications
Edited by Elizabeth Thomson and William Armour

Forthcoming:

The Texture of Casual Conversation: A Multidimensional Interpretation
Diana Slade

A Multimodal Approach to Classroom Discourse
Kay O'Halloran

Reading Visual Narratives: Inter-image Analysis of Children's Picture Books
Clare Painter

An Introduction to the Grammar of Old English: A Systemic Functional Approach
Michael Cummings

Morphosyntactic Alternations in English: Functional and Cognitive Perspectives
Edited by Pilar Guerrero Medina

From Language to Multimodality
New Developments in the Study of Ideational Meaning

Edited by
Carys Jones and
Eija Ventola

LONDON OAKVILLE

Published by Equinox Publishing Ltd.

UK: 1 Chelsea Manor Studios, Flood Street, London SW3 5SR
USA: DBBC, 28 Main Street, Oakville, CT 06779

www.equinoxpub.com

First published 2008. This paperback edition published 2010.

British Library Cataloguing-in-Publication Data
A catalogue record for this book is available from the British Library.

ISBN-13 978 1 84553 911 5 (paperback)

Library of Congress Cataloging-in-Publication Data

From Language to Multimodality: new developments in the study of Ideational meaning: / edited by Carys Jones and Eija Ventola.
p. cm. — (Functional linguistics)
Includes bibliographical references and index.
ISBN 978-1-84553-347-2 (hb)
1. Semantics. I. Jones, Carys. II. Ventola, Eija.

P325.N489 2008
401'.43—dc22

2008017428

Typeset by S.J.I. Service, New Delhi
Printed and bound in Great Britain by Lightning Source, Milton Keynes, UK

Contents

Information about the authors

Lynne Flowerdew is a senior lecturer in the Language in Education Research Centre at the University of Leeds. Her main research interests include corpus linguistics, discourse analysis, genre analysis and systemic-functional linguistics. She has published very many articles on various aspects of corpus linguistics. Her forthcoming book, *Corpus-based Analyses of the Problem-Solution Pattern: A Phraseological Approach,* is to be published by John Benjamins in the Studies in Corpus Linguistics series.

Chris Gallagher is a lecturer in the English Language Program at the International Christian University in Tokyo, Japan. He holds an MSc in TESP from Aston University and has co-authored a number of articles on novice academic writing with Anne McCabe, including a short piece in the Language Awareness section of the *Macmillan Dictionary of English.* His research interests include genre-based literacy and register development in novice writing.

Sheena Gardner has recently joined Birmingham University as Reader in Educational Linguistics having been Associate Professor in the Centre for English Language Teacher Education at the University of Warwick for several years. She teaches Systemic Functional Linguistics, Grammar Teaching and TESP. Her research centres on the analysis of spoken and written educational discourse including the discourse of early years classroom-based assessment of English as an additional language, and genres of assessed university student writing in the British Academic Written English corpus.

Birgit Huemer studied German literature, applied linguistics and mathematics at the University of Vienna, Austria. After her studies she worked as web designer, technical project manager and usability engineer in industry. She is now research associate at the Department of Linguistics for a FWF funded project 'Supporting students' writing at Austrian universities.' She is working on digital arts for her PhD at the department of Linguistics in Vienna. Her scientific interests are academic writing, design, discourse analysis, digital arts, genre theory, human-computer interaction, multimodality, semiotics, systemic functional linguistics and usability.

Carys Jones is Coordinator of Academic Communication and Study Skills for the Florence Nightingale School of Nursing and Midwifery at King's College, University of London. She has also had a long association with the Department of Education where she completed her doctoral research into how language helps learning: an area which continues to engage her main interests. She founded and runs LIHERG (Language in Higher Education Research Group), an international organisation that supports novice and established researchers and practitioners in the field of academic language and literacy. Her publications include chapters and articles on the role of language in science, in nursing and midwifery; on Vygotskian and Hallidayan perspectives on language as a learning tool; and on discourse analysis from an SFL perspective.

Julia Lavid is Professor of English Linguistics at the Department of English Philology (Universidad Complutense of Madrid), where she lectures on a number of linguistic subjects from a functional perspective and co-edits the international journal *Estudios Ingleses de la Universidad Complutense.* Her research interests focus on leading-edge applications of functional analysis, especially those involving technological and multilingual issues with a special emphasis on English and Spanish. She has published extensively on these topics, and led a number of international and national projects. She heads an active research group at her University on the contrastive functional analysis of English and Spanish, and is currently working on a systemic-functional grammar of Spanish, contrastive with English, to be published by Equinox.

Arianna Maiorani teaches Systemic Functional Linguistics and Multimodal text analysis applied to advertising and websites. Her area of research also covers English and French Literature and Cultural Studies. Her most recent publications include: 'Karen Blixen in Africa: language as a means to preserve a disappearing world', *Cross-Cultural Encounters: Identity, Gender, Representation*, edited by M. Silver and G. Buonanno, Roma, Officina Edizioni, 2005, pp. 147–157, and '"Reloading" movies into commercial reality: a multimodal analysis of "The Matrix" trilogy's promotional posters', in *Semiotica* (2007) 166, 45–67.

Ana Martín-Úriz is Full Professor of English/Applied Linguistics at the Universidad Autónoma de Madrid. Her research and teaching interests include Second Language Acquisition/Learning, and Second/Foreign Language writing. In the last ten years she has directed several research projects on writing in English in Spanish schools, and published, with Rachel Whittaker, the results of the first stage in a book, *La composición como comunicación: una experiencia en las aulas de inglés en bachillerato* (2005). Her ongoing project 'Writing in English in secondary school: genres and registers' studies texts from a functional perspective.

Anne McCabe is Director of the ESL Program at Saint Louis University's Madrid campus, where she also teaches linguistics and writing. She holds a PhD in Language Studies from Aston University, UK, and has published a number of articles on student writing from a systemic-functional perspective. She has recently co-edited two books with Rachel Whittaker and Mick O'Donnell on literacy development: *Language and Literacy* and *Advances in Language and Education*, Continuum.

Ann Montemayor-Borsinger works at Instituto Balseiro, Cuyo National University: a graduate and postgraduate centre for physicists and engineers in Patagonia, Argentina. She is also Invited Professor and Researcher at the Institute of Linguistics, University of Buenos Aires. Her research focuses on discourse analysis and systemic functional theory in English and Spanish. Her most recent publications include 'Text-type and Texture: the potential of Theme for the study of research writing development', 'El análisis de la organización del discurso literario en español: una propuesta desde la lingüística sistémico funcional', and the book *Tema: una perspectiva funcional de la organización del discurso* (Ediciones Universitarias de Buenos Aires – EUDEBA).

Nick Moore is a Senior Lecturer at Etisalat University College, United Arab Emirates. He has also worked with language learners and teachers in Turkey, Brazil, Oman, and United Kingdom. His research interests centre on the Textual metafunction.

Susana Murcia is a lecturer at the Universidad Autónoma de Madrid (UAM) within the Department of Filología Inglesa. She completed her PhD on instructional texts in English and Spanish in 1999, under joint supervision between the Universities of Stirling and Córdoba. She has taught Spanish in several UK universities (Stirling, Strathclyde, The Open University), and English in Spain (Córdoba, Jaén and UAM). She has worked for the international branding company Enterprise IG developing language guidelines for Spanish companies.

Mick O'Donnell is currently a research fellow in the Informatics Department at Universidad Autónoma de Madrid. He completed his PhD in computational treatment of Systemic Grammar in 1995, under Christian Matthiessen. Since 1990, he has worked in research centres in Sydney, Los Angeles, Edinburgh, Darmstadt and Trento, typically applying Systemic Functional Linguistics computationally. He has worked in dialogue, museum artefact description, hypertext generation, sentence parsing and machine translation. He has developed several tools to help linguists hand-code text, including UAM CorpusTool, Systemic Coder and RSTTool.

Kay O'Halloran is Associate Professor in the Department of English Language and Literature, and Director of the Multimodal Analysis Lab at the Interactive and Digital Media Institute (IDMI) at the National University of Singapore. Her research areas include multimodal analysis, social semiotics and systemic functional linguistics, with a special interest in the multimodal analysis of mathematics and scientific discourse. She has published widely in these areas in international refereed journals, books and edited collections. She is currently developing interactive digital media technology for multimodal analysis with her interdisciplinary research team in the Multimodal Analysis Lab.

María J. Pinar Sanz is a lecturer in linguistics and discourse analysis at Castilla-La Mancha University. Her research interests are in multimodal discourse analysis and most specifically in aspects related to the analysis of election campaigns and political advertising. She is the main investigator in a research team analysing multimodal discourse analysis and has published several articles on the generic structure of political ads and the relationship between the verbal and visual elements not only in political texts, but also in children's narratives. Applied Linguistics is a further area of interest: she has been the co-coordinator of the project, *Access to Language Learning by Extending to Groups Outside,* for three years and now co-coordinates the VIVACE project, both with the financial support of the European Union.

Claire Scott is a doctoral research student at Macquarie University, studying with David Butt and Annabelle Lukin. Her research is a diachronic, systemic-functional investigation of war reporting in Australia, covering 104 years from the Boer War to the Iraq War, and involves issues of register and multimodality. She also teaches at undergraduate and postgraduate level in the Department of Linguistics at Macquarie.

Sridevi Sriniwass is Senior Lecturer in the University of Malaya. She teaches *systemic functional linguistics, syntax, theory of grammar* and *child language* in The Faculty of Languages and Linguistics. Her primary research interest is in the analysis of expository, academic and scientific texts using the theory of Systemic Functional Linguistics. Her recent publications include *Systemic Perspectives on the Clause Complex in English: Logico-semantic Relations in Chemistry* (2006), *A Systemic-semantic Investigation of Textuality Through the Resources of Ideational Lexis* (2004) and *Transitivity and Cognition: Looking Beyond the Surface of Chemistry Texts* (2003).

Geoff Thompson is a Senior Lecturer in Applied Linguistics in the School of English at the University of Liverpool. He previously taught EFL and Applied Linguistics in a number of countries. Recent publications include *Introducing Functional Grammar* (Arnold, 2nd edition 2004), and papers on topics such as conjunction, Theme and grammatical metaphor. With Susan Hunston he co-edited *Evaluation in Text: Authorial Stance and the Construction of Discourse* (OUP, 2000) and *System and Corpus: Exploring Connections* (Equinox, 2006).

Eija Ventola is a Professor in the Department of English, University of Helsinki, Finland. She has also held professorial posts in Germany and Austria and guest professorships in many other countries. Her research on discourse analysis includes studies on casual conversations, chats and service encounters of various kinds, as well as developing dynamic modelling for analyses of interactional discourse. She has written on Australian literature and its reception, the language of literature and translation, and linguistic stylistics. Her current interests include language and gender issues; the language of conferencing and 'internetting'; the language of business, communication and tourism; multimodality and multimediality. Major authored, edited and co-edited books are: *The Structure of Social Interaction* (1987), *Functional and Systemic Linguistics. Approaches and Uses* (1991), *Approaches to Literary Analysis* (1991), *Academic Writing: Intercultural and Textual Issue* (1996), *Coherence in Spoken and Written Discourse* (1999) *Discourse and Community* (2000), *The Language of Conferencing* (2002), *Perspectives in Multimodality* (2004).

Karina Vidal is a lecturer in English at the Universidad Autónoma de Madrid (UAM), where she currently teaches courses in the School of Economics. Her research and teaching interests include English for Specific Purposes, Research Methods in Applied Linguistics and Acquisition of

Vocabulary. She completed her PhD on 'Academic listening: a source of vocabulary acquisition?' in 2001 in the Department of English Philology at the UAM. Her research has appeared in *Applied Linguistic* and *RESLA*, and has been presented in International Conferences of Applied Linguistics.

Casey Whitelaw received his PhD in computational linguistics from the University of Sydney, Australia. His research has investigated ways of representing semantic information for statistical systems such as text classification and named entity classification. Casey is currently working for Google, Inc. in New York City.

Rachel Whittaker is a lecturer in English at the Universidad Autónoma de Madrid, specialising in discourse analysis and academic writing. She has been working with Ana Martín-Úriz on a number of research projects on writing in English in Spanish high schools, and together they have published a first stage of this research in *La composición como comunicación: una experiencia en las aulas de inglés en bachillerato* (2005). She has recently co-edited two volumes on literacy, *Language and Literacy: Functional Approaches* (2006), and *Advances in Language and Education* (2007).

Dai Fei Yang is Associate Lecturer in the Student Learning Unit, University of Western Sydney. She has a doctorate from the University of Western Sydney for her research into language functions and educational design in higher education. Since the completion of her Masters in SFL in 1986 at the University of Sydney she has maintained a strong research interest in SFL and multimodality in academic discourse. She has been involved in language education for 20 years in Australia.

Michele Zappavigna is a research associate in the Linguistics Department at Sydney University. She is currently working with Jim Martin and Paul Dwyer on a project investigating how reconciliation is enacted multimodally in youth justice conferencing (a form of restorative justice). She holds a PhD in Information Systems on using Systemic Functional Linguistics to understand tacit knowledge about technology.

Introduction

Carys Jones and Eija Ventola

This volume deals with a branch of linguistic inquiry that explores the understanding of meaning-making. It is positioned within the field of linguistics and, more specifically, within systemic-functional linguistics (SFL), introduced by Michael Halliday some fifty years ago. Over the years, SFL has proved itself to be a highly effective research tool for accommodating and addressing change. It views language as having evolved functionally, as an intrinsic part of human evolution, and continually evolving, as it is used for meaningful communication in human societies. Meaning is positioned along a cline of instantiation, from the meaning potential at the theoretical level to the instance of occurrence in such a way that the genesis of language, including change in language usage, can be accommodated within the framework. In addition, meaning is perceived as culturally and situationally construed, thus needing a metafunctional system to understand its richness and complexity.

More specifically, SFL views meaning-potential as something through which we construe our experiences of the world (within and outside us) and which is highly organised. This organisation is most crucially observable at the level of lexicogrammar, which can be seen to be organised through three metafunctions: Ideational, Interpersonal and Textual. In SFL, these three have been considered to be systematically related to contextual social semiotic structures shaped by the Field, Tenor and Mode of situational contexts respectively. The Ideational metafunction is activated by the Field: 'the nature of the social action that is taking place ... that the participants are engaged in' (Halliday 1985: 12). The Interpersonal metafunction is activated by the Tenor: 'the negotiation of social relationships among participants' (Martin 1992: 523), and the Textual metafunction is activated by the Mode: how social action is realised. The choices of Field, Tenor and Mode have, through the metafunctions, repercussions on the actual choices specifically in the discourse semantic and lexicogrammar strata of language and ultimately to phonological / orthographical (and other modal) realisations as structures.

The role of the Ideational function of language in meaning-making processes is always the most widely focussed and studied: hence the reason for this book. Of the three metafunctions, the Ideational function is particularly helpful in capturing the ways we construe meaning, and how we understand and represent the world around us in terms of the Field (i.e. that which is to do with the representation of knowledge and content) through the use of language. As the global society around us continually changes, at times it is necessary to re-evaluate the tools for describing this change and reconsider how the Field is captured through the linguistic systems, especially at the level of lexicogrammar: to see which tools still function, which need further development or adaptation and what kinds of new tools are needed. From this perspective, the Ideational function is an extremely useful organising principle for investigating new ways of making meaning, and it provides the tools that are best able to accommodate the complexities of changes as they are realised.

In terms of understanding language in use, the Ideational may also be the most complex and the most challenging of the three metafunctions because it is concerned with the representation of meaning as experience, i.e. where meaning is at its most invisible and unstable. This particular characteristic is always interesting to the development of the system as a whole. Hence we have felt it important to bring together a collection of chapters that explore new approaches and methods to analysing meaning making, thus offering new and deeper insights into how language works.

The metafunctional principle has shaped the organisation of meaning in language so that each unit of meaning embodies all three metafunctions. This book would be incomplete if it did not feature interactions of the Ideational with the two other modes of meaning-making: the Interpersonal and Textual metafunctions. The Interpersonal function serves to represent the enactment of relationships, encounters and personal attitudes as they occur, from brief passing encounters in daily life to those that occur within highly institutionalised social structures. The function of the Textual is to organise the message as discourse, as a coherent text. This involves both the organisation of the lexicogrammar from the level of clause to the level of text and the inclusion of non-structural cohesive devices that bind the text together as 'discourse flow' (Halliday 2003: 17).

At this point it is necessary to expand on the Ideational metafunction to give some indication of how it is organised to cope with representing the indeterminacy of meaning that is an essential feature of the world of experience. In SFL, the Ideational metafunction has always been viewed as divided into two kinds of suborganisation of systems: on the one hand, the Experiential, and on the other, the Logical. The Experiential function works to theorise experience through the construal, then the deconstrual and reconstrual of meaning (Halliday 1985). In other words, it functions to enact the process of making sense of the world through language. The Logical function extends the experiential power of the grammar by realising the logico-semantic relations between two units of meaning. This works most powerfully in lexicogrammar in the creation of clause complexes, where simple clauses are combined paratactically or hypotactically. This book concentrates largely on the former, the Experiential, and it is this side of the Ideational metafunction that is elaborated upon next.

The Experiential function is structured as a configuration of Process types that is realised grammatically as a system of Transitivity. This is accompanied by the Participant(s) involved in the Process and any attendant Circumstances. A Process represents a flow of events, that is both action and reflection at the same time. Thus it is realised by a verbal group. The Transitivity system in English is underpinned by the idea that human experience with the world is divided into three main types: doing, sensing and being. These are represented by three main processes: Material, Mental and Relational respectively. Material processes are to do with doing, happening, creating; Mental processes have to do with feeling, seeing and thinking; Relational processes are to do with having identity, having attribute and symbolising. At the borders of these three Processes, three further Process types have been identified: Behavioural, Verbal and Existential. Each of the six Process types configures the Participant that accompanies it. For example, in a Material Process the two most frequent Participants will be the Actor and the Goal. In a Mental Process two Participants must be involved, the Senser (active) and the Phenomenon (inactive); and in a relational process, one type of relationship might be causative where the Participants could be the Agent, the Carrier and / or the Attribute.

The Transitivity systems, which are more extensive and elaborate, are constantly inspiring a considerable amount of new research and discussion, as shown in several chapters of this book. Chapter 1 discusses generalised patterns of Transitivity configurations while Chapters 2 and 3 demonstrate different approaches to dealing with the difficulties of classifying certain Process types. An additional concept in Participant / Process analysis is that of Ergativity, which explains how clausal meaning might be represented in different ways. For example, a Material Process could have two Participants as Actor and Goal, one Participant as Medium or two Participants as Agent and Medium. Such problematic options need to be addressed at the semantic level and Chapter 6 examines how this might best be done.

Clearly Participant and Process are closely intertwined. Less close to Process is Circumstance. The function of Circumstances is to contribute something more to the meaning of the Process if desired or necessary. This might happen in one of the three ways: Extension, Elaboration or Enhancement. Circumstances are classified into two types: the simple type, which represents a quality, such as manner, and is realised as an adverbial group; and the macro circumstance, such as location, role or reason, and is realised as a prepositional phrase. But, the Process can also be augmented with an adverbial clause thus creating the types of clause complex mentioned earlier as a function of the Logical. These types of augmentation are closely examined in Chapter 7.

One significant feature of language that demonstrates the indeterminacy of meaning within the experiential function is Nominalisation, which Halliday (1993) has shown to be particularly evident in the writing of science. Processes can become reconstrued as Participants through rank-shifting from the level of clause to the level of nominal group, thus taking on the status of grammatical metaphor and functioning to introduce a further Process of meaning-making. Three chapters, 8, 9 and 10, focus on different academic contexts and show in different ways how Nominalisation features in the development and coding of academic writing.

However, what is most interesting about SFL is the way it has been able to evolve so as to highlight interdependence among the metafunctions and to accommodate shifts in perspective, thus providing deeper insights into how language works in practice. Chapter 4, for example, draws on the interaction of the Interpersonal with the Transitivity system by exploring the semantic construal of emotion in two different languages, Spanish and English, with an analysis that enhances our understanding of the grammar of emotion. Chapter 6 links the Textual and Ideational metafunctions by examining cohesion through Participant tracking at the level of semantic relations within a Field. Both chapters, in different ways, show how the lexicogrammatical level can be informed by examining the construal of meaning at the higher rank of discourse semantics and, when that is not enough, at an even higher contextual level. The discourse semantic level is ever-present throughout the book, sometimes as background and sometimes as foreground. It is there that the system of Appraisal (Martin 2000, Martin and White 2005) is situated. The Appraisal system has been extensively developed and shown to go far beyond a reliance on Interpersonal resources. Thus it demonstrates how well the foundations of the SFL framework cope with new perspectives. Appraisal is explored here in Chapter 5 where it is shown to interact with the Transitivity system. Another chapter that makes extensive use of rank-shifting is Chapter 11, where the concept of Genre provides the umbrella for Register in examining the lexicogrammar of Process in students' writing.

The dimension of rank-shifting in SFL has proved very helpful to our understanding of language as a complex system of meaning-making and, furthermore, about the nature of human communication and of transmitting knowledge, where the Textual function may no longer be restricted to language but is manifested through a variety of modes. To this end, the book aims to enhance recent debates that have been engaging linguists not only within SFL but also in other linguistic forums: extending from how meaning is made and transmitted to representations of meaning in our increasingly globalised and technological society. Thus, it draws on investigations into how we use language to make meaning of the world around us through the Experiential systems and structures of language for two purposes. The first, as we have explained, is to explore further and more deeply our knowledge and understanding of how language works. The second is to examine the use of other semiotic means that offer a representation of the rapidly changing society of today and how these have the potential to further our understanding of the directions of change. Therefore, the main concern of the book is how these questions and the systemic resources they concern are anchored so effectively by SFL.

Having examined the resources of the Ideational function at the level of lexico-grammar, the later chapters in the book explore multimodal ways of meaning-making. These chapters display the richness of SFL approaches in explaining the various discourse and learning phenomena in the information society. Chapter 12 proposes a multimodal discourse approach based on a systemic functional socio-semiotic perspective to examine the discourse of mathematics. The following chapters, 13, 14, 15 and 16 highlight the diversity of multimodal discourses that now challenge the resources of the system. In all four cases, the ability of the Experiential function to develop new tools of analysis is well demonstrated. These 16 chapters together comprise the book. Below they are introduced in more detail.

The book represents the work of experienced SFL scholars working within different contexts, disciplines and languages in many parts of the world and is organised into four parts. Part I focuses solely on theoretical developments concerning the Experiential function. In Part II, the interactions of the Experiential function with the other three functions, i.e. Logical, Interpersonal and Textual, are examined. Part III presents studies within the academic context, focusing mainly on the Experiential function. The final part, Part IV, is devoted to systemic studies of multimodality that are so representative of our meaning-making society today.

The three chapters in Part I enhance the ways in which linguistic phenomena can be studied through the Experiental function. They examine the potential of the resources within the Experiential component of the system to carry out in-depth discourse analyses, which extends our understanding of the Experiential function as a methodological tool and of how language works ideationally.

In Chapter 1, Thompson explores the resources of Transitivity choices to investigate the ideology underlying, and constructed and maintained by, the discourse. He shows how three methodological resources can be combined to reveal the distinguishing qualities of a text and its register. These are Transitivity concordances, the Cline of Dynamism within different Transitivity configurations, and generalised Transitivity configurations, which he refers to as 'transitivity templates'. With sample text analyses, he demonstrates how the system can handle comparison between texts or generalisations across registers.

Flowerdew, in Chapter 2, shows how a Transitivity analysis of corpus data can be useful for shedding light on the area of problematic Processes and for disambiguating between Process types. She argues that an analysis of multiple concordance lines can indicate whether a Process should be coded as Material or Relational, for example. She shows that this is most useful when, as is frequently the case, Process identification is not clear-cut.

In Chapter 3, the difficulties of identifying and coding some Process types are examined in more detail. Furthermore, the authors, O'Donnell, Zappavigna and Whitelaw, question whether or not differences in Transitivity coding can be attributed to different communities of practice. They find that practitioners tend to code either at a semantic level ('what kind of action is being reported in the clause'), or at a syntactic level ('what kind of clause structure is being used'). This, they propose, could be very useful for refining coding practices and could be used as an important criterion for making Process types explicit, particularly in the areas of Verbal, Mental and Behavioural Processes.

As revealed in Part I, the most interesting aspect of SFL is its flexibility to accommodate new insights into language in use and meaning-making. It provides a framework that easily lends itself to being developed and re-shaped. But this also means that the complexity of language in use becomes even more highlighted. Inevitably, interactions, and the nature of those interactions among the metafunctions of the system, become realised as a feature of SFL. In Part II, the flexibility of the system is further demonstrated in the four chapters that show how the Experiential function combines with other functions to provide deeper insights into how knowledge is construed.

In Chapter 4, Lavid draws on the lexicogrammars of two languages, English and Spanish, in a corpus study that investigates how the emotive domain of human experience is construed in everyday language. She presents an analysis of language-specific preferences in the categorisation of four basic emotions to produce a model of experience preferred by each language: 'joy', 'anger', sadness' and 'fear'. Lavid's contribution is a tightly focused study combining qualitative, quantitative and contrastive analyses of Experiential parameters such as the semantic construal of the emotion and the model of experience preferred by each language. The author shows how such a lexicogrammatical exploration contributes to a better understanding of the grammar of emotion in English and Spanish.

Scott, in Chapter 5, explores the interaction between Field and Tenor in a study that is based on the idea of simultaneous inter-dependence, as a feature of the metafunctional system, such that an understanding of the inter-dependence between metafunctions is vital to our understanding of meaning-making. She does this with the Transitivity system (within the Experiential function) and the Appraisal system (within the Interpersonal function) through an analysis of the ways experience and attitude are construed in two texts about one event of the tsunamis of December 2004 in South-East Asia. Scott develops her argument by showing that, in these texts, slight differences in Tenor and Mode actually result in quite different orientations to Field which then has implications for how we invoke 'metafunction' in our theorisation of meaning-making.

Chapter 6 considers the interaction between the Ideational and Textual functions by tracking Participants through taxonomic relations. The author, Moore, views taxonomies of semantic relations that circumscribe a Field of discourse as a major organising principle of the Ideational metafunction. He thus asserts that these resources contribute to the texture of a text as Participants make cohesive ties within and between taxonomies. He builds up a convincing argument suggesting that this interaction might be better understood through the cohesive function of Participant Tracking rather than through the concept of bridging the metafunctions. He proposes an alternative model: one which provides a more unified linguistic and psychological account of Participant Tracking. His thesis is based on a re-analysis of texts found in seminal bridging papers and in undergraduate textbooks, and is illustrated through the use of system network diagrams. He concludes that it is through the cohesive function of Participant tracking that lexical and grammatical relations combine, and that it is through semantic relations within a Field that cohesion bridges the Textual and Ideational metafunctions.

Chapter 7, the final chapter in this section, explores the meaning-making resources of the Experiential and the Logical functions, with a focus on Augmentation. The author, Shrinwass, explores the representation of Logical relations of Enhancement – one type of Circumstance – and its relationship with the Experiential function in the construction of knowledge in tertiary chemistry books. From her analysis of the semantic load carried by the grammatical resources of Complexing and Circumstantial Transitivity in the creation of Field meanings in chemistry, she suggests that 'time', 'space', 'manner', cause' and 'condition' may be encoded by either Tacit or Circumstantial Augmentation whereas in the case of 'spatial' meanings the preference is for encoding by the latter. Her study reveals distinctive contributions to understanding Clause Augmentation, with particular reference to chemistry textbooks.

Academic texts for analysis have already featured in earlier chapters: 2, 6 and 7. Part III focuses on the writing of academics and students at different levels of study. All four chapters display the richness of SFL approaches in explaining the various discourse and learning phenomena in the information society. In the knowledge-oriented, global, learning society, the expression of Field, i.e. knowledge about the world around us, and about the phenomena associated with this world, has become extremely influential in our understanding of what language does and can do. Those who succeed best in producing and distributing knowledge also succeed best in the global society. Language as a coding system for knowledge plays a crucially important role in knowledge distribution. Thus, the more we know about how language codes these knowledge Fields through the Experiential function, the better are our chances of being effective in our communication about the world and the knowledge produced in it. Therefore, linguistic description and applications of SFL in diverse academic contexts are particularly important in the globalisation of knowledge.

In Chapter 8, Montmayor-Borsinger discusses how a physicist develops his Ideational representational practices through subject position over time. Her developmental study captures how increased experience provides the writer with resources to represent grammatical subjects differently, thus significantly enhancing the communication and negotiation Processes of scientific knowledge. The changes are examined through drawing on *instantial* and *conventional* representations. The author shows that scientific knowledge construction may be enhanced by instantial combinations of content and argumentation in subject position. She concludes that a strategic use of unmarked Theme for new, sometimes controversial, meanings simultaneously function as the 'nub of the argument'.

Gardner, in Chapter 9, continues the issue of knowledge formation through the initial subject positioning and the role of grammatical metaphor in it. Her chapter explores the extent to which an analysis of initial sentence subjects (ISS) in a corpus of student writing allows us to map differences in how knowledge is construed across disciplines and across undergraduate years of university study. The question is whether an analysis of only the initial sentence subject of each text can provide a snapshot of similar distinctions across many disciplines and years. Students' written texts in English, History, Psychology, and the Sciences are analysed; the findings are compared with earlier studies of all sentence subjects. A framework for the ISS-approach is proposed to capture differences in angle on Field in university student writing across many disciplines and years. This is tested with texts from Philosophy, Economics and Business.

The next chapter, Chapter 10, is a detailed study of the Nominal group and its role in capturing Experiential meaning in academic writing. The authors, McCabe and Gallagher, provide a comprehensive analysis of the function of the Nominal group in novice and proficient writing in English at the undergraduate level. Their examination of the role of each Nominal group in the Transitivity of the clause, along with the internal Experiential structure, shows that novice writers often use relatively simple Nominal groups, and their discourse thus is more informal, even spoken-like, in register. A comparison of the data sets indicates that novice students need help in learning to compact their Nominal groups in a more academic register when constructing writing. The pedagogic activities recommended by the authors help novice writers to improve their encoding and decoding of academic texts in their courses.

In Chapter 11, the authors (Martín-Úriz, Whittaker, Murcia and Vidal) discuss the construal of Experiential meanings in EFL students' texts. The data are carefully elicited, pre-university student essays of three types: Recount, Exposition and Report. The chapter focuses on Recounts of a personal experience and explores how pre-university Spanish EFL students and English native speaker students, express their experience, how they represent themselves and the events, and how they structure the whole text. The study examines which Process types were selected to express the events, how the Processes were distributed in the essays and whether the students were making conscious, systematic meaning choices when they built up their recounts in English. The study reveals a gap between the Spanish and the English students. The authors conclude that, in order to bridge the gap, SFL-oriented pedagogy for EFL-writing should include more activities that would raise Spanish students' awareness to Genre structure and Register.

The last section of the book, Part IV, captures some of the most recent developments in SFL. Many systemicists have begun developing new ways of capturing the representation of the Field beyond linguistic aspects. The Experiential meaning-making is coded not only through the systems of language but also through other modes of meaning-making, and the systemic-functional focus is extended to explain how the linguistic and other semiotic systems are integrated in discourses. When experience is happening multimodally, we urgently need to develop our tools of capturing the systems and structures that work together with the systems and structures that all linguistic approaches have been describing. New ways of modelling this multimodal realisation of human experience is a challenge for linguists, linguistic description and linguistic application as is demonstrated in the five chapters in this final section.

Chapter 12 is the key opening for the section. Here the author, O'Halloran, discusses the problem of dealing with the multi-semiotics of mathematics discourse. She defines multimodality as a theory and practice of multi-semiotic mediation where language, visual images and other semiotic resources function integratively to construct meaning. She argues the case for developing a new, systemic functional-multimodal discourse approach (SF-MDA), to capture the concept of multimodal grammaticality, where the grammatical systems of semiotic resources are seen as interlocking phenomena. By drawing on SF-MDA to analyse one example of mathematics discourse she shows how visual images and mathematics symbolism are reconfigured and realigned to address mathematical problems. Processes, Participants and Circumstance configurations undergo metaphorical transformation across semiotic choices giving rise to Semiotic Metaphors (SM). The chapter shows how semantic shifts in SM do not follow the pattern of grammatical metaphors in language which leads to the author's argument that tools for multimodal discourse analysis need further development.

The final four chapters of the book demonstrate four innovative approaches to capturing meanings created multimodally. Chapter 13 shows in practice what happens when the different semiotic Modes – language, image, sound and music – combine to model experience in the digital artwork of *Listening Post*, the winner of the Golden Nica 2004, the international prize for interactive art from Ars Electronica. This multimedia art installation culls English text fragments in real time from a large corpus of unrestricted internet chat rooms, bulletin boards and other public forums. The texts are ordered by lexical phrases or key words, read (or sung) by a voice synthesizer, and simultaneously displayed across a suspended grid of more than two hundred small electronic screens. The author, Huemer, shows how two different 'readings' and 'visualizations' of these text fragments realise a contrast and tension between individual / private space / isolation and mass / public space / communication. She claims that the Experiential metafunction plays a principal role in realising an individual and mass voice in these texts.

In Chapter 14, the author, Maiorani focuses on the *The Matrix* movie trilogy. The first episode, *The Matrix* was released in 1999 and then considered to start a new trend in science fiction movies because these movies, with their use of the internet terminology and devices, brought the virtual world and virtual community to the big screen and turned things upside down. In the first movie, in fact, we discover that what at the beginning seems to be the present-day real world is actually a program where people unconsciously live a virtual life while functioning as energy providers for the artificial intelligences who created it. Maiorani analyses how the interplay between textual and visual semiotics develops through a select corpus of posters in the promotional poster campaign of this trilogy. She shows how the Experiential meanings and the representational structures are used (or not used) to create different kinds of advertisements for other products, which seem to vary for each of the three episodes of the trilogy. They actually turn motion pictures into types of interactive social events, especially for an audience of 'fans' who are well aware of the internet ways and means.

Then, in Chapter 15, Yang examines the co-articulation of verbiage and image in presenting Ideational meaning with children's social experience of crucial events and their conceptual understanding of the world around them. The combination of semiotic resources is illustrated by analysing an article from the *Sun Herald,* a weekly Sydney newspaper, dealing with the September 11, 2001 event and its impact on a group of Australian children. Yang draws on three levels of analysis, beginning with Bakhtin's concept of time and space to develop her argument that the Sun Herald was aware that the distinctive features in the children's drawings were the epitome of success for ensuring greater emotional connections with the readers than photographic images or language could offer. The deployment of children's work appears to have helped the editors achieve their social agenda and maximise the sensational nature of the news.

In the final chapter, Chapter 16, Pinar Sanz, looks at images, political cartoons, and considers how they transmit meaning and the ideological load implied in them. The chapter also explores some cognitive mechanisms involved in the creation and interpretation of cartoons. The question explored is whether the main aim of the cartoons is to be humorous or predominantly to display political criticism and debate on the relevant points and how they succeed in this. As in any multimodal text, cartoons display multiplication of meaning and meaning creation is an interactive, dynamic and symbiotic process. Pinar Sanz shows, through a focus on visual metaphor and semiotic spanning (Ventola 1999, 2002), how, in political cartoons, the combination of the Ideational function and the emotional power of the drawing and the critical analysis of social and political issues create a highly complex message.

SFL issues are now the concern of a highly active, world-wide community, having become a major linguistics discipline, taught and researched in many countries, and dealing with a wide range of languages from those used globally to those used in very small, hardly-known communities. This collection of research builds upon insights into potential ways of exploring meaning-making, drawing on recent seminal developments in Ideation. It is intended to be of theoretical and applied interest to the SFL global community and for linguists working with related networks in a wide range of academic contexts at post-graduate level. However, it is not designed as a textbook but rather as a research book or perhaps a secondary reference book as a resource for enrichment. We hope that the innovative thinking presented here will stimulate further debate and provide incentives for developing further the tools of analysis to address issues of socio-semiotic interest that penetrate much further than the linguistic system itself but are nevertheless anchored firmly in the metafunctional system that has consistently proved so fruitful to date.

References

Bloor, T. and Bloor, M. 1995. *The Functional Analysis of English: A Hallidayan Approach*. London: Arnold.

Halliday, M. A. K. 1978. *Language as Social Semiotic. The Social Interpretation of Language and Meaning.* London: Arnold.

Halliday, M. A. K. 1985. *Introduction to Functional Grammar* (1st edition). London: Arnold.

Halliday, M. A. K. 1994. *Introduction to Functional Grammar* (2nd edition). London: Arnold.

Halliday, M .A. K. and Hasan, R. 1985. *Language, Context and Text: Aspects of Language in a Social-Semiotic Perspective.* Victoria: Deakin University Press.

Halliday, M. A. K. and Martin, J. R. 1993. *Writing Science: Literacy and Discursive Power.* London: The Falmer Press.

Halliday, M. A. K. and Matthiessen, C. M. I. M. 1999. *Construing Experience through Meaning.* London: Cassell.

Halliday, M. A. K. and Matthiessen, C. M. I. M. 2004. *An Introduction to Functional Grammar* (3rd edition). London: Arnold

Kress, G. and van Leeuwen, T. 1996. *Reading Images: The Grammar of Visual Design.* London: Routledge.

Martin, J. R. 1992. *English Text.* Amsterdam: Benjamins.

Martin, J. R. 2000. Beyond Exchange: APPRAISAL systems in English. In Thompson, G. and Hunston, S. (eds) 2000. *Evaluation in Text.* Oxford: Oxford University Press, 142-175.

Martin, J. R. and White, P. R. R. 2005. *The Language of Evaluation: Appraisal in English,* London and New York: Palgrave Macmillan.

Thompson, G. 1996. *Introducing Functional Grammar.* London: Arnold.

Ventola, E. 1999. Semiotic spanning at conferences: cohesion and coherence in and across conference papers and their discussions. In Bublitz, W. Lenk, U. and Ventola, E. (eds). *Coherence in Spoken and Written Discourse. How to Create It and How to Describe It.* Amsterdam: Benjamins, 101-125.

Ventola, E. 2002. Why and what kind of focus on conference presentations? Ventola, E. Shalom, C. and Thompson, S. (eds). *Conference Language.* Frankfurt am Main: Peter Lang, 15-50.

PART I

Theoretical developments in representation: Experiential issues

1

From process to pattern: methodological considerations in analysing transitivity in text

Geoff Thompson

1.1 Introduction

It is widely recognised that an analysis of transitivity choices in a text or set of texts, using Halliday's model of transitivity (Halliday and Matthiessen 2004), is one of the most effective ways of exploring the ideological assumptions that inform and are construed by the texts (see, for example, Fairclough 1989; Hodge and Kress 1993; Butt *et al.* 2004). It is typically not just the choices in an individual clause that are significant in revealing the ideological substratum, but the patterns of choices across a text or texts. However, probing ideology via transitivity in this way involves a great deal of detail. The analyst needs to take into account not only the process types but also the entities represented in different participant roles, the kinds of meanings expressed as circumstances, etc. This means that the identification of the patterns is not always straightforward. What I aim to do in this chapter is to present and illustrate an approach to the investigation of transitivity choices which is designed to highlight the key patterns and to make the movement from the identification of these patterns to interpretation of their significance in ideological terms more transparent.[1]

1.2 Illustrating the approach: an analysis of a recipe

I will start by illustrating parts of the approach on a text type that is an easy target in transitivity terms: a recipe. Example (1) below is a short extract from a recipe for making blinis (from *Delia Smith's Winter Collection*, 1995, BBC Books). The analysis that follows is based on the whole of the instructions section of the recipe, but the extract gives a sufficient flavour of a text type that will be very familiar to most readers.

(1) Begin by sifting the salt, buckwheat flour and plain flour together into a large roomy bowl and then sprinkle in the yeast. Place 220 ml/7 fl oz of the crème fraîche into a measuring jug and add enough milk to bring it up to the 425 ml/15 fl oz level.

1.2.1 Transitivity concordances

The first step in setting out the patterns is to draw up a **transitivity concordance**: that is, to gather together all the clauses in which each entity or group of entities in the text is represented in a particular participant role.[2] Clearly, some interpretation is involved in deciding on groupings, although in my experience it is usual to find a high level of agreement between readers on what groupings are appropriate. In some texts, the infrequency (or absence) of certain entities in participant roles may be significant.[3] But normally it is those which occur often which are most rewarding to focus on. It may be important to track whether entities are assigned core participant roles in the clause or relegated to circumstances, and whether they appear as head of the nominal group or as a modifier of some kind within the nominal group (see the discussion of the academic history text in Section 3).

The most frequently recurring participant in the recipe is *you* (typically not explicit because it is associated with imperative clauses). In 90 per cent of its occurrences (47 out of 52), it is Actor in a material: dispositive process (i.e. acting physically on something that already exists), e.g., *[**you**] sprinkle in the yeast.* The next most frequently occurring participant is made up of a number of entities which can be grouped together as 'dish/ingredients'. In 65 per cent of the occurrences (24 out of 37), this group realises the function Goal, e.g., *sprinkle in **the yeast**.* No other entities occur more than once or twice as participants. However, the group 'equipment' occurs 16 times in Circumstance, either of Location (*into a measuring jug*) or Means (*with a whisk*), and there are 18 Circumstances involving 'time', either Location (*then*) or Extent (*for about 1 hour*). Thus the initial analysis results in three main transitivity concordances: for 'you', 'dish/ingredients' and 'equipment'.

1.2.2 Transitivity templates

Transitivity concordances, especially when derived from a group of texts of the same type, allow generalisations to be drawn about the ways in which significant entities are represented in a particular register or genre. In the recipe, as one would of course expect, the central participant is the addressee, who is typically represented as acting on things. The other main participant, the ingredients/dish, is typically acted on rather than acting. However, with many text types the picture that emerges is more complex: a major disadvantage is that different entities which appear as participants in the same clauses are separated in the concordances. Thus, the ways in which the entities are represented as relating to each other in the text still have to be accounted for. In order to do this, the next step is to look at the transitivity structures of whole clauses rather than just focusing on single participants. By bringing together the concordances for different entities, it is possible to identify **transitivity templates**, i.e. schematic representations of transitivity structures in which there are recurrent patterns of one or more of the entities appearing in complementary distribution, in particular participant roles or circumstances. In the case of the recipe, there is one dominant template, shown in Table 1.1 (the parentheses show that not all clauses fitting the template include a circumstance of the type shown).

No fewer than 80 per cent of the clauses in the recipe are covered by this template. This is an unusually high percentage. It is indeed one of the characteristics of recipes in general that the main body, the instructions section, typically repeats this template with relatively few deviations into other patterns.

Of course, this analysis does not show anything that a description of recipes based purely on intuition would not include. We already know that a recipe is about the addressee acting on ingredients which gradually transform into a dish, using certain kitchen equipment, with timing being an important consideration. The aim has simply been to demonstrate the concepts of the concordance and template on data where the validity of the analysis can be confirmed precisely by the fact that the results match intuitions. The next step is to apply these concepts to data where the

Table 1.1: Transitivity template for a recipe

ACTOR	+ PROCESS: MATERIAL dispositive	+GOAL	(+CIRCUMSTANCE) location/means/time
[you]	*act on*	*dish/ingredient*	*equipment/time*

patterns are somewhat less obvious, in order to test their potential value as an analytical tool.

1.3 Exploring ideology through transitivity choices in history texts

To do this, I will take texts which construe different views of history. The texts deal with the reign of Queen Elizabeth I; working with texts which are comparable in some ways (in this case in broad subject matter) makes it easier to highlight the choices which each writer has (or has not) made in deciding how to represent the events. There is only space to quote a few lines of each text; but even the short extracts given below should bring out the differences.

1.3.1 Transitivity in a popular history text

The first extract, Example 2, is from a website aimed at a non-specialist readership.[4] The findings reported will again apply to a longer stretch of text – in this case, the whole webpage (513 words, 65 processes).

(2) She [Elizabeth] also managed to contain the Catholic threat to her monarchy. Mary, Queen of Scots, fleeing from her rebellious subjects, took refuge in England in 1568 and was detained as a prisoner by Elizabeth. The latter regarded Mary as a dangerous rival, because the English Catholics wished to raise her to the throne of England, and formed several plots and conspiracies to make that happen. Elizabeth had Mary beheaded on February 8, 1587.

The entities that are represented in the text are overwhelmingly human, either individuals (e.g. *Elizabeth, Mary*) or groups of individuals (e.g. *the English Catholics*). Of the 65 processes in the text, 58 (89 per cent) have humans in one or more participant roles. The other, much smaller, group consists of what can be roughly termed 'concepts'; these are abstract ideas, often realised as nominalisations, such as *the darkest* ***stain*** *on the memory of Elizabeth* or *the* ***stability*** *of her throne*. A few other entities appear, such as events (e.g. *plots and conspiracies*), but there are five or fewer occurrences of each of these groups, and they play only a minor role in the representation construed in the text.

Table 1.2 summarises the concordances by showing the distribution of the two main entity groupings across transitivity roles, in order of frequency

Table 1.2: Transitivity concordance results for a popular history text (Example 2)

Roles	*human(s)*	*concepts*
Actor +Goal	15	—
Actor –Goal or +Scope	14	—
Goal	10	2
Senser	7	—
Sayer	7	—
Carrier	7	4
Assigner/Initiator	4	—
Token	3	1
Behaver	2	—
Beneficiary	2	—
Phenomenon	2	—
Scope	1	—
Value	—	2

(the totals add up to more than the number of processes, since most processes have two participants).

Table 1.2 shows that humans appear in nearly all the possible participant roles: that is, in this text they are represented 'in the round', rather than as being engaged in only one or two types of processes. However, there is a clear pattern of humans being involved in Material Processes, as Actor or Goal (over 50 per cent of the 74 cases). If we then combine the concordances, they translate into two closely related major templates, as in Table 1.3.

Here 22 per cent of the clauses are covered by the first template, and a further 15 per cent by the second – together, 37 per cent of the clauses are covered.

Table 1.3: Transitivity templates for a popular history text

Template 1	ACTOR	+ PROCESS: MATERIAL	–GOAL [+SCOPE]
	'human' (*typically individual)*	*'acts'*	—
Template 2	ACTOR	+ PROCESS: MATERIAL dispositive	+ GOAL
	'human' (*typically individual)*	*acts on*	*('human')* *(typically individual)*

Examples of these two templates are:

(3)	She	narrowly	escaped	death,	
	Actor	*circumstance*	*Pr: material*	*Scope*	

(4)	She	retained	several Roman Catholics	in her privy council,
	Actor	*Pr: material*	*Goal*	*circumstance*

History, in the Example (2) text, is thus construed as a human narrative in which it is primarily the actions of people (mostly 'important' people) that determine the course of events, and in which, when these actions are represented as impacting on anything, it is typically humans that are affected. When the emotions or speech of the historical personages are represented, these are usually introduced as appendages to the main textual thread of the actions: they are construed as being the cause of action (e.g., from (2) above, *The latter* ***regarded*** *Mary as a dangerous rival* – and therefore had her beheaded), or as reactions to action as in *Elizabeth* ***ascended*** *the throne* [action] *and the majority of the people* ***rejoiced*** *at her accession* [reaction].

This centrality of actions by individuals is, of course, the popular view of history. It therefore seems 'natural', and few of the intended readers would question its validity as one – perhaps the only – appropriate form of representation. But a comparison with alternative ways of seeing history brings out clearly the extent to which the human narrative view is one choice amongst several possible representations (albeit a culturally prioritised one in terms of its wide dissemination).

1.3.2 Transitivity in an academic history text

To illustrate one of these alternative representations, I will use an extract from an academic journal article dealing with Elizabeth I and Mary, Queen of Scots, aimed at specialist historians.[5] I analyse only part of the text, chosen to be roughly equivalent in length to the webpage: 558 words, 50 processes. Example (5) is representative of the style of the text.

(5) But to understand the genesis of English anti-Catholicism, we must return to the sixteenth century and to the problem of the two queens. Let us begin by exploring the linkage between gender and religion that fuelled fears of female role in the early modern period. Early modern culture defined 'male' and 'female' as polar opposites. This hierarchical dual classification system categorically differentiated between male and female, privileging men over women as both spiritual and rational beings in ways that underpinned social order and hierarchy.

It is immediately noticeable that historical individuals are almost entirely absent as participants. They occasionally appear in the text, but in grammatically oblique ways; for instance, in Example (5) *the two queens* are represented not as a transitivity participant but in the form of the post-modifier of an evaluative head noun *problem* within a circumstance. A number of human groups fill participant roles, but these are mostly represented not as groups of individuals but as generalised embodiments of ideological or societal issues: for example, *virile Catholic males of the blood royal.*

By far the largest grouping of entities in the text consists of what I have termed 'concepts' above: abstractions such as *the linkage between gender and religion* and *fears of the female role.* Of the 50 processes in the extract analysed, 38 (77 per cent) have 'concepts' in one or more roles. Table 1.4 summarises the concordances.

In the Example (5) text, it is concepts which are represented 'in the round', as metaphorically acting (Actor) and being acted on (Goal), being equated with other concepts (Token and Value), thought about (Phenomenon), and so on. It is also worth noting the appearance of 'researcher(s)' – named individuals or 'we' (author plus peer researchers as readers) – whose views are reported or whose cognitive processes are invoked, as in *As Carol Weiner wrote in her important study* or *Let us begin by exploring the linkage.* Whereas the popular history text presents the events as unquestionable 'facts', with no explicit indication that an author has been involved in the process of selection or wording – the text as transparent conveyor of information – the academic text signals that

Table 1.4: Transitivity concordance results for an academic history text (Eg. 5)

Roles	*Concepts*	*Groups*	*Individual(s)*	*Researcher(s)*
Actor –Goal or +Scope	11	2	—	—
Token	9	—	—	—
Value	9	—	—	—
Actor +Goal	8	3	—	—
Goal	7	3	—	—
Phenomenon	5	—	—	—
Assigner/Initiator	2	3	—	1
Carrier	2	—	1	—
Scope	2	—	—	—
Target	1	—	—	—
Senser	—	2		2
Sayer	—	—	1	2
Total	56	13	2	5

what is being represented is an interpretation mediated through the consciousness of academic researchers.

When the concordances are combined, three main templates emerge, as shown in Table 1.5.

Examples of the templates are:

(6)	The spectre of a feminine succession	ended	with Mary's execution
	Actor	*Pr: material*	*Circumstance*
(7)	certainty of male succession	reinforced	the shift in the episteme
	Actor	*Pr: material*	*Goal*
(8)	the threat to English Protestantism	[which was] posed	by Catholicism
	Value	*Pr: relational*	*Token*

Here 36 per cent of the clauses in the text are covered by the first two templates, both with 'concept' as Actor; and a further 18 per cent are covered by the third template, making a total of 54 per cent coverage. In this view of history, in terms both of what counts as appropriate content and of what it means to write history, individuals and events are subordinated to ideas. This ideational subordination permeates, and is construed by, the grammatical structure, in that individuals typically appear only as modifiers within nominal groups with abstract heads, and events are typically nominalised into concepts which can then be represented as participants within the templates (on nominalisation in academic text in general, see Halliday and Martin 1993; on the discourse of history, see Coffin 2006). The nominal group *Mary's execution* in Example (6) above illustrates both of these tendencies (and the event is further marginalised by appearing in a circumstance). On the relatively few occasions when events are the focus of a clause, these are typically represented as the cause of, or sometimes evidence for, the abstract phenomena which make up the main thread of what might be called the 'narrative of interpretation' that forms the core of the text. The events merely provide the starting point for a textual movement reminiscent of the 'distillation' explored by Martin (1991), in which the raw material of events is refined into its conceptual essence which is the true focus of this academic text. More often, however,

Table 1.5: Transitivity templates for an academic history text

Template 1	ACTOR *'concept'*	+PROCESS: MATERIAL *Acts*	[+SCOPE] *['concept']*
Template 2	ACTOR *'concept'*	+PROCESS: MATERIAL dispositive *acts on*	+GOAL *'concept'*
Template 3	TOKEN *'concept'*	+PROCESS: RELATIONAL identifying =	+VALUE *'concept'*

it is just the end product of this distillation which is represented in the text; it is assumed that the reader can 'recover' the raw material as necessary. A simple illustration is Example (6) above: the fact that Mary was executed appears in this text only in nominalised form, represented as something already known to the reader (no doubt from having at some much earlier time read about it in 'narratives of events', such as the Elizabeth text).

A connection can be made between the kinds of experiential patterns captured in templates and Lemke's concept of 'thematic formations' (Lemke 1995, 1991; Thibault 1991). The latter are also built up from repeated patterns of representation across many texts and reflect the core meanings that are taken as valid for a particular field in a particular culture at any particular time. However, there are important differences. Thematic formations are generally larger-scale than templates, in that the formations may comprise clause complexes or even longer stretches of discourse. That is, they encompass not only the transitivity structures within clauses but also the rhetorical relationships (especially of cause and effect) between clauses. At the same time, in other ways, they are more detailed than templates, in that the particular entities involved in a thematic formation (the 'thematic terms') may be specified (e.g. 'molecules'), whereas templates seem to work more effectively when the entities are generalised groupings (such as 'ingredients/dish' or 'concepts'). A further difference is that, although firmly based on text analysis, thematic formations are less bound to the wordings of individual texts. They do not necessarily occur in their full form in a particular text, but the coherence of the text relies on the underlying relationships:

> [L]isteners and readers are expected to be able to supply the canonical semantic relations of thematic terms, which are often underspecified or omitted. This is done by familiarity with a canonical pattern of semantic relations (the *thematic formation*), either from another text or discourse, or from an earlier section of the present one. (Lemke 1998: 96)

Although intertextuality is also important in regard to templates, it is not in the sense of 'supplying relations' between terms. Rather, intertextuality comes into play through the repetition of templates across many texts in a register: it is the occurrence of the templates which signals that a text belongs to the register of, say, academic history rather than popular history.

1.3.3 The cline of dynamism in popular history texts

The third analytical tool that can be used to illuminate transitivity patterns is Hasan's (1985/1989) **cline of dynamism**. This attempts to capture the basic intuition that some transitivity roles construe the entity in that role as having greater dynamism. At the crudest level, this is the distinction between the doer (dynamic) and the done-to (passive). However, that distinction only applies easily to Actor and Goal in material processes, and the cline of dynamism extends the intuition to the full range of transitivity roles. Table 1.6 arranges most of the transitivity roles identified in the model on a scale from most to least dynamic: the cline is slightly adapted from that proposed by Hasan, on the basis of analysis of a range of text types. (The division into six bands will be explained below.)

The extreme points on the cline are reasonably self-explanatory. Initiator/Assigner is the most dynamic in that one entity is represented as causing other entities to engage in processes. Actor in a clause with a Goal is also high on the scale in that it performs an action which 'carries through to', and typically affects, the Goal in some way. On the other hand, Goal is affected by the actions of other entities and is thus lowest on the scale.

The distinctions between the intermediate points are less clear-cut, although some gradation can be observed. For example, Actor in a process without Goal or with Scope is fairly high on the scale but is less dynamic than when a Goal is involved; what is represented is activity which does not affect other entities (see Halliday and Matthiessen (2004: 192) on the status of Scope as not affected by the process). When Phenomenon is Subject, the mental process is encoded as one entity impinging on the consciousness of a Senser. It is thus represented as dynamic to the extent

Table 1.6: The cline of dynamism (adapted from Hasan 1985/1989, via Driscoll 2000 and McLaughlin 2002)

Band	*Role*	*Example*
1	Initiator/Assigner	**She** had Mary beheaded/**She** appointed William Cecil secretary of state
2	Actor (+Goal)	**They** took Mary to Stirling Castle
3	Actor (–Goal or +Scope)	**She** fled/**She** took refuge in England
	Phenomenon (Subject)	**Elizabeth** frightened her sister
	Behaver	**She** learned Latin
	Sayer	**They** entreated her to marry
	Senser	**Mary** feared Elizabeth
4	Token	**She** was the last Tudor sovereign
	Carrier	**She** was a Roman Catholic
5	Beneficiary	Philip of Spain made **her** an offer of marriage
	Phenomenon (Complement)	Mary feared **Elizabeth**
	Scope	James VI of Scotland succeeded **her**
↓ 6	Goal	They took **Mary** to Stirling Castle

that it affects the Senser, but there is no inherent implication that the impinging was intended to occur. However, lower down the scale, when Phenomenon is Complement this degree of dynamism is absent. The question of dynamism does not seem particularly relevant to participants in relational processes (Carrier and Token in Table 1.6). But, of course, the representation of entities as participants in relational processes rather than in other kinds of process still has to be seen as a choice, and therefore these roles are placed at the mid-point of the cline.

Although most of the distinctions shown in Table 1.6 appear to be valid, the precise sequencing of some of the roles on the cline is uncertain. In practice, we have found that it is more workable to group the roles into the six bands shown in the table, with each band including one or more roles which seem to have roughly the same degree of dynamism. It is perhaps worth stressing that dynamism in itself is not necessarily positive. It can be used to reinforce the negative representation of an entity if the processes in which the entity plays a dynamic role are destructive or otherwise negatively valued. For example, in a study of Canadian government documents on immigration, McLaughlin (2002) found that, especially in documents from earlier periods, immigrants were assigned negative dynamic roles which increased the sense of threat that was conveyed and thus made the sanctions imposed on them appear more justified.

To illustrate in greater detail the ways in which the cline can be used, I will take another popular history text, this time about Mary, Queen of Scots, and compare it with the Example (2) text about Elizabeth I analysed above. Example (9) gives the flavour of the text. The analysis again uses the whole webpage (694 words, 82 processes).[6]

(9) The following year, despite the warnings of her friends, Mary decided to go back to Scotland, now an officially Protestant country after religious reforms led by John Knox. She was a Roman Catholic, but her half-brother, Lord James Stewart, later Earl of Moray, had assured her that she would be allowed to worship as she wished and in August 1561 she returned, to an unexpectedly warm welcome from her Protestant subjects.

The transitivity concordances and templates for Example (9) are, as one might predict, very similar to those of the Elizabeth I text. The overwhelming majority of participants are humans, nearly all individuals: 70 of the 82 processes (85 per cent) have humans in one or more participant roles. The same templates dominate: 27 per cent of the clauses have a human Actor in a material process with no Goal or with a Scope, and a further 32 per cent have a human Actor in a material process with a Goal (more than two-thirds of which are human). The total of 59 per cent coverage for these two templates is even higher than the 37 per cent for the Elizabeth I text.

So far, the analysis has brought out the similarities and confirmed the picture of popular history discourse. However, if we focus on the representation of the two queens in terms of the cline of dynamism, a very clear difference in the patterns for each of them emerges. Table 1.7 shows the number of times in which Elizabeth and Mary appear in each of their participant roles.

It is worth noting that, although the absolute numbers of instances are comparable (38 and 41), Mary appears in a narrower range of participant roles. However, the most striking difference is in the dynamism of their roles. Elizabeth is represented as acting and, to a fair extent, affecting the world, whereas Mary is above all acted on. Examples (10) and (11) show typical clauses in which Elizabeth and Mary, respectively, appear.

(10)

Elizabeth	had	Mary	beheaded	on February 8, 1587.
Actor	Pr:-	*Goal*	*-material*	*Circumstance*

[she]	to promote	the stability of her throne
Actor	*Pr: material*	*Goal*

Elizabeth	died	on March 24, 1603
Actor	*Pr: material*	*circumstance*

(11)

Mary	escaped	from Lochleven	in 1568,
Actor	*Pr: material*	*circumstance*	*circumstance*

she	was kept	in captivity	in England	for 19 years
Goal	*Pr: material*	*circumstance*	*circumstance*	*circumstance*

Table 1.7: Role dynamism for the two queens

	Elizabeth	*Mary*
Assigner/Initiator	2	0
Actor +Goal	7	0
Actor –Goal and/or +Scope	9	11
Behaver	2	0
Sayer	4	0
Senser	2	3
Token	3	2
Carrier	5	4
Beneficiary	2	2
Phenomenon	1	0
Scope	1	1
Goal	3	15
Total	41	38

The differences can be seen even more sharply if, as a somewhat crude guide, a measure of dynamism is calculated by weighting the roles positively or negatively in accordance with the bands shown in Table 1.6 and adding up the 'scores'. This is shown in Table 1.8.

At first sight, these results might not seem significant; this is, after all, how the two Queens are typically seen, with Elizabeth as 'Gloriana', a dynamic, commanding figure who defeated the Spanish Armada, fended off suitors of royal and noble blood, wielded absolute rule in a male-dominated world, etc., while Mary is the archetypal passive victim, spending apparently the major part of her life in imprisonment and ending up on the executioner's block. However, this is precisely why the results are significant. They reflect a view of the Queens, and the events which have been handed down over the years, becoming increasingly the culturally ratified version, through countless texts which construe the history of the two women in these contrasting terms. If one considers the record dispassionately, Mary was in many ways an equally commanding figure. She was Queen of not one but two countries (France and Scotland), and in Scotland also wielded absolute rule; she took command of an army in two campaigns; she outlived three husbands including a King of France (and may well have had her second husband murdered); and, however innocently, she served as a focus for Catholic resistance to Elizabeth. But history is written by the victors, and in this case the writing has been extremely successful. Although there is no space to give examples here, it is easy to find texts – especially of popular history – in which the relative dynamism of the Queens identified above is repeated.

What this discussion of just two texts has been designed to do is to show how such an analysis can indicate lines of enquiry that could guide a more extensive analysis across a wide range of texts. We can in fact see

Table 1.8: Role dynamism 'scores' for the two queens

			Elizabeth		*Mary*	
band	*p*	*weighting*	*no.*	*score*	*no.*	*score*
1	Assigner/Initiator	*+3*	*2*	*+6*	*0*	*0*
2	Actor +Goal	*+2*	*7*	*+14*	*0*	*0*
3	Actor –Goal and/or +Scope, Behaver, Sayer, Senser	*+1*	*17*	*+17*	*14*	*+14*
4	Token, Carrier	*0*	*8*	*0*	*6*	*0*
5	Beneficiary, Phenomenon, Scope	*–1*	*4*	*–4*	*3*	*–3*
6	Goal	*–2*	*3*	*–6*	*15*	*–30*
	Total		*41*	*+27*	*38*	*–19*

the results as reflecting a localised case of what Hoey (2005) calls 'lexical priming'. For nearly all who are familiar with them as historical personages, the names of Elizabeth and Mary bring with them an association, more or less unconscious, with the specific kinds of transitivity choices illustrated above. When we come across the names in text, we feel it natural to find them in those transitivity roles because of the accumulation of the instances in which we have previously met them in grammatically similar contexts. This clearly does not apply only to these two names but has wider implications. There are many other fields in which the transitivity primings associated with specific individuals or groups might be explored – most obviously politics and the media, where, for example, the construal of different in-groups and out-groups is a central function of many kinds of discourse (see e.g. Wodak *et al.* 2000). An examination of the relative dynamism attributed to different entities (along with the templates in which they occur) can provide important insights into the values embedded in the discourse.

1.4 Conclusion

For the purposes of the chapter, I have consciously set aside the inescapable fact that the initial transitivity analysis still has to be done, and that it can be extremely time-consuming. There is software which is available to help speed up the process of functional analysis, such as O'Donnell's *Systemic Coder*.[7] As yet, however, these programmes cannot easily handle different layers of analysis (e.g. of the transitivity choices in embedded clauses), and in any case some basic steps in applying the analytical methods outlined here are difficult to do except by hand – for example, the identification of relevant entities and groups of entities, and of the transitivity concordance lines which involve only those entities. In addition, it is often difficult to decide on a single analysis for each relevant clause. Nevertheless, once the initial stage of transitivity analysis is completed, the remaining steps can usually be carried out fairly rapidly. Indeed, although the concordances, which are the basis for working with the templates and the cline of dynamism, may be based on a transitivity analysis of the full text(s), it is often possible to take a more economical approach. The relevant entities can be identified in advance, from a preliminary reading and/or a comparison with other texts, and only those clauses in which they appear singled out for analysis.

The three forms of analysis have been applied in studies which are inspired by Critical Discourse Analysis, e.g. McLaughlin (2002, 2006), but also in studies which aim to increase our understanding of important aspects of our culture without necessarily emphasising the role of language in maintaining inequalities in the distribution of resources (e.g. Driscoll (2000) on how the roles of doctors, patients and carers are construed in medical leaflets). We have found that the transitivity concordances, while often illuminating in themselves, are usually preparation for either of the next steps. As the sample analyses above have suggested, the templates and the cline of dynamism lend themselves to slightly different kinds of investigation. The templates are more appropriate for the identification of the experiential characteristics of registers, whereas the cline of dynamism can in particular illuminate imbalances in power of whatever kind. Both can, of course, be combined in the exploration of how a world-view is construed in text or across texts. The three approaches together are designed to capture in a relatively precise and replicable way the significant patterns in transitivity choices in text and to facilitate the move from identification of the patterns to interpretation of their socio-cultural significance.

Notes

1 The forms of analysis presented in this chapter have been developed in collaboration with some of my research students (particularly Driscoll 2000 and McLaughlin 2002; see also McLaughlin 2006 for an example of the approach applied to a corpus of children's writing).

2 As with any grammatical analysis, it is possible to work at several different levels of delicacy: one can analyse the transitivity choices only in independent clauses, or in all ranking clauses, or in all clauses including embedded clauses. The last of these alternatives is adopted as most appropriate for the kinds of issues explored in this chapter, since I am interested in the ways in which a particular entity or group of entities is represented across a text rather than whether the message makes that representation informationally salient (by realising it in independent clauses) or backgrounds it (by embedding it within other clauses).

3 See, for example, Thompson (2003) on 'elided' participants in certain kinds of academic discourse.

4 http://ilil.essortment.com/queenelizabeth_rrva.htm; last accessed 1.9.2006.

5 From McLaren, Anne (2002). Gender, religion and early modern nationalism: Elizabeth I, Mary Queen of Scots and the genesis of English anti-Catholicism. *American Historical Review* 107/3: 739-767. Available at http://

www.historycooperative.org/journals/ahr/107.3/ah0302000739.html; last accessed 1.9.2006.

6 http://www.royal.gov.uk/output/Page134.asp; last accessed 1.9.2006.

7 A list of the software that is available and links to download it can be found at http://www.isfla.org/Systemics/Software/index.html

References

Butt, D., Lukin, A. and Matthiessen, C. M. I. M. (2004). Grammar: the first covert operation of war. *Discourse and Society*, 15/2–3: 267–290.

Coffin, C. (2006). *Historical Discourse: The Language of Time, Cause and Evaluation.* London: Continuum.

Driscoll, J. (2000). The representation of doctors and patients in medical discourse. Unpublished MA dissertation. Liverpool: University of Liverpool.

Fairclough, N. (1989). *Language and Power.* London: Longman.

Halliday, M. A. K. and Martin, J. R. (1993). *Writing Science: Literacy and Discursive Power.* London: The Falmer Press.

Halliday, M. A. K. and Matthiessen, C. M. I. M. (2004). *An Introduction to Functional Grammar* (3rd edition). London: Arnold.

Hasan, R. (1985/1989). *Linguistics, Language and Verbal Art.* Melbourne: Deakin University Press. Reissued 1989. Oxford: Oxford University Press.

Hodge, R. and Kress, G. (1993). *Language as Ideology* (2nd edition). London: Routledge.

Hoey, M. (2005). *Lexical Priming: A New Theory of Words and Language.* London: Routledge.

Lemke, J. L. (1991). Text production and dynamic text semantics. In E. Ventola (ed.) *Functional and Systemic Linguistics: Approaches and Uses.* Berlin and New York: Mouton de Gruyter, 23–38.

Lemke, J. L. 1995. Intertextuality and text semantics. In M. Gregory and P. Fries (eds) *Discourse in Society: Functional Perspectives.* Norwood, NJ: Ablex, 85–114.

Lemke, J. L. 1998. Multiplying meaning: visual and verbal semiotics in scientific text. In J. R. Martin and R. Veel (eds) *Reading Science.* London: Routledge, 87–113.

Martin, J. R. (1991). Nominalization in science and humanities: distilling knowledge and scaffolding text. In E. Ventola (ed.) *Functional and Systemic Linguistics: Approaches and Uses.* Berlin and New York: Mouton de Gruyter, 307–337.

McLaughlin, S. (2002). The inside out of Canadian immigration discourse: a linguistic analysis of ideology. Unpublished MA dissertation. Liverpool: University of Liverpool.

McLaughlin, S. (2006). Each one of us owns a story – childhood in the second Intifada: a linguistic analysis of conflict and hope. Unpublished PhD thesis. Liverpool: University of Liverpool.

Thibault, P. J. (1991). Grammar, technocracy, and the noun: technocratic values and cognitive linguistics. In E. Ventola (ed.) *Functional and Systemic Linguistics: Approaches and Uses*. Berlin and New York: Mouton de Gruyter, 281–305.

Thompson, G. (2003). The elided participant: presenting an uncommonsense view of the researcher's role. In A-M. Simon-Vandenbergen, M. Taverniers and L. J. Ravelli (eds) *Grammatical Metaphor: Views from Systemic Functional Linguistics*. Amsterdam: Benjamins, 257–278.

Ventola, E. (ed.) (1991). *Functional and Systemic Linguistics: Approaches and Uses*. Berlin and New York: Mouton de Gruyter.

Wodak, R., de Cillia, R., Reisigl, M. and Liebhart, K. (eds) (2000). *The Discursive Construction of National Identity* (translated by A. Hirsch and R. Mitten). Edinburgh: Edinburgh University Press.

2 Using corpus data to have a closer look at the Experiential function

Lynne Flowerdew

2.1 Introduction

In the past few years, corpus linguistic techniques have been applied to exploring various metafunctions (see e.g., Butler 2004; Coffin *et al.* 2004; Flowerdew 2003). One application has been to test the robustness of the system networks on a corpus to see if the functional theories stand up, a point initially raised by Halliday and reiterated by de Beaugrande (1997).

Using published corpus observations to compile a database of verb senses known as the Process Type Database (PTDB), which comprised around 5,400 process types (i.e. verb senses), Neale (2006) identified a set of verb senses missing in the Cardiff Grammar Transitivity network. Neale found that 'matching' verbs of the type *combine, merge, blend, mix, match* and *join* could not be satisfactorily accounted for in the present system with their classification as circumstantial relations, which, as she points out, is a semantically very diverse category. Accordingly, Neale (2002) proposed a new relational process type known as 'matching' to complement the existing types of relational processes, i.e. intensive, possessive, circumstantial (Matthiessen 1999), for inclusion in the system network for transitivity in English.

In this chapter, following Neale's (2006) research where she demonstrated that corpora can be used as a test bed for expanding and modifying the system networks, I would like to propose that corpora can also be very useful for disambiguating between different types of process verbs. Stubbs (2001) has argued that the conventionalised view that pragmatic meanings are usually inferred by the reader/listener, making them highly context dependent, may be overstated and that large-scale corpus studies can provide evidence to show that pragmatic meanings can also be conventionally encoded in linguistic form. In a similar vein, I would like to argue that corpus data can provide evidence to show that process types can also be conventionally encoded in text and that analysis of multiple concordance lines can aid in the semantic disambiguation of verbs.

2.2 Corpus and methodology

The data for the analyses in this chapter are drawn from a specialised 250,000-word corpus of 60 Environmental Impact Assessment (EIA) reports from 23 different environmental consultancy companies in Hong Kong. These reports document the potential environmental impacts of the construction and operation of proposed buildings and facilities, and also contain a section on suggested mitigation measures to alleviate any possible environmental impacts. The Concord function in WordSmith Tools (Scott 1999) was used to obtain KWIC (key-word-in-context) concordances of items selected on the basis of problematic classification, either as relational/material processes, or existential/material processes.

2.3 Corpus-based findings

Two process types which have caused difficulties in categorization are material and relational verbs: 'The frontier between relational and material processes is typically fuzzy' (Halliday and Matthiessen 1999: 504). Existential and material processes also have boundaries which are not easy to delimit sometimes. In Section 2.3.1, the prepositional verb *associated with* has been chosen to elucidate differences between material and relational processes, and in Section 2.3.2 existential *there* will be used to examine differences between existential and material processes.

2.3.1 'Associated with': relational or material?

Thompson (1996: 81) refers to a 'blending' of relational and material processes, with one being dominant. In Example (1), Thompson argues that the relational ('state') meaning is the dominant one, but that the choice of a more dynamic verb brings in a material process colouring.

(1) Hope Street *runs* between the two cathedrals.

But, Martin *et al.* (1997: 123) view tense as a deciding factor in classification. They state that the present continuous is the unmarked choice in a material clause, as in Example (3) and that the verb in Example (2) is relational by virtue of the tense used, even though on the surface the verb is a material one. They state that what process should be construed can also be probed by exploring agnate verbs (for example, in (2) below 'runs' could be replaced by the locative 'is located').

(2) The road runs along the river. (relational)

(3) The jogger is running along the river. (material)

Verb choice and colligational patterning (i.e. the grammatical company a word keeps) may both play a role in construing the meaning potential of process verbs, and these are factors that will also be considered in the corpus analysis of *associated with.*

Before examining the concordance output for *associated with* it would be instructive to look at the dictionary definitions for this prepositional verb. Both the Macmillan dictionary and COBUILD, which are corpus-based, define *associated with* as being connected or related to something: in other words, as relational. However, an examination of this verb in my specialised corpus of environmental reports shows it to have a different meaning.

The phrase *associated with* was found to occur 139 times in the corpus of environmental reports and, most significantly, across all the 23 different companies, indicating it was not just a feature of an in-house company style of writing. In 135 instances it seemed to be somewhat ambiguously involved in a causal effect with a negative semantic prosody, as illustrated by the examples shown in Table 2.1.[1]

In order to substantiate my interpretation of this phrase and to see whether it also had a negative prosody involving a causal effect in general scientific texts, I consulted the seven-million-word Applied Science domain of the 100-million-word British National Corpus, BNC, (Aston and Burnard

Table 2.1: Concordance lines for *associated with* in EIA corpus

tprint. Blasting activities	associated with	with the removal of the headl
sediment concentrations	associated with	backfilling at the two
the engineering difficulties	associated with	hydraulic dredging and
lines.. Health hazards	associated with	proximity to high tension
vehicular emission impact	associated with	the traffic from the roadw
memorandum. The noise	associated with	tunnel drilling, or a tunnel
in place. The problems	associated with	continued pollution of the
residual impacts remain	associated with	the stream works between

1998). In this sub-corpus, *associated with* was found to occur 1,327 times in 162 different texts. As it was not feasible to trawl through all 1,327 lines of concordance output to examine the data qualitatively, concordance lines were selected on a one per text basis. This examination revealed that in 40 per cent of cases this phrase clearly has a negative semantic prosody, as in Example (4).

(4) The commission is concerned about the possible risks associated with releasing genetically altered organisms ...

Following Thompson (1996), this could be considered as a blending of both material and relational processes, with the material process very much the dominant one in this context. Here I would argue that a relational verb has most likely been chosen as an attenuated form of the material process verb *cause*, in line with Hyland's (1998, 2000) observation that such hedging devices would be used when scientists would avoid claiming a direct causal effect, thereby forestalling any challenges from their peers, especially when controversial issues are involved. Although Hyland's research is concerned with academic writing, it could be surmised that the same principles apply to writing in the professions, which have their own conventions and discourse practices.

Another salient observation about the occurrences of *associated with* is that out of the 135 instances only two occur as part of a main verb (e.g., *No adverse impacts will be associated with vehicle movements...*). All the other occurrences are found in a reduced relative clause. There are no examples of relative clauses containing this verb, such as: *which are associated with...*, a construction which would give the information in the clause more emphasis. The grammatical choice of a reduced relative clause would therefore also seem to have an attenuating effect in addition to the choice of verb.

The next question to ask is why there is a discrepancy between the dictionary meaning of 'associated with' and its meaning in the specialised corpora covering science-related issues. Both the dictionaries consulted are corpus-based, with Macmillan based on the 100-million word BNC, a general corpus. However, it has to be borne in mind that dictionaries are constructed on the most frequently occurring senses found in large-scale general corpora. The fact that *associated with* in the sense of 'caused by' is not listed in either dictionary strongly suggests that it does not frequently appear with this causative function in a general corpus and is mainly confined to science-related texts.

Moreover, the fact that *associated with* was found in reports produced by all 23 different environmental consultancy companies in the small, specialised corpus indicates that this sense is very much genre-related and not just an idiosyncratic usage of a few writers. The genre, or discourse domain, in addition to an item's colligational preference, would therefore also be a factor in determining the sense of a word, and hence its categorisation as a member of a particular process type under certain circumstances. In the fields of lexicography and computational linguistics, syntactic preferences (i.e., colligational choices), collocational networks, lexical relations and discourse domains (i.e., genres) are all employed as clues in word sense disambiguation (Kilgarriff and Rundell 2006). This chapter proposes that the same set of clues can also be usefully applied to process-type verb disambiguation in SFL.

2.3.2 'There + be': existential or material?

Existential *there* is another structure which defies an exact categorisation. Halliday and Matthiessen comment thus:

> there is the phenomenon of existing - still construed, grammatically, as a type of process. What is said to exist may be an entity, something that persists through time, like *there's a letter for you*; but it may also, in many languages be a happening, as in *there was a fight*. Here we have something that could alternatively be construed as a material process (*people were fighting*), which suggests that 'existential' processes are another intermediate type, something between the relational and the material. (Halliday and Matthiessen 1999: 514)

Halliday (1994) discusses this intermediary process type, giving examples of verbs falling into this category:

> Existential clauses typically have the verb *be*; in this respect also they resemble relational processes. But the other verbs that commonly occur are mainly different from either the attributive or the identifying. One group is a small set of closely related verbs meaning 'exist' or 'happen': *exist, remain, arise, occur, come about, happen, take place*. The other group embody some circumstantial feature; e.g. of time (*follow, ensure*), place (*sit, stand, lie, hang, rise, stretch, emerge, grow*). (Halliday 1994: 142)

The corpus-based *Longman Grammar of Spoken and Written English* (Biber *et al.* 1999) provides the following information about existential 'there'.

> Existential *there* is a formal device used, together with an intransitive verb, to predicate the existence or occurrence of something (including the non-existence or non-occurrence of something). Most typically, a clause with existential *there* has the following structure:
>
> *there* + *be* + indefinite NP (+ place or time position adverbial)
>
> (Biber *et al.* 1999: 943)

Although this reference grammar mentions that this structure can indicate 'the existence or occurrence of something', we do not know under what conditions this structure construes an existential or a material process indicating occurrence. In order to disambiguate when existential *there* with *be* takes on the semantics of existential or material process verbs, I extracted a concordance of *there* from the EIA corpus. Out of a total of 326 occurrences, four of these were discarded as they referred to location. An analysis of the remaining 322 concordance lines of existential expressions revealed that, without exception, they all occurred with *be*; none of the other 'existing' and 'happening' verbs mentioned by Halliday were found to occur with 'there'. This led me to surmise that *be* is not only being used in an existential sense, but also as an agnate verb for the 'happening' material process verbs.

In order to test this hypothesis, I classified all the occurrences according to temporal reference, as shown in Table 2.2, as this has implications for the subsequent analyses. Given that these environmental reports concern potential environmental impacts, it is not surprising to find that nearly half the tokens refer to future time.

Table 2.2: Breakdown of tokens for existential *there* according to time reference in EIA corpus

Time reference for existential 'there'	*Tokens*
Present	
There is / are ...	165
Past	
There has / have been ...	3
There was / were ...	10
There may have been ...	1
Future	
There will / would be ...	104
There shall / should be ...	12
There may / could be ...	13
There is potential for ...	8
There is / are unlikely to be ...	6
Total no. of tokens:	322

When *there* + *be* refers to a present state of the existent, i.e. participant, it would seem to be best construed as existential, as illustrated by Examples (5) and (6).

(5) There are various disposal options for dealing with the waste ...

(6) There is little evidence of significant losses to the water column ...

However, an examination of existential *there* with reference to past and future time reveals that in many cases the process is encoded within a somewhat different type of semantic frame. Here *be* could be substituted by *arise*, a causative verb of the result/effect variety, when the existent is a negatively evaluated Inscribed or Evoking item, based on Martin's (2000, 2004) system of Appraisal for classifying Evaluative lexis. The Inscribed option refers to lexis that is explicitly evaluative, in which the evaluation is encoded in the word, e.g., *problem, difficulty*. The Evoking option, meanwhile, 'draws on "ideational" meaning to "connote" evaluation ... by selecting meanings which invite a reaction' (Martin 2004: 289). Items in this category, such as *noise* and *impact*, would have an intrinsically less negative connotation than an Inscribed item such as *problem*, having the status of hyponyms for the more superordinate Inscribed items (see Flowerdew 2003, 2004 for corpus-based studies using this sub-classification from Martin's Appraisal system). In Examples (7–9) the existents (indicated in bold) are negative Evoking items.

(7) ... it is expected that there will be no significant residual **impacts**.

(8) ... there may be limited **erosion** of soft surface material ...

(9) There would also be some **loss** of diversity.

Sometimes the cause is also mentioned after the effect, introduced by *due to, from, arising from* or *associated with*, which are a reflection of the unfolding discourse of a chain of cause and effect events, as illustrated in Examples (10–13):

(10) There will be a net **loss** of 86.95 ha of fish pond area due to the ...

(11) During operation, there will be no **adverse water quality impact** from active effluent.

(12) ... and there will not be any additional **noise impacts** arising from the ...

(13) There should be no **significant sources** associated with ...

The usage of *potential* with *be* also renders the verb a causative material one, as suggested by the rephrasing of the pattern *There is potential for ...*. Here the existents are negative Evoking items in the form of grammatical metaphor nouns (e.g., eutrophication, intrusion).

(14) ... where there is potential for **contamination** ...

(15) ... where **contamination** may arise ...

In this specialised corpus, therefore, the semantics of the verb *be* in existential clauses would seem to be dependent on the existent noun and its connotation. Where the existent does not have a negative connotation, the semantics of *be* tends more towards existential processes, as illustrated in Examples (16-18):

(16) ... there will be a short period of time before completing ...

(17) ... but there will be some light equipment used for sorting of ...

(18) ... there will be a 22-lane Toll Plaza and an Administration building ...

2.3.3 Discussion: 'Priming' and Process Verbs

Hoey's (2005) theory of 'priming' holds that words are primed for collocational and grammatical use:

> ... every time we encounter a lexical item it becomes loaded with the cumulative effects of those encounters, such that it is part of our knowledge of the word that it regularly co-occurs with particular other words or with specific grammatical functions. (Hoey 2004: 21)

An illustration of this concept with regard to nested combinations involving *winter* (e.g. *in winter, in the winter, during the winter*), Hoey (2005: 41) has shown that in a 95-million-word corpus of *Guardian* news and features text '*in the winter* and *during the winter* are likely to be quite strongly primed to occur with Material process verbs and that *in winter* will probably be primed to occur with Relational process verbs'.

Taking up Hoey's concept of priming, I would argue that when the verb *associate with* is found in a reduced relative clause, as illustrated by the multiple concordance data in Section 2.3.1, it is primed to have the meaning of 'caused by' in an attenuated form rather than its usual dictionary meaning of 'related to'. In other words, different senses of a word are primed to occur in different grammatical structures.

The analysis of *there* + *be* in Section 2.3.2 lends further weight to Hoey's notion of priming. We could tentatively conclude that when negative Inscribed or Evoking items (there were no examples of positive items in my corpus) occur in existential clauses, they 'prime' *be* to be construed as a material rather than an existential process verb. Or, conversely, when existential *there* + *be* has a negative semantic prosody, *be* is primed as a material process verb, thus illustrating the inderdependency between lexis and grammar (Stubbs 1996).

2.4 Conclusion

Hunston (2006) has shown how various patterns can be mapped on to the clause complexes, demonstrating the dependency of a clause or phrase upon a lexical item. In this chapter, I have attempted to show how recurring syntagmatic features, such as colligation and semantic prosody of the phraseological approach usually adopted in corpus-based studies, can, likewise, be mapped on to the different process types in Halliday's paradigmatic system in order to disambiguate between different verbal processes. However, for the time being, this kind of analysis can only be done manually:

> computational analysis tools cannot yet cope with the combination of rich analysis and a flow or registerially unrestricted text. For example, it would not be possible to analyse a large corpus automatically in terms of the system of process type. (Matthiessen 2006: 141)

The challenge for future work in this area lies in how the different types of processes could be identified through automatic means. A corpus analytic perspective, making use of Hoey's concept of 'priming', may provide some clues as to how this might be achieved.

Notes

1 In the other four instances *associated with* was found with budget considerations with the meaning of 'in connection with', e.g. *The recurrent cost **associated with** the operation and maintenance of ...*

References

Aston, G. and Burnard, L. (1998). *The BNC Handbook.* Edinburgh: Edinburgh University Press.

Aston, G., Bernardini, S. and Stewart, D. (eds) (2004). *Corpora and Language Learners*. Amsterdam: Benjamins.
Biber, D., Johansson, S., Leech, G., Conrad, S. and Finegan, E. (1999). *Longman Grammar of Spoken and Written English*. London: Longman.
Butler, C. (2004). Corpus studies and functional linguistic theories. *Functions of Language*, 11 (2): 147–186.
de Beaugrande, R. (1997). *New Foundations for a Science of Text and Discourse*. Norwood, NJ: Ablex.
Coffin, C., Hewings, A. and O'Halloran, K. (eds) (2004). *Applying English Grammar: Functional and Corpus Approaches*. Milton Keynes: Open University.
Flowerdew, L. (2003). A combined corpus and systemic-functional analysis of the problem-solution pattern in a student and professional corpus of technical writing. *TESOL Quarterly*, 37 (3): 489–511.
Flowerdew, L. (2004). The problem-solution pattern in apprentice vs. professional technical writing: an application of Appraisal theory. In Aston, G., Bernardini, S. and Stewart, D. (eds) *Corpora and Language Learners*. Amsterdam: Benjamins. 125–135.
Halliday, M. A. K. (1994). *Introduction to Functional Grammar*. London: Arnold.
Halliday, M. A. K. and Matthiessen, C. M. I. M. (1999). *Construing Experience through Meaning*. London: Cassell.
Hoey, M. (2004). The textual priming of lexis. In G. Aston and L. Burnard, *The BNC Handbook*. Edinburgh: Edinburgh University Press, 21–41.
Hoey, M. (2005). *Lexical Priming: A New Theory of Words and Language*. London: Routledge.
Hunston, S. (2006). Phraseology and system: a contribution to the debate. In G. Thompson and S. Hunston (eds) *System and Corpus: Exploring Connections*. London: Equinox. 55–80.
Hyland, K. (1998). *Hedging in Scientific Research Articles*. Amsterdam: Benjamins.
Hyland, K. (2000). *Disciplinary Discourses: Social Interactions in Academic Writing*. London: Longman.
Kilgarriff, A. and Rundell, M. (2006). Lexicom-Asia. A training workshop in lexicography and lexical computing. 11–13 December, 2006, Hong Kong University of Science and Technology.
Martin, J. R. (2000). Beyond Exchange: APPRAISAL systems in English. In G. Thompson and S. Hunston (eds) *Evaluation in Text*. Oxford: Oxford University Press, 142–175.
Martin, J. R. (2004). Sense and sensibility: texturing evaluation. In J. Foley (ed.) *Language Education and Discourse: Functional Approaches*. London: Continuum, 270–304.
Martin, J. R., Matthiessen, C. M. I. M. and Painter, C. (1997). *Working with Functional Grammar*. London: Arnold.
Matthiessen, C. M. I. M. (1999). The system of transitivity: an exploratory study of text-based profiles. *Functions of Language*, 6 (1): 1–51.

Matthiessen, C. M. I. M. (2006). Frequency profiles of some basic grammatical systems: an interim report. In G. Thompson and S. Hunston (eds) *System and Corpus: Exploring Connections*. London: Equinox, 103–142.

Neale, A. (2002). More delicate TRANSITIVITY: extending the PROCESS TYPE system networks for English to include full semantic classifications. Unpublished PhD thesis. Cardiff: Cardiff University.

Neale, A. (2006). Matching corpus data and system networks: using corpora to modify and extend the system networks for Transitivity in English. In G. Thompson and S. Hunston (eds) *System and Corpus: Exploring Connections*. London: Equinox, 143–163.

Scott, M. (1999). *WordSmith Tools*. Oxford: Oxford University Press.

Stubbs, M. (1996). *Text and Corpus Analysis*. Oxford: Blackwell.

Stubbs, M. (2001). On inference theories and code theories: corpus evidence for semantic schemas. *Text*, 21 (3): 437–465.

Thompson, G. (1996). *Introducing Functional Grammar*. London: Arnold.

Thompson, G. and Hunston, S. (eds) (2006). *System and Corpus: Exploring Connections*. London: Equinox.

3 A survey of process type classification over difficult cases

Mick O'Donnell, Michele Zappavigna, Casey Whitelaw

3.1 Introduction

One distinct aspect of Systemic Functional Linguistics (SFL) is the analysis of clauses in terms of *process types*. According to the theory, the grammar provides a number of schemas for packaging information into a clause. For instance, *material* clauses consist of an Actor, a Process and a Goal, while *mental* clauses contain a Sensor, a Process and a Phenomenon. Each of these schemas corresponds to a *process type*. Normally, six process types are identified: material, behavioural, verbal, mental, relational and existential.

Process type analysis was first described in Halliday (1976), which stemmed from Halliday's attempt to develop the kind of grammar which would support teachers in teaching language. A fuller, more evolved description was given in *Introduction to Functional Grammar* (Halliday 1985, henceforth IFG), and its two later editions: Halliday (1994) and Halliday and Matthiessen (2004). However, these texts proved too technical for beginners, and easier introductions were introduced (e.g. Downing and Locke 1992; Eggins 1994; Bloor and Bloor 1995; Butt *et al.* 1995; Thompson 1996; Droga and Humphrey 2002). Apart from these works which more directly follow IFG, various works have offered alternative descriptions of process types (e.g. Fawcett 1980; Morley 2000; Neale 2002).

In each case however, the authors differ somewhat in the criteria used to classify process types, often to handle cases not covered by IFG, but sometimes because the author's interpretation differs. Because of this diversity of descriptions, SFL does not provide a single process type classification of any clause. The classification a coder makes rather depends on the model being employed. This situation has been confirmed by ongoing discussions on the Systemic discussion lists, *Sysfling*[1] and *Sysfunc.*[2] Difficult cases have been presented to the lists and rich discussions have followed, revealing a range of coding practices existing within the Systemic community.

The aim of this chapter is to explore how 'standard' is the application of process type analysis: to what degree does the community of practitioners concur in their application of the theory. To this end, we prepared 32 clauses, ranging from those reasonably clear as to process type to those which are very difficult to code. We placed these examples on a web-page, which allowed a coder to assign a process type to each clause, and invited the coder to comment on their reasoning. We then solicited readers of Sysfling and Sys-func to complete the coding. Seventy-five people responded.

The rest of this chapter will use the results of this study to explore the variation in the SFL community. We will look at the data from two directions:

1. In terms of clauses: What range of responses did each clause evoke, and what criteria motivated each coding? Does the community in fact vary in the criteria they use?
2. In terms of coders: Can we see patterns in the ways different people code? Do they form sub-communities within the greater SFL community? Can we talk about 'dialects' of SFL, as often suggested by Robin Fawcett?

Section 3.2 below will describe in more detail the data collection process. Section 3.3 will discuss some of the clauses in the study, and how the community coded them, while Section 3.4 will explore the community structure of the coders. Section 3.5 will draw conclusions from the findings.

3.2 Data Collection

The methodology for data collection and cleansing is described in this section.

Selection of sentences. Subscribers to the Sysfling mailing list regularly submit clauses that they have difficulty analysing in terms of process type, for general discussion. We have collected some of these over several years. There was also a 'Tough Clause Workshop' at Sydney University Linguistics Department (04/04/2003) analysing difficult clauses, and we obtained a list of clauses from the organiser, Geoff Williams. To this list, we added some more easily coded clauses, with the intention that these would allow us to verify that at least those examples were commonly coded (and if not, they would allow us to identify coders who were very different from the rest).

The examples discussed on Sysfling were often given out of their textual context, and we were unsure of any confidentiality restrictions on their use. For these reasons, we decided not to use these examples, but rather searched the web for similar cases and used these instead. Our final set included 32 sentences, most of them on the difficult side.

Web survey. We then constructed a web-page which presented each clause and its textual context, and allowed the coder to select one of material, behavioural, mental, verbal, relational or existential. There was also space for the coder to type a comment on why they had chosen that option, or what other options appealed. On clicking the 'Submit' button at the bottom of the page, the coder's responses were stored in a file online. At the end of the survey, there were 75 responses.

Eliminating coders. A small number of coders gave completely different responses to those of other coders. In some cases, this is because they were new to the field, but there were also cases where the coder had an individualistic approach to process types. For Section 3 however, we sought some notion of 'typical' response patterns. So, for that study, the seven most unconventional coders were eliminated. (See Section 3.4.1 for our study of coder nonconformity which informed these exclusions.)

Eliminating clause. One clause was excluded because our instructions of which verb to code were not clear. In *Escape, he thinks, is Jewish,* 37 coded 'think' and 25 coded 'is'. Given that the responses in this case did not reflect a particular coding approach, but rather a decision as to what we wanted coded, we excluded this case from the study.

3.3 Analysis of clauses

Given limited space, we have chosen to focus only on those clauses which shed light on the coding of verbal processes. We first explore the confusion between behavioural and verbal processes, and then explore some other aspects of verbal processes.

3.3.1 Behavioural clauses

According to IFG, behavioural processes are 'physiological and psychological behaviour, like breathing, dreaming, smiling, coughing' (Halliday 1985: 128). These processes are often a source of confusion because they border on other processes; they are similar to material processes in that they can include physical manifestation (e.g., *cough, dance*); they usually include the physical manifestation of verbal processes (e.g., *talk, yell*); and the physical manifestation of mental processes (*look, listen, worry*, etc.) and mental states (*cry, laugh, smile*).

There is some difference in the literature as to exactly what does belong in this category. Thompson (1996:100) notes that verbs Halliday includes such as '*dance*' and '*sing*' might just as well be classed as material.

Below we discuss three of the clauses which seem best to fit this category.

(1) *I laughed at that.*

Context: *Until they can find you a council flat. 'But the days of them are gone.' 'There are still some going and you're bound to get preferential treatment of some sort.' 'Why? Because I've had to spend a couple of nights in a porchway?' 'Because you're a genuine case.' I laughed at that. 'The hostels of London are stuffed full of genuine cases. Why pick on me?*
Situation: conceptually a bodily reaction manifesting a mental reaction to some phenomenon.
Result: behavioural: 63, mental: 3, material 2.

Explaining coding differences: This is a very prototypical behavioural clause; *laughing* is often used as an example of behavioural clauses. However, three coders coded it as mental, suggesting that, for them, the fact that the laughter is expressing a mental reaction is most important. Two coders selected material, and these coders did not use the behavioural category for any clauses in the study, suggesting that behaviourals are not part of their process type model. Both coders in fact commented that they tend to subsume 'behavioural' processes within 'material'.

(2) *We talked for hours*

Context: *Later, in the café, we put the flag into the salt cellar and waited. We talked for hours. Then we went back to our room, and Jim played the guitar, and I sang.*
Situation: the situation expressed by the clause involves verbal action, although the lexico-grammatical expression is not a projecting clause.
Result: behavioural: 40, verbal: 24, material: 4

Explaining coding differences: this clause is less clearly behavioural, as it is expressing a situation in which verbal action is taking place. However, the majority decision here, with 40 coders, is that this is behavioural. IFG mentions 'talk' as a behavioural of the 'near-verbal' kind.

Twenty-four of the coders chose to code it as *verbal*. These coders seem to look at the conceptual situation as their primary criteria when coding clauses, and since there is underlying verbal action, code it as such. As one coder commented:

> I define verbal process as a process of communication. I do not accept that [potential] projection is necessary.

The majority pay attention to its grammatical form (there is no projection), and coded as behavioural. They probably choose behavioural rather than material because it is bodily action without any indicated change of state. However, four coders did choose material, but two of these coders, as mentioned above, always code behavioural-like processes as material.

(3) *and talked about his hometown of Motown*

Context: *The talented junior sat down with Samantha Kilgore <u>and talked about his hometown of Motown</u> knowing what Coach expects and what its like to be Rick in this edition of Tiger Q&A.*
Situation: this clause is similar to the previous clause, except that there is a circumstance of Matter which seems to be realising the Verbiage.
Results: verbal: 36, behavioural: 27, material: 5.

Explaining coding differences: the presence of the circumstance of Matter swayed 12 coders away from the behavioural interpretation over to a verbal one. This was possibly because the 'about' circumstance could be taken as a type of Projection. As one coder commented:

> The presence of Matter clearly pushes it more towards verbal: there would certainly be a case for saying that 'talking' (also 'chatting', etc.) is behavioural, whereas 'talking about' is verbal.

Those who stayed with *behavioural* often commented on the lack of potential for projection. One person who coded the previous example as behavioural coded this one as material. This could be due to coder irregularity.

Part of the confusion here may stem from the confusion in Halliday and Matthiessen (2004). On page 251, 'grumbled about the food' is said to be behavioural. However, on the next page, the following sentence containing 'talk about' is said to be verbal: *Chiruma would find any opportunity to talk to that priest about Kukal.* This work was largely a revision of Halliday (1994) by Matthiessen, and we guess that this is one place where the coding difference between Halliday and Matthiessen becomes apparent (Matthiessen is more conceptual in his coding).

To summarise the results for sentences (1)–(3), we can see that there is a cline from hard behaviourals (e.g., *laughing*) to hard verbals (e.g., to say something). Coders fall into one of three groups: the first code *laugh, talk,* and *talk about* as behavioural. Group 2 follows group 1, except that they code *talk about* as verbal. Group 3 code any form of *talk* as verbal. See Table 3.1.

Here we have explored only the behavioural-verbal cline, but similar clines would probably be observed for near-mentals, and near-materials, with a gradual shift of codings from behavioural to the other category. For instance, in relation to the near-mentals: *I was thinking all day* > *I was thinking about the weather* > *I was thinking that I should go.* A brief survey of participants in a workshop supported this hypothesis.

3.3.2 Verbal clauses

Verbal processes involve a communication between a Sayer and an Addressee, where some message, the Verbiage, is communicated. The study showed clearly that there is no general agreement as to which clauses fit this description. For some coders, there needs to be an actual presence of grammatical projection (e.g., *He said that he was going; She said to eat*). For others, it is enough that the underlying situation is one of verbal communication, as in the examples above involving 'talk'.

For those who use grammatical criteria, people follow different criteria as to what passes for projection. For some, an 'about' adjunct is sufficient; for others, it needs to be a clausal projection. A middle case involves the use of a nominalised report, as in *he asked a question.* This case was not included in our study, but it would be interesting to see the distribution of codings for this example (Halliday and Matthiessen (2004) classes this as verbal, as does Thompson (1996)).

Table 3.1: The behavioural-verbal cline

	Group 1	*Group 2*	*Group 3*
He laughed	Behavioural	Behavioural	Behavioural
We talked	Behavioural	Behavioural	Verbal
We talked about...	Behavioural	Verbal	Verbal
He said...	Verbal	Verbal	Verbal

Below we consider some cases, some clear, some difficult, which shed light on the criteria people are using to code. The first case, (4), is prototypically verbal. Those which follow are more peripherally verbal.

(4) *'There is nothing I can do,' said the King.*

Context: *Despite being repeatedly arrested and brought back home, bruised and beaten by the police, she finally got to see the King by throwing herself into the road in front of the Royal car. 'There is nothing I can do,' said the King, as she was dragged away.*
Situation: conceptually verbal and expressed congruently in the grammar as a projecting clause.
Result: All 68 coders coded as verbal.

Explaining coding differences: since both conceptual and grammatical criteria lead to the same coding decision, there was no dissention here.

(5) *'Dear father, thank you so much,' her smile said.*

Context: *She smiled at him and then, once again, at her father from whose authority these vows released her. 'Dear father, thank you so much,' her smile said – for he had loved and cherished her most tenderly, claiming her obedience as his right, his due.*
Situation: this seems to present an act of communication, although it is not clear whether the communication was intentional. If an intentional communication, it is through a non-verbal channel. The situation might also be interpreted as one of body expression of internal mental states, and thus behavioural. Syntactically, the expression is a projecting clause, using a verb typically used for expressing verbal processes.
Results: verbal: 50, relational: 10, behavioural 5, mental: 3

Explaining coding differences:

Verbal: the majority of coders nominated this as a verbal clause. On one level, this is understandable, because the verb 'say' is a prototypical one for verbal processes, and there is projection in the clause. There are however three potential problems in this example which need to be addressed:

(a) *Non-human Sayer:* it is not the woman who is saying, but her smile. However, Halliday says explicitly that non-human agents can be Sayer:

> The Sayer can be anything that puts out a signal, like the notice or my watch; cf. the light in the light says stop, the guidebook in the guidebook tells you where everything is. (IFG, p. 140)

(b) *Intentionality*: for some, communication must be intentional before it can be classified as semiotic, and thus verbal. In this case, it is not clear whether the woman intended to communicate the message, or whether the message is just the interpretation of the observer.

(c) *Nonverbal communication*: some may query whether nonverbal communications should be classified as verbal processes. For example, is *He waved goodbye* a verbal process?

Most coders seem quite happy to accept a non-human sayer, that the message was intentional, and that verbal processes include nonverbal channels. It is also possible that some coders are purely responding to the grammatical container. Some commented that the clause is conceptually relational realised in a verbal container, but most of these coded on the container anyway.

Relational: 11 coders chose to ignore the grammatical form, looking more at the conceptual action, which is one of something 'meaning' or 'indicating' something, and thus coded relational. Some who coded relational did so because of the issue of intentionality. One coder indicated that if there had been some indication of intentionality in the process, they may have swayed to verbal.

Behavioural: there were also five cases of behavioural coded here, which perhaps relate to a bodily expression of mental states (what IFG calls 'near mental').

Mental: of the few mental coders, one commented that the clause could be viewed in terms of the perceiver, i.e., 'he interpreted her smile to mean …'.

(6) *A final line of analysis insists that the government has made little difference*

Context: *A third interpretation is to say that the strategy has not been implemented and therefore the government is not fully responsible for the outcome. A final line of analysis insists that the government has made little difference, particularly on unemployment.*

Situation: 'insisting' is usually carried out via a verbal channel, but also connotates some element of persistence, which might be mental. The agent of the insisting is non-human. The non-human agent is an abstract object, an 'analysis', which could be seen as the product of a process of analysing, which indirectly could make the people who make the analysis the hidden agents of the insisting. Grammatically, this is a projecting structure.

Results: verbal: 50, relational: 9, material: 5, mental: 3, existential: 1

Explaining coding differences:

Verbal: the vast majority coded verbal, as suggested by the presence of a projection. It seems that, as with the prior example, the non-human nature of the Sayer was not a problem, allowing a message-container to be the (personified) Sayer (e.g., *the message said to come*). One coder took 'line of analysis' as the Instrument of the process rather than the Sayer, with Sayer left unmentioned.

One argument against the verbal coding is that 'insist' cannot take an addressee, although other verbal processes such as 'demand' are similar in this regard. Another argument against a verbal coding is that the tense, simple present, places this as either a continuing action, or as a recurring action. Both are less likely for a verbal process, but more likely for mental or relational interpretations (see below).

Relational: some coders took 'insists' to be similar to 'shows', 'means', 'points to', etc. and the process would thus be relational. One comment was that 'insists' is like 'means' but with a connotation of forcefulness. The simple present tense is the unmarked form for such relationals.

Material: it is not clear what criteria lead to this coding. One of the five coders in this class commented that:

> in other contexts 'insist' could be verbal, but not in this case where the doer (a final line of analysis) is non-human.

One comment provided a possible criterion for the material coding: *if nothing else fits, code as material.*

Mental: it is possible these coders took 'insist' as a form of 'believe', with 'line of analysis' symbolically representing those people who make that analysis. The simple present tense is appropriate for stating permanence of belief.

(7) *They instruct people how to take binding directives*

Context: '*Three theses were presented as part of an explanation of the concept of authority. They are supposed to advance our understanding of the concept by showing how authoritative action plays a special role in people's practical reasoning. But the theses are also normative ones. They instruct people how to take binding directives, and when to acknowledge that they are binding.*'

Situation: the conceptual situation is again one where we have a message-carrying object functioning as Agent. The 'theses' are probably intended in the 'argument' sense rather than in the 'book' sense. The process of 'instruction' is one which is conceptually complex, typically involving verbal actions (*talking, writing*), but also possibly non-verbal elements (material demonstrations, etc.). The grammatical form is of a projecting clause, parallel with more clearly verbal clauses such as *He told her how to get there.*

Results: verbal: 41, material: 19, relational: 4, mental: 2, behavioural: 1

Explaining coding differences:

Verbal: this was the majority decision. These respondents focused on the fact that the instructing agent is an abstract message, personified as the Sayer (or perhaps as the Instrument of the saying). The grammatical form (projecting) supports this decision. Halliday (1985: 146) gives examples of 'explain' and 'show' as verbal processes, and 'instruct' is not too different. Some coders commented that while instruction involves material and mental aspects, they coded as verbal because in this case it happens through the medium of words.

Material: we think the complex nature of the instruction process (including verbal elements but not entirely) push some people to code this as material. If the context of the clause suggested a more material setting for instruction (e.g., a classroom), then more coders would possibly have taken this path. Several of the comments on this clause suggest that the coders were torn between verbal and material, showing the tension in coding criteria here.

Relational: four coders took this path. We are not sure why. One coder commented:

> I don't know!! teach and train and instruct always seem to be tricky, even with human agents, let alone abstract 'teachers' in the form of texts ... the general semantic field seems to be that of cognition, understanding, etc. but there is also a relational aspect to this in the 'showing/revealing' of knowledge.

Mental: the situation of instruction does involve cognitive processing in the instructed person. One coder glossed 'instruct' as 'cause people to know how to.' However, only two coders chose this option. As the comment above states 'the general semantic field seems to be that of cognition, understanding, etc.'

3.3.3 The coding community

In general, there seems to be a general spread of coding practices for most of the clauses discussed here. However, note that most of these clauses were selected exactly because they had given coders problems. Several means of coding sentences are evident, which will be discussed below.

First, the comments and coding patterns of individuals suggests that some coders depend primarily on the syntactic structure of the clause; if there is projection, or potential for projection, then it is a mental or verbal clause, and the choice of the verb decides between these options.

A second set of coders use conceptual criteria; they decide what underlying action is being represented by the clause, and code on that basis. For instance, if the situation expressed by the clause involves verbal action, then code verbal. This approach is problematical where the represented situation contains elements of different process types, e.g., teaching can involve elements of material, verbal and mental activity.

For difficult cases, some coders rely on the paraphrase test: rephrasing to a less difficult wording, and coding as that clause is coded. This approach has been common in discussions on Sysfling, but Martin at least finds it problematic:

> Paraphrase (having the same truth value in some possible world) is a graveyard for transitivity analysis, as case grammar and most other approaches have revealed ... and seems to be creeping into systemic descriptions. (Jim Martin, Sysfling email, 2001)

In response, John Haynes asked whether this put into question Halliday's notion of grammatical metaphor; the unpacking of a metaphor is in a sense a paraphrase. Our guess is that those who code on conceptual criteria can use paraphrase without too much danger, while for those who code grammatically, it is totally perilous.

Another criterion for coding is to defer to authority: to check how the textbooks coded similar examples. The problem with this approach is that we end up coding as we do because 'that is the way things are done'. What we really need to develop are explicit rationales for determining how each and every clause should be coded. As a community, we need to develop explicit statements of coding criteria, detailing how to determine a clause's type, in a manner similar to that used to classify plants into families (e.g., does it produce flowers or not? Does it have 1 or 2 seed leaves? etc.).

Note that this does not entail the need for a unified coding practice. As Halliday said in 'Syntax and the consumer' (Halliday 1964), the way you describe language depends on how you intend to apply the description, and as we as a community are exploring many different applications, differences in coding practice are bound to occur. However, it would be useful if there existed a number of explicit coding guides to facilitate students learning how to code, and also to provide a basis for discussion as to what criteria should be used.

3.4 Are there coding dialects?

In Section 3.3, we looked at a number of *clauses*, and analysed how coders responded to it. Here, we will instead look at each *coder*, and explore how they relate to other coders. We will first explore a measure which attempts to show how (non)conformist each coder is in relation to the other coders. Then we will explore whether the coders can be grouped together into coding *dialects*: where a set of coders follow a particular common set of coding criteria.

Robin Fawcett often talks of 'dialects' of SFL, distinguishing the 'Sydney dialect' (after Halliday, etc.) from the 'Cardiff dialect', (after Fawcett), and other dialects (although he attributes the concept to Halliday himself). In this section, we wish to explore whether the responses to our survey support the idea that there are such dialects in the SFL community.

The term 'dialect' suggests that there are groupings of individuals with common practices. The practices do not have to be exactly identical across all individuals in the grouping, but each individual should exhibit a sufficient number of the group's common practices for that individual to be recognised as part of the group.

We can define a *coding dialect* as a common set of criteria to use in the making of grammatical decisions, e.g., in the present case, as to what process type a given clause represents.

One of our goals is to identify whether the data of our study supports the hypothesis that there are actually distinct coding dialects, i.e., are there groupings of coders which tend to code a given set of clauses in the same way.

Unfortunately, the study included only one contributor from the 'Cardiff dialect'. The setup of the study itself biased against this group, as it assumed six primary process types, while the Cardiff grammar uses a different set of labels, and more of them. Our study thus really explores the dialectal variation within the Hallidayan strand of the school.

3.4.1 Measuring coder conformity

In any population of coders, there will be those who conform to a standard (conformists), and those who follow their own rules (individualists or nonconformists). It will help us to identify our dialects (standards) if we first eliminate all of those coders who do not belong to any dialect, whose responses are on the whole nonconformist.

We thus introduce a formula which allows us to rate each coder according to the degree to which their set of responses conform with other coders – their *conformity level.* We calculate conformity as follows:

We first calculate the probability of each response for each of the sentences (e.g., the probability of coding 'we talked for hours' as verbal). The formula here is simple:

$$\text{Prob(Rij)} = \frac{\text{Count of response i to clause j}}{\text{Number of responses to clause j}}$$

This provides a number between 0.0 and 1.0, with 1.0 representing 100 per cent. The probabilities of all responses to a given clause will sum to 1.0.

For each coder, we sum the probabilities of each of their responses, and then divide by the number of clauses they responded to. This gives us the *average response probability* (ARP) for the coder.

We can then rank all coders in terms of their ARP. The higher their ARP, the more conformist they are (their choices follow the general population more frequently than those with lower ARPs).

This approach does favour those who select the most popular response. However, coders who sometimes code the second or third most popular response may not necessarily come out as nonconformist. If the second-most popular choice for a clause is close in popularity to the favourite, then the difference in conformity ratings for that item will not be great. Only coders who regularly have few agreements with other coders will have low conformity ratings.

There is nothing good or bad about being 'conformist' or 'nonconformist' in regard to coding. It is just that for our purposes (modelling what it is that conformists are conforming to), we need to identify those who are not conforming to any dialect, so that they can be put aside for this study.

In preparation for the next stage, grouping users into dialects, we put aside the data for the six least conformist coders, since we wish to measure what people are conforming to.

Using the above measure, it is possible that a small set of coders with common coding practices (a coding dialect) all come out as nonconformists, and would thus be eliminated. A second means of identifying nonconformist coders was developed, which avoided this problem. Due to lack of space, no details can be given, but we note that the same six coders come out bottom using either approach.

3.4.2 Grouping users

The technique for grouping used here does not at first try to group coders. Rather, it makes the assumption that each coder approximates some ideal coder (a 'coding model'), and varies from that model because of errors, or idiosyncratic decisions on particular clauses. We then examine the data with the aim of positing a set of coding models which best explains the actual coders.

In the simplest case, we assume there are two coding models, and each coder approximates either one or the other. We assign each coder to the model which they are closest to in their choices. We measure the number of coder responses which differ from the model. A coding model is another term for the 'dialects' we mentioned earlier.

Ideally, we seek two coding models such that, over all coders, there are as few differences from the coder's closest model as possible. We call each case where a coder's response does not agree with their assigned coding model an 'unexplained coding'. We can thus rephrase our goal as seeking to minimise the sum of unexplained codings over all coders

Rather than two models, we might instead assume three or four, etc. In these cases, each model represents a distinct set of responses to the clauses to be coded. Around each model will cluster a number of coders, in that the coders are closer to that model than they are to any other model.

The problem thus becomes: how to locate the ideal coding positions which together minimise the unexplained codings. Our solution was to use a simple hill-climbing method, as described below. Note however, that such a hill-climbing method suffers from the problem of sometimes discovering a local minima, rather than a globally best solution. We leave it to later work to improve on this approach.

Step 1: Initiation:

(a) Start with a single model, which is arbitrarily given as the most popular coding of each clause. For each coder, we measure the number of cases where the coder differs from the model, and sum these together to get the Total Unexplained Codings (TUC).

(b) Introduce a second model, identical to the first.

(c) Search for a single change in this second coding model which will improve the TUC: for instance, changing the coding of the fifth sentence from material to mental might decrease the TUC by 5.

(d) Take the change which caused the highest reduction in TUC, and actually make that change to the second model. In case of a tie, the first found is used.

Step 2: Iteration:

Repeat steps 1c/1d but this time looking for the best change in *either* model. Repeat this process until no single change in either model decreases the TUC.

Two model results

Assuming a single model (to which all coders are assigned), we have a TUC (Total Unexplained Codings) of 493. For this sub-study, we included 60 coders, and 31 clauses per coder, giving 1,860 responses. As 493 are unexplained, this means the model explains 1367 responses, or 73.5 per cent.

By introducing a second model, the number of unexplained codings was reduced to 438 (55 more codings are explained), which means 1,422 are explained, or 76.5 per cent. The users were almost equally divided between the two models.

The next question is, are there qualities of the models that we can identify? In 24 of the sentences, both models agree. However, they differ in regards to the coding of seven sentences. See Table 3.2.

Model 1 prefers material/behavioural codings in some cases where Model 2 codes verbal (and in one case mental). In all of these cases, the clause is not a projecting clause, but does to some degree involve conceptually a verbal/mental element. It seems then that to followers of Model 1, syntactic criteria are important (no projection means it cannot be verbal/material), while to followers of Model 2, it is the conceptual structure that is important.

The other difference between the models is that the coders of Model 1 code two complex cases as relational, while the Model 2 coders treat them as material. It is difficult to understand why, but (a) it is good that these two similar cases are treated identically within the models; and (b) these

Table 3.2: Differences between coder 'dialects': the 2-model case

Text	*Model 1*	*Model 2*
the letter draws attention to the arrest ...	material	verbal
A roar greeted his effort at authority	material	verbal
We talked for hours.	behavioural	verbal
and talked about his hometown of Motown	behavioural	verbal
If you've gotta count the sheep	material	mental
The connoisseurship demonstrated in these two examples is built up from an accumulation of work by many scholars	relational	material
the Hamadryas makes do with only a handful	relational	material

cases are so difficult to code that they may represent noise to some degree, the responses not representing the coder's underlying model, but rather a random response where their understanding fails them.

Three model results

Assuming three models results in a reduction of the TUC from 493 to 415 (77.7 per cent of the responses fit the models). Model 1 was by far the most popular, with twice as many members as either other model.

Table 3.3 shows the differences between the three models. Models 1 and 3 are basically identical to the models in the 2-model case. Model 2 falls somewhere between these cases, sometimes siding with Model 1, sometimes with Model 3. Only in two cases (fifth and ninth) does it represent a distinct opinion. It agrees with Model 3 in those cases which are clearly conceptually verbal (*talking, roaring*), but sides with Model 1 in less clear cases (*coming to God, drawing attention*).

3.4.3 Interpretation

The goal of this section was to explore the issue of whether coding dialects exist within the community. To this end, we first applied techniques to identify those coders who were least conformist, and put these coders aside, as it is the conformists we are trying to categorise.

Table 3.3: Differences between coder 'dialects': the 3-model case

Text	*Model 1*	*Model 2*	*Model 3*
the letter draws attention to the arrest ...	material	material	verbal
A roar greeted his effort at authority	material	verbal	verbal
We talked for hours.	behavioural	verbal	verbal
and talked about his hometown of Motown	behavioural	verbal	verbal
If you've gotta count the sheep	material	verbal	mental
The connoisseurship demonstrated in these two examples is built up from an accumulation of work by many scholars	relational	relational	material
the Hamadryas makes do with only a handful	relational	material	material
When we come to God through Jesus Christ	material	material	mental
Nanny stood on the bridge that spanned the ornamental lake	material	behavioural	material

Second, we applied a technique to find the optimal division of our coders into sub-groups, first trying a two-group split, and then a three-group split. This grouping offered strong support for the hypothesis which we derived in Section 2, that some coders use conceptual criteria to code, and others code on grammatical grounds. The sentences which divide the groups are largely those which conceptually involve mental or verbal action, but syntactically do not involve projection.

However, on examining the locality of the coders in each group, there does not seem to be any geographical commonality within the groups. In some cases, teacher and student are in different groups, and each group is equally seeded with the big names. We thus conclude from this that, at least within the Hallidayan tradition (the Cardiff tradition was not represented enough to measure), there are not geographically defined 'dialects' of SFL. Rather, within each locale, each practitioner chooses for themselves from the variety of criteria which are available in the community as a whole.

3.5 Conclusions

Both our analysis of individual clauses (Section 3.3) and of the grouping of coders (Section 3.4) show that the divide between using conceptual vs. syntactic criteria is widespread throughout the community as a whole, and each individual chooses which path they follow. This is, we believe, the result of the lack of explicit coding criteria in general, and argue that what the community needs is explicitly stated sets of criteria for coding practices, and perhaps distinct criteria descriptions for particular applications. To a degree, this has already started; for instance, Robin Fawcett in Cardiff has developed coding criteria for his grammar, although these have not been published.

As a community, we need to develop our criteria, get them published, then use these published criteria as a basis for general discussion as to what criteria are valid (for particular applications), what problems they may have, etc. Only in this way can we avoid the claim of those outside SFL that our practice does not meet the scientific requirement of 'repeatability': that any two coders should produce the same analysis of the same text.

This chapter has only addressed one area of SFL analysis, transitivity, but we believe, similar conclusions would be reached for the analysis of multiple coder surveys of other areas of analysis, such as theme.

Notes

1. http://www.isfla.org/Systemics/Contact/Sysfling.html
2. http://listserv.uts.edu.au/mailman/listinfo/sys-func

References

Bloor, T. and Bloor, M. (1995). *The Functional Analysis of English: A Hallidayan Approach*. London: Arnold.

Butt, D., Fahey R., Spinks, S. and Yallop, C. (1995). *Using Functional Grammar: An Explorer's Guide*. Sydney: NCELTR, Macquarie University.

Downing, A. and Locke, P. (1992). *A University Course in English Grammar*. New York: Prentice Hall.

Droga, L. and Humphrey, S. (2002). *Getting Started with Functional Grammar*. Sydney: Target Texts.

Eggins, S. (1994). *An Introduction to Systemic Functional Linguistics*. London: Pinter.

Fawcett, R. P. (1980). *Cognitive Linguistics and Social Interaction: Towards an Integrated Model of a Systemic Functional Grammar and the Other Components of a Communicating Mind*. Heidelberg and Exeter: Groos and Exeter University.

Halliday, M. A. K. (1964). Syntax and the consumer. In Stuart, C. (ed.), *Report of the Fifteenth Annual Round Table Meeting on Linguistics and Language Study. Monograph Series in Languages and Linguistics 17*. Washington, DC: Georgetown University Press, 11–24.

Halliday, M. A. K. (1976). Types of process. In Kress, G. (ed.) *Halliday: System and Function in Language*. Oxford: Oxford University Press, 159–173.

Halliday, M. A. K. (1985). *Introduction to Functional Grammar* (1st edition). London: Arnold.

Halliday, M. A. K. (1994). *Introduction to Functional Grammar* (2nd edition). London: Arnold.

Halliday, M. A. K. and Matthiessen, C. M. I. M. (2004). *Introduction to Functional Grammar* (3rd edition). London: Arnold.

Morley, G. D. (2000). *Syntax in Functional Grammar: An Introduction to Lexicogrammar in Systemic Linguistics*. London and New York: Continuum.

Neale, A. (2002). More delicate TRANSITIVITY: extending the PROCESS TYPE system networks for English to include full semantic classifications. PhD thesis. Cardiff: Cardiff University.

Thompson, G. (1996). *Introducing Functional Grammar*. London: Arnold.

PART II

Interactions among Ideational, Interpersonal and Textual meanings

4 The grammar of emotion in English and Spanish: a systemic-functional approach

Julia Lavid

4.1 Introduction

The lexicogrammar of every natural language is a theory of human experience, a resource whereby experience is transformed into meaning:

> If we analyse the language of any experiential domain in lexicogrammatical terms, provided the categories used are not ad hoc but are part of a general theory-based description of the language, we are able to see how this domain is construed semantically – how the experience is transformed, by the grammar, into meaning. (Halliday 1998: 23)

At the same time, the grammar of a natural language is a system of probabilities. If we want to characterise a grammatical system adequately, we need to specify the probabilities attached to each of the paradigmatic options available to the speaker in a specific environment, since these relative probabilities are an essential part of the meaning that the system brings into the text (Halliday 1994b: 454).

Here, an attempt is made at characterising how emotion is construed lexicogrammatically in English and Spanish. This is achieved by analysing the semiotic potential shared by both languages in the construction of certain emotive domains and the preferred options selected by each language in terms of their probabilistic weightings.

The motivation for this study is twofold. First, emotion is one of the most challenging areas of human experience, having attracted the attention of several scientific communities (psychology, anthropology, social semiotics, linguistics), and having been the object of extensive research within different trends of the cognitive linguistic paradigm. Second, the predominant perspective adopted in the study of emotion in different cognitive accounts is one where language is treated as a kind of code in which pre-existing conceptual structures are expressed (Harkins and Wierzbicka 2001; Lakoff and Köveces 1987; *inter alia*).

This chapter adopts an alternative viewpoint based on systemic-functional theory, according to which language is seen as the foundation of human experience (Halliday and Matthiessen 1999). It presents a systematic contrastive analysis of the language-specific preferences in the lexicogrammatical construction of four basic emotions in English and Spanish: 'joy', 'fear', 'anger' and 'sadness'. This is achieved through an extensive empirical analysis based on comparable corpora in English and Spanish, which combines the qualitative, the quantitative and the contrastive dimensions. The purpose is to bring out the potential that lies behind emotional expressions in both languages through their corpus-based realisations and their associated probabilistic patterns.

Section 4.2 presents the research methodology used for the proposed investigation, focusing on the data and the analysis procedure. The latter includes an explanation of the different types of analysis carried out and the parameters investigated. Section 4.3 presents the results of the analysis for each emotive domain in both English and Spanish. Finally, Section 4.4 summarises the main points of the study and provides some concluding remarks.

4.2 Research methodology

4.2.1 Data

Two monolingual corpora were selected for analysis. For Spanish, a sample of one million words from the 1900s was extracted from the *Corpus del Español* (CE), a one hundred million word searchable corpus of historical and modern Spanish texts on the web which allows users to perform advanced searches based on parts of speech: lemma, synonyms, word and clause frequency.[1] In addition, a syntactic database of contemporary Spanish (*Base de datos sintácticos del español actual* (BDS) was also consulted. This consists of 160,000 analysed clauses of the contemporary section of the *Archivo de Textos Hispánicos de la Universidad de Santiago* (ARTHUS). For English, the *British National Corpus Sampler* (BNCS) was selected for analysis. This is a one million word representative sample of the largest British National Corpus.

4.2.2 Procedure

The empirical analysis of the data combined three complementary types of analysis: the qualitative, the quantitative and the contrastive.

The qualitative analysis focused on the search for expressions of four basic emotion domains in English and Spanish (*joy, anger, sadness and fear*) and the organisation of those expressions into working paradigms for each domain and language. The purpose of this analysis was to examine expressions from the standpoint of transitivity (Halliday 1994a; Davidse 1992; Matthiessen 1995; Fawcett 1996; *inter alia*). The parameters investigated were the type of semantic construal and the model of experience preferred by each language. The former refers to prototypical semantic categories through which we construe experience (Halliday 1998; Matthiessen and Halliday 1999); the latter refers to two different clausal systems which characterise the experiential grammars of English and Spanish (Davidse 1992; Lavid and Arús 2007, 2004, 1998; Arús and Lavid 2001; Lemmens 1998). One of these is the *transitive* system, which realises a PROCESS-AND-EXTENSION model where the central variable is whether the Process extends to another Participant or not. The other is the *ergative* system, realising an INSTIGATION-OF-PROCESS model where the central variable is whether the process is externally caused or not.

The quantitative analysis examined the frequency distribution of the lexicogrammatical expressions in both languages in terms of their semantic construal and their model of experience. After normalising the raw counts into proportions per million words, the data were statistically analysed using the chi-square test. The results allowed the possibility of establishing reliable comparisons of language-specific preferences in the selection of expressions for a given emotive domain.

4.3 Results of the analysis

The results of the empirical analysis are presented in tabular form in Appendices 1–8 for each emotive domain and language, as shown in Tables 4.1 to 4.8, and explained in detail in each subsection. In all the tables the first column specifies the type of semantic construal of the emotion in the grammar. There are three possible types in both languages: construal as (a) Process, (b) Quality, or (c) Thing.

The second column (a) presents illustrative lexicogrammatical expression examples found in the corpus corresponding to each type of construal, preceded by a representative construction of each example. The source of the examples is specified in parenthesis.[2] The third column (b) offers an experiential analysis of the expressions in terms of their process type (material, mental, relational, behavioural, relational and verbal). This includes an analysis of the model of experience (transitive or ergative) selected in each language for those expressions where the emotive domain is construed as a process. The fourth column (c) analyses the main experiential functions of the structural elements of the expressions. The fifth column (d) presents an agnate expression from some other semantic domain, sharing the same primary grammatical features. Finally, the sixth column (e) shows the probability of occurrence of the expressions normalised to their proportion per million words.

4.3.1 'Joy' domain

With respect to the two parameters which were investigated contrastively through the empirical analysis, the following observations can be made. Both English and Spanish share the same paradigmatic potential in the semantic construction of the experiential domain of 'joy,' i.e., as Process, as Quality or as Thing. However, the probabilistic weighting attached to each of these options differs in both languages, as shown in Tables 4.1 and 4.2.

When comparing the frequencies in both tables, it can be observed that English prefers to construe this domain semantically as a Quality, as illustrated by Examples 4, 5 and 6 in Table 4.1, whereas Spanish prefers to construe it as a Process, as illustrated by Examples 1, 2 and 3 in Table 4.2. The difference in these proportionalities is statistically significant, as shown in Table 4.3 and in Figure 4.1.[3]

With respect to the model of experience preferred by each language, it can be observed that English prefers the transitive model, as illustrated by Examples 1, 2 and 3 in Table 4.1, whereas Spanish prefers the ergative model, as illustrated by Examples 1, 2 and 3 in Table 4.2. The difference in these proportionalities is statistically significant, as shown in Table 4.4.

4.3.2 'Anger' domain

The semantic potential of the emotive domain of 'anger' is common to English and Spanish. That is, 'anger' is semantically construed as a Process, as a Quality, or as a Thing in both languages. However, the probabilistic weighting attached to each of these options differs, as shown in Tables 4.5 and 4.6.

Table 4.1: Paradigm of 'joy' expressions in English

Semantic construal		(a) Joy expression	(b) Type of process	(c) Experiential functions	(d) Agnate expression	(e) Prob. (per million words)
Joy as Process	1	*X rejoice* The nation rejoices. (BNCS, g11)	Mental: transitive middle	Person = Senser	The nation mourns.	10
	2	*X rejoice in/at* We rejoice in your promise/at your skills. (BNCS, gx0)	Mental: transitive middle	Person = Senser Other = Circ.		2
	3	*X pleased Y* The name pleased the duchess. (BNCS, ccd)	Mental: transitive effective	Person = Senser Other = Phen	The game pleased the duchess.	1
						Total = 13
Joy as Quality	4	*X be pleased/happy (about/with)* I am pleased with that. (BNCS, kd8)	Relational: intensive attributive transitive	Person = Carrier 'joy' = Attribute	I am sad.	143
	5	*X feel pleased/happy* He'll feel pleased/happy. (BNCS, kp6)			He'll feel sad.	3
	6	*X is pleasing to Y* This is pleasing to you. (BNCS, ccd)	Relational: intensive attributive transitive	Other = Carrier 'joy' = Attribute Person = Beneficiary	This is frightening.	2
						Total = 148
Joy as Thing	7	*X be a joy* That was for me a great joy. (BNCS, j55)	Relational: intensive attributive transitive	Other = Carrier 'joy' = Attribute Person = Beneficiary	That was a great satisfaction.	1
	8	*It is sb's joy to+ inf.* It is our joy to pray for the queen and the government of this country. (BNCS, gx0)	Relational: intensive attributive transitive	Other = Carrier 'joy' = Attribute	It is our hope to..	1
	9	*X feel joy* 'I feel joy.' (BNCS, ccd)	Mental: transitive	'joy' = Phen. Person = Senser	I feel hope.	1
	10	*X give joy to Y* My plan will give joy to some and satisfaction to many. (BNCS, ccd)	Relational: attributive/ poss. transitive	Other = Agent Per. = Possessor 'joy' = Possessed S	My plan will give happiness to many.	1
	11	*X be joy* She was all lightness and joy. (BNCS, ccd)	Relational: intensive/ attributive transitive	Person = Carrier 'joy' = attribute	She was all anger and bitterness.	1
	12	*X jump with joy* She jumped with joy at the thought. (BNCS, fxr)	Material: transitive	Person = Actor 'joy' = Circ.	He cried with frustration.	1
						Total: 6

When comparing the frequencies in both Tables 4.5 and 4.6, it can be observed that English prefers to construe 'anger' semantically as a Quality, as illustrated by Examples 3, 4, 5 and 6 in Table 4.5, whereas Spanish prefers to construe it as a Process, as illustrated by Examples 1, 2 and 3 in Table 4.6. The difference in these proportionalities is statistically significant, as shown in Table 4.7 and in Figure 4.2.

With respect to the model of experience preferred by each language, it can be observed that English prefers the transitive model, as illustrated by Examples 1 and 2 in Table 4.5, whereas Spanish prefers the ergative model, as illustrated by Examples 1, 2 and 3 in Table 4.6. The difference in these proportionalities is statistically significant, as shown in Table 4.8.

Table 4.2: Paradigm of 'joy' expressions in Spanish

Semantic construal		(a) Joy expression	(b) Type of process	(c) Experiential functions	(d) Agnate expression	(e) Prob. (per million words)
Joy as Process	1	*Alegrarse* David se allegro. (BDS, Jóvenes: 80, 11)	Mental ergative:middle	Person = Senser	David se preocupó.	31
	2	*Alegrarse de* Me alegro de todo. (CE, misc)	Mental ergative: pseudoeffective	Person = Senser Other = Phen.	Me preocupo de sus cosas.	
	3	*X alegrar Y* Ese pequeño dolor me alegraba. (BDS, Jóvenes: 83,24)	Mental: ergative: effective	Person = Senser Other = Phen	Ese pequeño dolor me preocupaba.	12.4
						Total = 43.4
Joy as Quality	4	*X ponerse alegre/contenta* Olga se pone alegre/contenta. (CE, oral)	Relational: attributive/ intensive phase: inceptive ergative: middle	'joy' = Attr. Person = Carrier	Olga se pone furiosa.	1.8
	5	*Y poner a X contento/alegre* Eso me pone contento. (CE, lit)	Relational: attributive/ intensive phase: inceptive ergative: effective	Other= Phen/Agent 'joy' = Attribute	Eso me pone furioso.	0.17
	6	*Sentirse/ estar alegre/contento (por/de)* Me sentía alegre y confiado. (CE, lit)	Relational: attributive /intensive transitive	'joy' = Attribute Person = Carrier	Me sentía molesta.	0.4
						Total = 2.37
Joy as Thing	7	*Tener alegría* Los amigos han tenido alegría y solaz. (CE, lit)	Relational: attributive/ possessive transitive	'joy'= Attribute Person = Carrier	Los amigos han tenido pena.	0.1
	8	*X dar alegría* Eso le da alegría. (CE, oral)	Relational: attributive/ possessive/ agentive transitive	'joy' = Poss. A. Other = Agent	Eso le da pena.	0.7
	9	*Sentir alegría* Mario sintió alegría. (CE, lit)	Mental transitive	'joy' = Phen. Person = Senser	María sintió pena.	0.1
						Total= 0.9

Table 4.3: Semantic construal of 'joy' domain (comparative proportions) ($p < 0.0001$)

	Process	*Quality*	*Thing*
English	13	**148**	6
Spanish	**43.4**	2.37	0.9

Table 4.4: Models of experience in 'joy' domain (comparative proportions) (p < 0.0001)

	Transitive	*Ergative*
English	168	0
Spanish	1.3	45.37

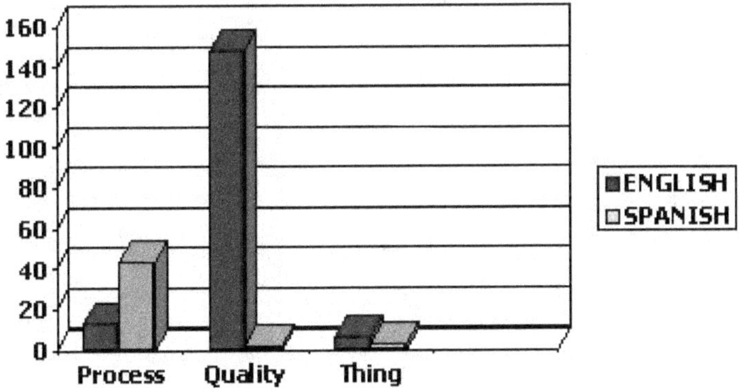

Figure 4.1: Comparative distribution of semantic construal of 'joy' domain

Table 4.5: Paradigm of 'anger' expressions in English

Semantic construal		(a) Anger expression	(b) Type of process	(c) Experiential functions	(d) Agnate expression	(e) Prob. (per million words)
Anger as Process	1	*X anger Y* The law has angered thousands of Russians. (BNCS, a87)	Mental: transitive Effective active	Person = Senser Phen. = Other	The law has bothered many people.	1
	2	*Be angered by* Mr.Bush has been angered by the personal nature of the criticism. (BNCS, aa4)	Mental: transitive effective passive	Other = Phen. Person = Senser	Mr.Bush has been bothered by…	6
						Total = 7
Anger as Quality	3	*Be angry* He was very angry. (BNCS, gv9) He felt angry. (BNCS, gw5)	Relational: intensive/ attributive /neutral transitive	'anger' = A. Person= Carrier	He was very sad. He felt sad.	54
	4	*Look angry* The girl looked worried and angry. (BNCS, gw5)	Relational: intensive/ attributive Phase:app. transitive	'anger' = A. Person = Carrier	The girl looked sad	1
	5	*Become angry* He became terribly angry. (BNCS, gwa)	Relational: intensive/ attributive Phase: inceptive transitive	'anger' = A. Person= Carrier	He became sad.	5
	6	*Sound angry* Peter's voice sounded angry. (BNCS, gul)	Relational: intensive/ attributive Phase: sense-perception transitive	'anger' = A. body part = Carrier	His voice sounded sad.	1
						Total = 61
Anger as Thing	7	*Be beside oneself with anger* She was beside herself with anger. (BNCS, ccd)	Relational: circumstantial/ attributive transitive	'anger' = Circ. Person= Carrier	She was beside herself with anxiety.	1
	8	*Be capable of anger* He was capable of fierce anger. (BNCS, jxl)	Relational: intensive transitive	'anger'= postm.of A. Person= Carrier	He was capable of profound love.	1
	9	*React with anger* He reacted with resigned anger to the news. (BNCS, a9v)	Mental: transitive	Person = Senser 'anger' = Circ.	He reacted with violence.	1
	10	*Fill voice with anger* She filled her voice with all the anger she had in her body. (BNCS, gw5)S	Material: dispositive transitive effective	Person= Actor 'Anger' = Circ.	She filled her glass with water.	1
	11	*Do sth. in anger* Never has it shot a gun in anger at a human being. (BNCS, jjv)	Material: dispositive transitive: effective	Person= Actor 'Anger' = Circ.	Shoot in despair.	1
	12	*Take anger out on sb.* (He) starts taking their anger out on her. (BNCS, kc7)	Material: dispositive transitive: effective	Person= Actor 'Anger' = Goal	He starts taking their anxiety out..	1
						Total = 6

Table 4.6: Paradigm of 'anger' expressions in Spanish

Semantic Construal		(a) Anger expression	(b) Type of process	(c) Experiential function	(d) Agnate expression	(e) Prob. (per million words)
Anger as Process	1	*Enfadarse* Mamá se va a enfadar. (BDS, Sonrisa, 200,17)	Mental: ergative: middle	Person = Senser	Mamá se va a molestar (contigo).	20.5
	2	*Enfadarse con* No te enfades conmigo. (BDS, Ochenta, 40,11)		Person = Senser Other = Circ.		6.8
	3	*Enfadar a alguien* Podía enfadar al abuelo. (BDS, Ternura: 22,9)	Mental: ergative: effective	Person = Senser Other = Phen.	El ruido molesta al abuelo	0.68
						Total = 27.98
Anger as Quality	4	*Estar enfadado* Juvenal está enfadado. (CE, lit)	Relational: intensive attributive transitive	Person = Carrier 'anger' = Attri.	Javier está molesto.	**Total = 0.4**
Anger as Thing	5	*Contener el enfado* Manolo no contuvo su enfado. (CE, lit)	Material: dispositive transitive	Person = Actor 'anger' = Goal	Manolo no contuvo su malestar.	2.80
	6	*Estar en el cenit del enfado de alguien* La princesa estaba en el cenit de su enfado. (CE, lit)	Relational: circumstance attributive transitive	Person = Carrier 'anger' = Circ. Attribute	La princesa estaba en el cenit de su desesperación.	0.68
	7	*El enfado de alguien ser Y* Tu enfado conmigo será mi muerte. (CE, oral)	Relational: intensive identifying transitive	'anger'= Token Other = Value	Tu malestar será mi preocupación.	0.68
						Total = 4.16

Table 4.7: Semantic construal of 'anger' domain (comparative proportions) ($p < 0.0001$)

	Process	*Quality*	*Thing*
English	7	**61**	6
Spanish	**27.98**	0.4	4.17

Table 4.8: Models of experience in 'anger' domain ($p < 0.0001$)

	Transitive	*Ergative*
English	7	0
Spanish	4.56	27.28

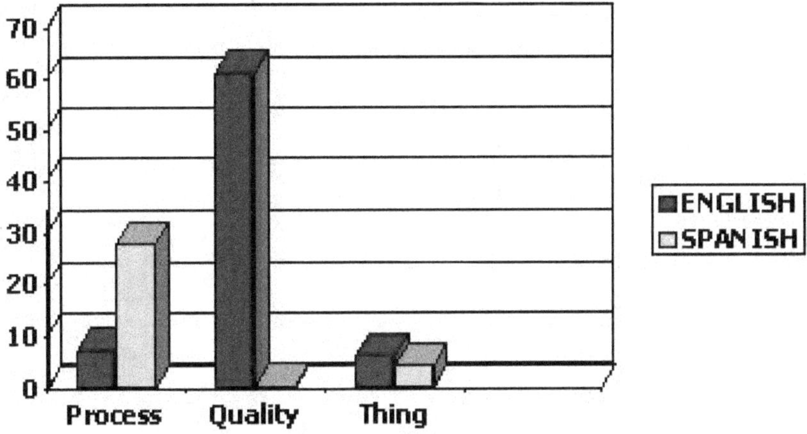

Figure 4.2: Comparative distribution of semantic construal of 'anger' domain

4.3.3 'Sadness' domain

The domain of 'sadness' behaves similarly to the domains of 'joy' and 'anger' with respect to the type of semantic construal and model of experience. As shown in Tables 4.9 and 4.10, English and Spanish attach different probabilistic weightings to each type of semantic construal and model of experience in this domain.

With respect to the type of semantic construal, English prefers to construe the emotive domain of 'anger' as a Quality, as illustrated by Examples 3, 4, 5, 6, 7 and 8 in Table 4.9. By contrast, Spanish prefers to construe this domain as a Process, as in Examples 1 and 2 in Table 4.10. The difference in these proportionalities is statistically significant, as shown in Table 4.11 and in Figure 4.3.

The language-specific preferences in the construction of the model of experience in this domain follow the tendency observed for the 'joy' and the 'anger' domains. English prefers the transitive model, as illustrated by Examples 1 and 2 in Table 4.9, whereas Spanish prefers the ergative model, as illustrated by Examples 1 and 2 in Table 4.10. The difference in these proportionalities is statistically significant, as shown in Table 4.12.

Table 4.9: Paradigm of 'sadness' expressions in English

Semantic construal		(a) 'Sadness' expression	(b) Type of process	(c) Experiential function	(d) Agnate expression	(e) Prob. (per million words)
Sadness as Process	1	*X saddens Y* It saddens me. (BNCS, h4a)	Mental: emotive transitive effective: active	Other =Phen Person = Senser	It surprises me.	1
	2	Many readers will be saddened by the news. (BNCS, cf9)	Mental: emotive transitive effective: passive		They will be surprised by..	4
						Total = 5
Sadness as Quality	3	*Feel/Be sad* I felt sad for my parents. (BNCS, fsb)	Relational: inten. attributive; neutral transitive	Person = Carrier 'Sadness'= Attri.	I was /felt surprised.	23
	4	*Seem sad* The men seemed very sad. (BNCS, aab)	Relational: inten. phase: app. transitive		The men seemed very surprised.	5
	5	*Look sad* She looked sad. (BNCS, g0a)	Relational: intensive.: attrib. sense-perception transitive		She looked surprised.	5
	6	*It be sad* It's terribly sad! (BNCS, kc0)	Relational: intensive transitive	Impersonal setting	It's shocking!	25
	7	*It be a sad sth.* It was a sad, tired face. (BNCS, fry)	Relational: intensive identifying transitive	body part = Token 'sadness'= Value	It was a happy face.	1
	8	*Sth. be sad* His eyes were always sad. (BNCS, gv9)'	Relational: intensive attributive neutral transitive	Body part = Carrier 'sadness' = Attr.	His eyes were always cheerful.	1
						Total =60
Sadness as Thing	9	*Experience sadness* 'I experienced the sadness of France.	Mental: perception: general, transitive	Per.= Senser 'sadness'= Phen.	I experienced another shock.	1
	10	*Do sth with a feeling of sadness* I looked with an odd feeling of sadness and relief. (BNCS, g0a)	Behavioural: transitive	Per. = Behaver 'sadness'= Circ.	I looked with amusement.	1
						Total = 2

4.3.4 'Fear' domain

The domain of 'fear' seems to follow a similar tendency to the one observed for the other emotive domains with respect to the investigated parameters, i.e., the type of semantic construal and the model of experience, as shown in Tables 4.13 and 4.14.

However, if we compare the language-specific preferences in the type of semantic construal, it can be observed that, whereas English prefers to construe the emotive domain of 'fear' as a Quality, as illustrated by Examples 5–11 in Table 4.13, Spanish distributes its preference between the construal as a Process, as in Examples 1–4, and the construal as a Thing, as in Examples 8–13. The difference in these proportionalities is statistically significant, as shown in Table 4.15 and in Figure 4.4.

Table 4.10: Paradigm of 'sadness' expressions in Spanish

Semantic construal		(a) 'Sadness' expression	(b) Type of process	(c) Experiential functions	(d) Agnate expression	(e) Prob. (per million words)
Sadness as Process	1	*Entristecerse* David se entristeció. (BDS, Jóvenes: 157,23)	Mental ergative: middle	Person = Senser	David se preocupó.	5.47
	2	*X entristece a Y* Una idea repentina entristece a Renato. (BDS, Sonrisa: 138,9)	Mental: ergative: effective	Person = Senser Other= Phen/Ag	Una idea preocupa a Renato.	9.65
						Total= 15.12
Sadness as Quality	3	*Ponerse triste* El profesor se puso triste. (CE, oral)	Relational: intensive attributive ergative: middle	'sadness' = Attri. Person = Carrier	El professor se puso alegre.	1.4
	4	*X pone triste a Y* El mar la ponía triste. (CE, lit)	Relational: intensive attributive ergative: effective	'joy' = Attri. Other = Attributor Person = Carrier	El mar la ponía alegre.	0.3
	5	*Estar triste* María estaba triste. (CE, lit)	Relational: intensive attributive transitive	Person = Carrier 'sad'= Attribute	María estaba alegre.	4.2
	6	*Sentirse triste* Me sentí triste. (CE, lit)			Me sentía alegre.	0.9
						Total=6.8
Sadness as Thing	7	*Dar tristeza* Me da tristeza dejar esta vida. (CE, oral)	Relational: attributive possessive/ agentive transitive	'sadness' = Attr. (possessed) Other = Agent	Me da alegría.	0.7
	8	*Sentir tristeza* Sentí tristeza. (CE, lit)	Mental: transitive	'sadness' = Phen. Person = Senser	Sentí preocupación.	0.3
						Total = 1

Table 4.11: Semantic construal of 'sadness' domain (comparative proportions) ($p < 0.0001$)

	Process	*Quality*	*Thing*
English	5	**60**	2
Spanish	**15.12**	6.8	1

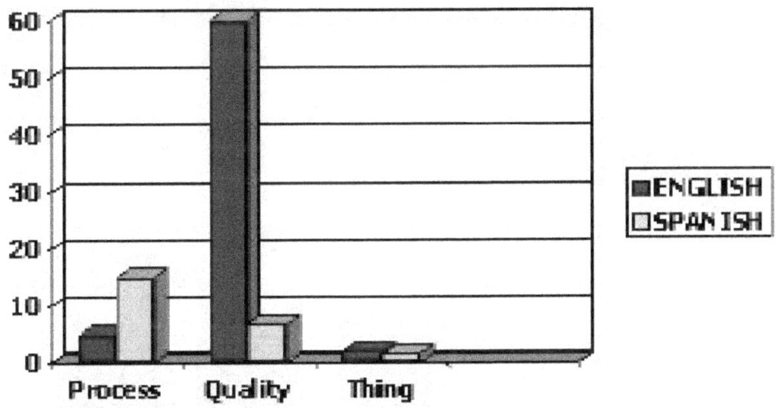

Figure 4.3: Comparative distribution of semantic construal of 'sadness' domain

As for the model of experience preferred by each language in this domain, it can be observed that both English and Spanish prefer the transitive model, as illustrated by the Examples in Tables 4.13 and 4.14. But in Spanish the ergative model also occurs, as illustrated by Examples 3 and 4 in Table 4.13. Here the difference in the proportionalities presented by both languages is not statistically significant, as shown in Table 4.16.

Table 4.12: Models of experience in 'sadness' domain ($p < 0.0001$)

	Transitive	*Ergative*
English	67	0
Spanish	6.1	16.82

Table 4.13: Paradigm of 'fear' expressions in English

Semantic construal		(a) 'Fear' expression	(b) Type of process	(c) Experiential functions	(d) Agnate expression	(e) Prob. (per million words)
Fear as Process		*Fear sth.* I fear a political Balkanisation. (BNCS, a9m)	Mental: transitive effective	Person = Senser Other = Phen.	I want a political change.	44
		Fear for sth. I fear greatly for their safeness. (BNCS, ccd)			I suffer for their safeness.	1
	3	*Fear to +inf.* I fear to see you hurt. (BNCS, ccd)			I like to see you.	1
	4	*Fear that + clause* I fear (that) we shall be denied all contact with the outside world. (BNCS, ccd)			I think that we shall be ok.	17
						Total = 63
Fear as Quality	5	*Feel afraid* Conway felt afraid. (BNCS, gwa)	Relational: intensive attributive: transitive	Person = Carrier 'fear' = Attribute	I felt sore.	2
	6	*Be afraid that* They were afraid that she was very ill. (BNCS, jjs)			I was glad that she was ok.	36
	7	*Be afraid of* Peter was afraid of seeing the station. (BNCS, fry)			I was scared of seeing..	25
	8	*Be afraid* Don't be afraid. (BNCS, kdh)			Don't be sad.	61
	9	*Be afraid to + inf* I was afraid to speak. (BNCS, fsb)			I was scared to speak.	10
	10	*Become afraid* Children will never become afraid of animals. (BNCS, fsb)	Relational: Intensive attributive phase: inceptive transitive		Children will never become fond of animals.	1
	11	*Get afraid* He'll begin to worry and get afraid. (BNCS, gul)			He'll begin to get impatient.	1
						Total = 145

Table 4.13: Paradigm of 'fear' expressions in English (continued)

Semantic construal		(a) 'Fear' expression	(b) Type of process	(c) Experiential functions	(d) Agnate expression	(e) Prob. (per million words)
Fear as Process		*Fear sth.* I fear a political Balkanisation. (BNCS, a9m)	Mental: transitive effective	Person = Senser Other = Phen.	I want a political change.	44
		Fear for sth. I fear greatly for their safeness. (BNCS, ccd)			I suffer for their safeness.	1
	3	*Fear to +inf.* I fear to see you hurt. (BNCS, ccd)			I like to see you.	1
	4	*Fear that + clause* I fear (that) we shall be denied all contact with the outside world. (BNCS, ccd)			I think that we shall be ok.	17
						Total = 63
Fear as Quality	5	*Feel afraid* Conway felt afraid. (BNCS, gwa)	Relational: intensive attributive: transitive	Person = Carrier 'fear' = Attribute	I felt sore.	2
	6	*Be afraid that* They were afraid that she was very ill. (BNCS, jjs)			I was glad that she was ok.	36
	7	*Be afraid of* Peter was afraid of seeing the station. (BNCS, fry)			I was scared of seeing..	25
	8	*Be afraid* Don't be afraid. (BNCS, kdh)			Don't be sad.	61
	9	*Be afraid to + inf* I was afraid to speak. (BNCS, fsb)			I was scared to speak.	10
	10	*Become afraid* Children will never become afraid of animals. (BNCS, fsb)	Relational: Intensive attributive phase: inceptive transitive		Children will never become fond of animals.	1
	11	*Get afraid* He'll begin to worry and get afraid. (BNCS, gul)			He'll begin to get impatient.	1
						Total = 145

4.3.5 Interaction between metafunctions in the emotive domain

An interesting feature which emerges from the experiential analysis is the different tendency observed in both languages in the interaction of the experiential and the interpersonal with the textual metafunction: more specifically, with the thematisation choices preferred by each language.

Thus, in English constructions of the type '*X is happy/angry/sad/afraid*' tend to structure the emotional experience as one where the person is presented as the Theme. If it is the first person singular, the unmarked way of getting it into thematic position is to map it on to the Subject. Hence, the preferred form of expression will be with the Subject 'I'.

If we compare this with what happens in Spanish, we can observe a different type of interaction between the experiential, the interpersonal and the textual metafunctions.

Table 4.14: Paradigm of 'fear' expressions in Spanish

Semantic construal		(a) 'Fear' expression	(b) Type of process	(c) Experiential function	(d) Agnate expression	(e) Prob. (per million words)
Fear as Process	1	*Temer* No temas. (CE, lit)	Mental: transitive: middle	'fear'= process Per = Senser	No ames.	7.58
	2	*Temer por/a/ +inf.* Temes por tu seguridad. (BDS, Coartada: 57, 14)	Mental: transitive: effective	'fear' = process Per = Senser Other = Phen.	Esperáis a Dios/ encontrarlo..	82.75
						Total= 90.33
	3	*Atemorizarse por* Los tres se atemorizaron por el hecho. (CE, lit)	Mental: emotive ergative: middle	'fear' = Process Per= M/Senser	Los tres se asustaron.	
	4	*X atemoriza a Y* El próximo paso le atemorizaba más. (CE, lit)	Mental: emotive ergative: effective	'fear' = Process Per= M/Senser Other = Inducer	Le asustaba.	**Total= 4.4**
Fear as Quality	5	*Estar/ parecer temeroso* ..parecía temeroso de cuanto le rodeaba. (CE, misc)	Relational: inten. attributive: transitive	'fear' = Attribute Person = Carrier	Estoy esperanzado.	1.1
	6	*Sentirse temeroso* 'Un viejo que no consigue dejar de sentirse temeroso' (CE, lit)	Relational: inten. attrib.: transitive	'fear' = Attribute Person = Carrier	Sentirse esperanzado.	0.1
	7	*Estar/ parecer atemorizado* Nuestro valle estaba atemorizado por la presencia de un tigre. (CE, lit)	Relational: inten. attributive: transitive	'fear' = Attribute Person = Carrier	Estaba angustiado por su presencia.	0.1
						Total = 1.3
Fear as Thing	8	*Dar miedo* Me da miedo la enfermedad. (CE, lit)	Relational: possessive attributive / agentive transitive	'fear'= Poss. Attribute Other = agent Person = Ben.	Me da rabia la injustice.	12.8
	9	*Infundir miedo* A los viejos les infunde miedo. (CE, oral)			El gato le inspiraba ternura.	0.6
	10	*Causar miedo* Sus relatos nos causan miedo. (CE, oral)			Sus relatos nos causan placer.	0.2
	11	*Producir* miedo Algunas cosas me producían miedo. (CE, lit)			Algunas cosas me producían desazón.	0.4
	12	*Tener miedo a/de* Tengo miedo/temor a/de la muerte. (CE, lit)	Relational: poss. attributive: transitive	'fear'= Poss. Attrib. Person = Carrier	Tengo deseo de desaparecer.	58
	13	*Siento miedo de (obj/inf/clause)* A veces siento miedo de que todo esto no sea más que un sueño. (CE, oral)	Mental transitive	'fear' = Phen. Person = Carrier	Siento alegría de.	4.3
						Total = 75.2

Table 4.15: Semantic construal of 'fear' domain (comparative proportions) ($p < 0.0001$)

	Process	*Quality*	*Thing*
English	63	145	28
Spanish	90.33	1.3	75.2

Table 4.16: Models of experience in 'fear' domain ($p < 0.21$)

	Transitive	*Ergative*
English	63	0
Spanish	166.83	4.4

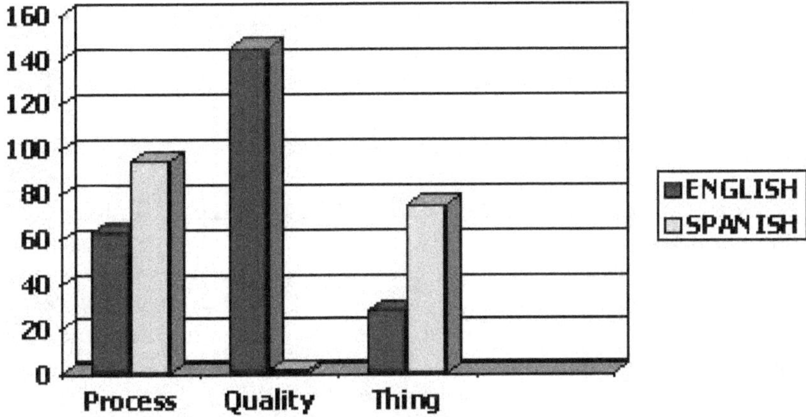

Figure 4.4: Comparative distribution of semantic construal of 'fear' domain

With respect to the experiential metafunction, we can observe that Spanish shares with English the same tendency to construe the emotional experience as one where the person is presented as the Theme in expressions of the type '*Me alegra/enfada/entristece/da miedo*', even though the type of semantic construal is different. While English opts for the construal as a Quality, Spanish prefers the construal as a Process. Experientially speaking, English and Spanish favour a similar type of thematic selection.[4]

Interpersonally speaking, however, English and Spanish behave rather differently. English opts for the interpersonal role of Subject as the Theme of the message in all three types of semantic construal in the emotive domain, favouring on many occasions the passive construction (which is not possible in Spanish in a similar context) when the construal of the emotion is as a process (e.g.: *Mr Bush has been angered by the personal nature of the criticism*, BNCS aaa4; *Many readers will be saddened by the news*, BNCS, cf9).

Spanish, by contrast, distributes thematic selection more evenly among the different roles of the interpersonal structure of the clause. Thus, alongside the conflation of Subject and Theme (*David se alegró*, BDS, Jóvenes: 80, 11) in middle constructions, the predominant type of conflation is of the Theme with the Complement function (realised by the personal pronoun) in effective expressions of the type *Me alegra/enfada/entristece/da miedo*.

Therefore, the dynamics of the interaction among the three metafunctions is different in English and Spanish. In English, a poorly-inflected language, the need to include the Subject function in preverbal position imposes restrictions on the thematic options at the speaker's/writer's disposal. In Spanish, the optionality of the Subject function allows a wider range of thematic choices.[5]

4.4 Discussion and concluding remarks

As the results of the analysis in Section 4.3 have shown, English and Spanish share similar resources for the expression of emotions but differ in their systemic probabilities along the contrastive parameters investigated in this chapter.

With respect to the semantic construal, English prefers construing emotions as qualities to be assigned to people as Carriers in relational-type processes, as illustrated by constructions of the type: *I am happy/angry/sad/afraid*, which have been found to predominate in the English corpus. The quality may also be assigned to a part of the body (*His eyes were always sad.*) or to attributes of the person (*Peter's voice sounded angry.*). Alternatively, it may simply be said to be present, as an element in a figure of 'being' (*It's terribly sad.*).

By contrast, Spanish prefers to construe emotions as processes in figures of 'sensing', as illustrated by constructions of the type *Me alegra/enfada/entristece*, where the person is typically assigned the experiential role of Senser and the interpersonal role of Complement. Another possibility is to construe the emotion as a thing in figures of 'being & having', as illustrated by constructions of the type *Tengo miedo* or *Me da/inspira/produce miedo* where the emotion is the Possessed Attribute.

With respect to the model of experience, English prefers the *transitive* model, whereas Spanish prefers the *ergative* model. This is a reflection of the different tendencies in the grammars of mental processes in both languages, where causation is a major motif in Spanish, but a minor motif in English (see Lavid and Arús 2004).

The analysis presented here can be relevant not only for theoretical-descriptive purposes, but also as the basis for applied work in a number of contexts. Lack of space precludes us from a full-length discussion of these contexts, but it is possible to envisage important implications for areas such as translation, second language learning or computational generation. For example, the probabilistic weightings attached to language-specific lexicogrammatical choices may serve as a guide in the process of contrastive generation deriving from a common systemic potential. Also, in areas such as translation and second language learning, the language-specific choices can be fruitfully used as the basis for the design of translation and second-language learning exercises which systematically compare the features of the emotive domains studied here. These and other issues, however, remain a matter for future research.

Notes

1. This large corpus has been created by Prof. Mark Davies of Brigham Young University and funded by funded by the NEH. It is available online at <http://davies-linguistics.byu.edu/corpus/>.
2. Here I follow the referencing conventions used in each of the consulted corpora. For the BNCS, the text code is provided. For the CE, the text type is provided; for the BDS the text name and line numbers are provided.
3. To be consistent with the proportionalities reflected in the tables, these are reproduced in Table 4.5 and Figure 4.1. Nevertheless, the chi-square test was performed on raw frequencies.
4. Although the experiential roles selected as Theme are not the same – Carrier in the English construction, and Senser in the Spanish construction – they can be subsumed under the general function of first participant role.
5. For a discussion of differences in the interaction between metafunctions based on an empirical study of choices in clause-initial position in English and Spanish see Lavid (2006).

Sources of data

Base de datos sintácticos del español actual (BDS) (http://www.bds.usc.es/)
British National Corpus Sampler (BNCS) (http://www.natcorp.ox.ac.uk/corpus/index.xml)
Corpus del Español (http://www.corpusdelespanol.org/)

References

Arús, J. and Lavid, J. (2001). The grammar of relational processes in English and Spanish: implications for machine-aided translation and multilingual generation. *Estudios Ingleses de la Universidad Complutense*, 9: 61–79.

Athanasiadou, A. and Tabakowska, E. (eds) (1998). *Speaking of Emotions: Conceptualisation and Expression*. Berlin and New York: Mouton de Gruyter.

Davidse, K. (1992). Transitivity/ergativity: the Janus-headed grammar of actions and events. In Davies, M. and Ravelli, L. (eds) *Advances in Systemic Linguistics*. London: Pinter, 105–135.

Fawcett, R. P. (1996). A systemic functional approach to complementation in English. In Berry, M., Butler, C. S., Fawcett, R. P., and Huang, G. W. (eds) *Meaning and Form: Systemic Functional Interpretations. Meaning and Choice in Language: Studies for Michael Halliday*. Norwood, NJ: Ablex, 297–366.

Halliday, M. A. K. (1994a). *Introduction to Functional Grammar* (2nd edition). London: Arnold.

Halliday, M. A. K. (1994b). Contexts of English. In Carlon, K., Davidse, K. and Rudza-Ostyn, B. (eds) *Perspectives on English: Studies in Honour of Professor Emma Vorlat*. Leuven: Peeters.

Halliday, M. A. K. (1998). On the grammar of pain. *Functions of Language*, 5/1: 1–32.

Halliday, M. A. K. and Matthiessen, C. M. I. M. (1999). *Construing Experience Through Meaning: A Language-based Approach to Cognition*. London and New York: Continuum.

Harkins, J. and Wierzbicka, A. (eds) (2001). *Emotions in Crosslinguistic Perspective*. Berlin and New York: Mouton de Gruyter.

Lakoff, G. and Kövecses, Z. (1987). The cognitive model of anger inherent in American English. In Holland, D. and Quinn, N. (eds) *Cultural Models in Language and Thought*. Cambridge: Cambridge University Press, 195–221.

Lavid, J. (2006). Contrasting textual choices in English and Spanish: a corpus-based exploration. Paper presented at the 18th EuroInternational Systemic-Functional Linguistics Conference and Workshop. University of Trieste (Gorizia, Italy), 19–22 July.

Lavid, J. and Arús, J. (2007). Processes of consciousness in English and Spanish: theoretical and applied perspectives. In Carretero, M., Hidalgo, L., Lavid, J., Martínez-Caro, E., Neff, J. and Pérez de Ayala, S. (eds) *A Pleasure of Life in Words: a Festschrift for Angela Downing*. Madrid: Universidad Complutense, 347–380.

Lavid, J. and Arús, J. (2004). Nuclear transitivity in English and Spanish: a contrastive-functional study. *Languages in Contrast*, 4/1: 75–103.

Lavid, J. and Arús, J. (1998). Exploring transitivity/ergativity in English and Spanish: empirical and computational findings. In Martínez Vázquez, M. (ed.) *Transitivity Revisited*. Huelva: Publicaciones de la Universidad de Huelva, 259–275.

Lemmens, M. (1998). *Lexical Perspectives on Transitivity and Ergativity. Current Issues in Linguistic Theory 166.* Amsterdam: Benjamins.

Matthiessen, C. M. I. M. (1995). *Lexicogrammatical Cartography: English Systems.* Tokyo: International Language Science Publishers.

5 Construing attitude and experience in discourse – the interaction of the TRANSITIVITY and APPRAISAL systems

Claire Scott

5.1 Introduction

Recently, Martin and White (2005) have acknowledged the interface between APPRAISAL[1] resources and field of discourse,[2] arguing that 'feelings are always feelings about something – about the activity sequences and taxonomies enacting one field or another'. In their analyses of ideational and evaluative meanings in historical and media discourses, they also go some way towards addressing the dependencies between the systems of TRANSITIVITY and APPRAISAL. Earlier work on appraisal attended to the relationship between TRANSITIVITY and APPRAISAL only in terms of realisational grammatical frames, particularly 'ideational meanings which rebound with affectual meanings' (Martin 2000: 155). The focus has largely been on the localised evaluative lexical content, rather than the global potential for appraisal selections afforded by semantic and contextual factors.

Some recent studies of psychotherapeutic discourse (Henderson-Brooks 2006) and war and media discourse (Scott 2003, 2004) have made use of the systems of TRANSITIVITY and APPRAISAL, PARTICULARLY THE SUB-SYSTEM OF JUDGEMENT, as complementary frameworks for discourse analysis. The results of parallel analyses with these systems have highlighted the semantic amplification achieved by the systematic and harmonious selection of experiential and attitudinal meanings. For example, in 'declaration of war' speeches, US President George W. Bush and Australian Prime Minister John Howard were shown to marginalise the enemy through their TRANSITIVITY selections, and their overwhelmingly negative appraisal of the enemy worked cooperatively with these meanings (Scott 2003, 2004). In other words, selections from each system simultaneously contributed to the construction of the enemy in these terms. These studies demonstrate that the two systems, one lexicogrammatical and the other semantic, are jointly implicated in the construction of particular points of view.

In this chapter, I further explore the interaction of the systems of TRANSITIVITY and JUDGEMENT by presenting a parallel analysis of these systems in two topically related texts. Whilst appraisal analysis is often conducted on texts as an end in itself, I wish to show the power of combining the two forms of analysis as a basis for understanding texts as registerial varieties, and for exploring their ideological tendencies. The analysis and interpretation of appraisal is presented first, in order to show the results of an analysis based on appraisal alone. Following that, I set out my analysis and interpretation of transitivity in order to illustrate the impact that an understanding of experiential meanings has on our interpretation of the appraisal in the text.

5.2 Texts

Two topically related texts are analysed: a newspaper article about one family's experience of the South-East Asia tsunamis of December 2004, and an internet discussion thread concerning reports of this same event. The story concerns Australian woman Jillian Searle and her family, who were holidaying in Phuket, Thailand, at the time of the tsunami. It attracted considerable attention in the media, being reported in all major Australian newspapers, as well as many international ones, and on Australian television and radio news broadcasts on 29 and 30 December. This particular news story appeared in the *Sydney Morning Herald* (henceforth SMH) on 30 December, 2004, entitled *Her baby or son: the choice almost tore them apart* (Granath 2004; see Appendix 1). It is considered an instance of the 'hard news' genre because of the way it functions to chronicle rather than interpret or explain events (see Section 3 in Iedema *et al.* 1994).

A number of discussion threads based on the Searles' story appeared on internet discussion forums in response to the media reports. The discussion thread analysed here appeared in a forum on Parenthood.com (2005), a US-based website providing information, support, and networking for parents. A discussion board moderator initiated the thread by posting a link to a news article about the Searles' situation, along with her own comment: 'I can't imagine the way this woman had to have felt. She was SO lucky in how it turned out! OMG[3] what an experience for them all.'

Nine other people, all mothers,[4] responded to the post with their own comments. The full text of the discussion thread is not included here for space reasons, however excerpts are given as relevant throughout the analysis.

Whilst the texts are topically related, there are a number of significant differences across the contextual parameters of mode and tenor. The newspaper article, as a monologic text created by one journalist at a fixed point in time and for a deadline, has a quite different contextual configuration from the discussion board, which is co-constructed by ten people over an ungoverned time period. The SMH text is a complete text and is not interactive apart from potentially (and indirectly) through the *Letters* page of the newspaper. The interactive Parenthood.com text is potentially never complete because contributors may post and re-post at any time. The 'final' post in this thread is only final because there had not been any further responses since it was posted; the text has no inherent 'conclusion' stage, so it could have been resumed at any time. The metafunctional implications of these shifts in tenor and mode will also be explored in the analysis.

5.3 Construing attitude

This section forms a preliminary investigation of the meanings construed in the texts by using the framework developed by Martin and colleagues (see Martin and White 2005) to present an analysis of the way attitude is construed. The TRANSITIVITY analysis in Section 5.5 will expand on the results of the appraisal analysis and bring into focus the complementarities between the two systems.

The meanings we are concerned with in this section are those of attitude, particularly judgement of human behaviour. Iedema *et al.* (1994: 212, 235) and Martin and White (2005: 170–173) argue that hard news stories generally avoid expressing explicit judgements of people's behaviour in the interests of presenting an 'objective'[5] account of events. If this is the case, and if we take the SMH text as an instance of the 'hard news' genre, we can expect that there will be observable differences between the number of appraisal instances (if indeed this is measurable in a reliable way)[6] in this text, and the number of instances in the Parenthood.com text, which is generically different. The main questions for this analysis will be addressed in the following sections:

3.1 What kinds of attitudes are expressed in the texts, and

3.2 How are the attitudes applied to people and things in the text?

The appraisal analysis involved identifying sections in the texts where emotional responses were expressed (*Affect*), or where there was some evaluation of a person's behaviour (*Judgement*) or of the appearance or value of a thing or person (*Appreciation*). Within these three subsystems, the attitudes can either be expressed explicitly (inscribed appraisal), usually including an evaluative lexical item, or implicitly (evoked appraisal), using 'apparently unevaluated descriptions of some event or state of affairs' (White 2004), and relying on the reader's understanding of the relevant social norms or aesthetic values (Iedema *et al.* 1994: 211–212; Martin 2000: 155). The subtypes of attitude are exemplified in Examples 1–5 using extracts from the two texts. Underlining is used to show attitudinal lexical items in inscribed appraisal. Note that there are no examples of positive *Appreciation* in the texts.

(1)	Parenthood.com	I'm glad that he is alive and safe (+Affect: Happiness)
(2)	Parenthood.com	I would be very hurt and angry (–Affect: Dissatisfaction)
(3)	SMH	he had held onto the pole for nearly two hours with his head just above water (+Judgement: Tenacity (evoked))
(4)	Parenthood.com	this woman is the dumbest, most thoughtless mom I've heard about in a loooong while (–Judgement: Propriety (inscribed))
(5)	SMH (quoted speech)	'it {the tsunami/ the situation} was so horrific' (–Appreciation: Reaction)

One of the difficulties with appraisal analysis is that there is as yet no simple way of reporting and comparing instances of appraisal proportionally, for example in relation to the number of clauses in a text, because of the possibility for appraisal 'instances' to cross clause boundaries or even cluster together in the one clause. This is a characteristic of the location of appraisal at the level of semantics (or discourse-semantics) rather than the level of lexicogrammar (eg. Martin and White 2005: 10–11). I will discuss the semantic and contextual implications of the appraisal amassed against particular people and things in the texts, rather than try to compare raw figures from two texts of different lengths.

5.3.1 What kinds of attitudes are expressed in the texts?

All APPRAISAL subsystems (AFFECT, JUDGEMENT, and APPRECIATION) are represented in the texts (see Examples 1–5). However, in both texts the main kinds of attitudes that are expressed are those from the subsystem of JUDGEMENT, as shown in Table 5.1. Table 5.2 shows that almost all the appraisal is sourced to the writers of the respective texts. However the SMH text also sources some appraisal to Jillian and Bradley Searle through direct quotation in the newspaper article.

Because it is dominant in the texts, the appraisal analysis in this chapter focuses on JUDGEMENT. Within APPRAISAL, JUDGEMENT is the subsystem from which speakers choose in order to express attitudes about human behaviour. The options within JUDGEMENT are presented diagrammatically in Figure 5.1 and outlined in Table 5.3. Essentially, there are two sets of options within JUDGEMENT: the social code on which the judgement is based – that is, whether the judgement is based on norms of *Social Esteem* or *Social Sanction* – and whether it is positive or negative.

In these texts, there are both positive and negative judgements of *Social Sanction* and *Social Esteem*. The distribution of the judgements, positive

Table 5.1: Number of instances of each APPRAISAL subsystem

	SMH	*Parenthood.com*
Affect	2	14
Judgement	12	55
Appreciation	1	0

Table 5.2: Source of appraisal and number of instances for each text

SMH				*Parenthood.com*			
Source	*Instances*			*Source*	*Instances*		
	Aff	*Judge*	*App*		*Aff*	*Judge*	*App*
author	0	10	0	author	14	55	0
Jillian Searle	2	2	0				
Bradley Searle	0	0	1				

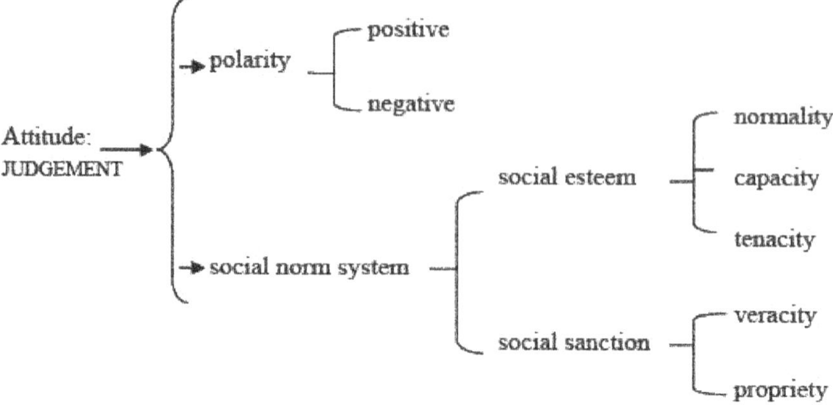

Figure 5.1: Categories of the subsystem of JUDGEMENT (DIAGRAM adapted from Martin and Rose 2003: 62)

Table 5.3: Categories in JUDGEMENT (Martin 2000: 155–156)

Judgement	
Social Esteem	Involving admiration and criticism, usually without legal implications
Normality	How usual (or unusual) someone is, e.g. lucky/unlucky, normal/peculiar, fashionable/daggy
Capacity	How capable someone is, e.g. powerful/weak, clever/stupid, sane/insane
Tenacity	How resolute someone is, e.g. brave/cowardly, reliable/unreliable, determined/unmotivated
Social Sanction	Involving praise and condemnation, with potential legal implications; morally based and institutionally enforced
Veracity	How honest someone is, e.g. truthful/deceitful, genuine/fake, direct/prevaricating
Propriety	How ethical someone is, e.g. good/bad, moral/immoral, just/unjust, law-abiding/corrupt

and negative, between the various subcategories of *Social Esteem* and *Social Sanction* is presented in Table 5.4. The instances in the table include judgements from all appraisers and of all the appraised. For example, in the SMH text this includes appraisal attributed to sources quoted in the article.[7] Despite the large difference between the numbers of instances in each text, which is due in part to a difference in text length (word and clause counts shown in Table 5.4), there are clear tendencies in the selection of appraisal polarity and subcategories in the texts. The SMH text tends towards positive appraisal of *Tenacity*, and equal numbers of positive and negative judgements of *Normality*. The Parenthood.com text leans towards negative appraisal, particularly of *Normality* and *Propriety*. Significantly, all categories of JUDGEMENT are represented in the Parenthood.com text, whereas the SMH text shows barely any use of *Social Sanction* subcategories. This finding resonates with the generic tendency (and expectation) for hard news reports, as reported in Iedema *et al.* (1994: 212, 235) and Martin and White (2005: 170–173).

The preliminary findings presented here give a broad overview of the appraisal in the texts. Both the appraised and the source of appraisal are important in interpreting the evaluative meanings in the texts, so the analysis will now be further detailed to discover whether particular people, things or events are appraised in consistent ways and by particular appraisers.

5.3.2 How are the attitudes applied to people and things in the text?

The main focus of the appraisal in both texts is Jillian Searle. In the SMH text, Lachie Searle, Bradley Searle, the Searle family, and the tsunami are also appraised. In the Parenthood.com text, journalists and Parenthood.com mothers also appear as targets of appraisal, whilst Bradley Searle does not. The numbers of instances where Jillian is the appraised are shown in Figure 5.2. The white bars in the chart indicate the frequency of positive

Table 5.4: Distribution of appraisal (Judgement) in SMH and Parenthood.com texts

	SMH (*473 words, 75 clauses*)		*Parenthood.com* (*929 words, 128 clauses*)	
	+	–	+	–
Social Esteem				
Capacity	0	0	2	4
Normality	3	3	4	10
Tenacity	5	0	4	2
Social Sanction				
Propriety	0	1	5	17
Veracity	0	0	7	2
Total	8	4	22	35

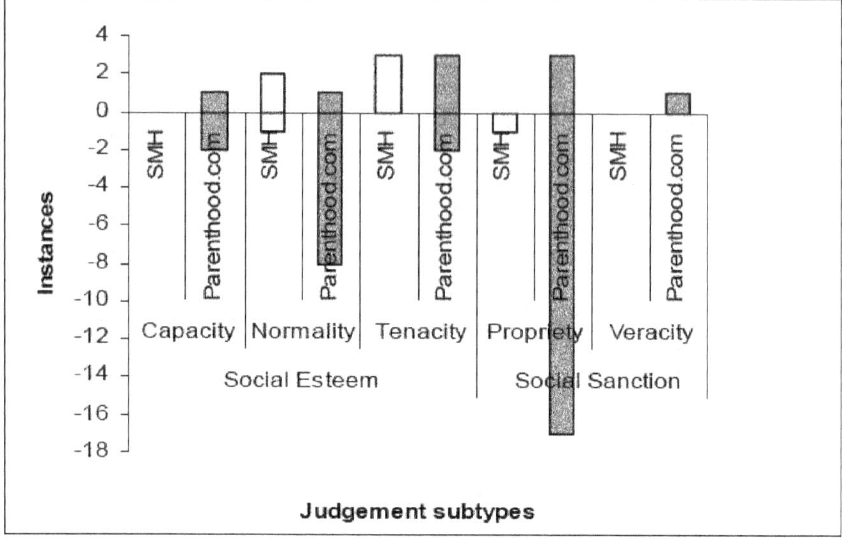

Figure 5.2: Instances and subtypes of appraisal with Jillian as the appraised

and negative appraisal in the SMH text, and the grey bars show these values for the Parenthood.com text. Bearing in mind the differences in the lengths of the texts, it can be seen that there are few instances of appraisal in the SMH text, tending towards the values within *Social Esteem*, and a substantial number of instances of appraisal in the Parenthood.com text, heavily weighted towards *Social Sanction*, particularly Propriety. (See Section 5.7 for a discussion of the implications of these findings for the conception of 'reporter voice'.)

In these texts, the evaluative meanings that appear most at stake are those concerned with Jillian Searle's choice to let go of her son, rather than, for example, the nature of the tsunami (another available choice, which would be realised through options in the subsystem of APPRECIATION). In the Parenthood.com text there is also some emphasis on the mothers' emotional responses (realised through choices in the subsystem of AFFECT). However it is their judgement of Jillian's behaviour that is foregrounded over all.

5.4 Summary of appraisal analysis

The SMH text is characterised by infrequent, predominantly positive appraisal of Jillian that is mostly based on the code of *Social Esteem*. In the SMH text, the journalist is concerned with how admirable Jillian is in terms of her resolve *(+Tenacity)* in trying to save herself and her children by whatever means possible. Jillian is also evaluated as being fortunate *(+Normality)* to have emerged from the situation with all family members safe (although this positive appraisal is attributed to Jillian rather than being authorially sourced). Jillian's resolve is a newsworthy 'stabilising' event in the midst of the extremely 'destabilising' circumstances of the tsunami, as it provides 'evidence that certain aspects of our world are permanent and consistent' (Iedema *et al.* 1994: 107).

The Parenthood.com text is characterised by a predominantly negative appraisal of Jillian that is used liberally and oriented towards the code of *Social Sanction.* The Parenthood.com mothers are concerned with acknowledging Jillian's misfortune (*–Normality*) in finding herself in such a difficult situation, and condemning her decision and resulting actions as morally questionable *(–Propriety)* despite the positive outcome. There are also a few mothers who defend Jillian *(+Veracity)* against the negative judgement of others. The general tone of the discussion, however, is highly judgemental.

Interestingly, the action the mothers construe as morally questionable (Jillian letting go of Lachie) is the very action the journalist presents as indicative of courage and determination. Two underlying ideologies seem to be at work here: 'try to keep everyone alive, no matter what it takes' (SMH) and 'never let go of your child, no matter what the consequences might be' (Parenthood.com). The mothers seem to want to distance themselves from Jillian's actions as a mother in order to define and reinforce their own norms about what a 'good mother' does. The journalist's evaluative position is perhaps less dependent on Jillian's motherhood status – the ideology would apply equally to anyone.

These evaluative meanings are construed semantically through appraisal resources, motivated by contextual factors such as the writers' relationship with their readers and the self-presentation function of the text. The SMH journalist is reporting a story as news to a general audience, whereas the writers in the co-constructed Parenthood.com text are responding to a version of this story, sharing their opinions with one another, and debating appropriate behaviour for mothers. In their communicative context they are licensed to evaluate Jillian more freely and explicitly than the journalist is, and Jillian is sufficiently distant from them (i.e. they would not expect her to appear as a participant in the forum) to do so without feeling self-conscious about it. These contextual factors permeate the meanings of the texts overall, at all strata, as will be demonstrated through the following analysis of the lexicogrammatical system of TRANSITIVITY.

5.5 Construing experience

We have seen that the evaluative meanings construed in the two texts result in two quite different portrayals of Jillian Searle. In this section, I present an analysis of the way the Searles' experience is constructed in both texts through selections in TRANSITIVITY. Since their evaluation of Jillian as a social actor differs so markedly, we can expect to find that the experiential meanings realised by the system of TRANSITIVITY, IN WHICH JILLIAN'S ROLE AS AN ACTOR IS GRAMMATICALLY RELEVANT, will also differ to some extent.

The inherent tenor roles in these different genres motivate the uptake of options for construing experience. The writers in the Parenthood.com text are allowed to construe both the experience of the Searles and their own experience as readers of the article and women who have children of their own. The writer of the SMH text is only warranted to construe the Searles' experience, not her own. The following sections show the analysis of transitivity with respect to:

5.1 What kinds of Processes are chosen to represent the 'goings on',

5.2 Which people or things are construed as Participants in the events, and

5.3 What kind of Participant roles these people or things are assigned.

5.5.1 What kinds of Processes are chosen to represent the 'goings on'?

A clause by clause TRANSITIVITY analysis was performed for the ranked clauses in each text, and the distribution of Process types is shown in Table 5.5. The frequency of each Process type is shown proportionally because of the large difference in clause numbers (again, number of clauses given as *n* in Table 5.5).

The SMH text predominantly uses Material Processes (48 per cent) to construe the events, whereas the Process types in the Parenthood.com text are more evenly distributed between Mental (30 per cent), Relational Attributive (26 per cent) and Material Processes (24 per cent). The SMH text thus systematically construes the events as involving concrete, dynamic actions or happenings, whereas the Parenthood.com text more frequently construes events using representations of inner experience (thoughts, feelings, perceptions) and descriptive relationships between one thing and another. Some examples from the texts are given in 6–11[8] below.

Table 5.5: Process types in SMH and Parenthood.com texts

	SMH n=75 (%)	*Parenthood.com* n=128 (%)
Material	48	24
Mental	18.5	30
Verbal	11	7
Rel:Attrib	18	26
Rel:Ident	0	7
Other	4	6
	100	100

(6) SMH — She clung {Material} to her older boy for as long as [[she could]], || but <<as her strength waned {Material}>> she appealed {Verbal} to a young girl nearby || to grab {Material} him.

(7)[9] SMH — 'The water had gone {Material} out || and ^IT just rushed {Material} back in again || and it was {Relational} so horrific || that <<when I got {Material} out [of the front [of the hotel]]>> I thought {Mental} || they were {Relational} all dead for sure.'

(8) SMH — When the water subsided {Material} || the couple began {Material} a frantic search of the hotel, in darkness, || wading {Material} through wreckage.

(9) Parenthood.com — I think {Mental} || that's {Relational } every mother's worst nightmare – [[having to choose between which child to save]]

(10) Parenthood.com — Admittedly, the first time [[I heard this]] I was {Relational} so choked up ... || her kids are {Relational} about the same age as mine. || ^IT'S {Relational} A horrible thing [[to have to decide]].

(11) Parenthood.com — How is this 5 year old going to feel {Mental}|| growing up {Material}|| knowing {Mental}|| his mama let him go to die {Material}

5.5.2 Which people or things are construed as Participants in the events?

Even from just this selection of examples, there are a number of Participants that seem to recur: Jillian Searle (realised as *she* and *his mama*), Lachie

Searle (realised as *her older boy, him,* and *this 5 year old*), the tsunami (realised as *the water* and *it*), and the authorial subject (realised as *I* in Examples 9 and 10). Table 5.6 shows the main people and things that occur in Participant roles for the two texts, including both the number and proportion of instances for each text (number of Participants in each text given as 'np'). I have included only the ones whose various lexical realisations can be transparently and cohesively grouped (eg. the entity 'Jillian Searle' is realised by a range of lexical items including *Jillian, his mother, she,* and *this lady*).

Jillian Searle is assigned a Participant role more than any other person or thing overall (although in the SMH text she and Lachie turn up equally frequently as Participants). This may seem to be a finding that could have been concluded without any detailed analysis at all, but the story of what happened to the Searle family involved a number of other people and things that could have been made Participants, and it could have been told from a number of angles, e.g. with a focus on Lachie or Bradley Searle's actions or the movements of the tsunami. What was considered most newsworthy,[10] however, was the sphere of action centred on Jillian and the choice she made at the time.

Whereas many of the entities in Participant roles in the SMH text belong to the same concentrated set of people or things, the Parenthood.com text involves a large number of dispersed and often abstract entities, e.g. *the problem, that (choice), my eyes, this story.* Table 5.6 reflects this difference and shows also that the Parenthood.com mothers have, in effect, 'zoomed in' on Jillian and Lachie, blocking out other potential Participants such as, notably, the tsunami or Bradley Searle. The central role of the tsunami in the events is effectively marginalised by its occasional inclusion only as a Circumstance of location (three instances: *in water, in the water,* and *on top of the water*). The Parenthood.com mothers appear as Participants almost as frequently as Jillian, which reflects both their

Table 5.6: Most frequent Participants in each text

	SMH *np=113*	*Parenthood.com* *np=208*	
Participant	Frequency	Participant	Frequency
Jillian Searle	22 (19%)	Jillian Searle	37 (18%)
Lachie Searle	22 (19%)	author	32 (15%)
tsunami	10 (9%)	Lachie Searle	20 (10%)
Bradley Searle	8 (7%)		
girl nearby	6 (5%)		

concern with presenting their own views on the situation (as Sensers), and the contextual appropriateness of writing in the first person.

5.5.3 What kind of Participant roles are these people or things assigned?

A crucial consideration in this analysis is what kinds of Participant roles, as activated through Process type selection (see Table 5.7), are assigned to the entities outlined in Section 5.2. In this section I will examine the patterning of Participant roles assigned to Jillian and explore how these meanings relate to our interpretation of the appraisal analysis presented above. The Participant roles assigned to Jillian in the SMH and Parenthood.com texts are presented in Table 5.8. Some Participant roles (e.g., Beneficiary, Phenomenon) and Process types (e.g., Existential and Behavioural) are not shown in Table 5.8 because Jillian does not turn up in these roles or the Process types occur very infrequently. The figures in bold type show the most frequent Participant role for Jillian in each text. As a general reference, Participants considered the main 'do-er' or 'be-er' in the Process (e.g. Actor, Senser, Sayer) will be referred to as Participant 1 roles (see e.g. Halliday and Hasan 1985).

In the SMH text, Jillian is constructed predominantly in Participant 1 roles particularly as Senser, and then as Actor. The text instances of these, including coding for subtypes of Mental Processes, are displayed as Examples 12–23. As Senser, Jillian engages in perceptive, emotive and cognitive Mental Processes (the option of 'desiderative' Mental Process, e.g. *want*, is not taken up in this text). So whilst Jillian's actions play a significant role in the story, her thoughts and emotions seem to be a dominant grammatical motif in the journalist's representation of events. And whilst Jillian's material actions are mostly to do with holding on to or letting go of Lachie (Examples 19–22), her Mental Processes are much

Table 5.7: Participant roles within each Process type

Process type	*Participant 1*	*Other Participants*
Material	Actor	Goal, Range, Beneficiary
Mental	Senser	Phenomenon
Verbal	Sayer	Verbiage, Receiver, Target
Behavioural	Behaver	Behaviour/Range
Relational: Attributive	Carrier	Attribute
Relational: Identifying	Token	Value
Existential	Existent	–

Table 5.8: Participant roles of Jillian in the SMH and Parenthood.com texts

Process type	*Participant*	*SMH: Jillian*	*Parenthood.com: Jillian*
Material	Actor	5	**13**
Goal	1	0	
Mental	Senser	**8**	8
Verbal	Sayer	5	8
Relational Attributive	Carrier	1	5
Attribute	0	3	
Relational Identifying	Value	0	1

more diverse, almost as if she had many thoughts occupying her mind, but only one of two actions that she could choose: *hold on to* or *let go of* Lachie. Jillian is construed as having the potential to affect others through her actions, and her son is construed as being affected by her actions. The examples also show that, as a Senser, Jillian is 'affected' by Lachie as Phenomenon (Example 14) and as part of Metaphenomena (Examples 12, 13, 10, 18): her thoughts, fears and senses in this event overwhelmingly involve Lachie.

(12) **she** feared {emotive} || that <<if she tried to hold both Lachie and her baby, Blake,>> they would all be lost.

(13) (**Jillian**) fearing {emotive} || she would never see her son again

(14) fearing || **she** would never see {perceptive}her son again

(15) and ^**SHE** learned {cognitive} || she had lost hold of Lachie

(16) **she** had already started to grieve {emotive}

(17) **'I** couldn't believe {cognitive} it'

(18) **'I** still can't believe {cognitive} || he's here'

(19) (**Jillian Searle**) to let go of her son Lachie

(20) so **she** could cling to her 20-month-old baby

(21) if **she** tried to hold both Lachie and her baby, Blake,

(22) **she** clung to her older boy for as long as she could

(23) Later, after the immediate danger had passed, **she** found the girl again

In the Parenthood.com text, Jillian again turns up mainly in Participant 1 roles, notably as Actor (see Table 5.8). She is less frequently portrayed as Senser and more frequently portrayed as Sayer than in the SMH text. Text instances of the construction of Jillian as Actor in the Parenthood.com text are shown in Examples 24–36.

(24) **she** could have left it at that

(25) **she** chose || to let him go

(26) (**this lady**) letting go of her child

(27) **his mama** let him go to die

(28) **she** should have never let this get out to the press

(29)[11] 'If **I** didn't let you go || we would have all died.'

(30) **'I** was dragging you under.'

(31) And **she** didn't just let him go, by the way

(32) I don't think || **she** should have to clam up about the story though

(33) How could **this woman** let one of her kids go!!

(34) But at first I thought || **she** let him go in the water by himself

(35) **She** gave him to a lady next to her

(36) So if this story really happened, || where **she** gave her eldest son to the woman close to her

As in the SMH text, most of these Material Processes involve Lachie as Goal and are concerned with 'letting go' of him (Examples 25, 26, 27, 29, 31, 33, 34). Much of the repetition in the Parenthood.com text is due to its co-constructed nature, as the mothers often reiterate ideas that others have already put forward. Again, Jillian is constructed as a dynamic Participant who has the potential to affect others, particularly Lachie.

5.6 Summary of transitivity analysis

Table 5.9 presents a summary of choices of Processes and Participants in the two texts, including the main roles of Lachie and the tsunami, which were not explicitly discussed in the analysis presented in Section 5.3. It is interesting to note that both texts construct Lachie as crucially affected by the actions of his mother, even though they differ with respect to the representation of Jillian herself. The SMH text constructs Jillian predominantly as Senser in a text of mainly Material Processes, whereas the Parenthood.com text presents Jillian mainly as Actor in the midst of a majority of Mental Processes.

The choice of major Participants in the texts is clearly influenced not just by the field of discourse, but also by the tenor and mode of the

Table 5.9: Summary of TRANSITIVITY selections in SMH and Parenthood.com texts

	SMH	*Parenthood.com*
Main Process Type	Material	Mental
Most Frequent Participants	Jillian (19%), Lachie (19%)	Jillian (18%), authors (15%)
Main Role of Jillian	Senser	Actor
Main Role of Lachie	Goal/Carrier	Goal
Main Role of Tsunami	Actor	Circumstance

interaction. The journalist passes on information as news to an unknown public readership. This information is known to her but as yet unknown to the readers, and the readers approach the news article expecting that it will present information 'objectively'. The SMH text therefore needs to present news and represent experience in the third person, and so it features a large range of Participants, including the tsunami and all members of the Searle family. However, the interaction in the Parenthood.com text has different characteristics: the mothers, who have about the same degree of knowledge about the topic, co-construct the text and are focused on sharing opinions about the Searles' story, particularly Jillian's actions. Other potential Participants, such as Bradley or the tsunami, are largely excluded in the Parenthood.com text. This may be explained by considering that the mothers are contextually positioned to emphasise their status as mothers, which concentrates their discussion on the mother-child relationship in the story. The mothers also feature frequently as Participants (Senser) because of the self-presentation function of the text. The journalist (Natasha Granath) may well be a mother also, but in this context her institutional and professional role as a journalist necessarily overrides her status as a mother. Thus, in her case, there is no option of including herself as a Participant, particularly in the role of Senser as a respondent to the story.

5.7 Discussion of findings

Each text singles Jillian out from the rest of the people and happenings, but in different ways. Through patterning of Process choices, especially of Material and Mental Processes, the SMH text conveys a dynamic, chaotic scene in which Jillian, against all odds, manages to remain rational and lucid. The Parenthood.com text evokes a situation that requires careful thought on Jillian's part; however, in their account Jillian acts rashly and without due consideration of the appropriate course of action for a mother. Jillian's feelings are frequently expressed in the SMH account through Mental Processes, but the higher order feelings in the Parenthood.com text are reserved for the mothers.

These findings from the transitivity analysis align with my expectations (following the appraisal analysis) about the version of events that would be represented in each text, as the different resources work together towards common semantic goals. The journalist's positive appraisal of Jillian's Tenacity in the situation is consistent with her construction of Jillian as a rational person, and the Parenthood.com mothers' negative appraisal of Jillian on the grounds of Propriety and Normality corresponds with their construction of Jillian as a rash, unthinking person.

These findings also resonate with the two contrasting ideological motifs (see Section 4) underlying the writers' responses to Jillian's actions: 'try to keep everyone alive, no matter what it takes' (SMH) and 'don't ever let go of your child, no matter what the consequences might be' (Parenthood.com). The SMH text shows Jillian rationally attending to this problem of keeping herself and both her children alive, thereby meriting positive appraisal, whereas the Parenthood.com text constructs her as someone who unthinkingly lets go of her child, thus warranting condemnation.

The ideational metafunction, particularly in the construction of Participant roles, has major semantic implications for the kind of evaluations expressed. In these texts, what is ostensibly the same topic interacts with two different configurations of tenor and mode variables, and they license quite different evaluative reactions and experiential orientations to the topic. We have seen that contextual shifts, particularly in mode and tenor, have metafunctional implications at the level of lexicogrammar, in the choices made from the system of TRANSITIVITY, and at the level of semantics, in the choices made from the system of APPRAISAL. We can see, therefore, that local appraisal and transitivity selections, although not strictly related metafunctionally, are still motivated by the same kind of global contextual and semantic considerations.

Appraisal has been used as a basis for distinguishing 'reporter voice' from other kinds of authorial voice in media texts (see Iedema *et al.* 1994: 220; Martin and White 2005: 170–173). Reporter voice, the authorial voice used in the hard news register, is purportedly distinguished by a lack of explicit judgement, especially that of Social Sanction. The SMH text, although displaying minimal explicit judgement compared with the Parenthood.com text, still contains *some* explicit judgement, and yet most readers would consider it 'hard news'. The combination of the different dimensions of grammar and semantics considered here indicates that there is greater complexity to reporter voice and hard news than simply the absence of appraisal. Lukin (2008) highlights the impact of the configuration of all contextual variables on conceptions of voice and register, and argues that a theory of reporter voice must take these into account. The results of this study suggest that even within the 'hard news' register there may be sub-registerial variation or a cline between 'hard' and 'soft news' that cannot be graded on the basis of appraisal analysis alone.

Tragic situations such as the tsunami inevitably lead to large volumes of news reports and other text types. A special issue of the journal *Discourse & Society*, dealing with media approaches to the tragedy of 11 September 2001, highlights the consistency with which some meanings become widely associated with tragic events through media coverage, while other equally legitimate meanings are largely excluded from public view. Chouliaraki (2004), for example, demonstrates the way television coverage of tragic events frequently has the effect of targeting particular constituencies with particular consistently constructed meanings.

Other recent examples of Australian media coverage of tragic situations involving mothers and their children show that mothers are not always glorified in the way Jillian is in this article. For example, in June 2005 the *Sydney Morning Herald* (among others) reported the death of four young children who were trapped in a burning house on the Central Coast of New South Wales. There had been seven children in the house under the age of 14 years: five siblings, a cousin, and a friend. Of the four who died, three were brothers (aged 15 months, 2 years and 7 years), and one was a 7-year-old school friend. A 13-year-old girl, the sister of the boys who died, had been left in charge of the children while their mother was out that evening. The reports in the *Herald* and elsewhere implicitly attribute some blame to the mother of the children by including non-essential, loaded 'facts', e.g. that her children were fathered by four different men, some of whom had spent time in jail, and that she had left the children to go to the local club to watch a boxing match with a male friend. In this case, the mother's behaviour is negatively appraised, and negligence is strongly suggested.

In the Searles' case no children died, and it is very likely the story would not have made it into the newspapers at all, had that been the case, as it would have been just one more death among thousands. But if it had, perhaps a report involving Lachie's death may have resembled the Parenthood.com perspective and the report of the Wyong house fire. That would suggest the presence of some underlying principles within journalism in which certain kinds of events and outcomes license the expression of negative appraisal. The suggestion of negligence in the house fire example, and the negative appraisal in the tsunami example, raise important questions: What is the social function of news reporting in contemporary Australian broadsheets? Is there a place in hard news reports for publicly judging the behaviour of ordinary people as portrayed in the reports, and if not, how is the use of appraisal justified in cases such as this?

An even more important consideration than whether or not a journalist expresses some kind of opinion is *how* this opinion is conveyed. If it is coded in explicit appraisal and perhaps labelled as opinion, then it can be read as such, as in labelled editorial articles in a newspaper. However, if opinion is coded in 'hard news' implicitly, through a kind of semantic 'groove' (cf. Coffin and O'Halloran 2005) created by patterning in grammatical resources (such as we have seen in the case analysed in this chapter) then it is more likely to be read as 'fact', and has a greater potential to unconsciously colour the reader's understanding of the events and the social context surrounding them.

The presence of appraisal in the news report analysed here indicates that hard news reports are not necessarily the objective, facts-only texts readers might assume them to be. This finding invites further questions about the extent to which the expression of attitude is warranted in hard news reports, the kinds of attitudes that are warranted, and the kinds of events that warrant such appraisal.

Notes

1. In this chapter, lower case letters are used to refer to appraisal and judgement in a general sense. Small capitals are used to denote appraisal or judgement as semantic systems.
2. A familiarity with systemic functional grammar (henceforth SFL) terminology is assumed; see Halliday and Matthiessen's *An Introduction to Functional Grammar* (2004) for a detailed framework.
3. OMG stands for 'oh my god'.
4. All participants in the discussion forum were mothers. They will be referred to as 'mothers' in this chapter to avoid confusion with the Participant function label (which is written with an initial capital).
5. Scare quotes are used here because, if language always involves choosing one option over others, there is always a subjective aspect to a text.
6. Since appraisal is a discourse-semantic resource, it is not necessarily realised by single, discrete lexical items, groups/phrase, or even clauses. Rather, 'the

realisation of an attitude tends to splash across a phase of discourse, irrespective of grammatical boundaries – especially where amplified' (Martin and White, 2005: 10), and so it is often hard to define the boundaries of what we would otherwise like to call an 'instance'.

7. Both authorially sourced and non-authorially sourced judgements are included because the journalist's inclusion of non-authorially sourced judgements can also be interpreted as contextually and ideologically motivated.
8. Key to notation conventions: Process; || clause boundary; [[embedded/rank-shifted clause]]; <<interrupting clause>>; {Process type}.
9. Example 7, from the SMH text, is a direct quotation of Bradley Searle.
10. See Iedema *et al.* (1994: 106–109) for a discussion of newsworthiness and angle choice.
11. Examples 29 and 30 are hypothetical reported speech in which the mothers try to explain how Jillian might justify her actions to her son in the years to come.

References

Chouliaraki, L. (2004). Watching 11 September: the politics of pity. *Discourse & Society,* 15/2-3: 185–198.

Coffin, C. and O'Halloran, K. (2005). Finding the global groove: theorising and analysing dynamic reader positioning using APPRAISAL, corpus, and a concordancer. *Critical Discourse Studies,* 2/2: 143–163.

Granath, N. (2004). Her baby or son: the choice almost tore them apart. *The Sydney Morning Herald,* 30 December: 3.

Halliday, M. A. K. and Hasan, R. (1985). *Language, Context, and Text: Aspects of Language in a Social Semiotic Perspective.* Deakin University, Victoria: Deakin University Press.

Halliday, M. A. K. and Matthiessen, C. M. I. M. (2004). *An Introduction to Functional Grammar* (3rd edition). London: Arnold.

Henderson-Brooks, C. (2006). 'What type of a person am I, Tess?' The complex tale of self in psychotherapy. Unpublished PhD thesis. Sydney: Macquarie University.

Iedema, R., Feez, S. and White, P. R. R. (1994). *Literacy in Industry Research Project: Media Literacy.* Sydney: Disadvantaged Schools Program, Metropolitan East Region, NSW Department of School Education.

Lukin, A. (2008). Journalistic voice, register and contextual configuration: a case study from the Spanish and Argentinian press. In Thomson, E. and White P. R. R. (eds), *Communicating Conflict: Multilingual Case Studies of the Rhetoric of the News Media.* London and New York: Continuum.

Martin, J. R. (2000). Beyond exchange: APPRAISAL systems in English. In Hunston, S. and Thompson, G. (eds) 2000. *Evaluation in Text: Authorial*

Stance and the Construction of Discourse. Oxford: Oxford University Press, 142–175.

Martin, J. R. and Rose, D. (2003). *Working with Discourse: Meaning Beyond the Clause*. London: Continuum.

Martin, J. R. and White, P. (2005). *The Language of Evaluation: Appraisal in English*. Basingstoke and New York: Palgrave Macmillan.

Parenthood.com. (2005). Discussion topic: Mother has to chose [sic] to save only 1 of her 2 sons. January 1. http://forums.parenthood.com/viewmessages.cfm–Forum=21&Topic=126206. Retrieved 30 January 2005.

Scott, C. (2003). Defending the indefensible: a systemic functional investigation of political discourse from the war on Iraq. Unpublished BA Honours thesis. Sydney: Macquarie University.

Scott, C. (2004). Experiential meanings, appraisal, and the construction of alterity in political war discourse. Paper presented at the Annual Conference of the Australia Systemic Functional Linguistics Association: 'SFL Ripples in the 21st Century', 30 June – 2 July, Brisbane, Australia.

White, P. (2004). Judgement: evaluating human behaviour. October 24. http://www.grammatics.com/appraisal/AppraisalOutline/Framed/Frame.htm. Retrieved 10 March 10, 2005.

Appendix 1 – SMH Text

From *The Sydney Morning Herald*, 30 December 2004

Her baby or son: the choice almost tore them apart

Natasha Granath

Jillian Searle was forced into an unimaginable decision: to let go of her son Lachie so she could cling to her 20-month-old baby as the tsunami crashed through their Phuket hotel.

For Lachie, only five and unable to swim, it was the beginning of a near-fatal nightmare that he survived by clinging to a pole in the hotel lobby, waiting for the raging waters to subside. All the while, Mrs Searle and her husband, Bradley, believed he was dead.

As the Perth mother and her two sons were swept up by the water, she feared that if she tried to hold both Lachie and her baby, Blake, they would all be lost.

She clung to her older boy for as long as she could, but as her strength waned she appealed to a young girl nearby to grab him. Mrs Searle, fearing she would never see her son again, screamed to the girl not to let go.

Later, after the immediate danger had passed, she found the girl again – and learned she had lost hold of Lachie.

Mr Searle had watched the scene unfold from a balcony, unable to reach his family and convinced the wave would kill everyone in its path.

'The water had gone out and just rushed back in again and it was so horrific that when I got out of the front of the hotel I thought they were all dead for sure,' he said.

He found his wife and youngest son just as a second giant wave swept through. They climbed on top of play equipment in the hotel grounds.

When the water subsided the couple began a frantic search of the hotel, in darkness, wading through wreckage. They were convinced their son was dead.

They had almost given up hope when they found him with a security guard and grabbed him from the man's arms. He told them he had held onto the pole for nearly two hours with his head just above water.

'I cried for Mum for a long time and then I was quiet,' he told his father, adding: 'My hands are all dirty and I need to wash my clothes.'

His father wept; his mother said she had already started to grieve. 'I was just so frantic for hours and the relief was just so strong,' she said. 'I couldn't believe it and I still can't believe he's here.'

The family returned to Perth yesterday, still astounded they had survived.

'We are just so lucky to walk away with the small children I've got, one of whom can't even swim and is petrified of water – even the pool at home – and one who is a little baby,' Mrs Searle said. 'I just can't believe they are still here.'

6 Bridging the metafunctions: tracking participants through taxonomies[1]

Nick Moore

6.1 Introduction: integrating cohesion into a model of discourse

The challenge presented to formal linguistics by theories of cohesion (Gutwinski 1976; Halliday and Hasan 1976) has resulted in a range of responses to integrate discoursal features of language into a fundamentally syntactic model (e.g. Grosz *et al.* 1995; Mitkov *et al.* 2000). In general, the approach taken by many formal syntactic-based approaches is to focus on anaphora (e.g. Fox 1987), and particularly in computational studies almost exclusively on pronominalisation (e.g. Beaver 2004; Bos 2003). While this has allowed formal theories to account for common referential surface features, progress has been hampered by a syntactic definition of language even when dealing with the fundamental issues of discourse and context (Grosz and Sidner 1998; Gundel *et al.* 2003; Lambrecht 1996).

In contrast, functional theories of linguistics have integrated the categories of Reference, Substitution, Ellipsis, Conjunction and Lexical Cohesion largely unchanged into theories of grammar and discourse (Halliday and Matthiessen 2004). One approach that develops Halliday and Hasan's (1976) theory is Martin's (1992), which extends Halliday's (1985) grammatical perspective to discourse semantics, stressing Halliday's insight of the ideational, interpersonal and textual metafunctions to describe the resources in English that make meaning in text.

This chapter investigates the textual metafunction in Martin (1992), exploring its model of reference and emphasising its dependence on the resources available in the experiential metafunction to create messages. Clearly choices from the textual metafunction are realised within clauses, but it is within the framework of discourse semantics that they can best be understood and related to other metafunctions. Martin's work is compared to one of the most influential approaches to incorporating cohesion into a formal model of language, i.e. Clark's (e.g. 1977) notion of *bridging*. While this model is influential enough for Martin to have included it in his systemic functional description of discourse, he also provides an opportunity to re-examine the model. This chapter utilizes Martin (1992) to determine an appropriate role for *bridging* in systemic functional discourse semantics.

6.2 Presenting and presuming reference: introducing and tracking participants

A typical clause in written English contains at least one Participant – an entity that enters a relationship with the process in a clause in the role of either Medium or Agent in an ergative analysis – or potential participant (Halliday and Matthiessen 2004). Participants are normally realised by nominal groups, but not all nominal groups contain participants (e.g. *nobody* or *it* in *It's raining.).* Potential participants can be derived from a circumstance, as a nominal group within a prepositional phrase or adverbial group, or from a process, as a nominalisation of a verbal process. A whole text, parts of it and all multi-modal elements are also potential participants in discourse.

Within Martin's (1992) model of discourse semantics, Participants are identified by Reference. One option for identifying a Participant is to use Presenting Reference: to *present* a participant to the context. Another is to presume its identity is retrievable elsewhere, using Presuming Reference: to *presume* that the audience already knows the participant's identity. The unmarked realisations for Presenting Reference include indefinite determiners, while Presuming Reference is typically realised by definite determiners (see Martin 1992: 102 *passim* for the complete system). The identity of a presumed participant may be located in: the context of culture (homophora) – as knowledge presumed common to all members of a community; the context of situation (exophora) – perhaps as something visible in the physical surroundings; or in the co-text (endophora) – possibly as a previously-mentioned participant (anaphora). The options for locating, or tracking, participants are illustrated in the network in Figure 6.1.

Whether the identity can actually be retrieved by a listener/reader is unimportant – the speaker/writer *presumes* that it can. Hence, unlike other functional (e.g. Firbas 1992) or formal (e.g. Beaver 2004; Bos 2003;

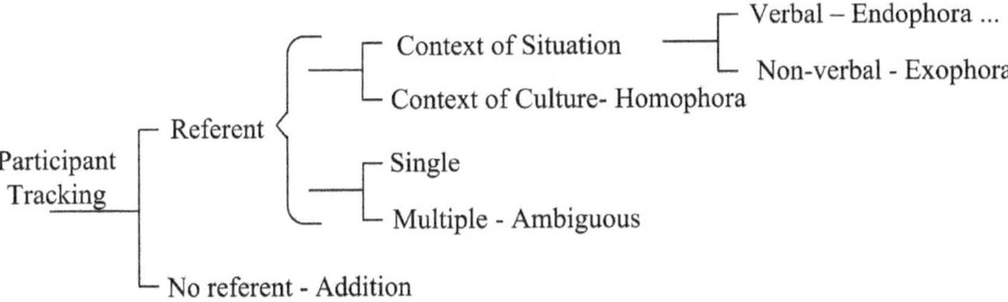

Figure 6.1: Initial options in the Participant Tracking network (from Martin, 1992: 126).

Fox 1987; Gundel *et al.* 2003; Lambrecht 1996) approaches to identifying referents in a text, Presenting and Presuming Reference are meaningful choices made by the speaker, independent of previous mention in the text. This difference is significant, as a failure to locate a previous mention of a referent in the co-text in Martin's model does not signify miscommunication or an 'ungrammatical' utterance. The model recognises that using Presuming Reference the first time a participant is introduced into a text, or using Presenting Reference more than once for the same participant, serves a communicative purpose (Fries 2000; Martin 1992: 102).

One function of Presuming Reference is to create cohesion in text, tying lexical items to other participants or to the context by compelling the reader to locate the identity of the presumed participant, rather than allowing the reader to find their own connections. While it is possible to analyse a text for all lexical relations (Hoey 1991), only lexical ties that are grammatically signalled for Participant Tracking are analysed in this study, because the grammatical resources of Participant Tracking make lexical ties explicit. Having outlined the grammatical resources for cohesive ties proposed by Martin (1992) this chapter offers a set of lexical relations, described in Section 6.3, that lead directly into the experiential metafunction.

6.3 Taxonomies: organising the experiential metafunction

A Field of discourse consists of a taxonomy of related elements. Both 'common-sense' and specialised knowledge structures depend on taxonomies. Indeed, a great deal of effort is involved in socialising young people into the counter-intuitive taxonomic systems developed by academic disciplines (Halliday and Martin 1993; Martin and Veel 1998). Experiential semantic relations that function to associate items in a taxonomy include the categories of Superordination and Composition, the Nuclear Relations of Enhancement, Extension and Elaboration (see Table 6.1) and Activity Sequences (Martin 1992). These relations, many based on Lyons (1977), are detailed in Figure 6.2 as a system network, with typical realisations.

Superordination consists of Hyponymy, covering unequal taxonomic relations of Class and Subclass, and Co-hyponymy, which covers relations of equal rank, including Contrast (of which Dichotomy is one type) and Similarity, including Synonymy, Repetition, Substitution (e.g. pronominalisation), and Derivation. Composition relations cover Constitution (part-whole relations, or meronymy), Collective (how items are grouped) and Consistency (what something is made of).

Nuclear Relations describe the grammatical nature of collocation in developing cohesion through and across clauses. The logical relations of Elaboration, Extension and Enhancement are employed to describe the grammatical expectations set up by the process in a clause (see Torsello (1996) on the logical metafunction across ranks). Table 6.1 illustrates the system, with typical examples. At the ranks of clause, and nominal and verbal group, logical relations function to categorise and relate elements, to make elements cohere and to make the type of element predictable from the grammatical pattern. Only those Nuclear Relations realised by participants are considered in this study. Similarly, as activity sequences

Table 6.1: Elaboration, Enhancement and Extension across clauses and groups (adapted from Martin, 1992: 317)

	Elaboration =	*Extension* +	*Enhancement* x
Clause	PROCESS = RANGE: PROCESS take shot (*take a shot*)	PROCESS + MEDIUM + RANGE: ENTITY shoot deer (*shoot the deer*)	PROCESS x CIRCUMSTANCE shoot field (*shoot in the field*)
Nominal group	CLASSIFIER = THING practice shot (*a practice shot*)	EPITHET + THING loud shot (*a loud shot*)	THING x QUALIFIER shot dark (*a shot in the dark*)
Verbal group	EVENT = PARTICLE shoot up (*shoot up*)	EVENT + EVENT try shoot (*try to shoot*)	EVENT x QUALITY shoot carefully (*shoot carefully*)

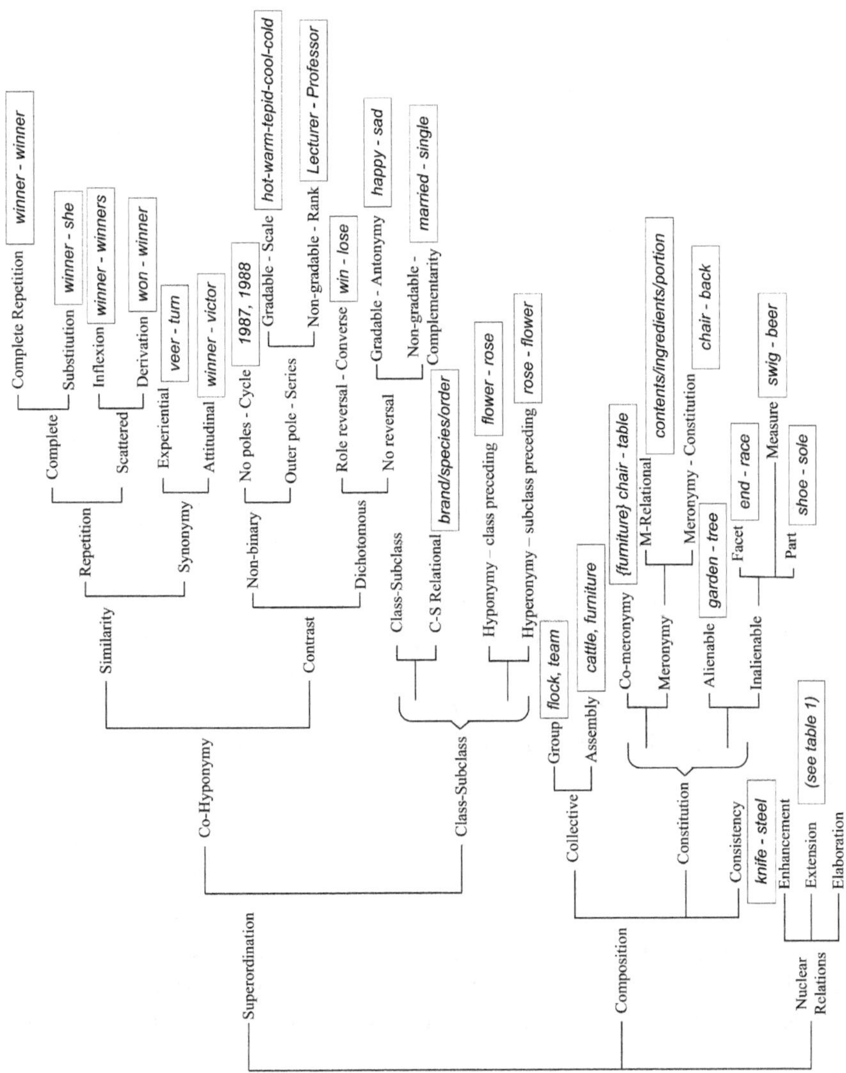

Figure 6.2: Network of Semantic relations to describe taxonomies (from Martin 1992: 299, 302, 304, 306, 307).

describe the relations between clauses typically covered by Conjunction, these relations are not considered in this study. Having looked at the main semantic relations between participants from the experiential perspective, Section 6.4 investigates the role of the textual metafunction in developing a taxonomy through a text.

6.4 Bridging: connecting grammatical and lexical participants in text

Martin (1992) proposes that an instance of Presuming Reference can be cohesively tied by either Direct or Indirect Phoric Reference in a Participant Tracking network. Clark and Haviland's (1974, 1977; Haviland and Clark 1974) concept of *bridging* is used to distinguish between Direct and Indirect reference:

> To this point the examples of endophoric reference given have all involved presuming information that has been made explicit in the co-text. However, as Haviland and Clark (1974) point out, phoric nominal groups may presume information that is implied rather than directly retrievable ... Haviland and Clark referred to indirect reference of this kind as **bridging**. (original emphasis, Martin 1992: 123–4)

However, no definitions of Direct, explicit or implied are offered. Figure 6.3 shows the options in Martin's (1992) network of Indirect and Direct Reference, but these are probably not the most delicate choices as they do not produce realisation rules (Fawcett 1988; Fawcett *et al.* 1993). It would therefore seem beneficial to identify the more delicate choices in this network.

The examples of direct reference given by Martin, and by Haviland and Clark, typically consist of pronouns and lexical repetition; i.e. the semantic relation of Repetition. That is, the options for Direct Reference can be made more delicate with the semantic relations of Repetition, as in Figure 6.4. The relationship between reference and semantic relations is described by Martin (1992) for Indirect Reference, or bridging, as: 'Bridging depends on experiential connections between presuming and presumed which facilitate the recovery of an implied identity' (1992: 124). That is, the

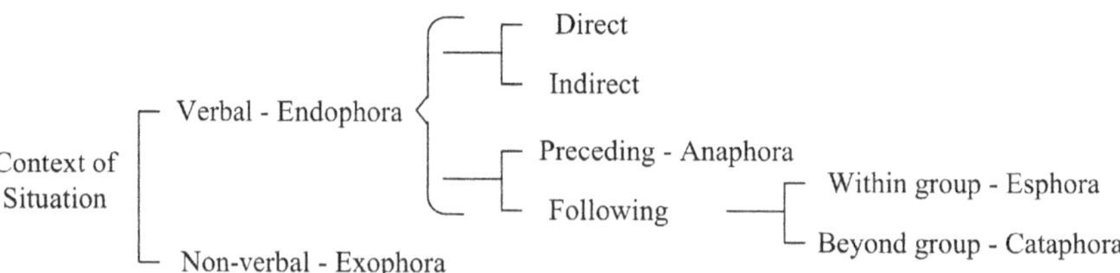

Figure 6.3: Network of further options in the system of participant tracking (from Martin, 1992: 126).

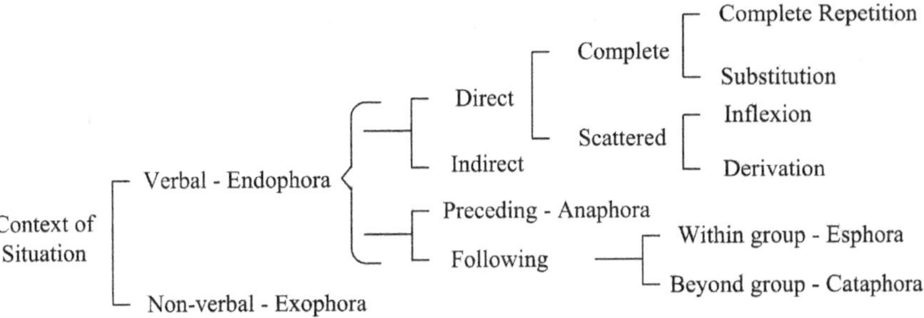

Figure 6.4: Network of more delicate options for Direct Reference in the system of participant tracking (adapted from Martin, 1992: 126)

operation of bridging probably depends on the same experiential relations that enable taxonomies to be construed in text, as detailed in Figure 6.2. This semantic explanation is essentially different to Clark and Haviland's (1977) psycholinguistic approach.

The examples for *bridging* and Indirect Presuming reference reveal a wide range of semantic relationships. In this example from Martin (1992: 124) the relationship between the presuming *tree* and the presumed *branch* is one of meronymy, or part-to-whole:

(1) He bumped into a branch;

he hadn't noticed the tree at all. (original emphasis, Martin 1992: 124)

The second line could also have used *it, the branch, the limb,* or *the obstacle,* relying on a relation of substitution, complete repetition, similarity, or hyperonymy respectively (see Figure 6.2). In each case, however, it is the Presuming Reference that requires the reader to make the connection between the two elements. Replacing *the tree* with *any trees* or *a branch* produces quite a different effect. While there may be semantic or lexical associations between the items, the reader is no longer required to *presume* that the identity can be tracked back in the text. Table 6.2 shows examples from Haviland and Clark's (1974) seminal work, with the semantic relationships for indirect reference provided. If Direct Reference depends on relations of Repetition, then, as the examples in Table 6.2 demonstrate, Indirect Reference, or bridging, can be shown to depend on other relations, including Similarity, Superordination, Composition, Nuclear Relations and Activity Sequences – the same semantic relations used for creating experiential taxonomies.

The tracking of participants in a text can thus be interpreted as exploiting the system of semantic relations in Figure 6.2. These relations also contribute

Table 6.2: Semantic relations for antecedents in examples from Haviland and Clark (1974: 514, 515, 517)

Context Sentence	*'Target' sentence*	*Semantic relationship of indirect reference*
We got **some beer** out of the trunk	**The beer** was warm.	REPETITION
We checked **the picnic supplies**.	**The beer** was warm.	MERONYMY
Last Christmas Eugene became **absolutely smashed**.	This Christmas he got **very drunk** again.	SYNONYMY
Last Christmas Eugene **couldn't stay sober**.	This Christmas he got **very drunk** again.	ANTONYMY
Last Christmas Eugene **went to a lot of parties**.	This Christmas he **got very drunk** again.	ACTIVITY SEQUENCE (CONJUNCTION)

to the texture of a text as the reader is required, through Presuming Reference, to build the relationships between participants and their collocates (Ward 2007) into complex taxonomies with multiple semantic relations within and between taxonomic fields.

As participants are woven through the processes realised by the verbal group, the identities of participants are established taxonomically in relation to processes, circumstances, and other participants in the text. Experiential taxonomic relations in a Field intersect with the textual metafunction by contributing to the tracking of Participants through predictable semantic relations, and so the textual metafunction draws on the resources available in the experiential metafunction to create messages.

The reader is expected to track participants through the use of Presuming Reference, no matter how direct or indirect the connection seems. More importantly, the grammatical realisations that signal this relationship are the same. Thus, if there is no difference between the realisation of direct and indirect reference, and if both depend on semantic relations, can direct reference be distinguished from indirect reference, or bridging? If not, at the entry point of 'Verbal-Endophora type' (Figure 6.4), Direct and Indirect can be replaced with the semantic relations in Figure 6.2. To answer this question, Section 6.5 looks more closely at the research undertaken to establish the concept of *bridging*.

6.5 Burning Bridges: combining grammatical and lexical resources in participant tracking

Clark and Haviland's description of *bridging* (1977) draws on a range of arguments. Objections to these arguments can be summarised as: problems with definitions; breaching and violation; methodology; and inconsistencies. While previous criticisms have been made (e.g. Asher and Lascarides 1998; Wilson and Matsui 1998), none question Indirect Reference. The objections below aim to replace the dual concepts of Direct and Indirect Reference with a single taxonomy of semantic relations.

This critique of bridging takes place in a socio-historical context quite different from the heyday of syntactic theory when Haviland and Clark took the radical step of performing experiments on the connections between sentences. Clark's work represents a significant step in establishing discourse as a focus of study. Bridging has subsequently become very influential, forming the basis of Prince's (1981) work, for instance, which in turn has inspired further study of cohesion and context. This rather intensive critique of bridging is necessary only because of its influence. However, its success must be re-examined in the light of current theories of discourse.

6.5.1 Definitions

The concept of Bridging was introduced as part of Clark and Haviland's (1977) 'Given-New' contract, which includes the Gricean 'maxim of antecedence':

> Try to construct your utterance such that the listener has one and only one direct antecedent for any given information and that it is the intended antecedent. (Clark and Haviland 1977: 4)

To claim the need for a Given-New contract, Clark and Haviland (1977) draw on definitions of Given and New by Halliday, Chafe, and Chomsky. While each of these linguists highlighted the importance of Given and New, none of their definitions refer to the same linguistic units, or to the same functions in language. On closer inspection, the 'maxim of antecedence' not only fails to define given information, but also appears to exclude the possibility of cataphoric reference. Furthermore, in relation to the maxim, *bridging* could be considered a 'patch' to allow for indirect antecedence. In short, the maxim of antecedence and the foundations of bridging remain poorly defined.

6.5.2 Breaching and violations

The 'Given-New strategy' can be violated negligently, covertly or overtly (Clark and Haviland 1977). Covert violations are distinguished from Negligent by intent. They 'are meant to deceive' (Clark and Haviland: 34). However, distinguishing *negligent* from *covert* violation by volition creates unfalsifiable categories. The violation is overt where the reader is dropped into an ongoing narrative, 'since the reader and writer are both aware that the reader cannot really compute the intended antecedents' (Clark and Haviland: 37). Clark and Haviland do not anticipate a breakdown in communication in this case, reasoning that, as with eavesdroppers, the reader accepts a situation of limited ambiguity. That is, even though an item is marked as having an antecedent, the reader or listener treats it as 'Addition' (Presenting Reference). It is not made clear how these cases are different from any other where Clark and Haviland proscribe ambiguity: 'On encountering ... a pronoun the listener must compute its intended antecedent' (Clark and Haviland: 27). That we can, and frequently do, suspend anaphoric resolution suggests that the maxim of antecedence is easily suspended, and bridging is not always required.

6.5.3 Methodology

The main evidence for bridging is provided in experiments which timed students on how quickly they indicated comprehension of the second in a pair of sentences which contains Direct or Indirect Reference (Haviland and Clark 1974). For example, the 'context' sentences (a) *We got some beer out of the trunk* or (b) *We checked the picnic supplies* were followed by *The beer was warm* as a 'target sentence'. Clark and Haviland (1977) conclude for the sequence using (b) that 'there is no direct antecedent, and so the listener must build a bridge' (1977: 21). That is, the listener (or, as in their experiments, the reader) must make an inference between the definite marker and something in the context or co-text so that the definite marker has an antecedent.

However, these experiments may contain a number of methodological flaws. Being exposed to an extended sequence of sentence pairs will surely produce effects that are unlikely to reflect real language processing. Without any kind of check on understanding, apart from 'Do you understand the sentence?', the accuracy of comprehension is not verified. This is particularly important in experiments where the sentence pairs make no sense.

As each sequence contains just two sentences with no context, and is presented in the confines of a psychology laboratory, it is doubtful whether the experiment accurately replicates real instances of text comprehension, inferencing or bridging. It seems incongruous to investigate a phenomenon that is dependent on context by removing context (of culture, situation and co-text: see Figure 6.1). It is extremely rare for a reader to look back for an antecedent, certainly physically and probably mentally (Just *et al.* 1982), since there appears to be very little backtracking during reading, while scanning forward in the text is commonplace (Shebilske and Reid 1979). These experiments left the subjects with no other option. Consequently, rather than attempting to disprove the null hypothesis, the experimental method appears designed to support only one interpretation.

6.5.4 Inconsistencies

One major inconsistency in Haviland and Clark's (1974) experimental data is found in the sequence that took longest for students to 'process'. This sequence had no indirect reference because there was simply no co-reference. The example given is *Andrew was especially fond of beer.* followed by the target sentence *The beer was warm.* Haviland and Clark claim that 'The indirect antecedent took about 140 msec. longer' (1974: 516), but there was in fact no antecedent, as lexical repetition does not entail co-reference. Offering a definite article for a Specified 'beer' in the second sentence when only Generic (Martin 1992) 'beer' is mentioned in the first caused more confusion than a taxonomically-related item (such as 'picnic supplies'). The 'inferential step' (Clark and Haviland 1974: 516) conjectured to connect the two lexical items may not take place. The subjects in the laboratory may instead realise that, despite the lexical repetition, the first and second instances of beer are unconnected, and indicate that they realise that the sequence cannot make sense.

Haviland and Clark also fail to account for why a 'Negative Antecedent' took **less** time to be 'understood' than an 'Indirect Antecedent'. The 'maxim of antecedence' predicts two inferences, or bridges, for the Negative Antecedent condition – one to turn the negative proposition to positive, and one to match the inference between the two terms – while only one is necessary in the Indirect Antecedent condition. This anomaly in the data is probably the result of ignoring the semantic features of 'bridging'. Haviland and Clark's (1974) experimental results suggest that complete (or direct) repetition may be the easiest relationship to recognise, followed by inflexion, derivation, different types of contrast, then hyponymy and hyperonymy. That is, the apparent anomalies in the data may be explained by the hierarchy of semantic relations in Figure 6.2 with all relations of Similarity, including Attitudinal Synonymy, appearing higher and so easier to process than relations of contrast.

The data still show a sizeable time lag before a Direct Referent is considered understood. The time to make an Indirect Reference (1097 msec.) is only 7 per cent longer than a Direct Reference (1023 msec.) (Haviland and Clark 1974: 517). It is possible therefore that a 'bridge' is made for Direct Reference. That is, the difference between matching a referent with its intended antecedent may be different in degree but not in kind between, for example, a pronoun and an item related by meronymy.

6.5.5 Summary

Using Clark and Haviland's (1974) experimental data as a base, one is forced to question the validity of the concept of bridging, as the data show no significant distinction between cohesive links in adjacent context-free sentences that use relations of repetition and those that use other semantic relations. There is a difference in response times, and one can posit a cline of semantic relations, but Clark and Haviland's (1974) methods seem designed to support an *a priori* view of language that separates grammar and lexis in discourse. Reinterpreting their data with the view that grammatical and lexical relations exist on a continuum allows greater adequacy of explanation. *Bridging* has done little to explain the actual processes or relations involved in creating referential ties, despite 30 years of research and its significant influence on other theorists (e.g. Prince 1981, 1985). It may instead have impeded research by consigning explanation to an impenetrable psychological *black box*.

Martin's (1992) taxonomy of experiential relations in text enables a semantic explanation of the concept of 'bridging'. The model proposed here suggests that there is no psycholinguistic distinction between Direct and Indirect Reference – either that there is no need for the concept of bridging, or that co-referential lexical repetition and pronominalisation depend on bridging just as much as tracking relations that use semantic relations of hyponymy, meronymy, superordination, nuclear relations or activity sequences. That is, the network in Figure 6.2 can replace the Direct/Indirect distinction in Figure 6.4, and so bridging, if it occurs, is explained by the various semantic relations between cohesively-tied participants. Corroboration for the intersection of these two systems is provided by analysis of sample texts and by system networks which show predictable patterns of distribution, as discussed in Section 6.6.

6.6 Applying the model: participant tracking in technical text

The model of participant tracking outlined in this chapter was tested against two sample texts: 'Amplifier Noise' (Horowitz and Hill 1989) and 'Milling Machine Elements' (Black 1997), which are typical undergraduate engineering texts. Although both are short, and from similar registers, the results are provided here as an initial indication that the model can be applied to authentic written text. Further research, including similar but improved psychological experiments to those carried out by Haviland and Clark (1974), and more text analysis could validate and further refine the model.

The overall results for semantic relations are illustrated as percentages in Figure 6.5, which is ordered to represent a hypothesised hierarchy of relations, with the most frequent, unmarked relations at the top, and the least salient relations, which in Haviland and Clark's experiments would take the longest to process, at the bottom. Options are ordered from left to right as in a system network. Prior to this system the results produced the following proportions (see Figure 6.1): Referent 63 per cent: No referent (Addition) 37 per cent; Context of situation 99 per cent: Context of culture 1 per cent; (simultaneous with) Single 97 per cent: Multiple (Ambiguous) 3 per cent; and Verbal (Endophora) 90 per cent: Non-verbal (Exophora) 10 per cent.

Of the 191 Endophoric relations that enter the simultaneous lexical and grammatical tracking relations in Figure 6.5, 141 (74.2 per cent) were judged to show a relation of Superordination. The results strongly suggest that the unmarked, or the most salient, lexical relationship in these texts is that of Complete-Repetition – a repeated word. Following the network from Superordination, the ratios of Co-hyponymy: Class-subclass; Similarity: Contrast; Repetition: Synonymy; Complete: Scattered; and Complete Repetition: Substitution are all approximately 9:1 – the same proportion identified by Halliday and James (1993) for markedness in other grammatical systems. Approximately 1 in 4.5 groups of all tracked participants terminate in Complete-Repetition. The alternative to Complete-Repetition is Substitution. Typically, a participant is substituted by a co-referential item, such as a pronoun. Complete-Repetition and

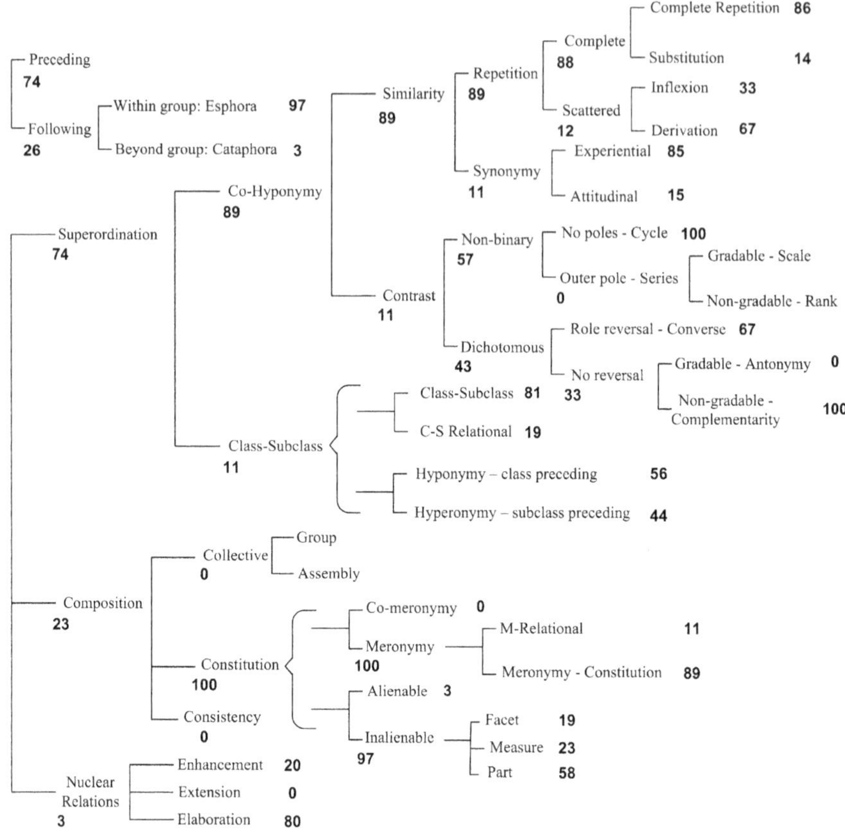

Figure 6.5: Choices as a percentage in two sample texts for semantic relations in participant tracking.

Repetition-Substitution together constitute 25.7 per cent of all participants and 40.8 per cent of all phoric groups across the two texts.

In Co-hyponomous relations, the choice is between Similarity, covering the Superordination choices discussed so far, and of relations of Contrast. In this analysis, Similarity relations account for 33 per cent of all participants with only 4.2 per cent Contrast relations. In these texts, all instances of Composition, accounting for 23.2 per cent of presuming reference, exhibit a relationship of Constitution. This is likely to be a result of the register; both pedagogic texts describe the component parts of a larger system. Nuclear Relations are disproportionately represented by relations of Elaboration (80 per cent), with just one example of Enhancement (20 per cent). With such a small number of realisations (5), it is currently not possible to judge whether the hypothesised ordering of Enhancement,

Table 6.3: Typical examples of semantic relations provided by presuming reference (from Black 1997 and Horowitz and Hill 1989)

Presumed and **Presuming** Pair	Type of semantic relation
The *cutting-fluid reservoir* and contains the pump to circulate **the fluid** to the cutting area.	anaphora: meronymy-constitution-facet
The knee has guideways on its top **surface**	anaphora: meronymy-constitution: part
... it can be reduced the techniques of *low-noise amplifier design*. ... will launch into a discussion of Transistor and FET noise, including methods for low-noise design with a given signal source, and will present **some design examples**.	anaphora: experiential synonymy
The two keys again provide **the means** of *transmitting* the drive.	esphora: elaboration

Extension and Elaboration should be changed, or whether the results obtained here are a result of text selection. Table 6.3 provides examples of some of the typical relationships quantified and described above.

The aim of the results in Figure 6.5, and the examples in Table 6.3, is primarily to show the feasibility of the system. All examples of Presuming Reference in these sample texts revealed at least one of these semantic relations. Further applications may reveal more consistent results to support the current hierarchy, or consistent variations across genres and registers. Although this has been just a short overview of some of the proportions and frequencies of choices made in two sample texts, the analyses are offered to demonstrate that, first, any text is likely to exhibit a range of semantic relations dependent on Presuming reference, and, second, that these choices are likely to be distributed across the different semantic relations in largely predictable proportions dependent on genre.

6.7 Conclusion: bridging the metafunctions

One function of Presuming Reference in discourse is to draw a reader's attention to participants that are semantically related to other participants and processes. The development of these relations through discourse contributes simultaneously to the building of taxonomies in a Field and to cohesion through a text. It is here that the Textual and Experiential metafunctions draw on the resources that each has to offer.

This chapter has largely been a review and application of one part of Martin's (1992) approach to discourse semantics – with one major change. It has called into question the distinction between Direct and Indirect Reference by suggesting that *all reference*, once it has been signalled as trackable through Presuming Reference, uses the same processes. That is, the difference between Direct Reference, which depends on the semantic relations of Repetition, and Indirect Reference, or bridging, which depends on a far wider range of semantic relations, is one of degree rather than kind.

This perspective provides a number of advantages to a systemic functional analysis. Participant tracking can be analysed to a greater level of delicacy, and to the point where it is possible to formulate realisational rules. The quantitative analysis exemplified here can be applied and compared across registers to reveal predictable proportions (Halliday 1991), and the principle of viewing lexico-grammar as a cline is further embedded in text analysis.

Another advantage is that the construal of taxonomies in text, made possible through a system of participant tracking dependent on semantic relations, does not depend on a representationist view of text which struggles to account for the kind of rapid semantic change witnessed in new Fields such as computer science (Bloor 1998). Through the textual and experiential resources described in this chapter, a discourse community is able to constantly (re)negotiate its taxonomies to ever-finer degrees of delicacy. While the Semantic Relations in Figure 6.2 remain constant, the realisations and proportions in the network are reconstrued instantially as a matter of (sub-)cultural convention. As a register draws on the predictable set of semantic relations to describe its taxonomies, the discourse community's context of situation is continually reconstrued in text. This reconstrual circumscribes the community's understanding of a Field. As tokens in taxonomies take on specific values, the only difference between instantial (Halliday and Hasan 1976, 1985) and 'permanent' lexical relations is their frequency in text and subsequent acceptance by a (sub-)culture. Through frequent use in a culture, instantial use becomes permanent.

This chapter has attempted to reveal the role played by semantic Experiential relations as they are employed by the Textual metafunction to develop taxonomies, thereby providing a link to semantics for the Textual metafunction. It is through the cohesive function of participant tracking that lexical and grammatical relations combine, and it is through Experiential semantic relations within a field that cohesion bridges the Textual and Experiential metafunctions.

Note

1. This chapter has benefited greatly from discussions with, and advice from, Geoff Thompson and Michael Hoey, both of whom I thank for their patience and inspiration. It has also benefited from guidance by the editors and George Needham. None of these people, however, should be held responsible for any remaining errors, for which I take full responsibility.

References

Asher, N. and Lascarides, A. (1998). Bridging. *Journal of Semantics*, 15: 83–113.

Beaver, D. (2004). The optimization of discourse anaphora. *Linguistics and Philosophy*, 27: 3–56.

Black, B. J. (1997). *Workshop Practices and Materials*. London: Butterworth-Heinemann.

Bloor, M. (1998). Lexical and grammatical choices in innovative language use in computer science. In Sanchez-Macarro, A. and Carter, R. (eds) *Linguistic Choice Across Cultures: Variation in Spoken and Written English*. Amsterdam: Benjamins.

Bos, J. (2003). Implementing the binding and accommodation theory for anaphora resolution and presupposition projection. *Computational Linguistics*, 29 (2): 179–210.

Clark, H. H. (1977). Bridging. In Johnson-Laird, P. and Wason, P. (eds) *Thinking: Readings in Cognitive Science*. Cambridge: Cambridge University Press.

Clark, H. H. and Haviland, S. (1974). Psychological processes as linguistic explanation. In Cohen, D. (ed.) *Explaining Linguistic Phenomena*. Washington, DC: Hemisphere.

Clark, H. H. and Haviland, S. (1977). Comprehension and the given-new contract. In Freedle, R. (ed.) *Discourse Production and Comprehension*. Norwood, NJ: Ablex.

Fawcett, R. 1988. What makes a 'good' system network good? Four pairs of concepts for such evaluation. In Benson, J. D. and Greaves, W. S. (eds) *Systemic Functional Approaches to Discourse*. Norwood, NJ: Ablex.

Fawcett, R., Tucker, G. and Lin, Y. (1993). How a systemic functional grammar works: the role of realization in realization. In Horacek, H. and Zock, M. (eds) *New Concepts in Natural Language Processing: Planning, Realization and Systems*. London: Pinter.

Firbas, J. (1992). *Functional Sentence Perspective in Written and Spoken Communication*. Cambridge: Cambridge University Press.

Fox, B. (1987). *Discourse Structure and Anaphora*. Cambridge: Cambridge University Press.

Fries, P. H. (2000). Issues in modelling the textual metafunction. In Scott, M. and Thompson, G. (eds) *Patterns of Text: In Honour of Michael Hoey*. Amsterdam: Benjamins.

Grosz, B. and Sidner, C. (1998). Lost intuitions and forgotten intentions. In Walker, M. Joshi, A. and Prince, E. (eds) *Centering Theory in Discourse.* Oxford: Oxford University Press.

Grosz, B., Joshi, A. and Weinstein, S. (1995). Centering: a framework for modelling the local coherence of discourse. *Computational Linguistics*, 21 (2): 203–225.

Gundel, J. K., Hegarty, M. and Borthen, K. (2003). Cognitive status, information structure, and pronominal reference to clausally introduced entities. *Journal of Logic, Language and Information*, 12: 281–299.

Gutwinski, W. (1976). *Cohesion in Literary Texts.* The Hague: Mouton.

Halliday, M. A. K. (1985). *An Introduction to Functional Grammar.* London: Arnold.

Halliday, M. A. K. (1991). Towards probabilistic interpretations. In Ventola, E. (ed.) *Functional and Systemic Linguistics: Approaches and Uses.* Berlin: Mouton de Gruyter.

Halliday, M. A. K. and Hasan, R. (1976). *Cohesion in English.* London: Longman.

Halliday, M. A. K. and Hasan, R. (1985). *Language, Context and Text: Aspects of Language in a Social-Semiotic Perspective.* Victoria: Deakin University Press.

Halliday, M. A. K. and James, Z. (1993). A quantitative study of polarity and primary tense in the English finite clause. In Sinclair, J., Hoey, M., and Fox, B. (eds) *Techniques of Description.* London: Routledge.

Halliday, M. A. K. and Martin, J. R. (1993). *Writing Science: Literacy and Discursive Power.* London: Falmer.

Halliday, M. A. K. and Matthiessen, C. M. I. M. (1999). *Construing Experience Through Meaning.* London: Continuum.

Halliday, M. A. K. and Matthiessen, C. M. I. M. (2004). *An Introduction to Functional Grammar* (3rd edition). London: Arnold.

Haviland, S. and Clark, H. (1974). What's new? Acquiring new information as a process in comprehension. *Journal of Verbal Learning and Verbal Behavior*, 13: 512–521.

Hoey, M. (1991). *Patterns of Lexis in Text.* Oxford: Oxford University Press.

Horowitz, P. and Hill, W. (1989). *The Art of Electronics.* Cambridge: Cambridge University Press.

Just, M. A., Carpenter, P. A. and Woolley, J. D. (1980). Paradigms and processes in reading comprehension. *Journal of Experimental Psychology: General*, 111 (2): 228–238.

Lambrecht, K. (1996). *Information Structure and Sentence Form.* Cambridge: Cambridge University Press.

Lyons, J. (1977). *Semantics.* Cambridge: Cambridge University Press.

Martin, J. R. (1992). *English Text.* Amsterdam: Benjamins.

Martin, J. R. and Veel, R. (eds) (1998). *Reading Science* London: Routledge.

Matthiessen, C. (1992). Interpreting the textual metafunction. In Davies, M. and Ravelli, L. (eds) *Advances in Systemic Linguistics*. London: Pinter.

Mitkov, R., Lappin, S. and Boguraev, B. (2001). Introduction to the special issue on computational anaphora resolution. *Computational Linguistics*, 27 (4): 473–477.

Prince, E. F. (1981). Toward a taxonomy of given-new information. In Cole, P. (ed.) *Radical Pragmatics*. New York: Academic Press.

Prince, E. F. (1985). Fancy syntax and 'shared knowledge'. *Journal of Pragmatics*, 9: 65–81.

Shebilske, W. and Reid, L. (1979). Reading eye movements, macro-structure and comprehension. In Kolers, P. A., Wrolstad, M. E. and Bouma, H. (eds) *Processing of Visible Language*. New York: Plenum.

Torsello, C. T. (1996). On the logical metafunction. *Functions of Language*, 3 (2): 151–183.

Ward, J. (2007). Collocation and technicality in EAP engineering. *Journal of English for Academic Purposes*, 6: 18–35.

Wilson, D. and Matsui, T. (1998). Recent approaches to bridging: truth, coherence, relevance. *UCL Working Papers in Linguistics*, 10: 1–28.

7 Tactic augmentation and circumstantial augmentation in the creation of field meanings

Sridevi Sriniwass

7.1 Introduction

This chapter reports on findings from a study investigating the construction of knowledge in tertiary chemistry through the resources of taxis (hypotaxis and parataxis) and logico-semantic relations (elaboration, extension, enhancement and projection). The focus of attention is on the creation of temporal meanings through two grammatical resources: logical complexing and circumstantial transitivity.

The resource of transitivity will be examined in relation to clause complexing for the realisation of temporal meanings. Halliday and Matthiessen (2004: 367) suggest that there are 'patterns of agnation' that hold between circumstance types in the clause and the logico-semantic types in the clause complex. However, in the creation of text the basic consideration of whether clauses may be augmented internally by means of a circumstantial element or externally by means of another clause in a complex depends on the amount of textual, interpersonal and experiential 'semiotic weight' (Halliday and Matthiessen 2004: 369) apportioned to the unit.

This chapter first presents a general overview of SFL perspectives on scientific texts. Then it outlines the aims, research methodology and theoretical framework of the study in Sections 7.3, 7.4, and 7.5 respectively. Section 7.6 comprises the findings. It first maps out the resources of logical complexing and circumstantial transitivity for temporal meanings. This is followed by the semantic contributions of both kinds of augmentation: circumstantial and clausal. Section 7.7 discusses the value of the study on clausal augmentation and circumstantial augmentation in the interpretation of scientific text and the pedagogical implications in an ESL context. Section 7.8 will conclude the study and offer directions for further research.

7.2 SFL perspectives on scientific texts

SFL perspectives on scientific discourse have demonstrated that the grammar of scientific texts has evolved and developed to serve its changing needs (e.g. Halliday and Martin 1993). From the SFL view, the grammatical resource of the clause complex to construe meanings in science is believed to have evolved first in the history of scientific language (see Halliday and Martin 1993; Halliday 1998). The SFL claim is that the clausal *mode* of meaning has evolved to become highly metaphorised to enable more information to be packed into its grammatical structure and for the technicalisation of common-sense terms into scientific terms. Halliday (1999) and others (e.g. Unsworth 2000; Rose 1997 and 1998; Veel 1997) have repeatedly emphasised that, for handling more abstraction and information, the metaphorical mode is preferred to the congruent mode. It is also generally believed that the use of clause complexing is rare in the written medium of expository texts and is more a feature of spoken discourse. Thus, prevailing research efforts within systemic traditions in the study of scientific texts have concentrated on literacy issues, discursive power, evolution and recontextualisation of science, verbal and non-verbal semiosis, congruent and metaphorical uses of language, genre theory and metafunctional analysis.

However, the genre of the textbook has been little studied in terms of the role of clause complexing relations in the construal of knowledge. Also, with respect to the genre of the textbook, little is known about the proportion of use of the more congruent *mode* of expression as opposed to the more abstract nominalised variety. Hence, an exploration into how knowledge is constructed through the congruent forms of language, the clause complex, could be of great value, particularly to ESL readers of scientific texts. Also, a method is proposed for the analysis of temporal meanings and for the comparison of meanings drawn from two different grammatical resources: circumstantial transitivity and logical complexing.

Hence, this study not only applies the theoretical model proposed by Halliday and Matthiessen (2004) for the analysis of temporal meanings to a specific *field* of study but also describes the congruent forms of language, which have been little researched in SFL studies in the genre of scientific texts. An investigation into the semantic load carried by both the complexing and circumstantial transitivity resources invariably reveals the system of Theme predication and reflects the textual motivations behind the complexing sequences for information flow.

7.3 Aim

The general aim of the study is to analyse the functions of temporal relations in clause complexing and circumstantiation in a context of use. Drawing on the strand of research on clause complexing in the larger study (Sriniwass 2006a, b), particularly in relation to enhancing relations, an attempt will be made to present the results in relation to two research questions:

1. How does the grammatical resource of clause complexing compare with circumstantial transitivity to encode *time?*
2. What is the semantic load carried by the grammatical resource of clause complexing and circumstantial transitivity?

7.4 Methodology

This section will provide a description of the data and an overview of the methodology for the analysis of data.

7.4.1 The sources of the data

The macro genre, comprising the factual genres of procedures, procedural recount, report, and explanation (Martin 1989), best represents the kinds of texts undergraduates engage with in the doing of science, in this case, chemistry.

The data for the study consist of whole chapters in the genre of analytical chemistry taken from three textbooks used at undergraduate level at the University of Malaya: Chapters 13 and 14 from Textbook A (Rubinson and Rubinson 1998); Chapters 24, 25 and 26 from Textbook B (Skoog *et al.* 2000) and Chapters 19, 20 and 21 from Textbook C (Christian 2004). The eight texts taken from these eight chapters are referred to as A1, A2, B1, B2, B3, C1, C2 and C3 respectively. These textbooks were selected because they contain suitable models of written chemistry exposition covering fundamental, traditional and practical aspects of analytical chemistry. They cover the range of applications of analytical chemical methods involving the principles of spectroscopy, chromatography, spectrometry, electrophoresis, electrochemical methods, electrogravimetry and classical polarography.

To enable a systematic collection of texts to be analysed, boundaries were set up to distinguish the 'running verbal texts' (after Lemke 1998: 97) from other modalities such as figures, tables, photographs, pictures, in-box texts, and annotations, as are typically found in any science textbook. The analysis excludes verbal texts accompanying images, diagrams, photographs, action boxes, annotations, end notes, spreadsheet calculations and mathematical symbolism. However, chemical equations, which were codified in mathematical terms and incorporated into the clause, were included.

7.4.2 The methodology for the data analysis

The methodology employed for analysing the data is a clause-based manual qualitative descriptive text analysis following the traditions of SFL to identify and interpret syntactic interdependency patterns and circumstantial transitivity.

The first step in the analysis was the identification of the text boundary. The running verbal texts were retyped and displayed as a sequence of numbered clauses. The text was set off orthographically with all section and sub-section labelling retained in its original form. Sub-sections without enumeration were given enumeration for ease of reference.

Since the unit of analysis was the clause complex, the orthographic units were further divided into ranking clauses, clauses having units functioning according to their rank as opposed to rank-shifted or embedded clauses. Each section and sub-section was displayed as texts with numbered sequences of simplexes and ranking clauses. Ranking clauses were analysed for taxis and logico-semantic relations. Paratactic and hypotactic links as well as the various logico-semantic relations were counted. In the original study, 57 coding categories were used for the analysis of logico-semantic relations remodelled after Halliday and Matthiessen's (2004) categorisation of clause complexing resources in English. The logical relations of enhancement were then compared with circumstantial transitivity in terms of their critical role in furthering the proposition or argument in the discourse.

7.5 Theoretical framework

The framework for the identification of circumstantial elements and logico-semantic relations is drawn from Halliday and Matthiessen (2004). The study focuses on analysing temporal meanings from two different systems – circumstantial augmentation, involving the system of transitivity, and tactic augmentation, involving the system of taxis and logico-semantic relations. Their theoretical models are briefly outlined in Sections 7.5.1 and 7.5.2 respectively.

7.5.1 The system of circumstantial transitivity

Table 7.1 provides the framework adopted for the study of enhancing circumstantial elements for the encoding of temporal relations.

Circumstances are associated with process types and participants in the system of Transitivity. They are usually not obligatory constituents and contribute towards the flux of experience in the clause. The grammatical distinction of constituents into process, participants and circumstance is given in Table 7.2 in relation to the following clause.

> Figure 24-5 shows concentration profiles for the bands containing solutes A and B on the column in Figure 24-4 at time t_1 and at a later time t_2 (Text B1 [24F-5/1]).

The experiential centre of the clause is the relational process, *shows.* The two participants, involved in the process are the token, *Figure 24-5,* and the value, *concentration profiles.* The clause above is also expanded through circumstantial means. Purpose augmentation is realised for *for the*

Table 7.1: Types of enhancing circumstantial elements for the encoding of temporal relations (adapted from Halliday and Matthiessen 2004: 262)

Wh-item	*Examples of realisation*
duration how long?	for; throughout 'measured'; nominal group
frequency how many times?	'measured' nominal group
time when? [then, now]	at, in, on; to, until, till, towards, into, from, since, during, before, after adverb of time: today, yesterday, tomorrow, now, then

Table 7.2: Experiential functions of elements in transitivity

Type of element	*Typical realisation*	*Realisation*
Process	Verbal group	Shows
Participant	Nominal group	Figure 24-5; concentration profiles
Circumstance	Adverbial group/ Prepositional phrase	for the bands containing solutes A and B; on the column; in Figure 24-4; at time t_1 and at a later time t_2.

Table 7.3: Constituent function in a multivariate relationship

Text	*Circumstance: Temporal*	*Participant: Actor*	*Process: Material*	*Participant: Goal*	*Circumstance: Spatial*
Text A1 [13 .2/5]	During all separations,	the components of the sample	are carried	by the mobile phase	through a volume or layer of particles of solid material
Text B3 [26/26B/8]	In the early 1980s,	Scientists	began to explore	the feasibility [of performing these same separations]	on micro amounts of sample in fused-silica capillary tubes.

bands containing solutes A and B, spatial for *on the column* and *in Figure 24-4,* and temporal for *at time* t_1 *and at a later time* t_2.

The examples in Table 7.3 further illustrate how constituents function in a 'multivariate' structure to realise different semantic functions. 'Univariate' structures link units of interdependency whereas 'multivariate' structures link units of constituency (Halliday and Matthiessen 2004: 369, for further discussions on this, see Halliday, 1979; Matthiessen 1992; Martin, 1992).

7.5.2 The system of taxis and logic-semantic relations

Tables 7.4 and 7.5 (from Table 7 (10) Halliday and Matthiessen 2004: 411) display the categories for enhancing relations and logico-semantic markers.

Halliday and Matthiessen (2004) suggest that two basic systems which determine how one clause relates to another are:

(a) The system of taxis or interdependency;

Table 7.4: Categories of enhancement and principal markers for paratactic relations.

Category	*Meaning*	*Paratactic*
Temporal	same time – A meanwhile B	(and) meanwhile; (when)
	different time: later – A subsequently B	(and) then; and + afterwards
	different time: earlier – A previously B	and/but + before that/first

Table 7.5: Categories of enhancement and principal markers for hypotactic relations

Category	*Meaning*	*Hypotactic*		
		Finite	non-finite: conjunction	non-finite: preposition
temporal	same time A meanwhile B	[extent] as, while	while	in (the course/ process of)
		[point] when, as soon as, the moment	when	on
		[spread] whenever, every time	—	—
	different time: later A subsequently B	after, since	since	after
	different time: earlier A previously B	before, until/till	until	before
		[point] where	—	—
		[spread] whenever, everywhere	—	—

(b) The system of logico-semantic relation.

Here, clause complexing is represented explicitly using the Greek letters of α, β, γ etc. to relate clauses which are in a Hypotactic (dependent) relationship, and the numerals 1, 2, 3, ... to relate clauses in a Paratactic (equal status) relationship, following Halliday and Matthiessen's (2004) notational conventions.

Any one pair of clauses related by a relationship of interdependency is called a 'clause nexus' (Halliday and Matthiessen 2004: 376). The clauses making up such a nexus are primary and secondary as illustrated in Table 7.6.

Table 7.6: Primary and secondary clauses in a clause nexus

		Primary	*Secondary*
parataxis		*1 (initiating)*	*2 (continuing)*
Example	Text C1 19.3/RFC/3	However, large capacity factors mean increased elution time,	**so** there is a compromise between separation efficiency and separation time.
hypotaxis		α (dominant)	β (dependent)
Example	Text A2 [14.1/28]	That is, the average rate of motion is still inversely proportional to the average cross section	**even though** it is not a single sphere.

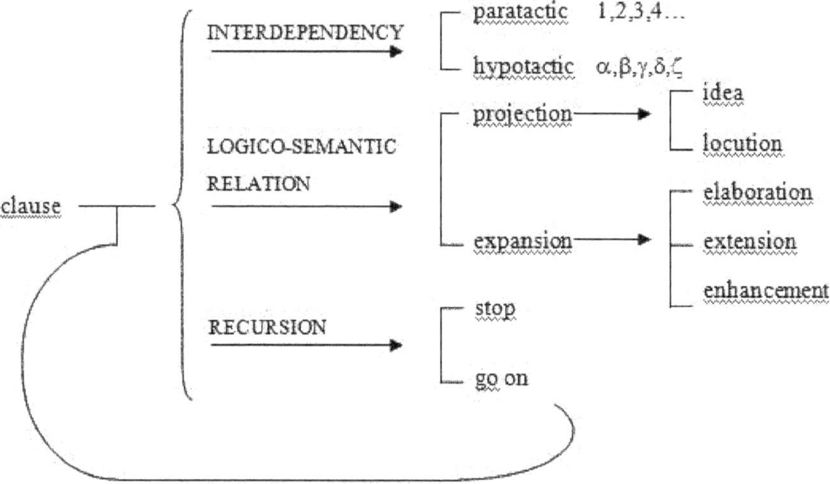

Figure 7.1: The systems of clause complexing.
(adapted from Figure 7-3, Halliday and Matthiessen, 2004: 373)

The system network in Figure 7.1 shows the degree of interdependency or Taxis and the logico–semantic relations that together form the system of the clause complex. As Figure 7.1 shows, the system of clause complexing involves three major systems: choice of interdependency, choice of logico-semantic relations and choice of recursion. The focus of this chapter will be on the system of interdependency and temporal expansion.

The technical name for the degree of interdependency in clauses forming a complex is Taxis. The two different degrees of interdependency are Parataxis, linking clauses of equal status as demonstrated in Example 1

(Text C1 [19.3/RFC/3]), and Hypotaxis, linking clauses of unequal status as demonstrated in Example 2 (Text A2 [14.1/28]).

(1) However, large capacity factors mean increased elution time, so there is a compromise between separation efficiency and separation time. (Text C1 [19.3/RFC/3])

(2) That is, the average rate of motion is still inversely proportional to the average cross section, even though it is not a single sphere. (Text A2 [14.1/28])

As suggested by Halliday and Matthiessen (2004) and as validated by research evidence (Sriniwass 2006a, b), clauses are usually made up of mixed taxis within a single clause nexus as shown in Example 3 (Text A2 [14.1/5]).

(3) Negative ions tend to migrate toward the higher (positive) voltage and positive ions tend to migrate toward the lower (negative) voltage whether the ions are in solution or in a gas. (Text A2 [14.1/5])

Temporal relations in the system of clause complexing correspond with extent/duration and location/time in transitivity. For the purposes of the current discussion and for ease of reference, all discussions on temporal augmentation will subsume both extent/duration and location/time functions.

7.6 Results and discussion

Section 7.6 presents and discusses the results of the study pertaining to how the grammatical resource of clause complexing encodes time and how it compares with circumstantial transitivity to encode the same meanings.

Section 7.6.1 presents the findings pertaining to temporal meanings from two different systems: tactic augmentation involving the system of taxis and logico-semantic relations and circumstantial augmentation involving the system of transitivity whereas Section 7.6.2 presents a comparison of both kinds of augmentation.

7.6.1 The encoding of time – tactic augmentation and circumstantial augmentation

Finite hypotactic temporal same time extent relations, introduced by *as* and *while* as in Examples 4 and 5 respectively, serve the purpose of linking two clauses to express timeless-present scientific statements. (In the examples throughout this chapter, the grammatical markers signalling logical relations are in bold, ellipsed subjects are indicated by Ø and embedded phrases or clauses are in double square brackets.)

(4) (Text A1[13.5/QT/7])
α The measurement is made on a small volume of the effluent
xβ **as** it passes through the detector.

(5) (Text C3 [21.2/36])
α A gel with a low exclusion limit, such as Sephadex 25, will allow the proteins to pass right through the column
xβ **while** the salts are retained.

Hypotactic Temporal Same Time Point relations introduced by *when* is used to link two habitual timeless events as in Example 6.

(6) (Text A2 [14.1/7])
xα **When** a charged body is placed in an electric field,
β it has a force on it [[that is proportional to the charge on the moving particle and on the voltage applied to it.]]

Hypotactic Temporal Same Time Spread marked by *whenever* is used to mark unspecified time as in Example 7.

(7) (Text C2 [20.3/GCE/10])
α... But
<xβ> **whenever** a sample component is eluted with the carrier gas,
...α a small resistance change will occur in the effluent arm.

Paratactic Temporal Later Time relations introduced by *and then,* is used to refer to events fixed in time and also to create an event line as in Example 8.

(8) (Text C2 [20.6/6])
1 Or the pressurized vapor is allowed to expand into 1 1-mLsample loop at atmospheric pressure,
x2 **and then** an auxiliary carrier gas carries the loop contents to the GC loop injector.

Hypotactic Temporal Later Time relations, introduced by *after,* is used to refer to the certainty of the event occurring and to create an event line as in Example 9.

(9) (Text A2 [14.4/3])
xβ As a result, **after** a separation is performed,
α further treatments must be done to make the bands detectable.

Finite Hypotactic Temporal Earlier Time relations, expressed by *until* and *before,* is used to refer to events up to a point in time as in Examples 10 and 11 respectively.

(10) (Text A1 [13.3/21])

α Notice

'β α that some of the peaks reach the baseline

xβ **before** the next peak begins.

(11) (Text C3 [21.1/HMD/10])

1 In adsorption chromatography the adsorbent is usually kept constant,

+2 α and the eluting solvent polarity is increased

xβ **until** elution is achieved.

Temporal relations may be encoded by the system of Circumstantiation in Transitivity, such as the Circumstance of Duration as shown in Examples 12 and 13 with the use of the prepositions *during* and *for* respectively.

(12) (Text A1 [13.2/5])

During all separations, the components of the sample are carried by the mobile phase through a volume or layer of particles of solid material.

(13) (Text C1 [19/3])

Tswett's original experiments went virtually unnoticed in the literature **for** decades

Clauses augmented circumstantially encoding earlier time and later time were also commonly found in the data, as in Examples 14 and 15 respectively.

(14) (Text B3 [26/26B/6])

Until the appearance of capillary electrophoresis, electrophoretic separations were not carried out in columns but ∅ were performed in a flat stabilized medium such as paper or a porous semisolid gel.

(15) (Text A1 [13.6/E/10])

After the extraction, we determine the concentrations of iodine in both aqueous and organic phases.

Examples 14 and 15 are both instances of marked information focus with the fronting of the circumstances of time: *Until the appearance of capillary electrophoresis* and *After the extraction.*

There are also instances of metaphorised later time relations augmented circumstantially as in Example 16.

(16) (Text C3 [21.5/TLC/6])

Following development, the individual solute sports are noted or ∅ are made visible by treatment with a reagent that forms a colored derivative.

Temporal circumstances may also be found in predicated theme structure as shown in Example 17.

(17) (Text C3 [21.1/5])

But it was not **until** the early 1970s that the technology of producing small silanized silica particles allowed the use of small-volume longer columns necessary to give the high-resolution performance.

In the theme predication illustrated in Example 17, the temporal circumstance *until the early 1970s* functions as an obligatory element of clause structure, as complement of direct object; therefore it is essential to the situation and functions as participant rather than circumstance.

Circumstantial transitivity encoding time may also post-modify a head noun as indicated in Example 18.

(18) (Text A1 [13.4/PIB/9])
Each peak [[that elutes]] **after** the hold-up volume requires a number of other parameters to describe it.

7.6.2 A comparison of tactic and circumstantial augmentation

Although both circumstantiation and logical complexing encode temporal meanings, they have different semantic functions in the text, as exemplified by Examples 19 and 20.

(19)

Text	*Logical structure*		*Ranking clause*	*Logico-semantic relation*
20.4/13	α		The first 12 gaseous or light compounds are readily eluted and resolved at a low fixed (100°C) temperature for 5.5 min,	
	xβ		while the others require higher temperatures.	Extension: Addition

(20)

Text	*Logical structure*		*Ranking clause*	*Logico-semantic relation*
20.4/14	1		After 5.5 min, the temperature is linearly increased at 5°C/min for 20 min to 200°C,	
	x2	α	and then the temperature is held at that value	Enhancement: Temporal
		xβ	until the last two compounds are eluted.	Enhancement: Temporal

Circumstantial enhancement is realised in both Examples 19 and 20 by the elements *after 5.5 min, at a low fixed (100°C) temperature for 5.5 min* and *at 5°C/min for 20 min to 200°C.* Example 20 demonstrates two clausal enhancements: Paratactic temporal later time enhancement realised by *and then the temperature is held at that value* and Hypotactic Temporal earlier time enhancement realised by *until the last two compounds are eluted.* However, it has to be noted that only Example 20 has 'propositions in its own right and could thus be tagged' and therefore have arguability (Halliday and Matthiessen 2004: 373):

— the temperature is held at that value, isn't it?
— the last two compounds are eluted, aren't they?

The subject complements, *at a low fixed (100°C) temperature for 5.5 min, at 5°C/min for 20 min to 200°C* and *at that value* are also not open to further negotiation.

A comparison of the temporal enhancement of Examples 19 and 20 indicates that enhancement through temporal circumstantial means are attendant on the processes *are readily eluted and resolved* and *is linearly increased.* The paratactic logical enhancement introduced by *and then* and hypotactic temporal earlier time introduced by *until* move the discourse forward by creating new propositions.

In order to appreciate the semantic contribution of the clause complex in the advancement of new propositions, Example 15 is revisited here and compared with Examples 21 (hypotactic) and 22 (paratactic) depicting *temporal later time* meanings.

(15) (Text A1 [13.6/E/10])
After the extraction, we determine the concentrations of iodine in both aqueous and organic phases.

(21) (Text C3 [21.5/DOS/5])
xβ **After** the sports are identified,
α they may be scraped off and the solutes washed off (eluted) and determined quantitatively by micromethod.

(22) (Text C3 [21.5/SPT/23])
1 The gel is soaked in water for about 3 days to complete the swelling,
x2 **and then** ∅ spread on the plate.

Although Examples 15, 21 and 22 all encode *temporal later time* relations, only the clause complexing devices in Examples 21 and 22 enable new arguments to be built up.

Halliday and Matthiessen (2004) suggest that in assigning semiotic weight to the unit – in this case, augmentation of the clause – many factors are taken into consideration. This is more clearly seen in the context of a longer span of text. Research evidence from the genre of the chemistry textbook indicates that while both circumstantial and clausal resources provide the means for the realisation of circumstantial meanings, the selection of clausal enhancement enables the subject to remain constant as clauses may be linked successively. An example of the construction of an event line with the use of *hypotactic temporal same time point* relations introduced by *when* is shown in Example 23.

(23) (Text A1 [13.8/SA/16] to [13.8/SA/17])
α Derivatization can also be useful
xβ **when** components are reacted to yield chemical groups [[that provide strong responses to the detector [[used with the instrument]]]].
α An example is to add chlorines (such as a —$CC1_3$ group)
xβ **when** using an electron capture detector [[that is highly sensitive to halogens]].

However, *when* clauses in succession may also be encoded by different means: one circumstantially, *When in the mobile phase,* and the other clausally, *When a molecule is associated with the stationary phase,* as shown in Example 24.

(24) (Text A1 [13.6/KET/4 to 13.6/KET/5])
When in the mobile phase, the solute molecules are being carried along at the velocity of the mobile phase.
xβ **When** a molecule is associated with the stationary phase,
α it does not move.

Although both the *when* clauses encode Temporal Same Time Point relations and enjoy thematic prominence, they have different functions. The element *When in the mobile phase* enhances the material process *are being carried* whereas the clause *When a molecule is associated with the stationary phase* is a proposition in its own right and plays a significant role in advancing the argument. The *when* clause here constructs a provision line in that one clause acts as a condition for another similar to conditional positive clauses introduced by *if.*

When clauses are also typically used to express factual meanings or habitual timeless events with the use of the instantaneous present tense as in Example 25.

(25) (Text B3 [26/26B-2/2])
xβ **When** a high voltage is applied across a fused-silica capillary tube containing a buffer solution,
α electroosmotic flow usually occurs [[in which the solvent migrates toward the cathode]]

Although *when* clauses are typically in thematic position, it was noted that in longer spans of text as in Example 26, the flow of information is further influenced by thematic structure.

(26) (Span of text from 26/26C-2/4 to 26/26C-2/5)
α Micelles form in aqueous solutions
xβ **when** the concentration of an ionic species with a long-chain hydrocarbon tail is increased above a certain level [[called the *critical micelle concentration* (CMC)]].
At this point, the surfactant begins to form spherical aggregates [[made up to 40 to 100 ions with their hydrocarbon tails in the interior of the aggregate and their charged ends exposed to water on the outside]].

Example 26 suggests that in encoding Temporal Same Time Point meanings, the textual marker *At this point* is also semantically significant in re-orientating the development of the text.

The habitual meanings expressed by *when* clauses in Examples 25 and 26 indicate an unrestricted time span in single nexuses. Frequency adverbials, such as *usually,* are typically used in statements expressing habitual meanings as shown in Example 27.

(27) Text C2 [20.1/PGC/15]
α They usually also allow splitless injection
xβ **when** packed columns are used (split/splitless injectors).

As far as temporal complexing is concerned, Thematic reiteration (after Eggins 2004: 324) was also found. *Theme reiteration* is to do with how the text is kept focused with the use of a particular thematic pattern on a regular basis. Throughout the data, it was found that in cases where *when* clauses experienced shifting between thematic and rhematic positions, the hypotactic clause followed the dominant or it preceded it, as indicated in Examples 28 (Rhematic) and 29 (Thematic).

(28) (Span of text from 13.8/SA/16 to 13.8/SA/17)
α Derivatization can also be useful
xβ **when** components are reacted to yield chemical groups [[that provide strong responses to the detector [[used with the instrument]]]].
α An example is to add chlorines (such as a —$CC1_3$ group)
xβ **when** using **an electron capture detector** [[that is highly sensitive to halogens]].

(29) (Span of text from 24F-6e/7 to 24F-6e/8)
xβ When the retention factor for a solute <u>is</u> much less than unity,
α elution occurs so rapidly [[that accurate determination of the retention times is difficult]].

xβ When the retention factor is larger than perhaps 20 to 30,
α elution times become inordinately long.

Hypotactic structures realising very congruent styles for encoding temporal relations were found throughout the data.

So far the discussion has focused on the finite logico-semantic complexing resource and its contribution to the creation of text. Non-finite temporal relations are also used, though not as widely as finite ones to realise clausal augmentation. Examples 30 and 31 demonstrate the use of Hypotactic Temporal earlier time and later time respectively.

(30) (26/26B-4/MI/1)
xβ Before entering values into the spreadsheet for calculating mobilities,
α let us rearrange Equation 26-4 and solve for $\imath_e$.

(31) (26/26B-4/MI/5)
α The table of arrival times on page 712 is entered into B8 through B15
xβ after putting the appropriate labels in A8 through A15 and titles in A7 and B7.

The foregoing discussion has highlighted the variations in role of two grammatical resources for the realisation of circumstantial meanings: tactic augmentation and circumstantial augmentation. Primarily, it has shown that, unlike circumstantial augmentation, tactic augmentation contributes to the rhetorical development of the text.

7.7 Tactic augmentation and circumstantial augmentation

Following the categories of Enhancement and Principal markers according to Halliday and Matthiessen's (2004) framework, this chapter has provided a discussion of Temporal Enhancing relations in the construction of knowledge in the genre of tertiary chemistry textbooks. It has shown how the grammatical resource of clause complexing compares with circumstantial transitivity to encode time in the creation of field meanings.

While circumstantial augmentation functions to increase the Experiential content of the text by adding a degree of specificity to the information given in the main propositions, clausal augmentation has the full potential of a clause and can be assessed modally. Being a clause in a clause complex, it can form part of a chain. In the creation of text, a choice is made between augmenting a clause internally, via a circumstantial element, and augmenting it externally, via another clause in a complex. The study has shown how the circumstantial elements augment the process, unlike the clausal elements, which contribute to the rhetorical development of the text. It has also shown how clausal enhancement of time helps construct a chronology of events as they unfold in time.

Although field meanings may be created through both grammatical resources, those of tactic augmentation and circumstantial augmentation, this chapter has argued that clauses augmented clausally contribute more significantly to thematic focusing or thematic reiteration: a feature concerned with cohesion and information organisation.

The overall findings from the original study on clause complexing relations (Sriniwass 2006a, b) show that Hypotactic Temporal relations, Same time point relations, were the most significant in usage, making up 51.21 per cent (i.e. 63 out of the 123 relations) followed by Same time extent, making up 31.7 per cent (i.e. 39 out of 123 relations). Hypotactic Temporal same time spread, Hypotactic Temporal earlier time, and Hypotactic Temporal later time were insignificant in usage. It may be inferred that the resource of *circumstantiation* is widely used to encode *earlier time* and *later time* relations.

The principal markers for expanding a clause to express Temporal relations were: *when* to introduce Finite Hypotactic Temporal same time point relations, *as and while,* to introduce Finite Hypotactic same time extent relations, and *until* and *before* to introduce Finite Hypotactic Temporal earlier time relations.

Interestingly, many writers of introductory chemistry textbooks at the tertiary level acknowledge that efficient communication of chemistry ideas is of the utmost importance in the methods of chemistry for an understanding of concepts and principles. For example, Bodner and Pardue (1989) explicitly suggest that their course was designed to meet the objective of familiarising students with the language of chemistry. Therefore, the significance of deploying a systemic approach to the study of scientific texts is in being able to show the interrelatedness between the choice of grammatical resource and the construal of knowledge, and to validate the SFL claim that grammar facilitates the interpretation of text. Further, the descriptive insight gained from the analysis of circumstantiation and clause complexing relations may be used to interpret and evaluate the construction of knowledge in any academic text.

In the context of an ESL/EFL situation, particularly in Malaysia, where English has recently been reintroduced as the medium of instruction for the learning of science and mathematics at primary, secondary and tertiary levels, an understanding of chemistry at the congruent level paves the way for a more accurate understanding of ideas at the metaphorical level. ESL/EFL learners of scientific English may need more exposure to the congruent types so that they may gradually develop the skills necessary to understand more sophisticated expressions of scientific thought. Moreover, the genre of the scientific textbook has been little studied in terms of the role of lexicogrammar in the construal of knowledge. Also, with respect to the genre of the textbook, little is known about the proportion of use of the more congruent mode of expression as opposed to the more abstract nominalised variety. Hence, it is the contention of this study that an exploration of how knowledge is constructed through the congruent forms of language, the clause complex, is of great value, particularly to ESL/EFL learners of science. The resources of clause complexing, when deconstructed in a step-wise fashion, may facilitate an understanding of how science sequences, taxonomises, theorises and creates cause and effect relationships.

As students become users of scientific English, they need to become familiar with the genre of their discipline of specialisation and at the same time gain expertise in the English language. From their own surveys, both Wood (2001) and Kennedy (2001) attest to the fact that English is still the most widely used language for the dissemination and publication of scientific ideas. ESL/EFL undergraduates in science based disciplines will have to be trained in reading and writing scientific English in a variety of genres, namely: textbooks, reference books, research articles and laboratory reports. As Eggins (1994: 36) points out, 'the functions of each stage of the genre are expressed through language choices (discourse-semantic and lexico-grammatical) realized in a text'. Hence, explorations into the language of scientific prose continue to have validity and provide valuable insights into the nature of the complex organisation of science and how it may be accessed by its apprentices. Since the findings from the original study (Sriniwass 2006a, b) show that the textbook genre of chemistry appears to have a somewhat balanced distribution of congruent and non-congruent forms for the expression of chemistry, hopefully this will assist learners to recognise these modes of expression. Recognising the congruent or clausal mode of meaning is useful especially for ESL/EFL learners trying to verify and reinforce their understanding of science. Once they are able to interpret how sequencing, reasoning and arguments are encoded in grammatically intricate and semantically dense clause structures, they may be able to access disciplinary specific knowledge in highly metaphorised albeit less grammatically intricate language.

7.8 Conclusion and directions for further research

The variations in role of the two grammatical resources for the realisation of circumstantial meanings point to the need for much more vigorous exploration of scientific texts. The research reported in this chapter has focused on External Enhancing relations forming complexes in ranking clauses. The data need to be examined in more detail in relation to other circumstantial resources, namely those of *space, manner, cause* and *condition.* Taking up Martin's (1992) suggestion that the construal of circumstantial meanings may be realised by other grammatical packagings, the findings of this research may be complemented with the encoding of circumstantiation via the resources of cohesive adjuncts or nominalisations to obtain a holistic picture of the functions of circumstantiation in scientific discourse. The extent of transformation of congruent forms of linguistic expression into highly abstract ones may be sought.

An analysis of text as a semantic unit, showing rhetorical-relational meanings as in Mann, Matthiessen and Thompson's RST (rhetorical structure theory) (1992) may be pursued to further an understanding of the flow of discourse. Further study may also be carried out on any possible variations in the nature of the development of reasoning, sequencing and argumentation in the sub-genres of the textbook genre to appreciate rhetorical–grammatical dependencies.

References

Bodner, G. M. and Pardue, H. L. (1989). *Chemistry: An Experimental Science.* New York: John Wiley and Sons.

Christian, G. (2004). *Analytical Chemistry.* Seattle, WA: University of Washington; New York: John Wiley and Sons.

Christie, F. and Martin, J. R. (eds) (1997). *Genre and Institutions: Social Processes in the Workplace and School.* London: Continuum.

Eggins, S. (2004). *An Introduction to Systemic Functional Linguistics* (2nd edition). London and New York: Continuum.

Flowerdew, J. and Peacock, M. (eds) (2001). *Research Perspectives on English for Academic Purposes.* Cambridge: Cambridge University Press.

Halliday, M. A. K. (1979). Modes of meaning and modes of expression: types of grammatical structure and their determination by different semantic functions. In Allerton, D. J., Carney, E. and Holdcroft, D. (eds), *Function and Context in Linguistic Analysis.* London: Cambridge University Press, 57–79.

Halliday, M. A. K. and Martin, J. R. (1993). *Writing Science: Literacy and Discursive Power.* London: The Falmer Press.

Halliday, M. A. K. and Matthiessen, C. M. I. M. (2004). *An Introduction to Functional Grammar* (3rd edition). London: Arnold.

Halliday, M. A. K. (1998). Things and relations: regrammaticising experience as technical knowledge. In Martin, J. R. and Veel, R. (eds) *Reading Science: Critical and Functional Perspectives on Discourse of Science.* London: Routledge, 185–235.

Halliday, M. A. K. (1999). The grammatical construction of scientific knowledge: the framing of the English clause. In Halliday, M. A. K. and Webster, J. (eds) *Collected Works of M. A .K. Halliday, volume 5: The Language of Science.* London: Continuum, 102–133.

Kennedy, C. (2001). Language use, language planning and EAP. In Flowerdew, J. and Peacock, M. (eds), *Research Perspectives on English for Academic Purposes.* Cambridge: Cambridge University Press, 25–41.

Lemke, J. (1998). Multiplying meaning: visual and verbal semiotics in scientific text. In Martin, J. R. and Veel, R. (eds), *Reading Science: Critical and Functional Perspectives on Discourse of Science.* London: Routledge, 87–151.

Mann, W. C., Matthiessen, C. M. I. M. and Thompson, S. A. (1992). Rhetorical structure theory and text analysis. In Mann, W. C. and Thompson, S. A. (eds) *Discourse Description: Diverse Linguistic Analyses of a Fund-raising Text.* Amsterdam: Benjamins, 39–77.

Martin J. R. (1989). *Factual Writing: Exploring and Challenging Social Reality.* Oxford: Oxford University Press.

Martin, J. R. (1992). *English Text – System and Structure.* Amsterdam: Benjamins.

Martin, J. R. and Veel, R. (eds) (1998). *Reading Science: Critical and Functional Perspectives on Discourse of Science.* London: Routledge.

Matthiessen, C. M. I. M. (1992). *Lexicogrammatical Cartography: English Systems.* Tokyo: International Language Sciences Publishers.

Rose, D. (1997). Science, technology and technical literacies. In Christie, F. and Martin, J. R. (eds) *Genre and Institutions: Social Processes in the Workplace and School.* London: Continuum, 40–72.

Rose, D. (1998). Science discourse and industrial hierarchy. In Martin, J. R. and Veel, R. (eds) *Reading Science: Critical and Functional Perspectives on Discourse of Science.* London: Routledge, 222–244.

Rubinson, J. F. and Rubinson, K. A. (1998). *Contemporary Chemical Analysis.* Upper Saddle River, NJ: Prentice Hall.

Skoog, D. A., West, D. M., Holler, F. J. and Crouch, S. R. (2000). *Analytical Chemistry: An Introduction.* Orlando, FL: Harcourt College Publishers.

Sriniwass, S. (2006a). Systemic perspectives on the clause complex in English: logico-semantic relations in chemistry. In Mohd Don, Z. (ed.) *English in a Globalised Environment: Investigating an Emerging Variety of English.* Kuala Lumpur: University of Malaya Press, 55–85.

Sriniwass, S. (2006b). Knowledge construction in the genre of chemistry textbooks: a systemic functional perspective. Unpublished PhD thesis. University of Malaya..

Unsworth, L. (2000). Investigating subject-specific literacies in school learning. In Unsworth, L. (ed.) *Researching Language in Schools and Communities: Functional Linguistic Perspectives.* London: Cassell, 245–274.

Veel, R. (1997). Learning how to mean – scientifically speaking: apprenticeship into scientific discourse in the secondary school. In Christie, F. and Martin, J. R. (eds), *Genre and Institutions: Social Processes in the Workplace and School.* London: Continuum, 161–195.

Ventola, E. (1996). Packing and unpacking of information in academic texts. In Ventola, E. and Mauranen, A. (eds) *Academic Writing: Intercultural and Textual Issues.* Amsterdam: Benjamins, 153–194.

Wood, A. (2001). International scientific English: the language of research scientists around the world. In Flowerdew, J. and Peacock, M. (eds) *Research Perspectives on English for Academic Purposes,* Cambridge: Cambridge University Press. 71–83.

PART III

Applications of the theory to academic contexts

8 Instantial and conventional representations in scientific knowledge construction

Ann Montemayor-Borsinger

8.1 Introduction

Systemic Functional Linguistics has had a long-standing interest in the role language plays in the creation, communication and negotiation of scientific discourse. This chapter is a detailed case study of how a physicist changes his grammatical subject representations in two research articles published within a decade of each other in international refereed journals. Grammatical subject is crucial when composing texts as it represents the nub of the argument: 'something by reference to which the proposition can be affirmed or denied' (Halliday 1994: 76), and is the element 'on which the validity of the information is made to rest' (Halliday 1994: 76). A study over time of different representations in grammatical subject with increased experience provides significant information on changes in the communication and negotiation of scientific knowledge, and provides a better understanding of how established scientists choose to convey the results of their research.

Section 8.2 considers the situational context of the texts. Section 8.3 focuses on methodological aspects of the text analysis by discussing Halliday's concept of 'grammatical metaphor' and introducing the notions of 'Conventional' and 'Instantial' representations of scientific knowledge. Section 8.4 examines how representations of grammatical subject change with increased experience in publishing research articles. The last section discusses the linguistic and pedagogical implications of this case study, which is in agreement with statistical results obtained from studying a larger corpus of research articles.

8.2 The situational context of the two articles

Since this study derives its motives from a larger project concerning research writing in the sciences, an understanding of the context in which scientific articles are written is necessary to ensure the effective interpretation of the analysis of the texts. In what follows characteristic features of the corpus are briefly discussed in relation to the writing and publishing contexts.

8.2.1 The writing context

Montemayor-Borsinger (2005, 2008) presented a study of an extended corpus of research articles published in international refereed journals. It was set up to analyse representational changes in grammatical subject by asking ten established physicists to submit their first article and two later articles that they had written on their own. Publications of the articles in international refereed journals were necessary to ensure they were socially validated texts as regards both language and scientific ideas. The physicists concerned have all published well over fifty articles, sometimes co-authored, and regularly act as referees themselves. Here I examine in more detail conventional and instantial subject representations in two articles, written by one of the researchers: his first article and an article published a decade later.

With respect to co-authorship, clarification is needed. In physics, teamwork is the norm, and it is customary for young researchers to publish their first articles with their supervisors. They generally start by writing parts of the article, which are then edited and often rewritten by supervisors. Once physics students have completed their PhD, they carry on working in research groups. However, within these highly collaborative settings, there are physicists who tend to work on their own and publish on their own. Alternatively, there are physicists who carry out the research work in collaboration with others, but tend to be the ones who end up writing the article. A distinction has thus to be made between the writer of an article, i.e. the one who actually puts into words what has been done, and its co-authors, i.e. the team of researchers who, by actively taking part in the research process, make the writing of the final article possible. In other words, articles in physics may have several authors, which does not necessarily mean that all of them have actually written the article. This is because physics requires both mathematics and words. The research process necessarily involves many different aspects such as detailed calculations, computational and laboratory work, results under the form of equations, tables and figures, decisions to be taken about which equations, tables or figures should be presented, how they should be presented, in what order, etc. As one informant, working in theoretical physics, put it during an interview (personal transcription, slashes indicate pauses):

> physicists ... use mathematics and they couldn't not use mathematics/ but mathematics isn't all it is either/ it is also the words/.../part of the difficulty of physics I think is precisely the whole balance between the verbal qualitative conceptual description in words/ and the precise mathematical quantitative description in terms of symbols/ hum/ well mathematical symbols because words are symbols too/.../all of us have the same problem/ it's actually often easier to just derive a bunch of equations and 'do equations' as it were in your research/ but that isn't actually going to relate to any physics unless you've thought about what we call 'the physics'/ and what is meant by 'the physics' is a verbal conceptual description of what's going on/...

Once 'the physics' has been conceptualised, then comes the actual writing stage when, sometimes, only one of the co-authors writes the article. This can be due to many different factors, ranging from personal preferences to institutional constraints. Common scenarios for a first article might be when a physicist has finished his PhD thesis and moves to a new research environment, but still has PhD results to publish, and, for later articles, when a physicist is having to write an article alone because colleagues are travelling, or because the article is co-authored by visiting researchers who have travelled back to their own institutions, for instance.

The reason for selecting articles written by one writer has obviously nothing to do with the quality of the scientific work. Physicists who tended to write on their own had to be found because of the aim of the present research: i.e. to detect changes in the representation of scientific knowledge in research articles with increased experience. Finding these 'lone writers' was actually one of the difficulties in setting up the present study, because, as noted above, in physics working in a team is much more common than working alone.

8.2.2 The publishing context

Physics is a highly internationalised branch of research, with several hundred journals. The Journal Citation Report gives detailed information about their relative importance and, in particular, about their ranking sorted by Impact Parameter (IP). This parameter is the ratio between the number of published articles in a given journal and the number of citations referring to these articles, both within a period of two years. For instance, if a journal has an IP of 2, this means that its articles are cited twice on average in other ranked international journals within two years following publication. The higher the IP, the more frequently cited are the articles from a given journal, with fewer than 20 journals having an IP higher than 3.

The general distribution of the articles that constitute the whole corpus as a function of the IP centres around high IP journals of about 2, indicating that the articles tend to come from relatively high ranked and prestigious publications. The two articles studied here in detail are no exception. The first article was published in *Physica A* (by North-Holland, officially endorsed by the European Physical Society) and the later one in *Physical Review E* (published by the American Physical Society). Both are highly specialised journals that publish research in statistical mechanics, aimed at an audience of statistical physicists.

The two articles were published within a decade of each other, a sufficiently long period of time for capturing significant changes in meaning-making as a researcher gains experience. A serious problem affecting longitudinal studies is that they tend to suffer case losses: all the more so in the case of extended time spans. In order to prevent such loss of information, the present analysis was designed as a retrospective longitudinal study where there was one data collection point, when the researcher was asked to furnish his first article and a later article of relevance.

8.3 Changes in representational practices over time

Another important consideration for such a study is the setting up of coding frames that will capture these changes in the representation of scientific knowledge with increased experience. An effective approach is offered by taking as a starting point Halliday's examination of grammatical metaphor (1993: 69–85, 1998: 196–206). Halliday looks at metaphor, not as a variation in the meaning of an expression, but as a variation in how a meaning is expressed. In science registers he distinguishes two different types of grammatical metaphor: a referring or taxonomising type and an expanding or reasoning type. He highlights the different roles both types have in scientific discourse because of the different things they enable writers to do. 'Type 1' (the referring or taxonomising metaphor, so-called because it refers via heavily nominalised technical classes) is concerned with the way scientists name their objects of study. Examples of Type 1 referring metaphors are technical terms such as the following that are found in the present corpus: *The Boltzmann equation, The general solution, Numerical analysis, Reaction-diffusion systems, Global coupling, Internal deterministic noise* etc. ...Type 1 metaphor has also been named '*distillation*' by Martin (1993) because it has compacted and changed the nature of familiar expressions: 'just as a vat of whisky is both less voluminous and different in kind from the ingredients that went to make it up' (Martin 1993: 172).

'Type 2' (the expanding or reasoning metaphor) is used for building up technical classes into flows of argument. Two examples taken from the present corpus are: *A full understanding of the role of global coupling in the dynamics of extended complex systems* and *The question of the equivalence between these two sources of asymmetry* where, in both cases, the scientist has nominalised reasoning processes of argumentation.

Another way of considering Halliday's distinction between Type 1, referring/taxonomising metaphors, and Type 2, expanding/reasoning metaphors, is that the former is already part of the enduring technical jargon of a given field of research, while the second constructs new scientific representations. Halliday observes that there is a continuum between the two types since Type 2, expanding/reasoning metaphors, may become 'distilled' into Type 1, referring/taxonomising metaphors, if they have become part of the language system. Halliday's continuum has to do with time. He distinguishes three different types of time. The first is the time of the unfolding of the text – Logogenetic time. The second is the time of the evolution of the language – Phylogenetic time. The third is the time of growth and maturation of the user of the language – Ontogenetic time (cf. Halliday 1998: 222–223), the last being the main concern of the present research. Writers can base their scientific representations on the readily accessible wordings conventionally used in their field. Alternately, writers may want to create tailored wordings that precisely fit into a particular stretch of discourse to convey complex and sometimes controversial reasoning processes. They are in a position to do so once they have deeply reflected upon and assimilated the substance with which they are working, and have made the material their own, as it were: hence the concepts of 'Conventional' vs. 'Instantial' representations that was set up and discussed in detail in previously cited works (Montemayor-Borsinger 2005, 2008).

Conventional subjects are commonly used representations within the research field concerned, as in Example (1) from the present corpus (grammatical subject in bold).

(1) **Global coupling** plays a relevant role in models of many real systems driven by long-range interactions.

In contrast, instantial subjects are expressions which have been especially composed to express new, sometimes controversial representations, as in Example (2) from the present corpus (grammatical subject in bold).

(2) **A full understanding of the role of global coupling in the dynamics of extended complex systems – to the levels already reached in the case of diffusive coupling** – will require the study of other types of local dynamics.

The need for a new taxonomy originated from difficulties encountered in previous studies that examined changes in scientific knowledge construction (Montemayor-Borsinger 2001). It was found that most of the highly specialised terms used in physics articles were both 'phenomenal' and 'epistemic' in the sense given by Peck MacDonald (1992) because they identified both objects of study and knowledge making elements that push science forward. However, these highly specialised terms differ in the level of writer creativity involved. The 'Conventional' versus 'Instantial' distinction is an effective way of studying representational changes with increased knowledge related both to subject-matter and to ways of writing about it. Writers can base their language choices on the readily accessible representations conventionally used in their field. On the other hand, writers may want to create tailored representations that represent new, complex and/or controversial issues. Hence the importance of distinguishing between these 'Conventional' vs. 'Instantial' representations that will be discussed in detail in the case study presented in the following section.

8.4 A discussion of the differences between Text 1 and Text 2

I shall now compare and contrast the representation of scientific knowledge in grammatical subjects in two articles written and published by the same researcher at different times. His first article was published in 1988, and will hereafter be referred to as 'Text 1'. The other was published in 1997, and will hereafter be referred to as 'Text 2'. The researcher works within an area of theoretical physics: statistical mechanics. Work in this area of research is based on models for systems that can only be described in terms of statistical probabilities, because information concerning these systems is incomplete. As stated above, the two articles were published within a decade of each other in specialised journals aimed at an audience of statistical physicists.

8.4.1 Percentages of conventional and instantial subjects in each text

The relative distribution of grammatical subject choices in the two articles is shown in Table 8.1. Apart from the 'Conventional' and 'Instantial' representations proposed here, another class of grammatical subjects was necessary to account for all the subjects in the articles. These were 'Participant' subjects, based on a taxonomy initially proposed by Davies (1988) and discussed in Gosden (1993). This type of subject representation is relatively straightforward to recognise on the basis of lexical clues. Participant subjects represent writers, and are mostly worded as '*we*' or '*our work*', '*our results*', etc.

Table 8.1 shows appreciable differences between Text 1 and Text 2. In Text 2, the percentages of participant and conventional subjects are significantly lower than in Text 1, while those of instantial subjects are more than double. In Text 1 all participant subjects are worded as '*we*' as shown in Example (3) taken from Text 1.

(3) (Text 1)
We obtain exact solutions for inhomogeneous systems ...
We have extended the analysis of the discrete two-velocity model ...
We have found similar solitonic solutions ... etc.

In Text 2 participant subjects are both lower in quantity and expressed differently, with a particularly noticeable absence of '*we*' representations. When asked about this in an interview, the researcher pointed out that he had deliberately tried to avoid appearing at all by either using the impersonal '*one*' as shown in Example (4), or verbs in the imperative that enjoin the reader to 'consider' or 'suppose' as in Example (5):

Table 8.1: Subject representations in the two articles

Text	*Year*	*Participant*	*Conventional*	*Instantial*
1	1988	8%	77%	15%
2	1997	3%	63%	34%

(4) (Text 2)
One should be interested in characterizing the forms of collective evolution,...

(5) (Text 2)
Consider a set of *N* identical elements ... Without loss of generality, suppose $r > 0$ ...

8.4.2 Relative proportions of conventional vs. instantial subjects

Another way of looking at differences between the two articles is to look at the relative proportion of conventional and instantial subjects in each one. These proportions are as follows. In Text 1 there are five times more conventional subjects than instantial ones, whereas in Text 2 there are only just over twice as many. Tables 8.2 and 8.3 respect these proportions, and show some of the wordings found in conventional and instantial subjects in each article. Hence, for each 15 conventional subjects there are only three instantial subjects in Text 1, whereas in Text 2 there are seven instantial subjects. Tables 8.2 and 8.3 show the first 15 conventional subjects

Table 8.2: The first 15 conventional and corresponding three instantial subjects as Text 1 unfolds

	Conventional grammatical subjects	*Instantial grammatical subjects*
1	The Boltzmann equation ...	The interest in this equation ...
2	The Boltzmann equation ...	Simplified models for the considered systems ...
3	the velocity of a one-dimensional gas molecule ...	The interaction between a two-velocity gas and a background for the spatially homogeneous case ...
4	The general solution ...	
5	Numerical analysis ...	
6	Particular exact solutions ...	
7	The Boltzmann equation ...	
8	These processes ...	
9	Solitonic distribution functions ...	
10	The velocities for the one-dimensional model gas ...	
11	The Boltzmann equations ...	
12	The bilinear operator (2.2) ...	
13	The positive coefficients ...	
14	The 2′2 matrix A = (aii) ...	
15	The density n and the current j ...	

Table 8.3: The first 15 conventional and corresponding seven instantial subjects as Text 2 unfolds

	Conventional grammatical subjects	*Instantial grammatical subjects*
1	Reaction-diffusion systems	The study of complex behaviour in extended systems ...
2	Global coupling	Other coupling mechanisms – in particular, global coupling ...
3	Long-range interactions	Forms of collective behaviour produced by global coupling ...
4	This paper	This kind of ordered entrained evolution which has been observed in systems formed by either identical or slightly different elements ...
5	Models of coupled bistable elements	A full understanding of the role of global coupling in the dynamics of extended complex systems to the levels already reached in the case of diffusive coupling ...
6	Internal deterministic noise	The same models, added with suitable harmonic forcing, ...
7	The mathematical model	The behaviour of the coupled system for $k = 1$ ...
8	A critical phenomenon	
9	Section III	
10	Results	
11	The individual dynamics The evolution of *xi*	
12	The evolution of *xi*	
13	The solution to Eq. (1)	
14	Global coupling	
15	The coupling constant *k*	

and the corresponding proportion of instantial subjects as each article unfolds. As a reminder, conventional subjects are technical terms that refer, via heavily 'distilled' technical wordings, to methods, models and phenomena. Instantial subjects, on the other hand, are more complex realisations that have to do with particular reasoning and argumentation processes as the discourse unfolds.

In a similar way to what was noticed for participant subjects, these quantitative differences are accompanied by qualitative ones. Instantial subjects increase both in number and in complexity in Text 2. The fourth and fifth instantial subjects found in this text and shown in Table 8.3 are two good instances of particularly complex representations. In Example (6), they are reproduced in bold, in the context of their respective clauses.

(6) *Fourth and fifth instantial subject found in Text 2*
This kind of ordered entrained evolution which has been observed in systems formed by either identical or slightly different elements is part of a wide class of possible behaviors with nontrivial features, including clustering, chaotic collective dynamics, and desynchronization. [new paragraph]
Although much attention has recently been paid to these sets of globally coupled oscillators, **a full understanding of the role of global coupling in the dynamics of extended complex systems to the levels already reached in the case of diffusive coupling** will require one to study other types of local dynamics.

These particularly complex instantial subjects are found throughout Text 2, and are much rarer in Text 1, as shown in the concluding paragraphs of each article in Examples (7) and (8). The grammatical subjects are in bold.

(7) *Concluding paragraphs of Text 1*
For this Boltzmann equation, **we** have found similarity solitonic solutions, representing shape-preserving distribution functions moving along the spatial coordinate. **These solutions** were expanded in power series of the similarity variable, obtaining recursive algebraic equations for the coefficients. **This scheme** allows the calculation of the distribution function with an arbitrarily small error.
The recursive equations can be solved in a closed form if remotion and regeneration processes are neglected. In this particular case, **an acceleration in the relaxation to equilibrium** is observed when the density of the background increases. **This effect** applies for each point, as the step soliton passes on it. Furthermore, **the value of the equilibrium current** depends on the background distribution, through eq. (2.3b). **These results** are the generalisation to the spatially inhomogeneous case of the main conclusions obtained for the homogeneous system [7]. **They** are expected to hold for more realistic gas models. (Zanette 1988: 617)

In the concluding paragraphs of Text 1, only one of the eight main grammatical subjects could be considered as being instantial, i.e. *an acceleration in the relaxation to equilibrium*, which may be justified on the basis of post-modification of *acceleration*. But even so the function of this subject is not one of argumentation, but merely the presentation of a certain type of acceleration. There is one participant subject *we*, and the remaining six subjects are all conventional wordings. In contrast, most of the subjects in the concluding paragraph of Text 2 are instantial in nature:

(8) *Concluding paragraph of Text 2*

This interpretation of the model of globally coupled bistable elements inspires the proposal of several generalisations that are indeed worth considering. For instance, it would be interesting to analyse the effect of an asymmetry in the potential of Eq. (1), such that **only one stationary state** is truly stable whereas **the other** becomes metastable. **This intrinsic preference for one of the states** can be compared with the evolution in the bistable symmetric potential from an asymmetric initial condition, as described by Eq. (10). **The question of the equivalence between these two sources of asymmetry – the potential or the initial condition –** arises then quite naturally. **A second generalisation, which is certainly relevant to the model of opinion formation,** is to admit the possibility that the coupling constant is not the same for all the elements, but is chosen at random for each element from a prescribed distribution. In physical models, **this form of quenched disorder** would represent some kind of spatial inhomogeneity. To the author's knowledge, **the effects of inhomogeneities in the coupling strength** has not been considered, up to this moment, in the literature on globally coupled systems. (Zanette 1997: 3257)

Five of the eight subjects in the concluding paragraph of Text 2 are instantial wordings whose function is that of discussing results, i.e. *This interpretation of... , only one ..., This intrinsic preference for ..., The question of the equivalence between ..., A second generalisation, which is certainly relevant to ....* Example (8) shows a much more sophisticated use of argumentation strategies where the writer does not overtly comment on the results, but rather hands over the agency to abstractions that combine ideational representations of content with interpersonal meanings of evaluation and negotiation. The function of such a combination is to account for the writer's interpretations in ways that will be perceived as being more objective by fellow researchers.

8.5 Implications for pedagogy

This case study shows that, with experience, the researcher has been able to compose grammatical subjects that increasingly function as elements of negotiation and argumentation without overt authorial presence. This finding is in agreement with statistical results obtained from studying a wider corpus of 30 research articles by ten different writers, with the whole set of results having been discussed elsewhere (Montemayor-Borsinger 2005, 2008). This reinforces the findings of diachronic studies such as

Bazerman (1984), who not only agrees with the traditional view that science is a rational, cumulative, corporate enterprise, but also points out that it is realised by 'linguistic, rhetorical and social means and *choices*, all with epistemological consequences' (1984: 191, emphasis added). Bazerman further suggests that studies of scientific texts should consider the linguistic tools available to scientists, and the implications of those tools:

> Even as the conventions constrain a writer, they [the tools] may be mobilised and manipulated to the writer's advantage. In whatever form the conventions make their presence felt, they are the basis of many writing choices. (Bazerman 1984: 191, square brackets added).

One such linguistic tool of particular importance is the capacity of construing instantial representations that offer powerful means of packing strategic information in grammatical subject, thus enhancing text flow by concentrating complexity in unmarked Themes, which simultaneously function as the 'nub of the argument'.

Both instantial and conventional subjects are ideational in nature. The difference is in the complexity of instantial subjects, which by means of pre- and post-modification combine ideational meanings with interpersonal ones. For these interpersonal meanings, where writers interact with their readers by means of argumentation and evaluation, results show a shift from the overtly interactive participant subjects of the *we* type, that disappear, to more subtle and complex instantial subjects, that nearly double. In general, research has shown that interpersonal meanings are much more moveable to different parts of the sentence and can adapt to many different structures (Halliday 1994: 68–105; Martin 2000: 175; Martin and Rose 2003: 64; Thompson and Zhou 2000: 122). This accounts for the rise in instantial subjects, which offer the possibility of interweaving ideational meanings with interpersonal ones. The capacity of finding optimum ways of combining ideational and interpersonal meanings appears to be what established researchers have developed.

An important incentive for studying representational practices by established writers is to help novice researchers in their attempts at successfully publishing their work. In my experience with academic writing workshops, young researchers often want to know how their published work compares with that of the leaders in their field, not only regarding results per se, but also regarding ways of presenting these results. Researchers publishing their first articles are acutely aware of the importance of mastering optimal writing strategies in a highly competitive publishing world. Rather than just seeking advice at the editing level, there comes a point when they want to discuss in more detail how to communicate and negotiate new meanings. A systemic functional perspective takes into consideration these fundamental questions on meaning-making and the different ways the language of science may 'regrammaticise' experience by grammatical metaphor (Halliday and Martin 1993; Halliday 1998). It also considers simultaneously the discussion of content: i.e. ideational strands of meaning, the evaluation of content: i.e. interpersonal strands of meaning, and information flow organisation: i.e. textual strands of meaning.

A greater focus on grammatical subject choice can be a very effective way of enhancing novice researchers' awareness of how to communicate more effectively, especially when there is little time and heavy pressure to publish. The type of analysis presented here highlights possible options offered by grammatical subject to suit different communicative aims and to enhance effective discourse flow. Devising instantial subjects that are ideationally purposeful, interpersonally strategic and textually suitable is an important step towards improving the discussion of results, where the linguistic choices that scientists make affect the way in which findings are perceived by their respective research communities.

References

Bazerman, C. (1984). Modern evolution of the experimental report in physics: spectroscopic articles in Physical Review, 1893–1980. *Social Studies of Science*, 14: 163–196.

Davies, F. (1988). Reading between the lines: thematic choice as a device for presenting written viewpoint in academic discourse. *The ESPecialist*, 9/1–2: 173–200.

Gosden, H. (1993). Discourse functions of subject in scientific research articles. *Applied Linguistics*, 14/1: 56–75.

Halliday, M. A. K. (1993). Some grammatical problems in scientific English. In Halliday, M. A. K. and Martin, J. R. (eds), *Writing Science: Literacy and Discursive Power*. London: The Falmer Press, 69–85.

Halliday, M. A. K. (1994). *An Introduction to Functional Grammar* (2nd edition). London: Arnold.

Halliday, M. A. K. (1998). Things and relations. In Martin, J. R. and Veel, R. (eds). *Reading Science: Critical and Functional Perspectives on Discourses of Science*. London: Routledge, 185–235.

Halliday, M. A. K. and Martin, J. R. (eds) (1993). *Writing Science: Literacy and Discursive Power*. London: The Falmer Press.

Hunston, S. and Thompson, G. (eds) (2000). *Evaluation in Text: Authorial Stance and the Construction of Discourse*. Oxford: Oxford University Press.

Martin J. R. (1993). Literacy in science: learning to handle text as technology. In Halliday, M. A. K. and Martin, J. R. (eds), *Writing Science: Literacy and Discursive Power*. London: The Falmer Press. 166–202.

Martin J. R. (2000). Beyond exchange: appraisal systems in English. In Hunston, S. and Thompson, G. (eds), *Evaluation in Text: Authorial Stance and the Construction of Discourse*. Oxford: Oxford University Press, 142–175.

Martin J. R. and Rose, D. (2003). *Working with Discourse: Meaning Beyond the Clause*. London and New York: Continuum.

Montemayor-Borsinger, A. (2001). Linguistic choices in two research articles in Physics: study of an author's development. *The ESPecialist*, 22/1: 51–74.

Montemayor-Borsinger, A. (2005). Authorial development in research writing: coding changes in grammatical subject. *The ESPecialist*, 26/2: 82–104.

Montemayor-Borsinger, A. (2008). Text-type and Texture: the potential of Theme for the study of research writing development. In Thompson, G. and Forey, G. (eds) *Text-type and Texture*. London: Equinox.

Peck MacDonald, S. (1992). A method for analyzing sentence-level differences in disciplinary knowledge making. *Written Communication*, 9: 533–569.

Thompson, G. and Zhou, J. (2000). Evaluation and organization in text: the structuring role of evaluative disjuncts. In Hunston, S. and Thompson, G. (eds), *Evaluation in Text: Authorial Stance and the Construction of Discourse*. Oxford: Oxford University Press, 121–141.

Zanette, D. H. (1997). Dynamics of globally coupled bistable elements. *Physical Review E* 55: 3247–3259.

Zanette, D. H. (1988). Solitonic solutions for the generalised two-velocity Boltzmann equation. *Physica A* 153: 612–618.

9 Mapping Ideational meaning in a corpus of student writing

Sheena Gardner

9.1 Introduction

As part of the British Academic Written English (BAWE)[1] project which aims to build and characterise a corpus of 3,000 student assignments across disciplines and years of study, this chapter focuses on describing Ideational meaning, or what university students write about. It focuses on Field, for example on whether students write about kings or cabbages, and in particular on Angle on Field or how students approach their topics, whether they write about *Time, The soit-disant age of absolutism,* or *Recent literature reviews and meta-analyses.*[2] The aim is to develop and test a framework for such description. This chapter starts by arguing for an analysis of Angle on Field through Subjects. The framework is informed by understandings from studies on variation across disciplines and years of study. The adequacy of using Sentence Subjects for student writing is tested against descriptions of published research across disciplines. Finally a framework is proposed that maps clusters of Field across disciplines and progression across years. Designed to map Field across the 28 disciplines and four years of study of the BAWE corpus, the framework is applied to Assignment Initial Sentence Subjects only. The framework enables us to locate and compare field from specific disciplines and years on a large scale.

9.2 Subjects and Angle on Field

Systemic functional linguistics (SFL) has shed light on the importance of unmarked topical Theme in providing the Angle on the Field of a text (Martin 1993: 224). As our student assignments are almost entirely written in declarative mood, unmarked Theme generally conflates with Subject, as seen in these examples (Subjects in bold):

(1) **The Dutch Republic** was something of an anomaly in seventeenth century Europe.

(2) Until the last few decades, **the accepted view amongst historians of Mexico** was that the seventeenth century was indeed one of crisis ...

(3) **Memory** is a topic of study with which psychologists have grappled experimentally for over a century ...

(4) **The work of Jean Piaget (1896–1980)** has informed the developmental psychology paradigm for many years.

(5) **The pursuit of an acceptable definition of schizophrenia** has tested researchers and clinicians since the classifications proposed by K ...

(6) **Escherichia coli O157:H7** is a particularly high-profile bacterium in modern times, not least as a result of its ability to inflict ...

(7) **Examination of the subcellular distribution of molecules** is an important tool in cell biology.

Analyses of Sentence Subjects in academic writing have led to insights about the epistemological level at which meanings are explicitly construed (Macdonald 1994) and their Discourse Domain (Gosden 1993), both of which overlap significantly with Angle on Field for our data.

As suggested by the examples above, Subjects are congruently realised as nominal groups, and carry demarcated Ideational-Experiential meaning. In contrast with Textual and Interpersonal meaning, it 'is a general principle of linguistic structure that it is the experiential meaning that most clearly defines constituents' (Halliday and Matthiessen 2004: 328).

Moreover, while nouns congruently realize entities (or 'things') (Halliday 1998: 208), they can metaphorically represent qualities, processes or relators, as in (2), (5) and (7) above. In other words 'any semantic element can be construed as if it was an entity (i.e. grammaticised as a noun)' (Halliday 1998: 211) This means that writers have diverse resources for construing experiential meanings as Subjects. When processes such as 'pursue' are nominalised as 'pursuit', this not only allows them to occur as Subjects, but also ideationally 'creates a universe of things, bounded, stable and determinate' (Halliday 1998: 228).

With nominalisation, grammatical metaphor and technical language (such as *Escherichia coli O157: H7*) comes the representation of different orders of reality. For example, the Angle on Field is of a different order of reality (Halliday and Matthiessen 2004: 441) in 'schizophrenia' and metaphenomena such as *an acceptable definition of schizophrenia*. In this way 'ideational meaning is related to the construction of institutional activity ("naturalised reality"), or Field' (Martin 2002: 56). This involves not what real world entities are referred to, but rather how reality is construed across disciplines.

> It is characteristic of all Fields that they name the things concerning them ... and order them taxonomically ... Through technicality, a discipline establishes the inventory of what it can talk about and the terms in which it can talk about them. (Wignell *et al.* 1993: 159–162)

It is what concerns disciplines that we wish to capture with Angle on Field.

Before we test whether this construction of institutional activity is revealed through Sentence Subjects, we turn to research on variation across disciplines and years of study to inform our framework.

9.3 Disciplinary variation

Research on the construction of knowledge in sciences and humanities suggests that where sciences use technicality – they 'reconstrue its Domains of experience technically by establishing an array of technical terms which are arranged taxonomically' (Wignell 1998: 297) – the humanities use abstraction, shifting from context dependence (*The Cold War*) to context independence (*the accepted view amongst historians*). Wignell goes on to show how social science discourse uses

> much the same resources as scientific discourse in establishing a technical framework which is then used for interpretation. Social science differs from science ... in what it makes technical ... it is the abstract, hypothetical and generic which is being construed technically. (Wignell 1998: 324)

This is seen in Economics (*collusion*) and Business (*world mergers and acquisitions).*

Similarly, Parry (1998) in her analysis of disciplinary discourse in doctoral theses characterises the language of science as 'technical and concrete'; the language of social sciences and applied professions as 'metaphorical, technical and abstract'; and the language of the humanities as 'highly metaphorical and abstract' (1998: 297). In other words the social sciences have 'technical' language in common with the sciences, and 'metaphorical and abstract' language in common with the humanities.

In comparisons of scientific and technological discourse, White (1998) shows sciences' preference for classical terminology (which allows ready scientific classification; e.g. *angiosperm* and *gymnosperm* are two types of sperm), and technology's preference for lexical items derived from everyday words, e.g. *memory, local area network*, and acronyms (*CD ROM*). These studies all suggest that any framework for characterising Field across disciplines should attend to abstraction, metaphor and everyday vs. technical language.

While broad generalisations with typical examples are possible, the notion of 'discipline' is not unproblematic. Divergence is not uncommon across subdisciplines (e.g. physical vs. human geography), or within fields across genres. For instance, Lores (2004) analysed research articles within Applied Linguistics and showed two distinct patterns: those with IMRD (Introduction-Methods-Results-Discussion) structure selected more Real World Subjects, and those with CARS (Create A Research Space) structure used more Subjects from the Participant Domain. In the IMRD texts the writer 'tends to hide behind real world entities and processes, in the CARS structure, the writer chooses to present himself [*sic*] as a visible participant in the research community' (2004: 299). Sentence Subjects may also vary across instances of the same assignment written by students from different backgrounds: North (2005) shows clear differences in the use of Theme between Arts and Science students in a Philosophy of Science class. Similar findings emerge from a study of English, History and Science stream secondary students in Vietnam whose English compositions show clear disciplinary influences in Theme (Duong 2005). It will be important, therefore, not to generalise from limited data to disciplines or disciplinary groupings, but rather to develop a framework that allows such differences to be mapped for specific data sets. This will enable us to explore the extent to which student writing reflects the established differences in abstraction, technicality and visibility of participants across disciplines.

9.4 Disciplinary progression

There is evidence of a drift towards grammatical metaphor not only as children progress through secondary school English (Christie 2002), but also through 'the stages of a science apprenticeship, from junior secondary to post-graduate levels' (Rose 1998: 263). As Hartnett explains, 'because nominalization requires knowledge of the Field, it distinguishes the expert from the uninitiated' and greater use of grammatical metaphor positions the writer more as an insider, or member of the specialist group (2001: 106). Similarly, Samraj (2004), in her analysis of graduate research papers, finds that, while two science disciplines vary significantly in percentage of epistemic Sentence Subjects, the more successful papers have a greater frequency of sentence subjects concerning knowledge construction, researchers and previous studies. Hewings (2004) in her comparison of Year 1 and Year 3 geography essays suggests that first year undergraduate students frequently tend to use unmarked topical Themes identifying people, places, things or abstract qualities, and thus much of their writing is descriptive (2004: 140), whereas third year students adopt a more critical stance and make more references to the literature (2004: 142). It will be important, therefore, to develop a framework that can reveal across student writing any development in grammatical metaphor, or epistemic Subjects.

9.5 Studies of sentence subjects

Two earlier classifications of Sentence Subjects and descriptions of professional academic writing are fundamentally similar; Macdonald's distinction between Phenomenal and Epistemic classes is echoed in Gosden's Real-World vs. Hypothesised and Objectivised Domains. Each of these is subdivided. Thus 'Shakespeare' is Macdonald's example of a Particular of the phenomenal classes, and 'the evidence' exemplifies Reason in the epistemological classes. For Gosden, 'Shakespeare' might be a real world entity, and 'the evidence' a hypothesised-objectivised viewpoint.

The classifications differ in that Gosden has an additional two Domains which refer to Participants ('we', 'South 1987') and the Discourse ('this essay', 'previous studies'). So a Subject such as *our data* is classified as Participant Viewpoint for Gosden, and Reasons for Macdonald. This reflects Macdonald's aim of comparing how reality is represented across disciplines as opposed to Gosden's aim of showing variation in writer visibility within disciplines. Thus Macdonald compared across narrowly specialised English, History and Psychology articles, while Gosden compared across stages of IMRD Science articles. As a result, the classifications, and resulting descriptions, which reflect these differences in aim, discipline and scope, cannot simply be conflated. Nevertheless, the descriptions of published research across disciplines are useful for comparisons with student writing.

9.6 Sentence Subjects in BAWE student writing

Given the potential for Sentence Subject analysis, Macdonald's and Gosden's frameworks were tested on our student data, not only to decide whether they could be modified for our purposes, but also to explore how their descriptions of professional writing related to student writing.

9.6.1 Does student writing in English, History and Psychology exhibit features similar to those described by Macdonald for professional writers?

Fifty BAWE pilot corpus assignments from English, History and Psychology were selected: five similar (e.g., essays from a core module) assignments with the highest marks, for each of Years 1, 2 and 3. In addition to five from the Year 1 'Introduction to Psychology' module, five from the Year 1 'Psychology Practical' were chosen, on the (unwarranted) assumption that these might show different Subjects. Following Macdonald (1992: 564–566), initial quotes and 'it' in cleft and pseudo-cleft constructions are disregarded, and existential 'there' is replaced by the existent, as we are more interested in Field than given-new or thematic structure.

Macdonald found that 75–85 per cent of the Subjects in the English and History articles were from the Phenomenal Classes (Particulars, Groups and Attributes). These findings were echoed in the student essays where we find *Prince Arthur* and *Edmund Spenser* in English, or *The Cold War,* and *Mohandas Gandhi* in History. In Macdonald's analysis, English favoured Particulars and Attributes, whereas History favoured Groups. English essays favoured Particulars and Attributes over Groups, but the preference for Groups was not found in History essays. This difference is probably more attributable to subdivisions within History (Macdonald's articles were all on New England colonial migration and inheritance) than differences between professional and student writing.

In contrast, over 60 per cent of the Subjects in Macdonald's Psychology articles were from the Epistemic Classes. This was also the case in the student writing, as *The pursuit of an acceptable definition of schizophrenia,* or *Approaches to the study of eminence* suggest.

So there was support from student writing for Macdonald's two major categories and their ability to distinguish 'between the phenomena that the researcher writes about (does research on, investigates etc.) and the concepts, categories, abstractions, or methodological tools the researcher uses to reason about the Subject' (1994: 157). English and History students are also engaged in 'epistemic' work, but this is not explicit in their writing. They could begin with 'The theory I wish to propose is that Prince Arthur ...' or 'A clear case for the Cold War ...', but they do not. Thus Sentence Subjects reveal not only what entities are discussed (*war vs. schizophrenia*) but also an Angle on Field, or a view of the epistemological level at which meanings are explicitly construed.

It may not seem very surprising that student writers echo professional writers in their choices of Sentence Subjects, but when we look at the extent to which first year students are using epistemic subjects in some disciplines, this finding gains in significance. Macdonald interprets a study by Witte and Cherry (1986) of American writers in Grades 4, 8, 12 and 15 as suggesting that 'epistemic Subjects are not part of the ordinary repertoire of writers well into the undergraduate years' (1994: 151). Hewings' comments about the prevalence of persons, places, things and abstract qualities in first year geography essays might support similar conclusions for British students, but closer examination suggests that in disciplines such as Psychology and Philosophy epistemic subjects are the norm, even at first year undergraduate level. Supporting evidence also emerges from a Key Word analysis (WordSmith Tools) of the Year 1 psychology assignments where *theory, concept* and *findings* emerge as key words. Of course these disciplinary differences do not mean that the texts in one discipline are more 'advanced' than those in another; rather that some are conventionally more epistemologically explicit. The explicitness in some disciplines may reflect competing theories and lack of agreement on 'real-world' entities. In terms of Angle on Field, our small study of student writing suggests that in psychology Sentence Subjects refer to Psychology – its definitions, studies, major works and psychologists, whereas in English or History, more Sentence Subjects refer to Literary Characters, Literary works or Historical events and institutions.

9.6.2 Does student writing in the sciences exhibit features similar to those described by Gosden for professional writers?

Gosden's classification scheme differs from Macdonald's in that it groups 'audience' and 'research' in a Participant Domain, and adds a Discourse Domain. The separation of a Participant Domain relates to Gosden's objective of showing how writer visibility shifts throughout the stages of research articles. His continuum of Subject Role Domains ranges from more interactional to more topic-based; or from the Participant Domain (*we, Smith 1987*) through the Discourse Domain (*previous studies, Table 1*), and the Hypothesised and Objectivised Domain (*the probable cause*) to the Real-World Domain (*preparation, oxygen*).

> Towards one end, it is typified by the increasingly overt presence of the writer as a visible participant in the research/reporting process; towards the other, there is a greater focus on research-based, i.e. real-world physical and mental entities and activities. (Gosden 1993: 62)

The inclusion of a Discourse Domain is partly motivated by the number of grammatical subjects in science that refer to tables and figures, rising to 5 per cent in the Results section. The predominant Domain for Subjects in sciences is however the Real World, with 77 per cent of the total, 56 per cent of which are Real World Entities.

A similar finding emerged from the analysis of BAWE student assignments from Biology (the only Science available at the time). Real World Subjects were most frequent and, within this, real world entities such as *e-coli, viruses* and *bacteria*. Subjects from the Discourse Domain were also evident (*This analysis, This report, Figure 1*) and are important in characterising Angle on Field in the sciences as opposed to English, for example, where more typical Discourse Domain Subjects were *This essay, We* and *I*.

9.7 Issues in analysis

While the analysis[3] of student assignments broadly supports the findings for professional writing, attempts to apply the frameworks more widely proved problematic. For instance, when does a 'real world' author become an interactive participant? Gosden defines interactive participants as 'researchers referred to by name in citations' (1993: 65), which allows their views to be challenged. This works well in sciences, but for English it is not always clear whether critics and authors (*Anaïs Nin*) are represented as interactive participants or objects of study. Does it mean that *Plath's analysis of madness* in 'The Bell Jar' novel, being represented as her analysis, is an epistemic class or is Plath the 'researcher' whose views we are challenging? Here Lewin *et al.*'s distinction (2001: 112) between Writer, Researcher, Thinker and Practitioner might be useful, where writers and practitioners produce texts 'in the real world'. Similarly, if we are engaging with *Kant's Critique of Pure Reason,* does this make Kant an interactive participant? Here, Kant could be interpreted as a Thinker, in which case again we are seeing disciplinary differences in terms of how engagement with the research community is construed.

The decisions should ultimately reside in reactances in the grammar, although it is acknowledged that multiple readings may be possible. Research on business texts, for instance, has shown how certain linguistic choices can be construed and interpreted differently by members of the business discourse community and English language specialists (Forey 2004). Equally, more technical language was at times impenetrable, giving rise to questionable analysis. More confident analysis requires greater familiarity with the discipline as well as its means of expression.

9.8 Assignment Initial Sentence Subjects

In working through the analyses of all Sentence Subjects in the student assignments, it became clear that such analysis of the 3,000 texts in the corpus was beyond the scope of the project at present. It also became clear that the first sentence of each text often provided an excellent indicator of Angle on Field.

Theoretical justification for focusing on initial sentences comes from work on macro and hyperThemes (Martin and Rose 2003: 181–186). HyperThemes are similar to topic sentences that predict the development of the next phase of the discourse, which may be several paragraphs long. MacroThemes predict hyperThemes. Moreover,

> [in] many registers, hyperThemes tend to involve evaluation, so that the following text justifies the appraisal, at the same time as it gives us more detail about the Field of the hyperTheme (its 'topic'). (2003: 181)

This evaluation and detail is exactly the kind of Angle on the Field of the following text we want. A practical solution was therefore to plot Assignment Initial Sentence Subjects (AISS) only. This necessitates neither a prior analysis of hyperThemes and macroThemes, nor a full analysis of all Sentence Subjects, and yet should provide a characterisation of Angle on Field, or what students write about.

9.9 Angle on Field through AISS: a framework

Earlier studies of disciplinary variation, disciplinary progression and initial analyses of student writing following Macdonald and Gosden led to a framework for characterising Angle on Field across disciplines and years through the lense of AISS. In Table 9.1, the horizontal axis represents degrees of abstraction from 'Phenomena' through 'Perspectives on Phenomena' to 'Scholarly Phenomena', and 'Perspectives on Scholarly Phenomena'. Phenomena are construed as real world entities, whereas perspectives on phenomena state the Angle of consideration, usually through appraisal resources. Phenomena may 'be' concrete physical objects or abstractions or theoretical constructs. It is how they are construed in writing that characterises them as Phenomena. They are objects of study that do not belong primarily to the world of academia. Scholarly phenomena are essentially metaphenomena, one step removed from the real world phenomena into the world of scholarship – hence the labelling of this Domain as the 'academic' Domain.

The vertical axis captures the range from everyday to technical language. We have everyday language Subjects (*ordinary people*), technical terms derived from everyday language (*post traumatic stress disorder*), and less penetrable scientific technical language (*Escherichia coli O157:H7*).

The analysis in Table 9.2 is based on the AISS of the 65 student assignments[4] originally selected for this study. In order to focus on

Table 9.1: ANGLES on field: academic Domain (includes fabricated examples)

		<———*Abstraction in the academic Domain*———>			
		Phenomena	Perspectives on Phenomena	Scholarly Phenomena	Perspectives on Scholarly Phenomena
TECHNICALITY	Everyday language	The Great Wall of China Wall of China	The importance of the Great Wall of China	Research into the Great the GWC	The history of research into
		Post traumatic stress disorder			
		Schizophrenia	Possible schizophrenia	Grey's theory of schizophrenia	Approaches to the study of schizophrenia
	Technical language	Escherichia coli O157:H7	—	—	—

Table 9.2: Mapping AISS across Five Disciplines

	Phenomena	*Perspectives on Phenomena*	*Scholarly Phenomena*	*Perspectives on Scholarly Phenomena*
Groups of Conscious Individuals	Ordinary people EN1 The British H13		Psychologists PS1	
Political Entities	The Bolshevik Party HI1 The Dutch Republic HI2	—		—
Conscious Individuals	Prince Arthur EN1 Arthur EN1 Edmund Spenser EN1 Tennyson EN2 William Blake EN2 Edward Grey HI2 Mohandas Gandhi HI3	—	Barbara Lupini EN2 Anaïs Nin EN3 Max Weber HI3 John Robert Seeley HI3	—
Semiotic Entities	*The Canterbury Tales* EN1 Blake's *Songs* … EN2 *Maud* EN2 This papal bull HI2	The prevalence of eye-witness testimony PS1 A large part of the aim of Kant's … PH2 A central Fregan introduction into the philosophy of thought and language PH3 The epithet of 'Order and Progress' HI1	The Right Shift theory of Annett (e.g. 1999) PS2 The work of Jean Piaget (1896–1980) PS1 Russell's Theory of Descriptions. PH3 The liar paradox PH3	The history of psychological research PS1 Recent literature reviews and meta-analyses PS1

	Phenomena	*Perspectives on Phenomena*	*Scholarly Phenomena*	*Perspectives on Scholarly Phenomena*
Physical and Material Entities	? The development of the vertebrate limb BS3	—	? The Necker cube PS2 Numerous factors PS3	—
Cognitive Entities	Memory PS1 Plath's analysis of madness EN3 The author's chosen reading EN3	The priority HI1	Research into … PS1 The construction of an expectancy-based model of melodic complexity PS3 Examination of the subcellular distribution of molecules … BS2	The accepted view amongst historians … HI2 The pursuit of an acceptable definition of schizophrenia PS1 Approaches to the study of eminence PS3 Its status as a special case of logical consequence … PH3
Entities with duration	The Cold War HI1 The … Revolution HI1 The SA war HI3	The soit-disant 'Age of Absolutism' HI2	—	—
Abstract Entities	Time PH1 Qualia PH1 Music PS1 self-consciousness PS3	—	? Psychology PS1	—

	Phenomena	*Perspectives on Phenomena*	*Scholarly Phenomena*	*Perspectives on Scholarly Phenomena*
Psychological Qualities	Hand preference PS2 Stimulus-response compatibility PS2 ? Post Traumatic Stress Disorder PS3	—	—	—
Micro-Biological Entities	Escherichia coli O157:H7 BS2 The C … e … organism BS3 H. Adenovirus and Herpes. Virus. BS3	A requirement for packing of genomic DNA BS2	—	—
Groups of Micro-biological Entities	The o.m.s. group of cyanobacteria BS2 Viruses BS2	—	—	—

Key: HI = History; PS = Psychology; BS = Biological Science; PH = Philosophy; EN1 = 1st year English; EN2 = 2nd year English etc. ? = uncertain classification differences in Field across student writing, the analysis ignores initial quotes (3 cases); substitutes for 'it' (0 cases), and existential 'there' (2 cases); and replaces Subjects from the Discourse Domain such as *we, this essay* or *Figure 1* (4 cases). It further characterises the vertical dimension as types of entities, groups, and individuals which reflect this data.

As with other classifications, further delicacy is possible, and is desirable particularly in those classifications which currently run the risk of being circular (e.g. 'psychological qualities'). To explore what an AISS analysis might reveal about Angle on Field in other disciplines, we turn to research on the social sciences.

9.9.1 Does student writing in Social Sciences exhibit features similar to those described by Lewin *et al.* (2001)?

Lewin *et al.* (2001) outline a genre-based approach to the analysis of social science journal articles, which are reports of 'empirical, quantitative research ... [divided] into sections detailing the background of the study, the methods, the results, and the interpretation of the results' (2001: 24). Although not focusing on Sentence Subjects, in an examination of moves and lexical chains in the Introduction sections of these articles, there are useful distinctions among participants, which often, from our analysis of their examples, correspond to Sentence Subjects. Within an SFL analysis into participants and processes, a distinction is made among Producers of Research ('Darwin', 'investigators'), Products of Research (literature), and Phenomena under study ('cocaine abusers', 'higher mortality rate') (2001: 32). The Lewin *et al.* findings suggest that

> the participant common to all the texts (from the social sciences) is the group of humans being studied ... The subjects of a study are referred to variously (1) by their membership in the class 'human beings' ('individuals' ... 'persons' ... 'children' ...); (2) by their membership in the class 'subjects of inquiry' ('respondents', 'subjects' ...); or (3) by their membership in the class 'people who embody the variables of the study' ('smokers' ...). (2001: 134)

Similarly *People* and *the rail passenger* occur in Psychology, both from second year students. These are not the typical subjects, however, as Lewin *et al.* point out: 'Rather than an animate entity, the most frequently realized participant in the Introductions is "past research"' (2001: 135). 'Past research' features heavily in the psychology student texts too (see Table 9.2). To this extent, both professional social science writers, and student writers in Psychology approach their writing explicitly from the Angle of past research.

To test the AISS Angle map on further social sciences, we analysed assignments from Business (IB) and Economics (EC) (see Table 9.3).

Business and Economics do not follow Lewin *et al.*'s finding about prior research in that no previous studies occur as AISS. This may be explained in that all their texts were of the IMRD pattern, which was also common in psychology assignments.

Second Phenomena are largely either cases (*Sam, CRT technologies*) or economic abstractions (*the yield curve, mergers and acquisitions*) which are construed as real entities. This echoes Byrd's analysis of noun phrases in Accounting textbooks, which are 'characterised by the use of specialised terminology, constant reference to money and figures, and the use of case studies (with made up names and dates) and problem sets' (2005: 19). Again, this is in contrast to Lewin *et al.*

Third, Scholarship focuses on definitions of terms. In contrast with *TNC, yield curve* and *house prices* which are construed as 'real', as existing or happening in the real world, *collusion* is construed as something to be defined. This analysis is based on reactances in the grammar. We do not have 'Collusion happens when ...' but rather 'Collusion refers to where ...'

Thus our framework has allowed us to distinguish writing in Psychology, which resembles Lewin *et al.*'s Social Sciences, from Business and Economics, which resembles Byrd's Accountancy. This is exactly the type of mapping of Field across disciplines anticipated.

In conclusion, we present some tentative findings comparing the writing of university students across disciplinary groups and years of study.

9.10 Comparisons across disciplines

The mapping shows clearly the general, everyday wording of phenomena in those categories shared by English and History in contrast with the technical wording in Biology and other uncharted disciplines. It enables us to group Philosophy and Psychology in their shared use of abstractions and theories, and to group Economics and Business in their shared use of cases and economic entities. It thus affords a snapshot of what students write about across the disciplines.

Table 9.3: Mapping Business and Economics

ANGLE ON:	*Phenomena*	*Perspectives on Phenomena*	*Scholarship*	*Perspectives on Scholarship*
Conscious Individuals	Sam IB1			
Groups of Conscious Individuals		The traditional accountants IB2		
Semiotic Entities	An analysis table IB1	An important problem faced by financial economists IB4 the key issues involved with corporate governance in the UK EC2	The Law of One Price IB4 An event study IB4 Agency theory IB4	The main features of the second-generation currency attack model EC3 – The different methods of regulation available to the government EC1
Political/Economic/ Social Entities	A transnational company EC1 The yield curve EC2 CRT Technologies IB1 House prices EC2 South Korea's economy over the past half century EC3 World mergers and acquisitions IB 2 monthly returns for both an index of hedge funds and for the MSCI EC3		Economic growth EC1 Collusion EC2 laissez-faire EC1 Weak form efficiency IB4	

9.11 Progression across years

Similarly, the mapping suggests comparisons across years of study.

9.11.1 Abstraction in the Humanities

In English there is progression from Entities construed as Real World Phenomena (individuals and semiotic objects) in EN1 across to Scholars in EN3 (*Lupini, Nin*), and down to cognitive entities (*Plath's analysis ..., the author's chosen reading).* Supporting evidence of such a progression is found from looking beyond AISS where simple relational clauses feature in EN1; verbal clauses in EN2 and grammatical metaphor (*analysis, study*) in EN3. In History there is progression from Entities construed as Real World Phenomena (individuals, semiotic objects and groups in HI1) to Perspectives of Scholars in HI2 (the acceptable view amongst historians) and to Scholars in HI3 (Weber, Seeley). Although the data sets here are small, the progression echoes that described in the literature on progression in English and History. Interestingly, a similar progression is suggested in Philosophy, but from 'Material abstractions' (*time, qualia*) in PH1 to scholarly theories construed as entities (*Russell's Theory of Descriptions, the liar paradox*) in PH3.

9.11.2 Technology in the sciences

In Biology, Subjects are technical terms, often lexically dense, requiring expertise in the field to interpret. BS2 appears to be more factual and experimental, where BS3 appears to acknowledge research more, but this does not emerge from analysis of Sentence Subjects. Further examples are needed before claims can be made about progression in the physical and life sciences.

9.11.3 Abstraction and technology in the Social Sciences

While the scattering of Psychology shows that abstraction is not a feature of development in psychology, initial analysis suggests it is a feature in Business from specific cases (*Sam*) in first year to theories (*Agency theory*) in fourth year. Just as the Social Science Subjects are generally less technical than those of the sciences and yet used more technically than those in

Humanities, so too does progression in Social Sciences reflect a mixture of progression as identified through abstraction in Humanities and no clear progression as in the sciences so far.

9.12 Conclusion

This chapter demonstrates that by mapping assignment Initial Sentence Subjects on to a framework of abstraction and technicality, we can analyse and describe Angle on Field across disciplines and years of study. This reveals disciplinary differences and similarities of the type already documented. Its potential for undocumented and emerging disciplines is therefore promising. Moreover, it has the advantage of being manageable for large corpora, and as such is only one perspective on Field, and only one aspect of our characterisation of assessed writing. For instance we are currently working on describing generic stages across disciplines and years. As work on this project and others continues, it will be possible to provide a more comprehensive map of Angle on Field in British student writing, which can then be used for comparison with other academic writing.[5]

Notes

1. The project 'An investigation of genres of assessed writing in British Higher Education' (2004–2007, ESRC RES-000-23-0800) includes development of the British Academic Written English (BAWE) corpus at the Universities of Warwick, Reading and Oxford Brookes, with Hilary Nesi, Paul Thompson and Paul Wickens. The pilot project and corpus were funded by the University of Warwick Research and Teaching Development Fund.
2. Examples in italics are from the BAWE corpora.
3. I am indebted to Alois Heuboeck for collaborating on the analysis of Sentence Subjects, and for discussions of related issues.
4. The 65 Initial Sentences are listed in the conference presentation handouts on Angle on Field at www.warwick.ac.uk/go/BAWE
5. For example, the Michigan Corpus of Upper-Level Student Papers (MICUSP) project is developing a parallel American corpus.

References

Byrd, P. (2005). Nouns without articles: focusing instruction for ESL/EFL learners within the context of authentic discourse. In Frodesen, J. and Holten, C. (eds) *The Power of Context in Language Teaching and Learning.* Boston, MA: Thomson-Heinle, 13–26.

Christie, F. (2002). The development of abstraction in subject English. In Schleppegrell, M. and Colombi, C. (eds) *Developing Advanced Literacies in First and Second Languages.* London: Erlbaum, 45–66.

Duong, T. T. (2005). Thematic choice in Vietnamese school writing: thematic differences in argumentative writing of vietnamese students from different school disciplines. Unpublished MA dissertation. Warwick: University of Warwick.

Forey, G. (2004). Workplace texts: do they mean the same for teachers and business people? *English for Specific Purposes,* 23: 447–469.

Gosden, H. 919930. Discourse functions of subject in scientific research articles. *Applied Linguistics,* 14: 56-75.

Halliday, M. A. K and Matthiessen, C. M. I. M. (2004). *An Introduction to Functional Grammar* (3rd edition). London: Arnold.

Halliday, M. A. K. (1998). Things and relations: regrammaticising experience as technical knowledge. In Martin, J. R. and Veel, R. (eds) *Reading Science: Critical and Functional Perspectives on Discourses of Science.* London: Routledge, 185–235.

Halliday, M. A. K. and Martin, J. R. (eds) (1993). *Writing Science: Literacy and Discursive Power.* London: The Falmer Press.

Hartnett, C. (2001). When do sciences make nouns from verbs, and when don't they? *LACUS Forum XXVII.* Fullerton, CA: LACUS, 103–112.

Hewings, A. (2004). Developing discipline-specific writing: an analysis of undergraduate geography essays. In Ravelli, L. and Ellis, R. (eds) *Analysing Academic Writing: Contextualized Frameworks.* London: Continuum, 131–152.

Lewin, B., Fine, J. and Young, L. (2001). *Expository Discourse: A Genre-based Approach to Social Science Research Texts.* London: Continuum.

Lores, R. (2004). On RA abstracts: from rhetorical structure to thematic organization. *English for Specific Purposes,* 23: 280–302.

Macdonald, S. P. (1992). A method for analyzing sentence-level differences in disciplinary knowledge making. *Written Communication,* 9: 533–569.

Macdonald, S. P. (1994). *Professional Academic Writing in the Humanities and Social Sciences.* Carbondale, IL: Southern Illinois University Press.

Martin, J. R. (1993). Life as a noun: arresting the universe in science and humanities. In Halliday, M. A. K. and Martin, J. R. (eds) *Writing Science: Literacy and Discursive Power.* London: The Falmer Press, 221–267.

Martin, J. R. (2002). Meaning beyond the clause: SFL perspectives. *ARAL,* 22: 52–74.

Martin, J. R. and Rose, D. (2003). *Working with Discourse: Meaning Beyond the Clause.* London: Continuum.

Martin, J. R. and Veel, R. (eds) (1998). *Reading Science: Critical and Functional Perspectives on Discourses of Science.* London: Routledge.

North, S. (2005). Disciplinary variation in the use of theme in undergraduate essays. *Applied Linguistics*, 26: 431–452.

Parry, S. (1998). Disciplinary discourse in doctoral theses. *Higher Education*, 36: 273–299.

Rose, D. (1998). Science discourse and industrial hierarchy. In Martin, J. R. and Veel, R. (eds) *Reading Science: Critical and Functional Perspectives on Discourses of Science.* London: Routledge, 236–265.

Samraj, B. (2004). Discourse features of the student-produced academic research paper: variations across disciplinary courses. *Journal of English for Academic Purposes*, 3: 5–22.

White, P. R. R. (1998). Extended reality: protonouns and the vernacular. In Martin, J. R. and Veel, R. (eds) *Reading Science: Critical and Functional Perspectives on Discourses of Science.* London: Routledge, 266–296.

Witte, S. P. and Cherry, R. D. (1986). Writing processes and written products in composition research. In Cooper, C. R. and Greenbaum, S. (eds) *Studying Writing: Linguistic Approaches.* Beverly Hills, CA: Sage, 112–153.

Wignell, P. (1998). Technicality and abstraction in social science. In Martin, J. R. and Veel, R. (eds) *Reading Science: Critical and Functional Perspectives on Discourses of Science.* London: Routledge, 297–326.

Wignell, P., Martin, J. R. and Eggins, S. (1993). The discourse of geography: ordering and explaining the experiential world. In Halliday, M. A. K. and Martin, J. R. (eds) *Writing Science: Literacy and Discursive Power.* London: The Falmer Press, 136–165.

10 The role of the Nominal group in undergraduate academic writing

Anne McCabe and Christopher Gallagher

10.1 Introduction

The centrality of the Nominal group in the written language, especially in academic registers, has been stressed by researchers working within systemic functional linguistics (SFL) on the role of language in literacy development. In fact, Halliday suggests that:

> the written language is organised around the nominal group: and this – since the nominal group construes reality as entities (objects, including institutional and abstract objects, and their quantities, qualities and types) – creates a world of things and structures, discontinuous, rigid, and determinate (1996: 352).

This can be contrasted with the spoken language by considering the differing notions of complexity in each of these modes of language. In this regard Halliday (1987) further suggests that, in terms of complexity, the differences come about because of the use of different linguistic resources in each of the two modes: '[w]ritten language tends to be lexically dense but grammatically simple; spoken language tends to be grammatically intricate but lexically sparse' (1987: 66). For writing, this means dense, or 'packed' texts, which can convey a greater amount of information within a single clause (Bloor and Bloor 2004). Subsequently, written language allows for greater abstraction of ideas and concepts, the effect of which is to 'foreground nominal groups at the expense of clause complexes' (Martin 1993: 219). Also, the notion of complexity of the nominal group is clearly closely linked to greater sophistication in writing. Indeed, Halliday and Martin (1993: 211), using Theme to analyse the differences in writing between a sophisticated writer and a novice, show that the better writers use lengthier Themes. Fang *et al.* (2006: 253) contrast the simple nominal groups and pronominal referents typical of spoken language with the 'elaborated and abstract nominal participants with pre- and post-modifications, noun clauses, and nominalised forms' of written academic texts.

Leckie-Tarry (1995) further contrasts some key differences between spoken and written modes by demonstrating the role nominal constructions play in creating abstract texts with a low degree of iconicity, or congruence. In the congruent construal of the world through the clause, participants, or people, places and things are realised as nominal groups, processes as verbs or through the verbal group, qualities and attributes as adjectives, circumstances as adverbs and prepositional phrases, and logical connections as conjunctions. However, written academic texts utilise a high degree of symbolism or grammatical metaphor, where, for example, processes become participants. If we look at a clause such as *John helped Mary*, we can see that John is a congruent participant (Actor in Hallidayan terms) in a material process; John is actively doing something, to, or in this case perhaps more aptly *for*, another congruent participant, Mary (functioning as Goal). We can compare that clause with the nominal group (taken from the data analysed in our study): '*the reconstruction of theology and religion as a means of aiding the transformation process*'. Here we have two participants (in quotations marks), combined together to form a single nominal group, which are actually processes (*reconstruction* and *transformation process*) in a non-congruent relationship; the nominal group suggests that the first process is helping the second one. Here we are in the realm of abstract experience.

Of course, abstraction in writing emerges much earlier than the undergraduate level, as Francis Christie (2002) illustrates in her investigation of the use of abstraction in the writing of school children. In texts of writers aged 12, the structure of nominal groups is still relatively simple; young writers will tend to use subordinate clauses rather than prepositional phrases for specifying circumstances. Next, developing writers, usually around the age of 14 or 15, will begin using nominalisation of processes (especially through *–ing* forms, e.g. *the killing of animals*), but also begin using other forms (e.g. *the slaughter of animals*). They also start using more embedding within the nominal group, through the use of defining relative clauses, and they start using more prepositional phrases to give circumstantial information. Their writing begins to take on increasing levels of abstraction, and they gain in mastery of grammatical metaphor.

Thus it can be seen from the literature cited above that the nominal group contributes in a variety of ways to a mastery of abstraction in writing and particularly so in educational settings that require more sophisticated registers. In the case of native speakers it appears that this mastery develops over a period of time (Jones, 2005b). Just how the development occurs in the case of non-native speakers is not so clear, although some studies are being carried out in this area. Martín Úriz *et al.* (2005), for example, analyse the development of complexity in post-modification in nominal groups in Spanish high school students learning English, while Marshall (2006) includes an analysis of the development of nominalisation in the writing of a secondary school ESL student in Australia. Also in the Australian context, Jones (1991) looks at grammatical metaphor in native speaker and ESL writing. Murphy (2001) describes the role of the nominal demonstratives in the emergent texture of the written texts of Japanese university students. Colombi (2002) analyses the development of grammatical metaphor through the nominal group in bilingual Spanish university students, and Youping (2003) focuses on Chinese EFL learners and their mastery of grammatical metaphor.

While the different studies do not add up to a complete picture of how the development of complexity in student writing takes place, what they do show is that the nominal group is a crucial feature of written academic language development. It allows students to create abstract meaning; without its presence, student writing remains in the congruent, in the here and now. It gives student writing a level of sophistication that cannot be created by other linguistic elements. It helps create a distinct written register and allows novice writers to be more concise in their writing, an important feature of academic writing. It is our aim in this chapter to contribute to this body of work by analysing the similarities and the differences in the use of the nominal group between proficient and novice undergraduate writers, in two different institutional contexts (Japan and Spain), in order to determine ways in which we can help focus our novice student writers' attention to this resource in order for them to better understand and write academic texts. To this end, the following sections describe the data and how it was analysed, and also provide the results of the analyses, including implications in terms of the contribution of the nominal group to the creation of academic register, and in terms of focus in the writing classroom.

10.2 Data and initial analysis

The proficient-novice distinction of the two data sets is based on the socio-cultural background of the source of the data. The proficient student texts were collected from undergraduate courses, at an American university in Madrid, in which English L1 writers are enrolled along with L2 writers. Thus, while not all texts in this data set are from L1 writers, all were given high marks by the course instructors. The papers were collected from biology (2 papers), theology (3) and English literature (6), along with a research paper writing course from the freshman composition programme (4 papers), a requirement for all students, regardless of their first language background. The novice student essays (15) are from students enrolled in a writing course specifically geared for those whose first language is other than English, and in which they are working on developing their academic writing skills before they attempt to handle the above-mentioned courses. These texts are from writers in language programmes at English medium universities in Japan and Spain.

The texts in both data sets are argumentative essays; that is, they present a thesis, provide several supporting arguments, and include some consideration of opposing views. Four essays were chosen from each set: from the proficient writer data, a paper on feminist theology, one on Emerson's writings, one on routine neonatal circumcision, and one on chiropractic treatment; from the novice writer data, we included one paper on euthanasia, one on aphasia, one on eugenics, and one on informed consent for cancer treatment.

We divided the texts into clauses, and tagged all of the instances of nominal groups in each clause. We then analysed the nominal groups for their structure of Head noun and any pre- and post-modifiers, according to one of four categories (Table 10.1). For each set of texts, the total number of nominal groups was calculated, and then based on that total number, percentages for each of the categories were determined. The results showed differences between the two cohorts in their use of nominal groups (see Figure 10.1).

As Figure 10.1 shows, the novice student writers make similar use of Head and Head + 2 nominal groups to their more proficient counterparts. However, they use more Head + 1 nominal groups, while the proficient writers use more complex nominal groups.

On the use of pre- and post-modification, Biber *et al.* (1999: 579) suggest that across all registers, pre-modification of nouns is somewhat more prevalent than post-modification. We also analysed the nominal groups Head + 1, Head + 2, and Complex further to check the use of pre-

Table 10.1: Categories of nominal groups

Category	*Explanation*	*EXAMPLES*:*		
		Pre-modifier(s)	Head noun	Post-modifiers
Head	(head noun only)		stress	
Head + 1	(head noun plus one pre- or post-modifier)	these	rates	
			those	who suffer from headaches
Head + 2	(head noun plus two pre- or post-modifiers)	the incorrect grammatical	objective knowledge	of the study
Complex	(head noun plus more than two pre- or post-modifiers	their poor economic the socioeconomic, religious, and cultural	status factors	that must be taken into account ...

Note: *Examples are taken from the data analysed.

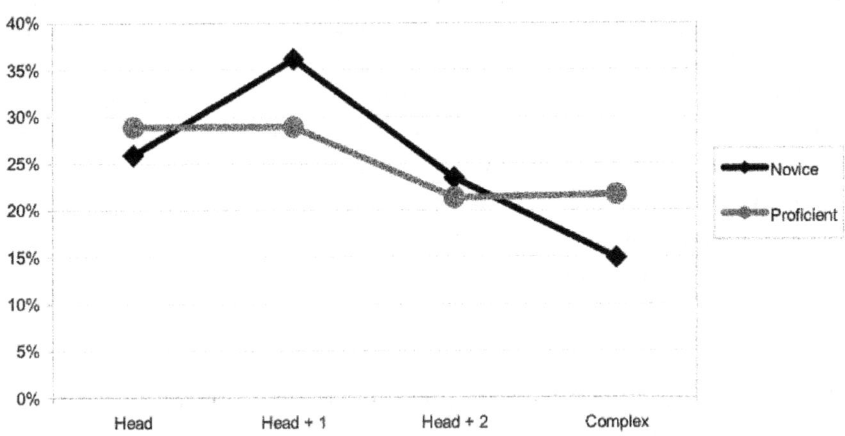

Figure 10.1: Nominal Group type results

modifiers vs. post-modifiers. The percentages in Table 10.2 demonstrate for each of the categories the portion of that category devoted to Head nouns modified through pre-modification, those modified through post-modification, and those combining pre- and post-modification:

There are some similarities across the two groups in terms of the favoured modification type, as both prefer pre-modification when there is only one

Table 10.2: Categories of nominal groups

	Novice			*Proficient*		
	Pre-mod (%)	*Post-mod (%)*	*Pre + Post (%)*	*Pre-mod (%)*	*Post-mod (%)*	*Pre + Post (%)*
Head + 1	83	17	–	86	14	–
Head + 2	39	7	54	45	1	54
Complex	22	13	66	13	5	82

modifier in the nominal group, and both prefer a combination of pre + post modifiers when there is more than one modifier, followed by pre-modification. It is clear, however, that novice writers use post-modifiers more frequently than do the proficient writers. One reason for this may be that these novice writers are not so comfortable with the kind of pre-nominal modification (using nouns as adjectives) that the English language allows for, but which Japanese and Spanish do not. We are unaware of any cross-linguistic studies that analyse greater frequency of one type of Head noun modification over another, which might help to shed light on these writers' interlanguage; however, we come back to this use of post-modification in our discussion of Qualifiers.

We then examined the types of modifiers the two cohorts used in their nominal groups, especially in terms of the Experiential function, as to how the nominal groups are used to help create the field in their written texts through two further analyses: one of the function of the nominal groups in the transitivity of the clause, and the second of the experiential structure of each individual nominal group.

10.3 Function of the nominal groups in the transitivity of the clause

The Experiential metafunction considers language as involved in expressing and constructing experience through the transitivity of the clause, which involves the encoding of circumstances, processes and participant types. We first analysed each clause to determine the process type, and then assigned a participant role to each nominal group based on its function within the process according to the framework in Table 10.3.

Table 10.3: Summary of process types and participants

Process type	*Meaning*	*Participants*
Material:		Actor, Goal
action	'doing'	Range, Beneficiary (Recipient and Client)
event	'happening'	
Behavioural	'behaving'	Behaver
Mental	'sensing'	Senser, Phenomenon
perception	'seeing'	
affection	'feeling'	
cognition	'thinking'	
Verbal	'saying'	Sayer, Target, Verbiage, Receiver, Reported
Relational		
attribution	'being' 'having'	Token, Value
identification	'attributing'	Carrier, Attribute
	'identifying'	Identified, Identifier
Existential	'existing'	Existent

Note: Based on Halliday and Matthiessen 2004: 260.

Figure 10.2 provides the results from the participant type analysis; frequency is shown per 100 nominal groups.

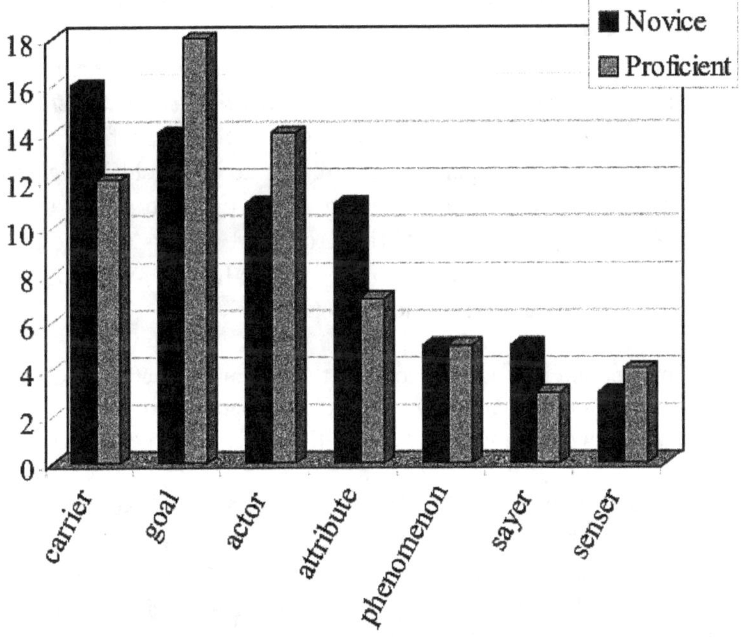

Figure 10.2: Nominal group participant roles.

For reasons of space, in Figure 10.2, we have not included the results for nominal groups which function within Circumstantial Adjuncts. Two examples of this use of the nominal group are underlined within the Circumstantial Adjunct, which is in italics, in Examples 1 and 2:

(1) ... other forms of oppression were found *in the home.* (PW1)
(2) Eugenics were applied in society often *in harmful ways.* (DW2)

In fact, this was the most frequent use of the nominal group in both of the data sets, with a similar frequency; in the proficient student data 24 per cent of the nominal groups were used as part of Circumstantial Adjunct phrases, and 22 per cent in the novice student data.

We have also left off minor participants, such as Recipient, Receiver, Target, Behaver, Identified, as their use was very infrequent across the two data sets. There are similarities in the use of the nominal groups to represent other participants, such as Phenomenon, Verbiage and Identifier, as can be seen in Figure 10.2. However, of greater interest here are the differences.

One difference is in the use of the nominal groups to represent Sayers. The difference is slight, the novice writers use 2 per cent more Sayers than the proficient writers, and can be explained through reference to the paper itself. Out of the 28 Sayers included in the novice writer data, nine refer to something that the paper itself has to say, what Hyland (2000) terms 'endophoric markers' and Dahl (2004: 1811) 'locational metatext'. In this sense, the Sayers are construed as metaphoric; that is, the process encoded in the verb is a verbal process, yet we do not normally think of 'papers' as 'talking' in the congruent sense. Examples from the novice writer data include e.g. ***this paper*** (six occurrences) *will explain/conclude,* ***this essay*** *will explain,* ***the following section*** *will describe.* In the proficient student data, all Sayers refer to a participant related to the field being written about, as in the case of an expert being called upon to support a point through the use of quote. None of the proficient writers use these meta-Sayers to describe the direction of the paper. Instead, they use direct statements of their overall argument such as:

> More information is needed to confirm the potential benefits of routine neonatal circumcision, and parents should be made aware of the issues before providing informed consent for this elective procedure. (PW4)

One reason for this may be that writing handbooks and websites used to teach undergraduates in composition courses admonish students learning to write for university not to 'make announcements', especially when laying out the scope and purpose of a paper through a thesis statement. For example, *The Brief Holt Handbook* suggests that an effective thesis statement is *not* of the type: 'The paragraphs that follow will show that intelligence tests may be inaccurate' (Kirszner and Mandell 2001: 14). Thus, the proficient writers, who have already been through college writing courses which give this type of instruction, may be avoiding this using locational metatext, which researchers of academic writing suggest is helpful for readers (Hyland 2000; Ventola and Mauranen 1996). At the same time, it has been suggested that attitudes towards this kind of textual metadiscourse are culturally bound (Dahl 2004) and Mauranen (1993: 8) reports that 'there is considerable variation in the attitudes of American writing pedagogues towards metatext use, and negative attitudes are not uncommon.' At any rate, the proficient student papers *were* considered successful, so perhaps this is a moot point for undergraduate writing, although it does suggest that composition programmes may not align with writing in other disciplinary areas.

What is even more striking is the difference in Carriers and Attributes – participants in relational processes, on the one hand, and Goals and Actors – from material processes, on the other. Martin (1993) suggests 'the effect of abstraction in the grammar of a text is to foreground relational clauses at the expense of material ones' (1993: 218–219). In a study of news reports, showing a greater number of material processes, vs. editorials, with more relational processes, Francis (1990: 53) further connects the greater use of relational clauses over material ones to nominalisation, which is

> a synoptic interpretation of reality: it freezes the processes and makes them static so that they can be talked about and evaluated. In other words they are no longer about *what is happening*, but what is being internalised and 'factualised' by society as to the status of *what has already happened*: the relationships *between events* rather than the events themselves. (original emphasis)

Thus, we had expected to find a greater use of relational clauses, along with its concordant relational participants, in the data analysed, given that the papers put forth arguments, and provide reasoning, rather than recounts of events that have taken place. As can be seen in Tables 10.4 and 10.5, there are marked differences in terms of use of relational and material processes.

The novice writers use their nominal groups more frequently to encode participants in relational processes; that is, the novice writers devote more of their text to describing – providing attributes of the entities they introduce – than showing what *happens*. Therefore, there is more description in their texts, making them more static in nature.

Table 10.4: Participants in relational processes (per 100 nominal groups)

	Novice	*Proficient*
Carrier	16	12
Attribute	11	7
Total	**28**	**19**

Table 10.5: Participants in material processes (per 100 nominal groups)

	Novice	*Proficient*
Actor	11	14
Goal	14	18
Total	25	32

The proficient writers, on the other hand, make greater recourse to participants of material processes. However, we do not perceive less abstraction in their papers. The proficient writers use non-congruent participants, such as abstract events and physical happenings, as Actors, which imbues their texts with a highly metaphorical nature. These non-congruent Actors abound in the texts, for example '*liberation and feminist theologies*' ... 'liberate people', '*increased patient satisfaction*' leads to 'more demand worldwide', '*education reform*' has 'brought about a shift towards Emerson's views on book learning', and '*United States Army hospital statistics*' ... 'skew ... socioeconomic, religious, custom and cultural factors'. While these more metaphorical Actors do appear in the novice writer data, the majority of the Actors in their texts refer to people, and thus are more congruent.

The greater number of material clauses in the proficient student data is perhaps due to a greater amount of explanation in their essays, explanation as to why things are as they are, along with explanations of why they should be different, summoning up more participants in material clauses. For example, there are more Goals in the proficient writer data – more things that are affected by, resulting from, etc. Examples 3–6 illustrate this use of Goals (Actors are in italics; Goals are underlined; processes are in bold):

(3) ... *the structural analysis of work conditions outside the home* **renders**
Actor

the economic basis of women's reproductive work unimportant. (PW1)
Goal resulting attribute

(4) the full humanity of women **has been concealed**. (PW1)
Goal

(5) and the idea that Scripture has justified the subordination and victimization of women
Goal
has been promoted. (PW1)

(6) *This method* **removes** less of the foreskin than the Gomco clamp: (PW4)
Actor Goal

Furthermore, the proficient writers use more dynamic material processes verbs, such as *promote, produce, conceal, preclude, eliminate, incorporate, analyse, obtain,* with organisations, people, abstract events, and physical happenings all acting as participants of these processes, e.g. *the full humanity of women (Goal), the American Academy of Pediatrics (Actor), the spinal manipulation that a skilled DC carries out (Actor)*. However, none of these verbs were used by the novice writers. The proficient writers use this kind of active encoding of events to strengthen arguments by making them more real, more visual. Thus, perhaps we could guide our novice writers in using these kinds of process verbs.

At the same time, we wonder if the proficient students may be overstating their cases in a way which is not done in other kinds of academic writing. Many students from American high schools have mentioned that their English teachers have told them to make their writing vivid, and to make their arguments strong. Indeed, college composition handbooks, such as *The Brief Penguin Handbook,* instruct students to '[t]hink about what the actions are and choose powerful verbs that express those actions' (Faigley 2003: 329) rather than use a form of the verb 'to be'. In addition, handbooks used for college writing instruction further instruct student writers to avoid the passive voice, in order to make agency clear and 'include people' (Faigley 2003: 330). However, the results from our study suggest that nominal groups in the proficient writer data act more as Goals than as Actors, demonstrating more of a focus on the receivers of action. Thus, we feel that these aspects of writing (more material processes, active/passive voice choices, and use of meta-discoursal announcements) warrant more research in undergraduate writing, along with comparison with other kinds of academic writing, as this type of research may help shed light on why some students may have difficulty in writing when they move into the graduate level. Also, if graduate and published academic writing uses greater amounts of metadiscoursal statements and more relational clauses at the expense of material ones, perhaps we need to rethink the ways in which students are being socialised into the writing process through the composition classroom and its accompanying handbooks.

In this section, we have analysed how undergraduate writers employ the nominal group to create different kinds of participants in their papers; thus the focus has been on the role of the nominal group in the experiential structure of the clause. We now move to the internal experiential structure of the nominal groups in the data.

10.4 The Experiential structure of the nominal groups

The internal experiential structure of the nominal group specifies the function of each of the modifiers to the Head, for example, as to whether the modifier in question further describes or provides an indication of the quantity, or qualifies it in some way. Table 10.6 (based on Halliday and Matthiessen, 2004: Chapter 6.2) indicates the types of modifiers we analysed in terms of their function within the nominal group, along with an explanation of the function.

We categorised the modifiers of all the nominal groups which consisted of more than just Head according to the functions in Table 10.4; Figure 10.3 displays the results. Here we see the novice writers constructing their nominal groups in similar ways to the proficient writers, with some slight differences in Epithets and Classifiers.

Table 10.6: The experiential structure of nominal groups

Function	*Explanation*
Thing	the main entity (usually, but not always, coincides with Head)
Deictic	indicates whether or not some specific subset of the Thing is intended
Post-deictic	identifies a subset of the class of 'thing' by referring to its fame (–)or familiarity, its status in the text, or its similarity/dissimilarity to some other designated subset.
Numerative	indicates some numerical feature of the Thing: either quantity or order, either exact or inexact.
Epithet	indicates some quality of the Thing, either an objective property, or some expression of the speaker's attitude towards it.
Classifier	indicates a particular subclass of the Thing in question.
Qualifier	further characterises the Thing; embedded constructions.

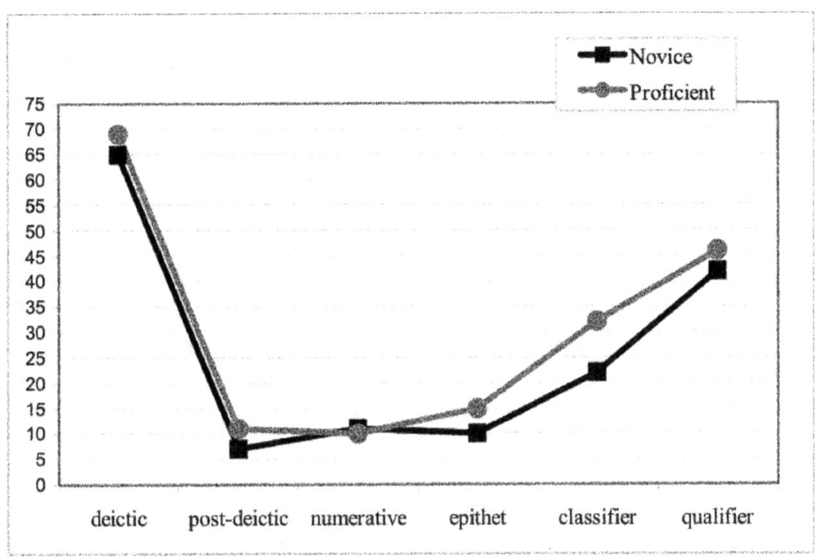

Figure 10.3: The experiential structure of all nominal groups (Head + X and Complex)

However, if we look at just the complex nominal groups, which the proficient writers use 7 per cent more frequently than the novice writers (see Figure 10.1), we see greater differences (Figure 10.4).

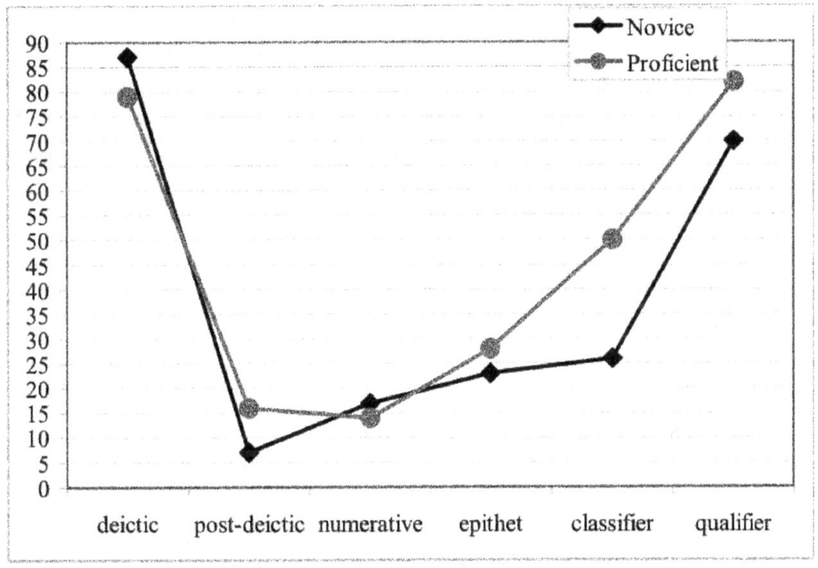

Figure 10.4: The experiential structure of only complex nominal groups

In the previous section, when we analysed the role of the nominal groups in the experiential structure of the clause, we needed to refer to metadiscourse to explain a difference between the novice and proficient writers. This is also the case for the internal structure of the nominal groups. The experiential structure takes in more than just experiential meanings, as through Post-deictics and Epithets, writers can encode their attitudes, and through Post-deictics and Numeratives, they can organise the text. While here we wish to focus more on experiential meanings, the differences in the experiential structure of the nominal groups across the two data sets warrants a brief mention of the textual and interpersonal functions.

The Novice students use far more overt techniques for inserting textual and interpersonal markings – textual adjuncts such as '*in addition*' and '*secondly*' and especially textual, through interpersonal adjuncts such as '*personally*'. However, the proficient writers are more likely to use the Post-deictic or Numerative position in the nominal group for organising their texts, and signalling that organisation, than they are to use textual adjuncts in Theme position, e.g. ***Three** different interpretations* have arisen. Also, the proficient writers use Post-deictics such as *further* or *additional*, to organise text; thus these writers are burying the logical structure of the text within the nominal group, rather than using more overt clause level positions.

There is also a wider range of Post-deictics in the proficient writer data, which serve a textual and an interpersonal function, and Epithets, which often serve an interpersonal function. Some Post-deictics, which the proficient writers repeat, but which are not used by the novice writers, and which give clues to the speaker's attitude, are *characteristic, general, main, mere, normal, original, possible, potential, purported* and *true*. Also, some Epithets, which are used by the proficient writers, especially for writing about research/arguments, are *absolute, appropriate, compelling, conclusive, considerable, contradictory, inconsistent, positive, problematical, significant* and *solid*. One of the novice writers, whose paper shows greater sophistication than the others in that data set, did use *crucial* and *inconsistent*; however, most of the Epithets in the novice writer data are more general ones, such as *best, appropriate, good, great, important, incorrect, notable*. Again, this allows the proficient writers to include their stance on an argument at the more subtle level of the nominal group, rather than in a modal adjunct at the clause level.

While we have needed to explain some of the differences in the experiential structure of the nominal groups by looking at how the textual and interpersonal functions are construed, we shall now focus on how the writers use the nominal groups to construct experience. As Figures 10.3 and 10.4 (especially 10.4) demonstrate, the proficient writers use a greater number of Classifiers, often nouns functioning as adjectives. These are problematic for the non-native speakers of English in this study as, in Japanese and Spanish, a noun cannot function in this way, and thus Classifiers need to be encoded as Qualifiers. For example, the Qualifiers (or part of the Qualifier) in the nominal groups in the left-hand column of Table 10.7 could be encoded as Classifiers (as in the right-hand column).

Given that the novice writers often resort to using Qualifiers, it might be assumed that their texts would show a greater frequency of Qualifiers than the proficient writers. However, it is still the case that the proficient writers use far more Qualifiers. One way of interpreting this phenomenon in the proficient student writing is by looking at instances where Head and Thing do not coincide (as in *a cup of* tea). Jones (2005a; 2005b) discusses the implications of abstract nouns, which appear as the Heads of nominal groups, where the Thing is represented separately, in a following prepositional phrase normally assigned to the Postmodifier. Jones (2005b: fn. 3) uses the term 'Pro-Head' to refer to these 'abstract grammatical Heads that compete for the reader's attention with what are usually more concrete "Things"'. Some examples in the proficient student data are:

(9) the possible considerations for misinterpretation of AIDS and circumcision related studies
(10) the issue of whether to routinely circumcise newborn males
(11) the effectiveness of this type of treatment and its relative benefits

According to Jones (2005a), we could say that, for Example 9, an abstract Head '*considerations*' foregrounds purely cognitive layers of experience, '*misinterpretations*', which, in turn, foregrounds a more concrete entity, 'studies'. These 'Pro-Heads', *consideration, misinterpretation, issue, effectiveness* 'focus the reader's attention on these abstract and analytic

Table 10.7: Novice writer: use of qualifier instead of classifier

Novice Writer: Original Wording		*Suggested Rewrite*
a patient's condition of cancer	→	a patient's cancer condition
an experience of learning	→	a learning experience
many serious problems in relation to racial issues	→	many serious race problems
the area of the brain that was injured	→	the injured area of the brain
inconsistent methods in reporting	→	inconsistent reporting methods

aspects of the Thing' (Jones 2005b); furthermore, the use of abstract Heads sets up a metaphorical universe made up entirely of analytic 'constructs' (Jones 2005a). We have seen that the proficient writers use significantly more Qualifiers, (especially in the Complex nominal groups), thus allowing them to set up these more complex metaphorical universes, while providing more analysis of abstract concepts in their essays.

The novice writers avoid these kinds of constructions, often by using a clausal encoding, therefore keeping the experiential meaning more congruent. Examples 12–14 show this kind of encoding:

(12) whether a patient should be informed of his/her cancer
(13) how a doctor informs a patient of his/her cancer
(14) how speakers put words and whether the sentences made by a speaker have meaning or not

These clausal encodings could be rewritten in ways that convey greater abstractedness, and thus they would be more appropriate for expressing meaning in an academic writing context as in Examples 15–17.

(15) the issue of informing a cancer patient
(16) the method/way of informing a cancer patient
(17) aspects of word order and sentence meaning

The more congruent clausal form of expression of the novice provides a clearer role for the participants involved in the event, while the more nominalised abstract way of academic writing obscures agents by embedding them within the nominal group, while giving a more prominent position to abstractions such as *issues, methods* and *aspects*. This is precisely the kind of writing which the college composition handbooks are so strongly opposed to, given that it can often seem bureaucratic and sometimes purposefully obscure. Indeed, we would want to avoid a pedagogic approach which would simply provide student writers practice in changing Qualifiers to Classifiers, perhaps leading them to feel that they have grasped appropriate register for academic writing. On the contrary, students need more than just to apply academic conventions and styles; they need to 'begin to understand how these styles and conventions can be used to represent and construct students' own meanings' (English 1999: 18). Through discussion with students of these different ways of constructing experience they can come to see how their language choices reflect their status as academic writers. Ivanič (1997: 267) suggests that through more nominalised forms of writing, 'writers identify themselves with those who engage in such knowledge compacting, objectifying and capturing practices' and thus put themselves forward as 'intellectual' and demonstrating 'reasoned thought'. Therefore, we argue that it is important to raise our novice writers' awareness of how these Pro-Heads function to put arguments on a more abstract plane.

10.5 Conclusion

The aim of this chapter has been to demystify a crucial area of academic register, the Nominal group, and show how an SFL approach reveals the linguistic resources of academic writing that are essential for novice writers to be able to use if they wish to achieve success in the academy. We have seen various ways the nominal group is exploited to create Experiential, as well as Textual and Interpersonal, meanings. Given its complexity, it deserves as much attention as the clause does in the writing classroom yet this is all too often not the case. In our experiences of teaching academic writing in two very different parts of the world, Europe and Asia, and working with materials produced for that end (within the American tradition of academic writing), there is a disproportionate focus on the clause. This predominantly involves text features such as getting the verb tenses right, sentence fragments, run-on sentences, to name some prime targets; yet all of these only highlight the verbal elements of a clause and can blind students to this other important linguistic resource in any academic text, the nominal group. Furthermore, we have seen instances where the nominal group sheds light on the differences between writing as it is taught formally to undergraduates, and other academic writing, i.e. in the use of metadiscourse and of material vs relational participant types, and focus on how this linguistic resource is exploited in different writing contexts can be of benefit not only to novice writers, but also to proficient undergraduate writers who wish to be successful in graduate level writing as well.

Martín Úriz *et al.* (2005) point out that the development of grammatical structures seems to emerge hand in hand with the need to express more complex ideas; thus, they suggest work on conceptual development prior to writing, in order to raise students' awareness of the syntactic and semantic relationships in the nominal group. Jones (2005b) also suggests a scaffolding approach in order to first familiarise students with increasingly complex concepts. In our work with novice writers in the undergraduate writing classroom, we take an approach following Martin and Rose in *Working with Discourse* (2003) – moving back and forth between an 'outside-in' perspective (working at more macro-levels, e.g. at the level of genre and overall text organization) and an 'inside-out' perspective, working, for example, at the level of the nominal group, helping students to be able to use it more effectively to create ideational, interpersonal and textual meanings. One way this can be achieved is by using sample student texts for analysis, and the students' own texts in revision exercises. Another approach, as Jones (1991) illustrates, involves rewriting more nominalised texts into more process-oriented texts, and vice versa, so that students are able to manipulate the linguistic resources of both spoken and written registers and identify in what kind of texts each should predominate. The Unilearning website, from the University of Wollongong, also provides activities along these lines. These kinds of activities can help call students' attention to the ways in which written expression mediates views of the world and interpersonal relationships, in a very different way to spoken language: an an awareness-raising exercise that can help them develop what Johns (1997) calls 'socio-literate awareness'.

Francis Christie writes:

> Whatever the particular text type sought in an EAP program, what is overwhelmingly valued in the texts of developing maturity – and hence of advanced literacy – is the capacity to deploy language in ways that abstract away from immediate, lived experience, to build instead truths, abstractions, generalizations, and arguments. (Christie 2002: 66)

Here we are in an ideational world. Martin (1993) also elaborates on the importance of abstraction: 'as far as education is concerned, students need to learn abstract discourse if they are to be functionally literate in our culture and write abstract discourse if they are to interpret their world in a critical way' (1993: 218). These statements resonate with Johns' view and our own beliefs as teachers of academic writing.

References

Biber, D., Johansson, S., Leech, G., Conrad, S. and Finegan, E. (1999). *Longman Grammar of Spoken and Written English.* Harlow: Pearson.

Bloor, T. and Bloor, M. (2004). *The Functional Analysis of English: A Hallidayan Approach.* London: Arnold.

Christie, F. (2002). The development of abstraction in adolescence in subject English. In Schleppegrell, M. and Colombi, C. (eds) *Developing Advanced Literacy in First and Second Languages.* Mahwah, NJ: Lawrence Erlbaum Associates, 45–66.

Colombi, C. (2002). Academic language development in Latino students' writing in Spanish. In Schleppegrell, M. and Colombi, C. (eds) *Developing Advanced*

Literacy in First and Second Languages. Mahwah, NJ: Lawrence Erlbaum Associates, 67–86.

Dahl, T. (2006). Textual metadiscourse in research articles: a marker of national culture or of academic discipline? *Journal of Pragmatics,* 36: 1807–1825.

English, F. (1999). What do students really say in their essays? Towards a descriptive framework for analysing student writing. In Jones, C., Turner, J. and Street, B. (eds) *Students Writing in the University: Cultural and Epistemological Issues.* Amsterdam: Benjamins, 17–36.

Faigley, L. (2003). *The Brief Penguin Handbook.* New York: Pearson Education, Inc.

Fang, Z., Schleppegrell, M. J. and Cox, B. E. (2006). Understanding the language demands of schooling: nouns in academic registers. *Journal of Literacy Research,* 38/3: 247–273.

Francis, G. (1990). Theme in the daily press. *Occasional Papers in Systemic Linguistics,* 4: 51–87.

Gallagher, C. and McCabe, A. (2001). Academic register and the nominal group. *Language Research Bulletin,* 16: 53–67.

Halliday, M. A. K. (1996). Literacy and linguistics: a functional perspective. In Hasan, R. and Williams, G. (eds) *Literacy in Society.* London: Longman, 339–371.

Halliday, M. A. K. (1987). Spoken and written modes of meaning. In Horowitz, R. and Samuels, S. (eds) *Comprehending Oral and Written Language.* London: Academic Press, 55–82.

Halliday, M. A. K. and Martin, J. R. (eds) (1993). *Writing Science: Literacy and Discursive Power.* London: The Falmer Press.

Halliday, M. A. K. and Matthiessen, C. M. I. M. (2004). *An Introduction to Functional Grammar* (3rd edition). London: Arnold.

Hyland, K. (2000). *Disciplinary Discourses: Social Interactions in Academic Writing.* Harlow: Pearson.

Ivanič, R. (1997). *Writing and Identity: The Discoursal Construction of Identity in Academic Writing.* Amsterdam: Benjamins.

Johns, A. (1997). *Text, Role, and Context.* Cambridge: Cambridge University Press.

Jones, A. (2005a). The head is the thing: metaphorical 'things' in a metaphorical universe, or discourse. Paper given at the *2005 International Systemic Functional Workshop,* Sydney, Australia.

Jones, A. (2005b). Conceptual development in technical and textbook writing: a challenge for L1 and L2 student readers. *Proceedings of the International Professional Communication Conference,* Limerick, Ireland, 12–15 July, 2005. Available at: http://www.ling.mq.edu.au/about/staff/jones_alan/Conceptual Development.pdf

Jones, J. (1991). Grammatical metaphor and technicality in academic writing: An exploration of ESL (English as a Second Language) and NS (native speaker) student texts. In Christie, F. (ed.) *Literacy in Social Processes.* Darwin: Centre for Studies in Language Education, Northern Territory University, 178–198.

Kirszner, L. G. and Mandell, S. R. (2001). *The Brief Holt Handbook* (3rd edition). Boston, MA: Heinle and Heinle.

Leckie-Tarry, H. (1995). *Language and Context: A Functional Linguistic Theory of Register*. London: Pinter.

Marhall, S. (2006). Guiding senior secondary students towards writing academically-valued responses to poetry. In Whittaker, R., O'Donnell, M. and McCabe, A. (eds) *Language and Literacy*. London: Continuum, 249–263.

Martin, J. R. (1993). Technicality and abstraction: language for the creation of specialized texts. In Halliday, M. A. K. and. Martin, J. R. (eds) *Writing Science: Literacy and Discursive Power*. London: The Falmer Press, 203–220.

Martin, J. R. (1991). Nominalization in science and humanities: distilling knowledge and scaffolding text. In Ventola, E. (ed.) *Functional and Systemic Linguistics*. Berlin: Mouton de Gruyter, 307–337.

Martin, J. R. and Rose, D. (2003). *Working with Discourse*. London: Continuum.

Martín Úriz, A., Blanco Paetsch, S., Hidalgo Downing, L. and Whittaker, R. (2005). Desarrollo y complejidad del sintagma nominal en composiciones en lengua inglesa de estudiantes de bachillerato. In Martín Úriz, A. and Whittaker, R. (eds) *La Composición Como Comunicación: Una Experiencia en las Aulas de Lengua Inglesa en Bachillerato*. Madrid: Ediciones de la Universidad Autónoma de Madrid, 99–114.

Mauranen, A. (1993). Contrastive ESP rhetoric: metatext in Finnish-English economics texts. *English for Specific Purposes*, 12/2: 3–22.

Murphy, T. (2001). The emergence of texture: an analysis of the functions of the nominal demonstratives in an English interlanguage corpus. *Language Learning and Technology*, 5/3: 152–173. Available at: http://llt.msu.edu/vol5num3/murphy/

Schleppegrell, M. and Colombi, C. (eds) (2002). *Developing Advanced Literacy in First and Second Languages*. Mahwah, NJ: Lawrence Erlbaum Associates.

Ventola, E. and Mauranen, A. (eds) (1996). *Academic Writing: Intercultural and Textual Issues*. Philadelphia, PA: Benjamins.

UniLearning: Academic Writing. University of Wollongong. Available at: http://unilearning.uow.edu.au/academic/

Youping, C. (2003). An analysis of the grammatical problems in Chinese EFL students' expository writing: a systemic functional perspective. *Singapore Tertiary English Teachers Society* (STETS). Available at: http://www.stets.org.sg/Vol2N1_2003ChenYouPing.pdf

11 The expression of Experiential meaning in EFL students' texts: an analysis of secondary school recounts

Ana Martín-Úriz, Rachel Whittaker, Susana Murcia, Karina Vidal

11.1 Introduction

> Language evolved, in the human species, in two complementary functions: construing experience, and enacting social processes (Halliday and Matthiessen 1999: xi).

In this chapter, we analyse evolving language systems in a corpus of recounts written by Spanish pre-university students of English. Learners' language, or interlanguage, has been defined by Selinker (1972, 1992) as the result of learners' attempts to reach the target system as they use the language, that is, while trying to fulfil the experiential and social functions of language. One important area in the study of interlanguage that has not been fully addressed is the question of how language learners acquire the different discourse types, or genres, of the target language.

Learning the formal, social and cultural features of written texts, that is, their generic features, is the result of a developmental process, as Halliday (1994) has suggested. This view has been supported by evidence from research on features of written text in productions by native speakers of English in the school context. Christie (1998, 2002; Christie *et al.* 2007) has found that school children and adolescents follow a developmental path in the acquisition of genres, their lexico-grammatical features and generic structure, and Rothery (1994, 1996), working on narrative, also describes development in junior secondary school writing. However, there are no studies conducted with foreign language learners that provide evidence of a developmental cline in the acquisition of generic competence during their period of schooling. Yet, in the European context, the Common

Curriculum Framework designed by the Council of Europe (2001) has been built on social and cultural bases, as well as on learners' competence in a variety of social contexts. Thus, studies that approach discourse competence from a genre and register perspective are vital if we are to evaluate students' linguistic abilities at all levels.

The recount, a subtype in the story genre, seems to be a popular genre in foreign language classes, especially at the pre-intermediate level with 17–18 year-old pupils. This is evident from the writing tasks that appear in standard textbooks and are given by teachers. Recounting personal experience through writing is thought to encourage immature foreign language writers to draw on their linguistic resources and make choices to represent their experiential world in a meaningful text, whereas more cognitively demanding genres and unfamiliar topics are prone to cause a mental block. Writing tasks in naturalistic language learning contexts are a social practice, but in foreign language learning classes they are a tool to express the students' inner world and to share feelings with their classmates. The study that we present here was designed to examine students' written texts about events deeply rooted in their experiences. This, we hoped, would encourage students with very low proficiency in the English language to write. Furthermore, the story genre has been recognised as an effective tool to help students develop their literacy as they learn to make the transition to academic genres (Barton 1994; Heath 1983).

Here, then, we examine the generic competence (Bhatia 1999) of Spanish learners of English as a foreign language (EFL) through their written recounts in English. After presenting the linguistic model used in the analysis, we give details of our study: the research questions, the participants who wrote the samples of texts, the task, and the tools and methods used for the analysis. We then examine the resources the students used to represent their experience. We also analyse a sample of texts addressing the same task written by native speakers of English: secondary school pupils of the same age as our Spanish EFL learners. Finally, the similarities and differences between the texts written by the EFL learners and those of their native-speaker counterparts are examined and discussed.

11.2 Genre theory: the recount genre as one of the story genres

We are working within the framework of the Sydney School model of educational genres, which has been implemented to develop literacy pedagogies in Australian primary and secondary schools (see Cope *et al.* 1993 and Veel 2006 for overviews of the projects on school genres led by J. R. Martin). The resulting pedagogical approach has also been applied to the adult immigrant population (Feez 2002). Research by the Sydney group has produced detailed analyses of the most common genres in the Australian education system. One of these is the story genre, highly valued in the school context.

It has been found that the story is not a homogeneous genre, but is composed of a variety of sub-genres, including observation, exemplum, recount and narrative (Rothery 1994). All story genres have the social function of entertainment, and they achieve their purpose by moving through identifiable stages, typically found in the structure of each genre (Martin and Rose 2003). The specific function of the recount is to review activities known to members of a culture: not surprising them, but rather reassuring them, so as to create 'a sense of solidarity among the members of a culture or subculture' (Rothery and Stenglin 1997: 239). Rothery (1994: 104) explains: "Recount deals with a sequence of events, how the characters get from point A to point B ... Unusual or problematic events may occur, but little is made of them.' To achieve its function, the recount is made up of three stages: Orientation, Event and Reorientation, with their typical register features. These are summarised in Table 11.1, based on the works of Christie (1986), Hammond *et al.* (1992) and Rothery (1994).

In the Orientation, the writer prepares the reader to understand the recount, giving the context for the rest of the text (Rothery and Stenglin 1997). After this, we find the Record of Events where the sequence of happenings is developed. Here we follow the participants moving from one point to another. The Reorientation 'brings the events full circle, with some reference to the starting point of the text' (Rothery and Stenglin

Table 11.1: The stages of the recount genre and their typical register features

Structure		*Register*	
		EXPERIENTIAL AND TEXTUAL	INTERPERSONAL
ORIENTATION		Material processes	Modality
RECORD OF	ACTIONS	Past tense	
EVENTS/	EVALUATION	Relational processes	Evaluation
EVENT STAGE		Specific participants	
REORIENTATION		(personal pronouns)	
		Circumstances (time, place)	Interaction
		Logical markers (temporal)	(writer/reader)

1997: 237). Interpersonal meanings can appear throughout the different stages, though they tend to cluster around key events and are frequently found in the Reorientation. Additional stages have been found in oral recounts, which may be prefaced by a Synopsis or an Abstract, and have a concluding Coda. Generic competence entails such knowledge of the structure and function of the recount, and this would be expected in texts written by mature native speakers of English. We set out to find whether our non-native writers would produce texts with a similar structure and function, and incorporate the features expected of native-speaker students of the same age.

11.2 The study

This chapter focuses on those features indicative of the stage of development of the EFL texts in the production of a written school genre and the construal of experiential meaning through addressing three questions:

1. Do the EFL learners in our study know how to construct the recount genre in a foreign language?
2. How do these students represent the events in their texts?
3. How do English native speakers of the same age complete the same task?

Question 1 focuses on generic structure, investigating the functional stages making up our EFL learners' recounts, which would reveal the degree to which they follow the expected stages. Question 2 asks about content: the kinds of activities our writers engage in: that is, how they represent their experiential world using English. Question 3 poses the same questions of the texts written by native speakers of English. Comparisons of the features found in the compositions written by the two groups of writers are expected to illustrate development along a continuum.

11.2.1 The sample

The sample of texts comes from two groups of pre-university students: 99 EFL Spanish learners and 25 English native-speaker students. The prompt given to both groups was designed to elicit written recounts of an important personal experience:

> 'The first time you went on a date' you went out with a boyfriend or a girlfriend. It is the first time you have gone out with him or her without other friends' company. Write a letter to your best friend, who now lives in a different city, telling him or her about that day.

The recounts produced by the EFL Spanish learners were collected in three schools in the Madrid area, from five different classes.[1] Of these, 11 were discarded, either because they did not respond to the task (topic or genre), or because the low level of the interlanguage made them un-analysable. This left 81 texts to be analysed. The total number of clauses written in these recounts was 2,183, the average length of the texts being just under 27 clauses. The corpus of native-speaker students' recounts[2] consisted of 25 compositions, of which two were rejected for being off topic, so that 23 texts were analysed, with 593 clauses in the recounts. The average length of the compositions written by the native speakers was 26 clauses. Table 11.2 summarises the corpus we analysed.

We are looking, then, at a fairly large sample of the writing of Spanish pre-university student writers and English native speaker students.

11.2.2 Instruments and procedure

For the analysis we used the Systemic Coder[3] (O'Donnell 2005), a semi-automatic coding tool based on system networks. We first carried out a pilot analysis on 27 texts taken at random from the five classes (Martín-Úriz and Whittaker 2003) in order to select the categories needed and adjust the instrument to the characteristics of the interlanguage texts. After this, we designed a number of system networks that would allow us to code for different features and their distribution through the generic stages of the recount. The systems in the networks included generic structure, process-type, writer-type, date-type, circumstance-type, writer-gender, syntactic complexity and frequent errors made by Spanish learners of English. The Coder allowed us to record the analyses, recover information, recover examples and perform different statistical operations on the results.

Table 11.2: The sample of texts

	Spanish EFL learners	*Native speakers of English*
Number of texts analysed	81	23
Number of clauses analysed	2,183	593
Mean number of clauses per text	26.95	25.78

Here, we report both on the analysis of generic structure, as evidence of our learners' control of the stages through which the recount unfolds, and on process types, which we felt were central to the representations of experience in the recounts in these stages.

11.2.3 Analysis: method, problems and solutions

We first identified the parts of the text belonging to the letter sections framing the recount in order to exclude them from the analysis.

Our unit of analysis was the clause. However, even the task of dividing the students' texts into clauses was not easy because of the pre-intermediate level of interlanguage, which sometimes required interpretation. For example, in the following instantiations we coded two clauses, interpreting that the second process – not realised in the student's text – had been elided: *They go out discotheque, cinema, etc. and Jose too; they miss you, but I very much.* In such cases, we also marked for ellipsis and error. Certain structures transferred from Spanish, e.g. *He wanted that I kiss him,* were coded as two finite clauses and marked as error.

Dividing the compositions into generic stages also offered problems. It was not always clear where the transition from one stage to the next was, again, mainly because of the interlanguage level, since the markers used by the EFL learners to signal stages often did not correspond with those described by Rothery (1994) for native texts. As we analysed the stages, we found that some recounts included some text before the Orientation, and, in some cases, more text following the Reorientation, which is typical of spoken recounts. Therefore, these segments also had to be excluded from the analysis of generic structure.

Finally, we coded the process-type in each clause, where there were also problems that had to be addressed. One difficulty was the analysis of verbs that had to do with saying and asking, which were prominent in the recounts. We decided to code clauses like *We were talking all the afternoon* as behavioural, and realisations such as *We were talking about the film; She always talked to me about him,* which included matter, as verbal. Some relational processes where the interlanguage gave evidence of transfer from Spanish, as in *we had very hot; The beach haven't end* were hard to classify. It was decided to code such clauses according to the correct English realisation; both these examples, then, were analysed as relational intensive attributive. Some clauses were difficult to interpret because they were simply "non-English" as in *It* [the hotel] *was inspirated in a s.XVIII house.* It was agreed that, for this item, the process should be classified as relational, interpreting the intended meaning as 'seem'. All problems were discussed by the coders and the same criteria applied in all cases.

11.3 Results

The results for the different features in the analysis are presented in four sections: clause type, generic structure of the recounts, process types in the recounts overall, and process types in the different stages. The results are described with examples of the realisations of these features in the texts of the two groups of writers, using tables to show how the texts of the two groups – the EFL learners and the native-speaker students – compare. The statistical analysis of the differences in the use of features by the two groups is given at the significance level of $p<0.01$, represented in the tables by +++, or $p<0.05$ represented by ++. Differences which were not statistically significant are indicated by NS in the tables.

11.3.1 Clause type

Table 11.3 gives the results of the analysis of clause type, i.e. the proportion of independent to dependent clauses, revealing one key characteristic of interlanguage data which should be compared with that of native speakers' texts. In the table, the first column identifies the features studied. Next comes the data for the Spanish EFL learners, and on the right the results for the native speaker students. For each, we give the total number of clauses in the recounts, and below this the average number of clauses per recount for each group.

Table 11.3: The proportion of independent to dependent clauses used by the two groups

	Spanish EFL learners			*Native speakers of English*		
	Number of clauses		*Sig.*	*Number of clauses*		*Sig.*
	2183 (Mean per recount 26.95)			593 (Mean per recount 25.78)		
Independent-clause	70.5%	1,539	+++	64.6%	383	+++
Dependent-clause	29.5%	644	+++	35.4%	210	+++

As Table 11.3 shows, there is a significant difference between the Spanish EFL learners' texts and those of the native-speaker students, the latter producing a higher proportion of dependent clauses.

11.3.2 Generic structure

Our first research question was about the structure of the genre. We found that all the EFL learners' texts included an Orientation and an Event stage. However, only 68 out of 81 included a Reorientation; this means that 16 per cent did not include a Reorientation. Of the 23 native-speaker students' texts, 3 (13 per cent) lacked a Reorientation.

We were also interested in the use the writers made of the stages. Table 11.4, then, shows how the clauses were distributed in the three stages of the recount. After identifying the stages in the left-hand column, we give the results for each group of writers: first the average number of clauses in each stage, with the percentage this represents of the total number of clauses for that group, then the total number of clauses in each stage and finally the statistical significance of the difference between the groups for each stage.

As can be seen in Table 11.4, a significant difference was found between the two groups in the number of clauses in the Orientation stage. The EFL learners wrote longer Orientations than did the native speakers. As regards the Event and Reorientation stages, no significant differences (NS) were found. The short mean length of the Reorientations in part reflects the fact that a number of writers did not include this stage. The EFL learners, then, differ from their native counterparts in writing significantly more clauses in the Orientation stage.

Table 11.4: Generic structure of the recounts: clause distribution

	Spanish EFL learners			*Native speakers of English*		
GENERIC STRUCTURE	*Mean Number of clauses*		*Sig.*	*Mean Number of clauses*		*Sig.*
	2,183			593		
Orientation	6.98			5.52		
	26.1%	570	++	21.4%	127	++
Record of Events	16.20			16.43		
	60.3%	1,316	NS	63.7%	378	NS
Reorientation	3.70			3.83		
	13.6%	297	NS	14.8%	88	NS

11.3.3 Processes

To answer Question 2, 'How do these students construct the events in their texts?' we examined the process types. Processes carry the core of the experiential meaning expressed in the clause, so that some process types will appear more than others in recounts, given the type of experience they construe. Since a sequence of actions is the most important part of recounts, material processes, which encode experiences in the world outside the self, are expected to be more frequent than the other process types. Verbal processes – saying – and mental processes – feeling, seeing and thinking – may also be a part of the story told in the recount. Description and evaluation also have a role, so relational processes are expected.

Use of processes in the recounts

Table 11.5 gives the result of the analysis of the processes used by the writers in their recounts. The different process types appear from left to right at the top of the table, with the data below – first for the Spanish EFL learners, and then for the native speakers. For each group, and each process type, we give the number of clauses (equivalent to the number of process types) and the percentage, which each process type represents in the sample.

No significant differences were found between the two groups for any of the process types. As expected, the most frequent type used by the EFL learners was material, found in 38.4 per cent of all the clauses they wrote, with examples like *Finally last Friday he telephoned me at midday.* Relational processes, in clauses like *in a couple of days my world just turn black to white,* made up 28.4 per cent, and mental processes, e.g. *I was only think about her, only her...,* made up 17.2 per cent. Verbal processes were less frequent, while behavioural and existential processes occurred very

Table 11.5: Distribution of process types in the recounts

		PROCESS-TYPE					
		Material	*Mental*	*Relational*	*Verbal*	*Behavioural*	*Existential*
Spanish EFL learners	No of Clauses	838	375	621	200	139	10
	%	38.4%	17.2%	28.4%	9.2%	6.4%	0.5%
Native speakers of English	No of Clauses	239	100	167	43	38	5
	%	40.4%	16.9%	28.2%	7.3%	6.4%	0.8%

infrequently. The native-speaker students distributed the main types in a very similar way. Material processes, in clauses like *We met when I went to Rachel's birthday party*, made up 40.4 per cent; relational processes, e.g. *All in all It was a great night*, made up 28.2 per cent; and mental processes, as in *because I've known him for ages*, made up 16.9 per cent.

We also studied the subtypes of mental processes – perception, affection and cognition (Halliday 1994: 118) – and of relational processes – intensive, possessive and circumstantial (Halliday 1994: 119). We found that our EFL learners used the same sub-types of mental processes as did the native speakers, mainly affection and cognition. However, among the sub-types of relation processes, the EFL learners used a significantly higher proportion of the circumstantial type, but tended towards a lower use of the possessive type. Regarding the types of circumstantial relational processes used, the EFL learners produced a higher proportion of circumstances of place than did the native-speaker students, though this difference was not significant. The native speaker students wrote a significantly higher proportion of circumstances of time than did the EFL learners, in examples like *after spending three hours with him.*

Distribution of processes in stages

Since the recount achieves its purpose by expressing different types of meaning in the different stages, we also studied the distribution of the process types by stage. Table 11.6 shows the types of processes used (calculated as percentages of the total number of clauses in each stage), excluding the very few existential processes. Again, the different process types appear from left to right at the top of the table, with the data for each generic stage below – first for the Spanish EFL learners, and then for the native speakers.

We found that here, too, our EFL learners and native-speaker students distributed the process types in the three stages of the recount similarly. In the Orientation, for both groups' texts, relational processes dominate, with examples like *she is very pretty, shy, gentle* (by a Spanish EFL learner) and *Seriously, she's more gorgeous than ever* (by a native speaker student). Both groups also used many material processes in the Orientation stage: clauses like *Two days ago I met a boy in the disco* (by a Spanish EFL learner) and *At the end of the night, we exchanged numbers* (by a native-speaker student). Mental processes, as in *And ... I love her!!* (by a Spanish EFL learner) and *I like him sooo much ...* (by a native-speaker student), were used less frequently by both groups. Verbal processes were infrequent in this stage, while behavioural processes were hardly ever found.

Table 11.6: Distribution of process types in the three stages

		PROCESS-TYPE					
GENERIC-STRUCTURE		*No. of clauses*	*Material*	*Mental*	*Relational*	*Verbal*	*Behavioural*
Orientation	Spanish. EFL learners	570	178 31.2%	104 18.2%	208 36.5%	58 10.2%	18 3.2%
	Native speakers of English	127	36 28.3%	25 19.7%	44 34.6%	16 12.6%	5 3.9%
Record of Events	Spanish. EFL learners	1,316	585 44.5%	184 14.0%	302 22.9%	127 9.7%	112 8.5%
	Native speakers of English	378	181 47.9%	55 14.6%	89 23.5%	21 5.6%	30 7.9%
Reorientation	Spanish. EFL learners	297	75 25.3%	87 29.3%	111 37.4%	15 5.1%	9 3%
	Native speakers of English	88	22 25.3%	20 23.0%	34 39.1%	6 6.9%	3 3.4%

In the Event Stage, the process type most frequently chosen by both groups was material. The EFL learners wrote examples like *to go out together saturday evening,* and the native-speaker students, *We went to the cinema for our first date.* The second most frequently used process type by both groups was relational processes, as in *He looked pretty handsome and very confident* from the EFL learner corpus, or *and she sounded fun, but not my type* from the native-speaker corpus. Mental processes, such as *because she would understand it* by an EFL learner and *I thoroughly enjoyed the evening* by a native speaker, were less frequent. Behavioural processes, while low in comparison to the main process types, were used more in this stage than in the others. Verbal processes were infrequent, especially in the native speaker students' texts.

For their Reorientation stage, both groups used relational processes to a greater extent than the other processes. Examples are *I is very happy because now he is my boyfriend,* and *She became my girlfriend* by EFL learners, and *It was sincerely the worst day in my life* or *I hope this lasts for a while* by native-speaker students. Mental processes were more frequent in the Spanish EFL learners' texts than in those of the native speaker students in this stage. The EFL learners wrote examples like *At present I love her with all my life* or *I feel that I know her better than another person thanks at tonight,* while native speakers produced clauses like *and I really enjoyed it, even the embarrassing parts.* Material processes appeared to the same extent in the texts of both groups, in a quarter of the clauses. An example from the EFL learner corpus is *The holidays finished and she must went to Belgium* and from the native-speaker student corpus *and I wouldn't trade that day – or Stuart – for the world.* Few verbal and behavioural processes were found in this stage.

Thus the analysis of the distribution of processes in all three stages across Spanish EFL learners' and native speakers' texts showed no statistically significant differences. There are some clear patterns of similarity between the two groups in the frequency of processes. In both the Orientation and Reorientation stages, relational processes were the most frequently found, whereas in the Events stage, material processes appeared twice as frequently as relational processes.

However, the fact that the three stages produced by the two groups of writers were different in length could mask possible differences in the use of processes in the EFL learners' and native-speaker students' texts. Because of this, we undertook another series of analyses, in which we studied the proportion of each process type in relation to the others in each of the stages. Here we summarise the most interesting results.

The analysis revealed statistically significant differences between the two groups of writers in the use of material, relational and verbal processes. Material processes were used significantly more by EFL learners than by the native-speaker students in the Orientation stage, with examples like *I have just came back of my first important date,* while in the Event stage it was the native speakers who used more material processes – a trend close to significance – with clauses such as *when I met this girl in a bar.* The higher percentage of relational processes in the EFL learners' Orientation stage, as in *I'm in the clouds,* also showed a trend towards significance. Verbal processes – *I finally asked her,* or *he asked me out* – were selected more by the native-speaker students than by the EFL learners in the Orientation, though the difference between the two groups of writers was not significant. However, the greater use of verbal processes by the EFL learners in the Record of Events, where they wrote clauses like *since he asked me shyly* or *and I said: 'OK; why not?' naturally,* did show a trend towards significance. There are, then, some important differences between our Spanish EFL learners' construction of the recount through the selection of process types in the different stages, and that of the native speaker students. We now discuss the results of our different analyses.

11.4 Discussion

Regarding the production of clauses in the recounts, it is interesting that the EFL learners succeeded in writing the same average number of clauses, 26, as the native-speaker pupils, as Table 11.3 shows. However, as can also be seen in this table, the native speakers' texts were constructed with a significantly higher proportion of dependent clauses. The ratio of independent to dependent clauses is considered to be a measure of syntactic complexity and one of the indexes that reflects development in interlanguages, as reported by Wolfe-Quintero *et al.* (1998). Chaudron *et al.* (2005) and Navés (2006) also came to similar conclusions in their research conducted in the Spanish school context. Thus, our learners have not reached the stage of development of the native speakers as regards the type of clauses that make up their texts. They are not yet able to manipulate the grammar of the clause in a way that native speakers can. Ability to use subordinate clauses allows the expression of a hierarchy among the meanings: a feature which we did not find exploited by our learners.

Turning to the distribution of the clauses in the stages, shown in Table 11.4, the fact that the majority of the EFL learners wrote the three stages indicates that these students do control the generic structure of the recount, at least to a certain extent. The lengthy Orientation stages written by the EFL learners included interpersonal features, which may be partly due to the task – a letter written to a close friend – as well as preparatory material: for example, a meeting before the date itself, or information about the circumstances of meeting. The EFL learners' written recounts seemed to use this stage to create the context for the date, involve the audience, and help readers understand the Event stage, as well as to evaluate the significance of the action for the writer, typically part of the Reorientation. Rothery and Stenglin (1997) have found that long Orientations tend to be found in spoken recounts, and that they have a strong interpersonal focus. These features in our sample of written texts, then, seem to be more appropriate for spoken than for written recounts. Features of orality have been found in other studies of Spanish EFL pupils' expository texts (e.g. Barrio 2004), and observed in young native speaker school children's writing (e.g. Christie and Humphrey 2007; Perera 1984). It seems that these EFL learners are still making the transition to the written mode.

The length of the Orientation may also reflect cultural narrative practices, as Melzi (2000) suggests. Berman and Slobin (1994) found that Spanish narratives devoted a good deal of attention to scene-setting, and studies of second language narrative writing have pointed out the influence of cultural patterns on text structure (Kaplan 1966; Sötter 1988). The fact that the native-speaker students produced shorter Orientations could be evidence of their generic competence in written recounts. The different lengths of the Orientation between the two groups' texts could, then, be due to different cultural norms. Orality, partly induced by the task and partly by immaturity, may also have contributed to the long Orientation in the EFL learners' texts.

We now move to the structure of the central stage, the Event stage. The main function of the recount is to share experience which unfolds as a sequence of actions. This is mainly achieved in the Record of Events, which would be by far the most extensive and elaborated part of the text. This was the case for both the EFL learners' and the native speakers' texts, indicating that both groups of writers have internalised the central function of this stage.

The main characteristic of the Reorientation is that the writer takes the reader back to the starting point of the recount. This seems to have been the most unsuccessful part of the recount for both groups; often it was very short and sometimes nonexistent. This may be due to the difficulty that immature writers have in moving from the local level of text to the global meaning, to the conceptual macro-structure (Bereiter and Scardamalia 1987). It could also indicate a lack of reader awareness (Blanco 2003). We have already found this inability to round off the text in this type of writer (Martín-Úriz *et al.* 2005). The EFL writers included a considerable number of interpersonal features in this stage, which also typifies spoken recounts.

Next, we consider the processes involved in the creation of the writers' representation of their experience, shown in Table 11.5. The high proportion of material processes represents the actions that the participants carry out, since 'The social purpose of Recount is to document the progression of events in sequence' (Rothery 1994: 105). In such a task as the one examined in this chapter, description, identification, evaluation of participants and events are included, which explains the large percentage of relational processes used. Both groups of writers also used mental processes, which are important in a recount for reporting expectations and reactions to events. The function of those clauses was mainly interpersonal, responding to the communicative situation specified in the prompt.

Table 11.6 shows the distribution of process-types in the texts of the two groups. The high proportion of material processes used by the EFL learners in the Orientation stage suggests a strong concern with preparing the reader for the Event, by giving a preview of what is to come and creating the context for the actions. Thus, in their texts, this stage seems to take on a function similar to that of the Abstract in spoken recounts (Rothery and Stenglin 1997: 237), thereby setting the scene for the hearer.

In the Event stage, the difference in the distribution of processes in the EFL learners' and native-speaker students' texts seems to reflect two different conceptions of what this stage is for. The native speakers focused more on the actual sequence of activities, but the EFL learners' recounts, which also used a considerable number of material processes, often allowed other voices to participate, as shown in the higher number of verbal processes found in them. While reported speech is also expected in this genre, these writers overused reported dialogue, which, in their texts, sometimes took the place of the narration of a series of events and the expected evaluation of the actions.

In the Reorientation stage, both groups used similar proportions of relational processes: the EFL learners mainly to evaluate their new relationship, which seemed to be the main focus of their Reorientation stage. The native-speaker students tended to make an overall evaluation of their experiences. The EFL learners also had a higher proportion of mental processes in this stage, completing their reflection on the date.

Hence, in a number of features, the native-speaker students showed more knowledge of the stages of the recount genre than did the EFL learners. The analyses suggest that the young native writers knew better which language choices would achieve the function, the social purpose, of the genre.

11.5 Conclusion

The study presented in this chapter has shown how native and non-native pre-university writers construe experiential meaning in their recounts. Our comparative analyses have revealed similarities between both groups' texts as well as points of divergence. The analysis of the construction of the three stages in the Spanish EFL learner corpus shows that for these students some of the expected features of the written recount genre are not fully developed. In comparison, the native-speaker writers' recounts reflect the genre conventions more closely. The differences between non-native and native recounts may be explained as stemming from the stage of their interlanguage and from cultural variations in narrative structures – lack of precise knowledge of the genre. Both problems hinder the full representation of patterns of experience and the subsequent reflection on them. In general terms, both groups' recounts reveal weaknesses at construing processes of inner consciousness.

From our analyses, then, we can conclude that these non-native secondary school students need to be made aware of the generic features of the target language texts, of the social purpose each genre serves in the culture in which it is used, and of the different sets of lexico-grammatical features for realising these generic values. At school level, work with EFL students on a basic genre such as the recount, focusing on the functions of the stages in the different culture, and on ways to achieve them in the foreign language, could be a way into the academic genres, and play an important role in the transition into literacy in English, before moving on to the language of the disciplines. The EFL classroom can provide a meaningful context where pupils can learn to construct their own personal representations and their interpretations of the world, and to share them with their peers and teachers, who serve as their audience. This can provide a base from which to move into the English language genres of higher education and the workplace.

Acknowledgements

This chapter presents part of a research project funded by the Spanish Ministry of Education: *Escribir en inglés en bachillerato: géneros y registros como base cognitiva del desarrollo del texto, y su relación con la calidad de la redacción* (Writing in English in secondary school: genres and registers as the cognitive basis of the development of the text, and relationship with composition quality.) HUM2004-06228; an earlier stage of which has recently been published (Martín-Úriz and Whittaker 2005).

Notes

1. We thank Concha Arribas, Ana Concostrina and Luis Ordóñez, who collected the data.
2. We are grateful to Angela Bradley for collecting these compositions.
3. The Systemic Coder is available free of charge from the website http://www.wagsoft.com/Coder/. We thank Mick O'Donnell for all his help with the Systemic Coder.

References

Barrio, M. (2004). Experimental study of textual development in Spanish students of English as a foreign language in 'Segundo de Bachillerato: Features of Written Register in Compositions of Argumentative Genre'. Unpublished PhD thesis. Madrid: Universidad Autónoma de Madrid.

Barton, D. (1994). *Literacy: An Introduction to the Ecology of Written Language.* London: Blackwell.

Bhatia, V. (1999). Analysing genre: an applied linguistic perspective. Keynote presentation. *12th World Congress of Applied Linguistics,* Tokyo.

Bereiter, C. and Scardamalia, M. (1987). *The Psychology of Written Composition.* Hillsdale, NJ: Erlbaum.

Berman, R. and Slobin, D. (1994). *Relating Events in Narrative. A Crosslinguistic Developmental Study.* Hillsdale, NJ: Erlbaum.

Blanco, S. (2003). *La calidad de la composición escrita en lengua extranjera: un modelo de composición centrado en la sensibilización del escritor ante la presencia del lector en el texto.* Unpublished PhD thesis. Madrid: Universidad Autónoma de Madrid.

Chaudron, C., Martín-Úriz, A. and Whittaker, R. (2005). Caracterización lingüística de las composiciones de los estudiantes de secundaria. In Martín-Úriz, A. and Whittaker, R (eds) *La Composición como Comunicación: Una Experiencia en las Aulas de Lengua Inglesa en Bachillerato.* Madrid: Ediciones UAM., 79–98.

Christie, F. (1986). Writing in schools: generic structures as ways of meaning. In Couture, B. (ed.) *Functional Approaches to Writing: Research Perspectives.* Norwood, NJ: Ablex, 221–240.

Christie, F. (1998). Learning the literacies of primary and secondary schooling. In Christie, F. and Misson, R. (eds). *Literacy and Schooling*. London: Routledge, 47–73.

Christie, F. (2002). The development of abstraction in adolescence in subject English. In Scheleppegrell, M. and Colombi, C. (eds) *Developing Advanced Literacy in First and Second Languages.* Mahaw, NJ: Erlbaum, 45–66.

Christie, F., Derewianka, B., Dreyfus, S., Humphrey, S. and Lewis, H. (2007). Developmental growth in control of literacy from the primary to secondary years. Paper presented at the 34th International Systemic Functional Linguistics Conference, Odense.

Cope, B., Kalantzis, M., Kress, G. and Martin, J. R. (1993). Bibliographical essay: developing the theory and practice of genre-based literacy. In Cope, B. and Kalantzis, M. (eds) *The Powers of Literacy: A Genre Approach to Teaching Writing.* London: Falmer Press, 231–247.

Council of Europe. (2001). *Common European Framework of Reference for Languages: Learning, Teaching, Assessment.* Cambridge: Cambridge University Press.

Feez, S. (2002). Heritage and innovation in second language education. In Johns, A. M. (ed.). *Genre in the Classroom.* Mahwah, NJ: Erlbaum, 43–69.

Halliday, M. A. K. (1994). *An Introduction to Functional Grammar.* London: Arnold.

Halliday, M. A. K. and Matthiessen, C. M. I. M. (1999). *Construing Experience through Meaning. A Language-based Approach to Cognition.* London: Continuum.

Hammond, J., Burns, A., Joyce, H., Brosman, D. and Gerot, L. (1992). *English for Social Purposes: A Handbook for Teachers of Adult Literacy.* Sydney: NCELTR.

Heath, S. B. (1983). *Ways with Words.* Cambridge: Cambridge University Press.

Kaplan, R. (1966). Cultural thought patterns in intercultural education. *Language Learning,* 16/1-2: 1–20.

Martin, J. R. and Rose, D. (2003). *Working with Discourse: Meaning beyond the Clause.* London: Continuum.

Martín-Úriz, A., Hidalgo, L. and Whittaker, R. (2005). El desarrollo del tema en la composición de estudiantes de secundaria: medición y evaluación de la coherencia. In Martín-Úriz, and Whittaker, R. (eds) *La Composición como Comunicación: Una Experiencia en las Aulas de Lengua Inglesa en Bachillerato.* Madrid: Ediciones UAM., 115–130.

Martín-Úriz, A and Whittaker, R. (2003). Composition in EFL in Spanish schools: linguistic features of different genres in writing. Presentation. *XV EISFL Workshop,* Leeds.

Martín-Úriz, A. and Whittaker, R. (eds) (2005). *La Composición como Comunicación: Una Experiencia en las Aulas de Lengua Inglesa en Bachillerato.* Madrid: Ediciones UAM.

Melzi, G. (2000). Cultural variations in the construction of personal narratives: Central American and European American mothers' elicitation styles. Discourse Processes, 30/2: 153–177.

Navés, T. (2006). The long-term effects of an early start on writing on foreign language learning. Unpublished PhD thesis. Barcelona: Department of Philology, Barcelona University.

O'Donnell, M. (2005). *The Systemic Coder Version 4.68*, July. Available at http://www.wagsoft.com.

Perera, K. (1984). *Children's Writing and Reading.* Oxford: Blackwell.

Rothery, J. (1994). *Exploring Literacy in School English. Write it Right Project.* Erskineville Disadvantaged Schools Program. Metropolitan East Region, NSW Department of School Education.

Rothery, J. (1996). Making changes: developing an educational linguistics. In Hasan, R. and Williams, J. (eds) *Literacy in Society.* London: Longman, 86–123.

Rothery, J. and Stenglin, M. (1997). Entertaining and instructing: exploring experience through story. In Christie, F. and Martin, J. R. (eds) *Genre and Institutions: Social Processes in the Workplace and School.* London: Cassell, 231–263.

Selinker, L. (1972). Interlanguage. *IRAL* 10, 209–31.

Selinker, L. (1992). *Rediscovering Interlanguage.* London: Longman.

Sötter, A. (1988). The second language learner and cultural transfer in narration. In Purves, A. (ed.) *Writing Across Languages and Cultures. Issues in Contrastive Rhetoric.* Beverly Hills, CA: Sage, 177–205.

Veel, R. (2006). The Write it Right Project – linguistic modelling of secondary school and the workplace. In Whittaker, R., O'Donnell, M. and McCabe, A. (eds) *Language and Literacy: Functional Approaches.* London: Continuum, 66–92.

Wolfe-Quintero, K., Inagaki, S. and Kim, H. Y. (1998). *Second Language Development in Writing: Measures of Fluency, Accuracy and Complexity.* Honolulu, HI: SLTCC, University of Hawaii.

PART IV

Exploring the Ideational function in multi-semiotic representation

12 Inter-semiotic expansion of Experiential meaning: hierarchical scales and metaphor in mathematics discourse

Kay L. O'Halloran

12.1 Introduction

Multimodality is concerned with the theory and analysis of language, visual images and other semiotic resources which integrate to construct texts, objects and events in print and digital media and everyday life (e.g. Baldry and Thibault 2006; Kress and van Leeuwen 2006; van Leeuwen 2005). In this chapter, the systemic functional (SF) social semiotic perspective (Halliday 1978, 2004; Martin 1992) is adopted in this chapter to examine the multimodal construction of experience in mathematics discourse. The semiotic resources under consideration are language, visual images (i.e. geometrical diagram and graph) and mathematical symbolism which together construct Example 14 (Teh and Looi 2001: 165–166), the mathematics problem reproduced in Figures 12.1(a) and 12.1(b).

O'Halloran (2007c) discusses the general functionality of language, visual images and the symbolism in Example 14 in relation to Halliday's (2004) metafunctions which are concerned with experiential, logical, interpersonal and textual dimensions of meaning. This chapter focuses specifically on Experiential meaning, and on the semantic expansions arising from choices from the three semiotic resources which enable Example 14 to be solved. In particular, metaphorical transformations of processes and participants which take place across the linguistic text, the visual images and the symbolic equations are investigated. The systemic functional multimodal discourse analysis (SF-MDA) framework for mathematics (O'Halloran 2005, 2007b) presented in Section 2 provides the theoretical basis for this investigation. First, the SF-MDA approach to mathematics discourse and

Example 14

A metal cube of side x cm has a hole of cross-sectional area 4 cm² drilled right through it in the direction perpendicular to one of the faces. The volume of the resulting block is V cm³.

Show that $V = x(x - 2)(x + 2)$.

Copy and complete the following table of values. Hence plot the graph of V against x.

x	3	4	4.5	5	6
V			73		

The block is now melted and made into a solid rectangular block whose sides are 3 cm, 3 cm and (15 – x) cm. Estimate the value of x by drawing a suitable straight line on the same axes.

Solution

Total volume of cube = x^3 cm³

Volume of the cylindrical hole = $4x$ cm³

∴ the volume of the resulting block is $V = (x^3 - 4x)$,
i.e. $V = x(x - 2)(x + 2)$

The table of values is as shown below:

x	3	4	4.5	5	6
V	15	48	73	105	192

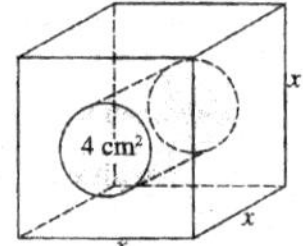

The graph is then plotted as in Fig. 8.14.

The volume of the solid rectangular block is

$$V_1 = 3 \times 3 \times (15 - x)$$
$$= (135 - 9x) \text{ cm}^3$$

Figure 12.1(a): Example 14 (Teh and Looi 2001: 165)

To find the value of x, the straight line function $V_1 = 135 - 9x$ is plotted on the same axes. The table of values is:

x	3	4	5
$V_1 = 135 - 9x$	108	99	90

From the graph, the curve and the line intersect at point A where x is approximately 4.8.

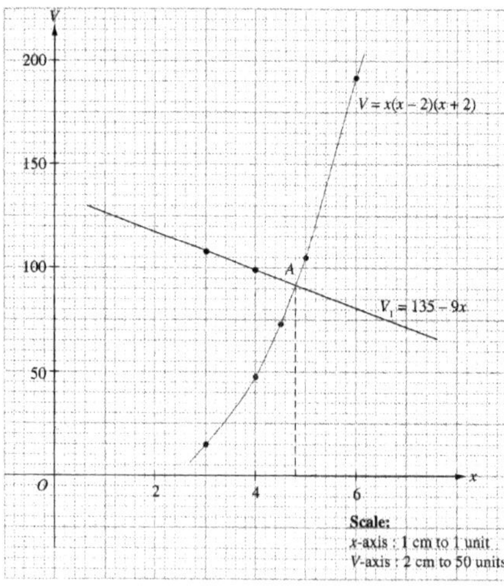

Figure 12.1(b): Example 14 (Teh and Looi 2001: 166)

the research leading to the present investigation are reviewed before the multimodal construction of experience in Example 14 is investigated.

12.2 SF-MDA approach to mathematics discourse

The SF-MDA approach to mathematics is based on Halliday's (2004) systemic functional (SF) model for language and O'Toole's (1994, 2005) extension of the SF model to the visual arts. Culture, social context and text are related in SF theory through the concept of realisation; i.e. culture and social context are realised as texts, which in turn are realised through grammatical and discourse choices. Table 12.1 displays the framework.

As Table 12.1 shows, the levels of abstraction in the SF-MDA model are the context plane (culture, social context); content plane (discourse and grammar); and display plane (graphology, typography and graphics). The context plane is concerned with the genre and register of the text, realised through choices from the grammatical and discourse systems, instantiated by system choices on the display plane which account for meaning arising in the materiality of the text.

Semiotic resources are viewed as interlocking semantic phenomena in the SF-MDA approach, giving rise to the concept of *multimodal grammaticality* (O'Halloran 2007a, 2007b) where linguistic, visual and symbolic choices function together to construct meaning in mathematics discourse. The semiotic collaboration extends to the structural organisation of the mathematics text where choices from the three semiotic resources appear together. For example, x appears in the linguistic text (e.g. a metal cube of side x), the diagram (e.g. length x), the graph (e.g. x axis) and the symbolic text (e.g. $V_1 = 3 \times 3 \times (15 - x)$) in Example 14. In addition, typography is an important aspect of multimodal grammaticality. For example, the italic font style for x functions to highlight the significance of this key participant in Example 14.

Halliday's SF model of language is based on *the general principle of hierarchy* where 'an element of any given rank is constructed out of elements of the next rank below' (Halliday 1994: 35). Accordingly, the SF-MDA content plane consists of grammar (with constituent ranks), and discourse semantics (at the rank of paragraph and text) for language, mathematical visual images and mathematical symbolism as displayed in Table 12.1 (see also Table 12.3). The SF-MDA grammar stratum consists of Halliday's (2004) SF grammar for language, and O'Halloran's (2005) grammatical

Table 12.1: SF-MDA Framework for Mathematical Discourse (O'Halloran 2005, 2007b)

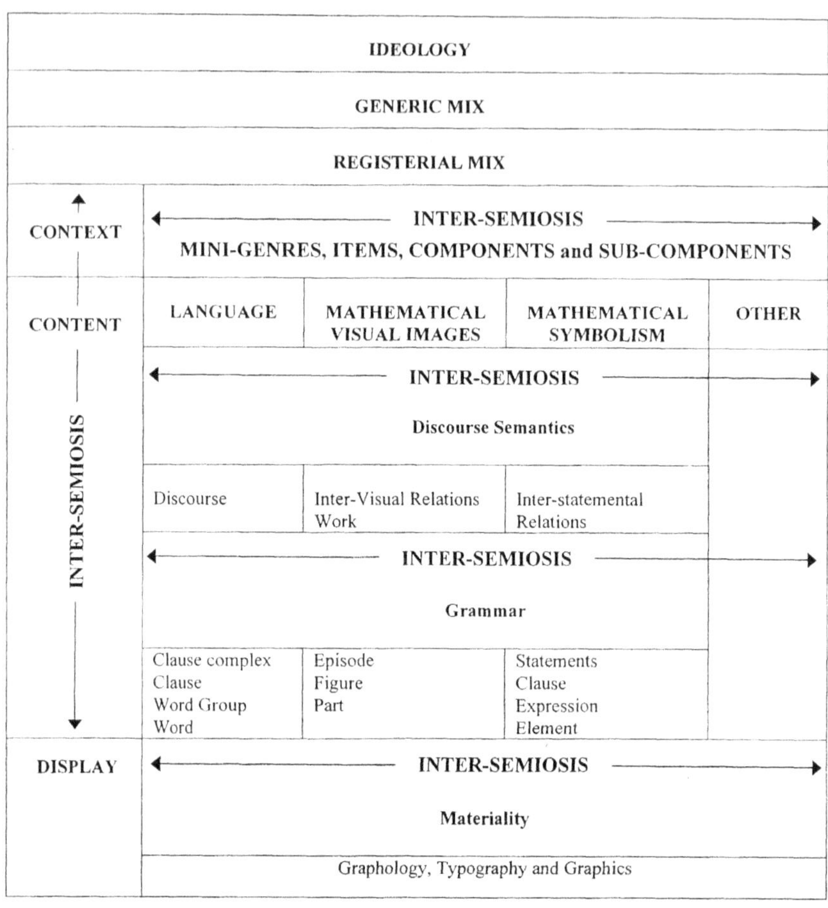

IDEOLOGY				
GENERIC MIX				
REGISTERIAL MIX				
CONTEXT	INTER-SEMIOSIS MINI-GENRES, ITEMS, COMPONENTS and SUB-COMPONENTS			
CONTENT	LANGUAGE	MATHEMATICAL VISUAL IMAGES	MATHEMATICAL SYMBOLISM	OTHER
INTER-SEMIOSIS	INTER-SEMIOSIS Discourse Semantics			
	Discourse	Inter-Visual Relations Work	Inter-statemental Relations	
	INTER-SEMIOSIS Grammar			
	Clause complex Clause Word Group Word	Episode Figure Part	Statements Clause Expression Element	
DISPLAY	INTER-SEMIOSIS Materiality			
	Graphology, Typography and Graphics			

framework for mathematical symbolism and visual images. The SF-MDA discourse stratum consists of Martin's (1992; Martin and Rose, 2007) discourse systems for language, and O'Halloran's (2005) discourse systems for visual images and mathematical symbolism (i.e. Inter-Visual Relations and 'Work' – i.e. the whole image following O'Toole (1994) – and Inter-Statemental Relations respectively). The SF-MDA context plane includes Mini-Genres, Items, Components and Sub-Components (see Figure 12.3), which add a further layer in the 'scalar levels of organisation' of multimodal texts (Baldry and Thibault 2006: 144). Mathematics discourse has a registerial mix of field (i.e. content) and interpersonal relations (i.e. tenor), and a generic mix of Genres which function to construct mathematical reality.

Halliday's (2004) principle of hierarchical ranks is significant for the SF-MDA approach because shifts of meaning take place across the layers of hierarchical organisation in the mathematics texts. However, the relationship between the hierarchical ranks in language is not straightforward and, as we shall see, the same applies to multimodal discourse. For example, Halliday (1994: 35) explains that 'there are variations on this pattern [of ranks in language]; in the clause as exchange [i.e. interpersonal meaning], there is slightly more layering in the structure, while in the clause as message [i.e. textual meaning] there is rather less.' Similarly, there are variations in the pattern of ranks and levels in multimodal discourse (Baldry and Thibault 2006; Djonov 2007; Lemke 2000). Baldry and Thibault (2006: 144) explain that the 'hierarchy of meaningful units and relations' in multimodal discourse are not simply building blocks or smaller parts of each other, rather they combine in complex ways. The ways in which hierarchical ranks and levels combine in mathematics texts are explored in this chapter. Baldry and Thibault (2006: 144) make the further point that 'larger-scalar units provide integrating contexts for smaller-scale ones,' adding to our understanding of how semantic expansions take place in multimodal discourse. That is, smaller-scale units are contextualised in relation to larger-scale units in multimodal discourse. Semantic expansions involve co-contextualizing and re-contextualizing relations (Baldry and Thibault 2006; O'Halloran 2005; Thibault 2000). In the SF-MDA model in Table 12.1, these inter-semiotic contextualising relations, which take place within and across the hierarchy of scales in mathematics discourse, are represented by vertical and horizontal lines with arrows.

O'Halloran (2007b) uses the SF-MDA framework to demonstrate the recursive nature of inter-semiotic contextualising processes in Example 6 from Teh and Looi (2001: 198). That investigation is undertaken through the formulation of *inter-semiotic systems* (i.e. 'inter-modal' in recent research projects by the Sydney SFL school) for grammar and discourse strata. The inter-semiotic systems for the construction of experiential meaning include discourse systems (e.g. Intersemiotic Ideation) and grammatical systems (e.g. Transitivity Relations, Lexicalisation, Symbolization and Visualization). Systems such as Colour and Font style are considered on the display stratum. In addition, O'Halloran (2005, 2007b) proposes inter-semiotic mechanisms to explore the ways in which linguistic, visual and symbolic choices integrate to produce semantic expansions in mathematics discourse. The inter-semiotic mechanisms include Semiotic Cohesion (multimodal reference), Semiotic Adoption (incorporation of semiotic choices across grammars), Semiotic Mixing (structural combination), Juxtaposition and Spatiality (spatial arrangement), Semiotic Transition (explicit shift to another semiotic resource) and Semiotic Metaphor (metaphorical forms of expression). In this chapter, semiotic metaphors (SM) are investigated in detail.

These explorations pave the way for examining in closer detail the processes through which experiential reality is reconfigured in Example 14 to solve the problem. The inter-semiotic grammatical construction of experience takes place within and across the hierarchy of scales: i.e. grammar and discourse on the content plane, and Mini-genres, Items, Components and Sub-Components on the context plane as shown in Table 12.1. While system choices on the display plane (e.g. colour and font style) function to construct experiential reality, the discussion focuses on the content and context planes. Semantic expansions take place as process, participant and circumstance configurations are reconfigured and realigned across hierarchical ranks and levels, in some cases leading to metaphorical transformation. As we shall see, inter-semiotic metaphorical transformations of experiential meaning in Example 14 include cases where entities are reconstrued as process and participant configurations (entity → clause), a semantic drift which flows in the opposite direction to grammatical metaphor (GM) in language (Halliday 1998, 2004, 2006; Halliday and Matthiessen 1999; Simon-Vandenbergen *et al.* 2003). *Semiotic metaphor* (SM) (O'Halloran 2003, 2005) is proposed to conceptualise these inter-semiotic metaphorical shifts in meaning occurring across semiotic resources. Therefore, GM in language is reviewed before extending the concept to SM in multimodal discourse. From this point, the multimodal analysis of experiential meaning in Example 14 is undertaken.

12.3 Ideational grammatical metaphor (GM) and semiotic metaphor (SM)

There have been three phases in the conceptualisation of grammatical metaphor (GM) in language: (a) as a counterpart of lexical metaphor; (b) in relation to the realignment between semantics and grammar; and (c) as the consequence of transgrammatical domains (Yang 2007). In the first case, lexical metaphor is viewed as 'variation in the meaning of a given expression' while GM is 'variation in the expression of a given meaning' (Halliday 1994: 342). In the second case, the stratification of the lexicogrammatical stratum permits GM to be defined as 'a realignment between a pair of strata: a remapping of the semantics on to the lexicogrammar' (Halliday, 1998: 192), leading to the formulation of congruent and metaphorical realisations of meaning which relate semantics

Table 12.2: Semantics and lexicogrammatical units in language

	Semantics	**Realisation**	**Lexicogrammar**
	Sequence	↘	Clause complex
Ranks	Figure	↘	Clause
	Element	↘	Word group or phrase
	Semantics	**Realisation**	**Lexicogrammar**
	Process	↘	Verbal group
	Participant	↘	Nominal group
Type of Elements	Circumstance	↘	Adverbial group, Prepositional phrase
	Relator	↘	Conjunction

and lexicogrammatical units. The congruent mappings are displayed in Table 12.2 (Halliday 1998; Halliday and Matthiessen 1999).

Recent theorisations characterise GM in relation to 'transgrammatical semantic domains' where fractal patterns of token-value relations between the metaphorical and congruent relations are seen as the key for representing GM in semantic system networks (Halliday 2004). That is, metaphorical elaboration is possible because fractal patterns, or transgrammatical semantic domains, run through the whole system (Halliday and Matthiessen 1999). The two main motifs in the latest theorisations are the remapping of semantics and lexicogrammar and the expansion of meaning potential.

GM is a lexicogrammatical resource which is related to the evolution of human language (phylogenesis), the development of language in an individual speaker (ontogenesis) and the unfolding of a text (logogenesis). Studies of scientific writing (Halliday 2006; Halliday and Martin 1993; Halliday and Matthiessen 1999; Martin and Veel 1998) and children's writing (Derewianka 2003) reveal there are two kinds grammatical movement with respect to ideational meaning (i.e. experiential and logical meaning), 'one in rank, the other in structural configuration' (Halliday 1998: 192). The first movement is downwards in rank, where sequences (congruently realised as clause complexes) are realised by clauses and word groups, and figures (congruently realised as clauses) are realised by word groups. The second movement is across in function, where individual elements are reconstrued by another type of element. Halliday (1998: 209–210) identifies 13 types of ideational GM and their subcategories in this second kind of movement, which he summarises in the following way:

relator → circumstance → process → quality → entity

Halliday (1998: 211) explains:

> (1) any semantic element can be construed as if it was an entity (i.e. grammaticalised as a noun); (2) a relator, a circumstance or a process can be construed as if it was a quality (i.e. grammaticalised as an adjective); (3) a relator or a circumstance can be construed as if it was a process (i.e. grammaticalised as a verb); (4) a relator can be construed as if it was a minor process within a circumstance (i.e. grammaticalised as a preposition, in a prepositional phrase).

The two types of movement arising from ideational GM result in a general semantic shift towards the construal of entities, through the process of nominalisation. '[T]he noun is the most metaphorically attractive category: everything else can end up as a noun' (Halliday 1998: 211). GM includes the introduction of new metaphorical entities with no congruent realisation e.g. 'the phenomenon of [x]'; 'the fact' (Halliday and Matthiessen 1999: 247). The general semantic shift in ideational GM in language is illustrated in Figure 12.2, where // indicates clause boundaries.

The parallel concept for GM in language is semiotic metaphor (SM) in multimodal discourse, where metaphorical shifts of meaning arise from the realignment of semantics and lexicogrammar within and across the hierarchical ranks for semiotic resources (O'Halloran 2003, 2005). For example, process and participant configurations in mathematical symbolism (e.g. x^2, i.e. $x \times x$) can be grammaticalised as linguistic entities (i.e. x to the power of two). In what follows, we further investigate how SM takes place across the scalar hierarchies of the SF-MDA framework. We shall see that the semantic shift towards the entity (i.e. noun) in GM in language is not the typical form of metaphorical construal arising from SM in mathematical discourse. The trend towards nominalisation in language may be the result

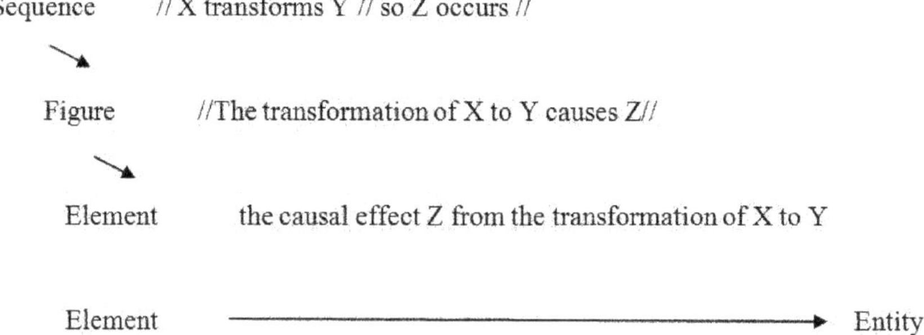

Figure 12.2: Down-ranking and cross-functional shift in ideational grammatical metaphor (GM) in language

of the metaphorical transformations of meaning which take place across linguistic, visual and symbolic semiotic resources in mathematical and scientific discourse. SM is explored in detail in the remainder of the chapter.

12.4 Experiential meaning across a hierarchy of scales in Example 14

Example 14 is an example of the Demonstration Problem, a Min-Genre from the textbook genre in school mathematics where new concepts are followed by worked examples to show how problems are solved based on the material presented. In this case, Example 14 is concerned with estimating the value of x when a metal cube with volume V, side x and a hole in the centre is made into a rectangular block with sides 3 cm, 3 cm and $(15 - x)$ cm. Example 14 involves questions (A)–(C), which are labelled in Figure 12.3.

(A) Show that the volume V for the cube is $V = x(x - 2)(x + 2)$.
(B) Complete the table of values, and plot the relationship between V and x.
(C) Estimate the value of x when the cube is made into a rectangular block with volume V_1 and sides 3 cm, 3 cm and $(15 - x)$ cm by plotting the relationship between V_1 and x.

Example 14 consists of two Items, the Problem and the Solution, which in turn are composed of the Components and Sub-Components displayed in Figure 12.3 and listed below:

(1) Problem: Statement of Problem Context, Questions (A, B and C) with Sub-Component Table (i) for Question (B).
(2) Solution: Question Answers (A, B and C), with Sub-Components Diagram for Answer (A), Table (ii) and Graph for Answer (B), and Table (iii) and Graph for Answer (C).

It is apparent from Figure 12.3 that language, the diagram and graph, and the mathematical symbolism combine in complex ways in the Components and Sub-Components in Example 14. In what follows, we trace the semantic shifts which take place across the linguistic, visual and symbolic texts in the solution to Questions (A)–(C). The resultant mappings reveal how the scalar hierarchy of ranks in the SF-MDA framework is traversed, in some cases giving rise to SM and metaphorical forms of expression. The semantic shifts and incidences of SM are described in Steps 1–4, and the mappings across the hierarchical ranks are recorded with arrows with

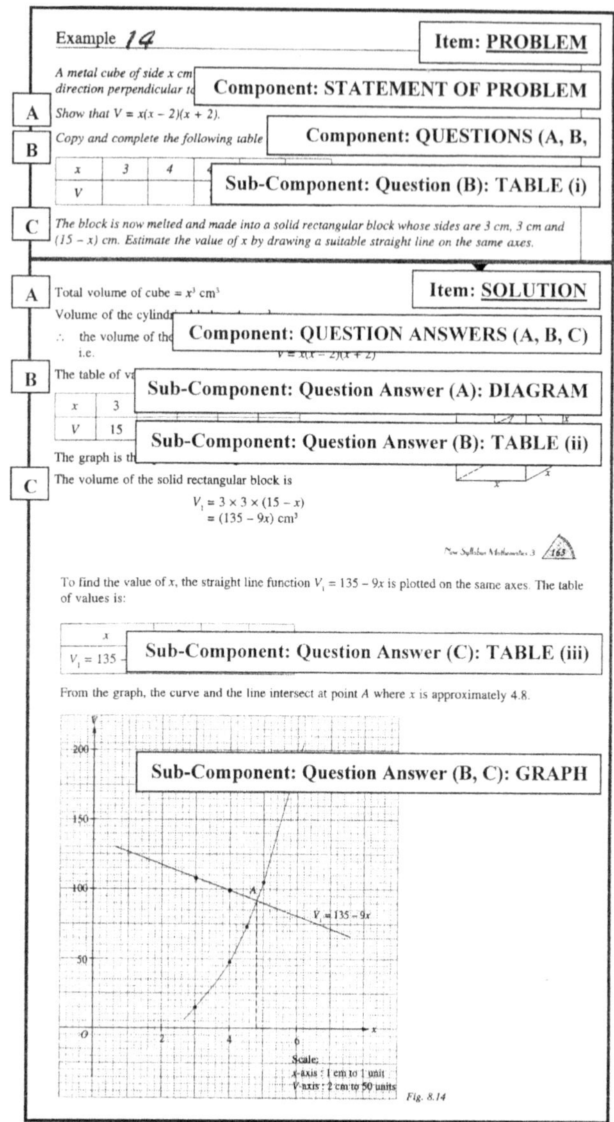

Figure 12.3: Items, Components and Sub-Components in Example 14 (Teh and Looi 2001: 165–166)

labelled boxes in Table 12.3. In addition, the dotted lines with the shaded labelled boxes in Table 12.3 link grammatical and discourse choices to their respective Sub-Component and Component structures. The down-ranking and cross-functional shifts found in ideational GM in language are mapped for comparison purposes in Table 12.3 (see bottom left hand corner), with Entity as the end point.

Table 12.3: Inter-semiotic semantic shifts across hierarchical ranks and semiotic metaphor (SM) in Example 14

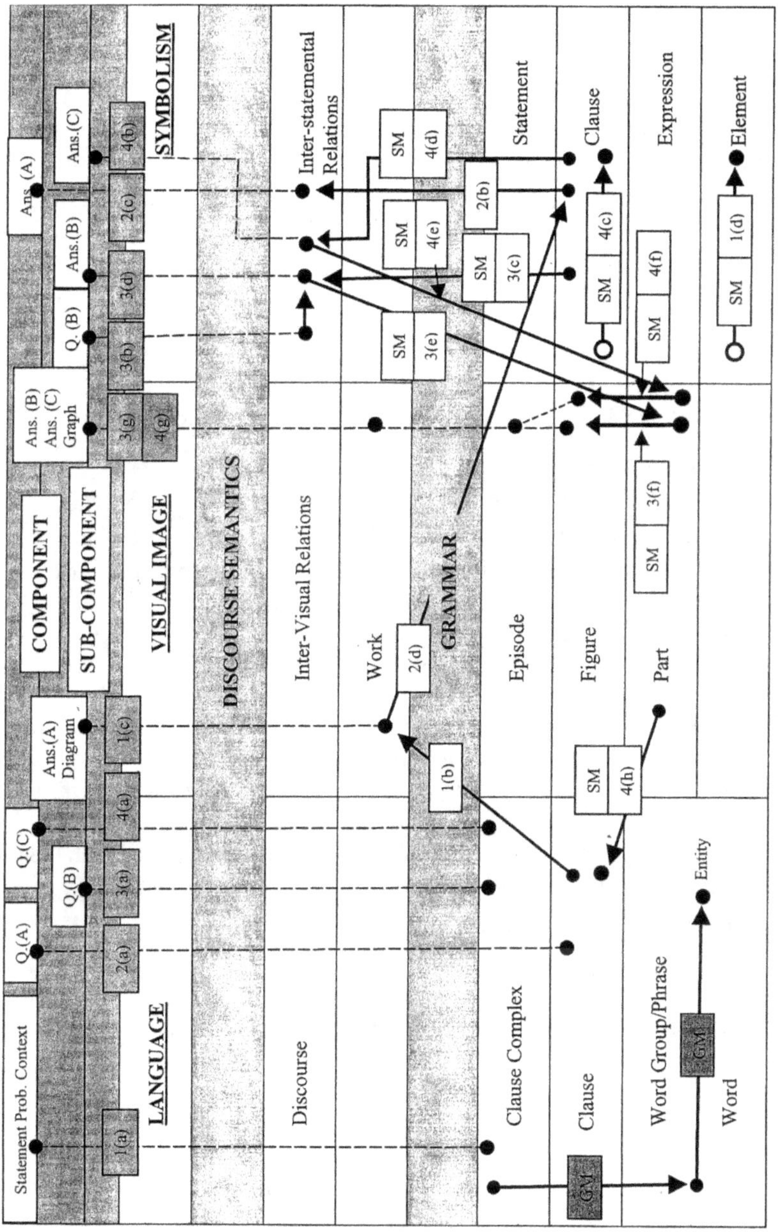

Table 12.3 is not a complete picture of the inter-semiotic experiential relations existing across linguistic, visual and symbolic choices in Example 14. The mappings only mark the significant semantic shifts which occur as the steps to the solution unfold. Steps 1–4 describe the semantic shifts within and across Items, Components and Sub-Components in Example 14, according to stages marked Item: Component: Sub-Component → Item: Component: Sub-Component. Table 12.3 and Steps 1–4 are complicated and at times difficult to follow. The need for effective methods for tracing and describing inter-semiotic expansions of meaning across hierarchical scales in multimodal texts is evident as Steps 1–4 unfold and we trace the mappings in Table 12.3.

12.4.1 Step 1

Problem: Statement of Problem Context → *Solution*: Question Answer (A): Diagram

The Statement of Problem Context consists of Clauses 1-2, which are cohesively linked through reference to the metal cube and the volume of the resulting block with the hole drilled in the centre. The square brackets '[[ ]]' in Clause 1 denote the presence of one rank-shifted clause using SF conventional notation (see Halliday and Matthiessen 2004). Clauses 1–2 are coded Statement Prob. Context 1(a) at the level of Component in Table 12.3.

Clause 1: //*A metal cube of side x cm* (Carrier) *has* (Relational, Attributive, Circumstantial) *a hole of cross-sectional area 4 cm*^{2} [[*drilled right through it*]] (Attribute) *in the direction perpendicular to one of the faces* (Location)//

Clause 2: //*The volume of the resulting block* (Token) *is* (Relational, Identifying, Intensive) *V cm*^{3} (Value)//

The Solution for Question Answer (A) involves the Sub-Component of the Diagram at the rank of Work, displayed in Figure 12.4.

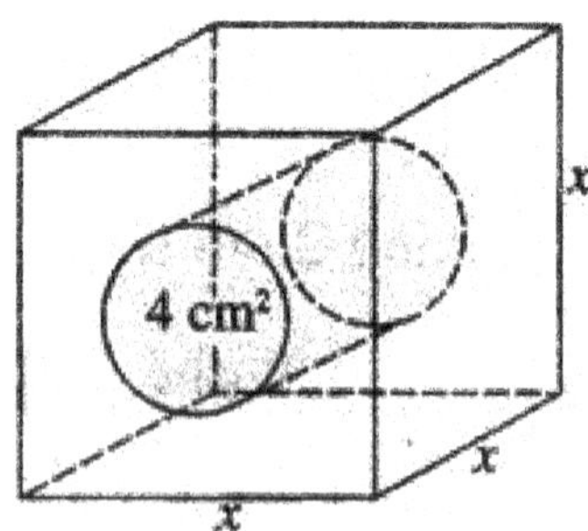

Figure 12.4: Question answer A: Diagram

The construction of the Diagram is based on the experiential relations encoded in Clause 1. That is, the Relational Attributive Circumstantial process *has*, with Carrier *a metal cube of side x cm*, Attribute *a hole of cross-sectional area 4* cm^2 [[*drilled right through it*]] and circumstance (Location) *in the direction perpendicular to one of the faces* are visualised so that the parts of the cube (the length, the sides and the hole) are perceived in relation to each other in the Diagram. There has been an inter-semiotic *up-ranking* where Clause 1 is reconstrued as Work, a move which gives access to the meaning potential of mathematical visual imagery. The semantic shift is recorded 1(b) in Table 12.3. The semantic shift is not classified as a SM because the attributive experiential relations of circumstance in Clause 1 are reconfigured visually as a Work consisting of Parts which bear a circumstantial relationship to each other. The semantic shift is important, however, because it gives access to the meaning potential of visual imagery and the logic of spatial relations. The Diagram subsequently becomes an important semiotic tool for reasoning about the cube, particularly with regards to formulating the symbolic description of the volume of the cube. The Diagram is labelled Ans. (A) Diagram 1(c) at the level of Sub-Component in Table 12.3.

Clause 2 has participant *the volume of resulting block*, which is implicitly realised in the Diagram through the shading of the cylindrical shape representing the hole drilled through the centre of the cube. The meaning potentials of language and visual imagery are inadequate, however, to exactly describe the volume of the cube. Consequently there is a shift to mathematical symbolism with the introduction of V in Clause 2. The Relational Identifying Intensive process means that *the volume of the resulting block* (Token) is V (Value), a semiotic choice from the grammar of the mathematical symbolism. It is a significant *cross-functional* move from language to mathematical symbolism, resulting in the introduction of the new entity V, which is defined symbolically in Step 2. Therefore, V is classified as a SM, following Halliday's (1998: 209–210) Type 10 category, where the class shift is zero → noun. The semantic shift is recorded SM 1(d) in Table 12.3, with the hollow circle to indicate the introduction of the new mathematical symbolic entity V.

12.4.2 Step 2

Problem: Question (A) → *Solution*: Question Answer (A)

Question (A) consists of Clause 3, where the reader is instructed to *Show that the volume* $V = x(x - 2)(x + 2)$. Clause 3 is labelled Q. (A) 2(a) at the level of Component in Table 12.3.

Clause 3: //*Show* (Material) [[*that* V (Token) = (Relational, Identifying, Intensive) $x(x - 2)(x + 2)$ (Value)]] (Range)//

There is an inter-semiotic shift from the linguistic command *show that* to the rank-shifted clause $V = x(x - 2)(x + 2)$ which functions as Range in Clause 3. Therefore, while the relations between the parts of the cube (length, breadth, depth and the hole) may be perceived in the Diagram, the mathematical symbolism is called into play to provide the exact description of those relations.

Question Answer (A) consists of Clauses 4–7, which are classified as Inter-Statemental Relations at the discourse rank for mathematical symbolism. The shift from Question (A) (i.e. clause) to Question Answer (A) (i.e. series of clause complex relations) involves grammatical *up-ranking.* The semantic shift from clause to Inter-Statemental Relations is recorded as 2(b) and Question Answer (A) is coded as Ans. (A) 2(c) at the level of Component in Table 12.3.

Clause 4: //*Total volume of cube* (Token) = (Relational, Identifying, Intensive) x^3 cm^3 (Value) //

Clause 5: //*Volume of the cylindrical hole* (Token) = (Relational, Identifying, Intensive) $4x$ cm^3 (Value) //

Clause 6: //∖ *the volume of the resulting block* (Token) *is* (Relational, Identifying, Intensive) [[$V = (x^3 - 4x)$]] (Value)//

Clause 7: //i.e. V (Token) = (Relational, Identifying, Intensive) [[$x(x - 2)(x + 2)$]] (Value)//

Clauses 4–6 consists of Relational, Identifying, Intensive processes with linguistic participants functioning as Token and symbolic participants functioning as Value. Clause 7 consists of a Relational, Identifying, Intensive process with symbolic participants functioning as Token and Value. That is, Clause 7 contains the symbolic description for V.

The Diagram provides the semiotic basis for the symbolic descriptions of the volume of the cube, the cylindrical hole and the resulting block in Clauses 4–6 because the relations between the parts of the cube can be perceived in relation to each other. Therefore, an inter-semiotic *down-ranking* from the Diagram (at rank of Work) to symbolic descriptions for volume (i.e. Clauses 4, 5 and 6) takes place, which in turn leads the required symbolic description for V in Clause 7. The semantic shift from Work to the symbolic clause is recorded 2(d) in Table 12.3.

In addition to using the Diagram, the derivations of the symbolic descriptions for volume in Clauses 4–7 are based on previous mathematical knowledge, including the volume formulae, algebraic laws and factorisation results listed in (a)–(e). Question Answer (A) demonstrates the hierarchical and layered nature of mathematical knowledge which depends on previously established results (Christie and Martin 2007; O'Halloran 2007a).

(a) The volume of a cube: V (cube) $= l \times l \times l$
(b) The volume of a cylinder: V (cylinder) $= A$ (base) $\times h$
(c) The volume of the resulting block: $V = V$ (cube) $-$ V (cylinder)
(d) Distributive Property of Multiplication over Addition (DPM/A): $a(b+c) = ab + ac$
(e) Factorisation: Common factor, and the difference of squares: $(a^2 - b^2) = (a + b)(a - b)$

The different grammatical strategies for encoding experiential meaning in language and mathematical symbolism are illustrated in Clause 6: i.e. nominalisation in language (*the volume of the resulting block)* and rankshift in mathematical symbolism $V = (x^3 - 4x)$ which is equivalent to $V =$ [[[[$x \times x \times x$]] $-$ [[$4 \times x$]]]]). The significance of the grammatical strategy of rankshift for encoding experiential relations in mathematical symbolism is discussed in the concluding section of the chapter.

12.4.3 Step 3

Problem: Question (B): Table (i) → *Solution*: Question Answer (B): Table (ii) and Graph

Question (B) instructs the reader to complete Table (i), displayed in Figure 12.5, and graph the relationship between x and V. Question (B) consists of Clauses 8–10 and Table (i) with Inter-Statement Relations ($x \leftrightarrow V$) which are labelled Q. (B) 3(a) and Q. (B) 3(b) respectively at the level of Sub-Component in Table 12.3.

Clause 8: //*Copy* (Material)//
Clause 9: //*and complete* (Material) *the following table of values* (Range)//
Clause 10: //*Hence plot* (Material) *the graph of V against x* (Range)//

Question Answer (B) involves Table (ii) and the Graph, displayed in Figures 12.6–12.7. Table (ii) and the Graph are labelled Ans. (B) 3(d) and Ans. (B) Graph 3(g) at the level of Sub-Component in Table 12.3. The semantic expansion from $V = x(x - 2)(x + 2)$ to Table (ii), and the ensuing

x	3	4	4.5	5	6
V			73		

Figure 12.5: Question (B): Table (i)

inter-semiotic shift from Table (ii) to the Graph are coded 3(c) and 3(e) respectively in Table 12.3. The semantic expansion within the Graph itself when the curve (i.e. Figure) is plotted is coded 3(f) in Table 12.3. These significant semantic expansions are discussed below.

x	3	4	4.5	5	6
V	15	48	73	105	192

Figure 12.6: Question Answer (B): Table (ii)

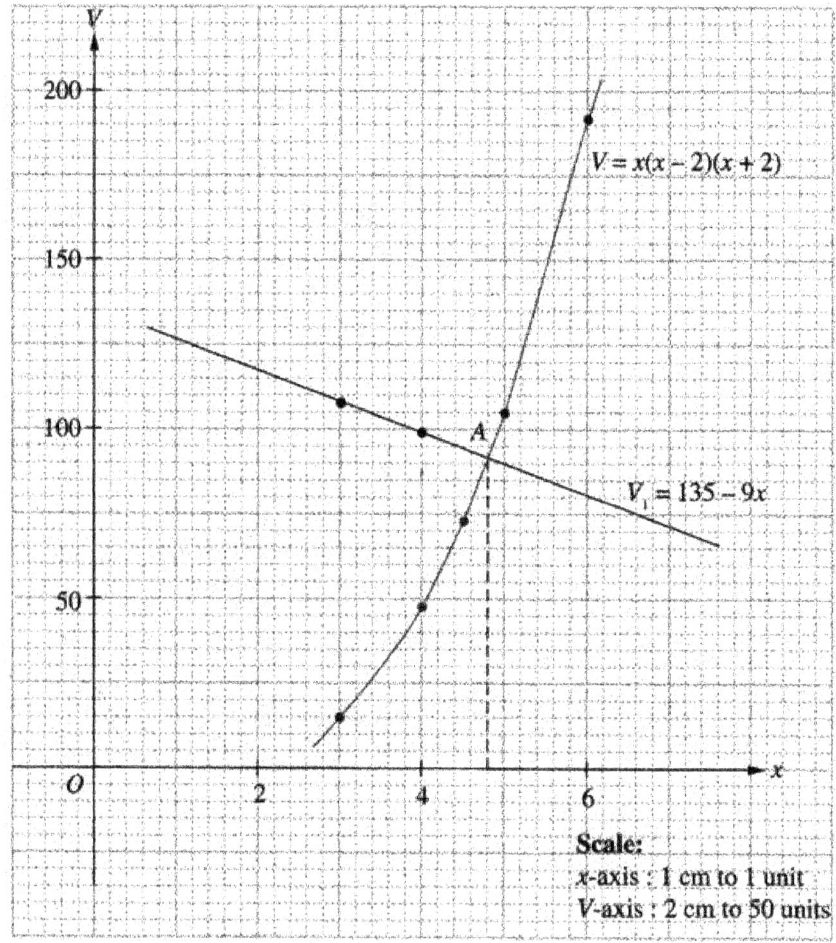

Figure 12.7: Question Answer (B, C): Graph

Question Answer (B) involves a semantic expansion shift from Table (i) to Table (ii). However, Table (ii) is completed by substituting the values for x in the mathematical equation $V = x(x - 2)(x + 2)$. However, the instruction to complete Table (ii) using the mathematical equation for V does not appear in Question (B). The implicit mathematical knowledge required to complete Example 14 is evident.

The semantic shift from clause $V = x(x - 2)(x + 2)$ results in a sequence of relational identifying clauses relations, (x ↔ V), (3 ↔ 15), (4 ↔ 48), (4.5 ↔ 73), (5 ↔ 105) and (6 ↔ 192), in Table (ii). The *up-ranking* semantic shift from figure (i.e. the symbolic clause) to a sequence (i.e. Inter-Statemental Relations consisting of clause complex sequence) is a SM which flows in the opposite direction to that found in GM in language (Halliday 1998; Halliday and Matthiessen 1999). The up-ranking SM is recorded 3(c) in Table 12.3.

The shift from Table (ii) to the Graph is marked 3(e) in Table 12.3. This is a significant semantic shift because the identifying relations between the x and V in Table (ii) become entities (i.e. points) on the Graph. That is, the identifying relations, (3 ↔ 15), (4 ↔ 48), (4.5 ↔ 73), (5 ↔ 105) and (6 ↔ 192), in Table (ii) are reconfigured as points in the Graph. The *down-ranking* semantic shift is a case of SM where identifying relational clauses become a sequence of entities. After the points are plotted, the new participant, the curve, is introduced in the Graph at the rank of Figure, in the move coded 3(f) in Table 12.3. This is a case of SM where a new Figure is introduced visually from the sequence of Parts (i.e. points). The Figure is part of the Graph at the rank of Word. The Graph is coded Ans. (B) Graph 3(g) at the level of Sub-Component in Table 12.3.

12.4.4 Step 4

Problem: Question (C) → *Solution*: Question Answer (C): Graph

The reader is required to undertake a series of material actions in Clauses 11–14 to estimate x when the metal cube is melted down to form a rectangular block with sides 3 cm, 3 cm and $(15 - x)$. Question (C), consisting of Clauses 11–14, is marked Q. (C) 4(a) at the level of Component in Table 12.3.

Clause 11: // *The block* (Goal) *is now melted* (Material)//

Clause 12: // *and made* (Material) *into a solid rectangular block [[whose sides are 3 cm, 3 cm and (15 – x) cm]]* (Range)//

Clause 13: // *Estimate* (Mental) *the value of x* (Phenomenon)//

Clause 14: // *by drawing* (Material) *a suitable straight line* (Range) *on the same axes* (Location)//

Question (C) does not explicitly state how the estimate for x should be obtained, apart from the instruction *by drawing a suitable graph on the same axes* in Clause 14. The steps involve (i) finding the mathematical expression for $V_{1,}$ (i.e. volume of the rectangular block) from the information given in Clause 12; (ii) constructing a table of values for x and V_1; (iii) plotting the line; and (iv) finding the point of intersection between the curve from Question (B) and the line, i.e. the value of x, which satisfies the conditions for V and V_1. The implicit knowledge required in Example 14 is demonstrated once more. Question Answer (C), involving Inter-Statemental Relations (i.e. Clause 15–16), is coded Ans. (C) 4(b) at the level of Sub-Component in Table 12.3.

Clause 15: //*The volume of the solid rectangular block* (Token) *is* (Relational, Identifying, Intensive) [[$V_1 = 3 \times 3 \times (15 - x)$ (Value)]]//
Clause 16: //[V_1] (Token) = (Relational, Identifying, Intensive) $(135 - 9x)$ cm^3 (Value)//

There is a shift from the linguistic nominal group *the volume of the solid rectangular block* (Token) to the introduction of a new mathematical entity, the rank-shifted clause $V_1 = 3 \times 3 \times (15 - x)$ (Value) in Clause 15. Therefore, the introduction of $V_1 = 3 \times 3 \times (15 - x)$ is classified as a SM, following Halliday's (1998: 209–210) Type 10 category, where the class shift is zero → noun. In this case, the class shift is zero → clause. The semantic shift is recorded SM 4(c) in Table 12.3, where the hollow circle indicates the introduction of the new process and participant configuration through the grammar of mathematical symbolism.

Clause 15 illustrates the different grammatical strategies for encoding experiential meaning in language and mathematical symbolism (see also Clause 6), which are further discussed in the concluding section of the chapter. The linguistic nominal group *the volume of the solid rectangular block* (Token) is equated with the rank-shifted mathematical expression $V_1 = 3 \times 3 \times (15 - x)$ (Value), which contains its own rank-shifted configurations of mathematical processes and participants; i.e. V_1 = [[3 × 3 × [[(15 – x)]]]]. The congruent form of encoding mathematical experiential relations in $V_1 = 3 \times 3 \times (15 - x)$ (as opposed to nominalisation in language) permits the easy rearrangement of process and participant configurations, which in this case leads to the simplification of the experiential relations for V_1. It is possible to ellipse V_1 in the resulting mathematical equation, $V_1 = (135 - 9x)$ cm^3, given the textual organisation of the symbolic statements where successive clauses are organised in lines underneath each other.

The symbolic description $V_1 = 135 - 9x$ cm^3 is used to complete the values for x and V_1 in Table (iii), displayed in Figure 12.8. The process is

x	3	4	5
$V_1 = 135 - 9x$	108	99	90

Figure 12.8: Question Answer (C): Table (iii)

similar to the semantic shift from $V = x(x - 2)(x + 2)$ to Table (ii) in Step 3, and hence the discussion is limited to a brief description of the semantic expansions which subsequently arise.

The semantic shift from the clause $V_1 = 135 - 9x$ cm^3 to the relational identifying clause relations (x $\leftrightarrow$ $V_1 = 135 - 9x$), (3 $\leftrightarrow$ 108), (4 $\leftrightarrow$ 99), (5 $\leftrightarrow$ 90) in Table (iii) involves semantic *up-ranking* from figure (i.e. clause) to sequence (i.e. Inter-statemental Relations). The resulting SM, where the semantic shift flows in the opposite direction to GM in language, is marked 4(d) in Table 12.3.

Plotting the values in Table (iii) on the Graph involves a similar semantic shift which occurred in plotting the values for Table (ii). That is, the sequence of identifying relations (3 $\leftrightarrow$ 108), (4 $\leftrightarrow$ 99), (5 $\leftrightarrow$ 90) is reconstrued as a series of entities (i.e. points) on the graph: a SM marked as 4(e) in Table 12.3. This gives rise to the introduction of a new entity: the line (i.e. Figure) in the Graph (i.e. Work), a semantic shift and a SM marked 4(f) in Table 12.3.

The curve from Question Answer (B) and the line in Question Answer (C) combine as two Figures, forming an Episode in the Graph. Question (C) is solved when the point of intersection between the curve and the line is found. That is, the two Figures intersect at point A (see Figure 12.7). The Graph (i.e. Work) is coded Ans. (C) 4(g) at the level of Sub-Component in Table 12.3. The accompanying description of the solution appears as Clauses 17–18.

Clause 17: //*From the graph* (Manner, Means), *the curve and the line* (Token) *intersect* (Relational, Identifying, Circumstantial) *at point A* (Value)//

Clause 18: //*where x is approximately 4.8*//

Point A, an entity on the Graph, is reconfigured linguistically in Clause 18. This is a SM involving an *up-ranking* grammatical movement from a visual entity (point A) to a linguistic clause (i.e. *where x is approximately 4.8*): a semantic shift which flows in the opposite direction to GM in language. The SM is marked 4(h) in Table 12.3. The corresponding symbolic identifying relational clause $x \approx 4.8$ would involve the same type of semantic shift, in this case involving mathematical symbolism rather than language.

Clause 18 contains the solution to Question (C), and Example 14 is completed.

12.5 Multimodal construction of Experiential meaning in mathematics

The inter-semiotic traversals across the hierarchical ranks in Table 12.3 illustrate how experiential meaning is expanded to produce the solutions to Questions (A), (B) and (C) in Example 14. In addition, the central role of mathematical symbolism is demonstrated in Table 12.3, where the bulk of semiotic activity seems to take place, as evidenced by the number of semantic shifts recorded for this semiotic resource. In what follows, the specialised grammar of mathematical symbolism is discussed to explain how this semiotic resource manages to expand experiential reality in such a profound way as it integrates with language and mathematical visual imagery in mathematical discourse. In addition, the metaphorical forms of experiential reality arising from grammatical up-ranking, down-ranking and cross-functional movements across hierarchical ranks and levels are discussed.

Language, visual images and mathematical symbolism integrate to construct experiential meaning in Example 14. The major functions of language are to contextualise the problem and to construct questions which involve undertaking material actions. The diagram provides an important bridge between the linguistic and the symbolic descriptions of the problem. Although the graph provides the semiotic means for answering the questions, the symbolism provides the semiotic tools for the exact description of the experiential relations for V and V_1 through which the graphical solution is found. The graphical method of solution is a precursor to solving the problem algebraically using mathematical symbolism.

The complex integration of linguistic and symbolic text in Example 14 is a consistent feature of mathematical discourse. The integration takes place effortlessly because the grammar of mathematical symbolism evolved in part from language. However, the symbolism developed its own grammatical systems according to the functions it was required to serve, which involve describing and rearranging experiential relations in a way which directly connects with the visual representation of those relations in order to solve problems.

The easy rearrangement of experiential relations in mathematical symbolism is possible through the grammatical strategy of rank-shift which functions to preserve *congruent forms of process and participant relations.* For example, experiential relations between participants are preserved in $V = (x^3 - 4x)$: i.e. $V = [[[[x \times x \times x]] - [[4 \times x]]]]$. The grammatical strategy of rank-shift in mathematical symbolism may be compared to nominalisation in GM in language, where information is packed into nominal group structures (e.g. 'the volume of the resulting block') which have lost their congruent process and participant configurations. Mathematical symbolism, however, adopts the opposite strategy to congruently encode experiential reality through the grammatical strategy of rankshift so that the process and participant relations may be reconfigured to solve mathematical problems.

The grammar and discourse systems, which aid the rearrangement of experiential relations in the rank-shifted configurations of mathematical processes and participants, include ellipsis of the multiplication process (e.g. $4x = 4 \times x$ and $x(x - 2)(x + 2) = x \times (x - 2) \times (x + 2)$), spatial index notation (e.g. x^3 and $V = (x^3 - 4x)$), and algebraic laws. Repetition makes for easy tracking of the mathematical participants which consist of simple nominal groups (e.g. V and x). The symbolisation of the processes and participants means that the mathematical solutions and formulae are reduced to the simplest possible format so they can be easily reconfigured according to the laws and theorems governing their existence.

The grammar of mathematical symbolism has evolved so that experiential meaning appears to transcend material reality with generalised processes and participants which describe relations and patterns in the world. Furthermore, mathematical symbolism restricts itself to a narrow range of process types, which are primarily confined to relational processes and mathematical operations. Mathematical reality becomes abstract reality, with a focus on mathematical process and participant relations which can be visualised. As a result, mathematical symbolism is a powerful semiotic tool for reasoning about experiential reality.

Mathematical symbolism integrates with language and visual imagery so that the meaning potential of the three semiotic resources can be accessed when required. The semantic expansions involve more than accessing the meaning potential of the three semiotic resources, however. Table 12.3 reveals the complexity of the inter-semiotic mapping across the hierarchy of SF-MDA ranks and levels where it is evident that the expansion of experiential meaning involves up-ranking, down-ranking and cross-functional semantic shifts across linguistic, visual and symbolic choices. The significant expansions of experiential meaning include incidences of semiotic metaphor (SM) where there is an inter-semiotic realignment between the grammar and semantics of semiotic choices. For example, symbolic identifying relations can be configured as visual entities in the shift from a table of values to a graph, and vice versa. In addition, mathematical symbolism gives rise to the introduction of new entities and experiential relations (e.g. V and $V_1 = 3 \times 3 \times (15 - x)$) which otherwise would not exist.

The multimodal grammatical approach to mathematics suggests that ideational grammatical metaphor (GM) in language functions as a down-ranking and cross-functional semantic phenomenon because significant semantic meaning expansions take place through other semiotic resources, in particular, mathematical visual imagery and symbolism. Multimodal analysis reveals the necessity of incorporating the hierarchical organisation of multimodal texts and looking beyond the contributions of individual semiotic resources in order to understand the inter-semiotic expansions of meaning and metaphorical transformations which take place in mathematics and science.

This chapter has demonstrated the multimodal semantic construal of experiential meaning as a multi-directional and multi-layered process which transverses the hierarchy in the SF-MDA framework. The SF-MDA approach is based on the concept of integrated grammatical and discourse systems with hierarchical ranks and levels. The result is a complex view of the construction of experience as inter-connected, layered systems of meaning where choices for experiential meaning unfold in conjunction with system choices for logical, textual and interpersonal meaning. The orchestration of the semantic flow of meaning, which is carefully choreographed in mathematics, is traced to demonstrate how mathematics successfully realigns experiential relations across language, visual images and mathematical symbolism in order to solve mathematical problems.

The chapter is confined to the analysis of experiential meaning where the complexity of tracing and mapping the semantic shifts demonstrate the need for alternative methods for SF-MDA. One alternative method may involve the development of interactive digital platforms to dynamically model the semantic expansions which unfold in multimodal discourse. In any event, much research remains to be done if we are to understand the functionality of mathematics and science, particularly in the age of interactive digital technology where computer algorithms and scientific visualisation are playing an increasingly significant role for the construction of mathematical and scientific reality.

References

Baldry, A. P. and Thibault, P. J. (2006). *Multimodal Transcription and Text Analysis.* London: Equinox.

Christie, F. and Martin, J. R. (eds). (2007). *Language, Knowledge and Pedagogy: Functional Linguistic and Sociological Perspectives.* London and New York: Continuum.

Derewianka, B. (2003). Grammatical metaphor in the transition to adolescence. In Simon-Vandenbergen, A-M., Taverniers, M., and Ravelli, L. (eds) *Grammatical Metaphor: Views from Systemic Functional Linguistics.* Amsterdam: Benjamins, 185–219.

Djonov, E. (2007). Website hierarchy and the interaction between content organization, webpage and navigation design: a systemic functional hypermedia discourse analysis perspective. *Information Design Journal* 15/2, 144–162.

Halliday, M. A. K. (1978). *Language as Social Semiotic: The Social Interpretation of Language and Meaning.* London: Arnold.

Halliday, M. A. K. (1994). *An Introduction to Functional Grammar* (2nd edition). London: Arnold.

Halliday, M. A. K. (1998). Things and relations: regrammaticising experience as technical knowledge. In Martin, J. R. and Veel, R. (eds), *Reading Science: Critical and Functional Perspectives on Discourses of Science.* London: Routledge, 185–235.

Halliday, M. A. K. (2006). *The Language of Science (Collected Works of M. A. K. Halliday)* (Vol. 5). London and New York: Continuum.

Halliday, M. A. K. and Martin, J. R. (1993). *Writing Science: Literacy and Discursive Power.* London: Falmer.

Halliday, M. A. K. and Matthiessen, C. M. I. M. (1999). *Construing Experience through Meaning: A Language Based Approach to Cognition.* London: Cassell.

Halliday, M. A. K. and Matthiessen, C. M. I. M. (2004). *An Introduction to Functional Grammar* (3rd edition). London: Arnold.

Kress, G., and van Leeuwen, T. (2006). *Reading Images: The Grammar of Visual Design* (2nd edition). London: Routledge.

Lemke, J. L. (2000). Opening up closure: semiotics across scales. In Chandler, J. and Vijver, G. V. D. (eds), *Closure: Emergent Organizations and their Dynamics.* New York: Academy of Science Press, 100–111.

Martin, J. R. (1992). *English Text: System and Structure.* Amsterdam: Benjamins.

Martin, J. R. and Rose, D. (2007). *Working with Discourse: Meaning Beyond the Clause* (2nd edition). London: Continuum.

Martin, J. R. and Veel, R. (eds). (1998). *Reading Science: Critical and Functional Perspectives on Discourses of Science.* London: Routledge.

O'Halloran, K. L. (2003). Intersemiosis in mathematics and science: grammatical metaphor and semiotic metaphor. In Simon-Vandenbergen, A-M., Taverniers, M., and Ravelli, L. (eds) 2003. *Grammatical Metaphor: Views from Systemic Functional Linguistics.* Amsterdam: Benjamins, 337–365.

O'Halloran, K. L. (2005). *Mathematical Discourse: Language, Symbolism and Visual Images.* London and New York: Continuum.

O'Halloran, K. L. (2007a). Mathematical and scientific forms of knowledge: a systemic functional multimodal grammatical approach. In Christie, F. and Martin, J. R. (eds) 2007. *Language, Knowledge and Pedagogy: Functional Linguistic and Sociological Perspectives.* London and New York: Continuum, 205–236.

O'Halloran, K. L. (2007b). Systemic functional multimodal discourse analysis (SF-MDA) approach to mathematics, grammar and literacy. In McCabe, A., O'Donnell, M. and Whittaker, R. (eds), *Advances in Language and Education.* London and New York: Continuum, 205–236.

O'Halloran, K. L. (2007c). The role of language, symbolism and images in mathematics: a systemic functional multimodal discourse analysis (SF-MDA) approach. *New English Language Teacher* 1/1, 73–89.

O'Toole, M. (1994). *The Language of Displayed Art.* London: Leicester University Press.

O'Toole, M. (2005). Pushing out the boundaries: designing a systemic functional model for non-European visual arts. *Linguistics and the Human Sciences* 1/1, 83–97.

Simon-Vandenbergen, A-M., Taverniers, M., and Ravelli, L. (eds) (2003). *Grammatical Metaphor: Views from Systemic Functional Linguistics.* Amsterdam: Benjamins.

Teh, K. S. and Looi, C. K. (2001). *New Syllabus Mathematics* (5th edition). Singapore: Shinglee Publishers Pte Ltd.

Thibault, P. (2000). The multimodal transcription of a television aadvertisement: theory and practice. In Baldry, A. P. (ed.) *Multimodality and Multimediality in the Distance Learning Age.* Campobasso, Italy: Palladino Editore, 311–385.

van Leeuwen, T. (2005). *Introducing Social Semiotics.* London: Routledge.

Yang, Y. (2007). Grammatical Metaphor in Chinese. PhD Thesis, Department of English Language and Literature. National University of Singapore, Singapore.

13 Representations of individual and mass: modelling Experience through multiple modes in digital art

Birgit Huemer

13.1 Introduction

Nowadays digital artworks are increasingly generated multi-modally. One of the most recent trends is to combine sound and visuals in live performances or interactive installations. Another practice is to transform the 'invisible' space of electronic data flows and give the so-called information space a physical form in the material world: a form that has a structure, a politics and a poetics (see Manovich 2006 for a discussion about information space in today's computer culture). In order to explore the meaning-making potential of these artworks, a theory is needed that enables researchers to analyse the different semiotic modes of communication and their intermodal relations. In this chapter, I show that the systemic functional model (Halliday 1978, 1994) can productively be applied to multimodal forms of communication. It is particularly useful in investigating the intermodal relations between the verbal, the visual and the aural modes, which commonly co-occur in digital art.

The specific work of art explored in this chapter is called *Listening Post.* It is a digital art installation assembled by Ben Rubin and Mark Hansen which was originally created for public presentation at the Brooklyn Academy of Music in 2001. In 2004 it was presented in Linz, Austria and won the 'golden nica' (category: Interactive Art), which is the highest international prize for digital arts in Austria awarded at the Ars Electronica festival. The following analysis mainly uses material from the latter exhibition and the artist's website.[1]

Listening Post is a multi-semiotic installation in the sense that it is composed of the aural, the visual and the verbal modes of communication.

The central theme of the artwork is the magnitude and diversity of online communication.

> The advent of online communication has created a vast landscape of new spaces for public discourse: chat rooms, bulletin boards, and scores of other public on-line forums. While these spaces are public and social in their essence, the experience of 'being in' such a space is silent and solitary. A participant in a chat room has limited sensory access to the collective 'buzz' of that room or of others nearby the murmur of human contact that we hear naturally in a park, a plaza or a coffee shop is absent from the online experience. The goal of our project is to collect this buzz and render it at a human scale. We use sound, text, motion and space to create sensual encounters, abstracting the communication spaces away from their familiar on-screen presence. (Rubin and Hansen 2002: 1)

In the following analysis of *Listening Post,* the social functions and meanings realised in this installation will be explored, revealing that representations of an individual and mass voice are realised by multi-semiotic modes of communication in this work of art. Combining Halliday's systemic functional model with a multimodal approach (Kress 2001; van Leeuwen 1999; O'Toole 1994), I focus on the ideational and interpersonal metafunctions and show how the different semiotic modes – language, image and sound – act in concert to model experience and enact social relationships.

To begin, this chapter provides a brief description of the artwork itself, focusing on the installation design by considering its physical appearance and the scene concept. Then in Section 13.3, I briefly outline the functional model that my analysis is based on and investigate the installation scene by scene to show which resources of the aural, the visual and the verbal modes are activated to realise representations of individual and mass. Finally, I explore how the three different modes interact to reinforce representations of individual and mass as well as how the different modes are put in opposition to each other so as to produce tension and engage the audience.

13.2 Listening Post

13.2.1 Installation design

Listening Post is composed of a grid of more than 200 small text displays, which are arranged in 21 columns and 11 rows. Each display is able to hold four lines of 20 characters. The small screens are connected with wire cables, which hang down from the ceiling. At the Ars Electronica in 2004 and at the Whitney Museum of American Art in 2002, *Listening Post* was presented in a dark room (see Figure 13.1).

The verbal messages are displayed on the screens and read by a voice synthesizer at the same time. Sampled sounds and mechanical clicks of the relays go with the synthetic voice. The sonic design is rather complex and consists of several speakers, subwoofers and other acoustical devices arranged in the exhibition space. The installation is made of four different scenes in sequence which are repeated in cycles. Each scene has its own programming logic. The program filters English text fragments in real time from thousands of internet chat rooms, bulletin boards and public forums of the English speaking community. The software and the computer programs are run by a network of several machines. (For a detailed description of the visual, technical and acoustic design of *Listening Post,* see Rubin and Hansen 2001, 2002.)

13.2.2 Physical appearance

The materiality and physicality of the installation, the light conditions and the way the artwork interacts with the surrounding space tells us something

Figure 13.1: Whitney Museum of American Art, December 2002 (Photo by David Allison).

about the scale to which we relate to this space with our bodies. To analyse these features, I draw on the systemic functional model outlined in O'Toole (1994), which provides an explanation of the way paintings, sculptures and architecture can be interpreted in terms of semiotic systems.

Room arrangement and dimensions

The installation is placed at the centre of the exhibition room. While the audience can walk beyond the grid and watch the screens from the backside, the curved form of the installation is oriented to the front and places the visitor in a watching position as in a cinema or theatre. The association with a cinema screen is reinforced by two aspects: first by the installation itself, which is about the size of a small cinema screen, and second by the exhibition room, which is about the size of a small theatre or cinema.

Lighting

At the Ars Electronica in Linz, the artwork was presented in a dark room. The only light in this dark environment comes from the screens themselves. At the back, they produce small dots of red light whenever they become active, and the fonts on the front side are of a shining blue-green colour. The lighting creates a stark contrast between the dark room and the shining screens, which serves to focus the visitors' attention on the action that is taking place on the displays. Observing the people at the exhibition in Linz in 2004, I could see that most of them actually sat down in front of the installation and remained there for a while, watching the four scenes. At another exhibition, the installation was placed in a lit room. Although I was unable to personally attend this exhibition, a photograph shows a room-arrangement with daylight conditions. My impression is that daylight evokes a very different atmosphere, which anchors the audience more in their present surroundings rather than allowing them to retreat into the darkness.

Materiality and physicality

The main materials used by the artists for their installation are small metallic text displays and wire cable. Metal is a cold, inorganic material used for machines that, in functional terms, realise non-natural realities, provoking social distance. The screens are connected with each other through the wire cable to build the grid. The grid is vertically oriented; it hangs down from the ceiling and is not merged with the ground. Its design is fragile, light and reminiscent of a meshed curtain.

All three features combined realise abstract truth and position the viewer in a setting of unreality like watching a movie in a darkened room.

This unreal setting stands in opposition to the real time data extracted from people's online discourse, which is displayed on the screens.

13.2.3 Scene concept

Listening Post comprises four different scenes, which are repeated in cycles, each cycle lasting about ten minutes. Each scene basically uses the same semiotic resources in all modes to produce meaning. However, the resources are composed individually, and each scene has a different programming logic which extracts text segments from English-speaking public communication channels.

The installation is structured by rhythm. Each scene is marked with a clear visual and acoustic starting and ending point. First, at the end of each scene, all screens turn black and then the sound ceases. The exhibition visitor experiences a sensation of 'drama' through constant comings and goings of loud and low frequency sounds and of visual appearance and disappearance.

Listening Post filters text-fragments and reorganises them in a new context as in a montage. The scenes are composed as a sequence of snapshots extracted from ongoing internet-communication, temporally and visually structured into the four scenes described above, with each new scene extending the others by simply adding new information.

> This is the kind of linking – or lack of linking – which dominates in contexts where people move from topic to topic on the basis of ad hoc associations, or in information media that adhere to the 'isolationistic' view of information as the accumulation of separate morsels or fact. (van Leeuwen 2005: 224)

In terms of composition in space, *Listening Post* is visually balanced. There is no difference in what is displayed left or right, or high or low. The grid is the background or context, upon which the visually and verbally realised meanings are displayed in the foreground. The synthetic voice is most often placed in the foreground as well. The mechanical clicks are mainly employed to provide background information.

The installation itself has a front and a back side. Communication takes place at the front, where the verbal messages are displayed, and the visitor can watch the visual patterns moving over the grid. However, the installation is placed in the exhibition room in such a way that the audience can also walk behind it and look at its back side. At the back, the relays do not carry text information. But whenever they become active the mechanical click of the relay initiates an action and the back side of the relay shows a red light at its centre.

13.3 Representations of individual and mass: aural, visual and verbal

The analysis of *Listening Post* that follows is based on the systemic-functional language theory proposed by Halliday (1978, 1994). This approach has inspired work in many disciplines: Kress and van Leeuwen (1996) in developing their grammar of visual design; van Leeuwen (1999) in expanding these insights to develop a systemic functional model for analysing speech, music and sound; and O'Toole (1994) in applying the systemic functional theory to visual arts, sculpture and architecture. In order to explore the meaning-making potential of digital artworks, which are increasingly generated multimodally, I use a functional multimodal approach that is mainly based on the work and theories mentioned above. Furthermore, I expand this approach to show how the three different modes interact to engage the visitor through reinforcement and opposition. This approach has turned out to be very productive for the analysis of digital art. First, it enables researchers to analyse the different semiotic modes of communication and their intermodal relations, using the same functional terminology for every mode. Second, the functional view allows researchers to interpret what you can do or how you can act upon people by activating specific semiotic resources of the different communicative modes. Third, the multimodal approach does not only deal with analysis and interpretation but can also be applied to production and design.

I will now outline how representations of an individual and mass voice are realised in the installation design in all three modes of communication by briefly highlighting the main semiotic resources that are used to compose *Listening Post*. In analysing the scenes, I focus on the following questions: who is represented or who is speaking, where does communication take place and which social relationships are enacted? First of all, however, I want to show how metaphors of 'online communication' (what kind of exchange is taking place) and 'virtual space' (where people meet) are realised through semiotic systems in *Listening Post*.

The 'online communication room' in this installation is represented as an organism of its own. Semiotic resources that are usually related to living beings are employed to animate this organism. Visual motion is one of the main features that needs to be discussed in this context. The verbal messages appear and disappear on the grid in unpredictable order like the coming and going of people in public places. In terms of acoustics, the artists choose to use sounds that are human or related to human beings. There is the synthetic male voice, realised in a friend-like social distance. There is the murmuring of many voices realising a crowd of people speaking all at once; and there are the 'peep-sounds' that have the tone-quality of a heart rate machine. Different personal statements and assertions appear on the screens representing a possible dialogue or an abstract idea of communication and exchange.

The virtual space is physically realised through the conceptual design of the installation. Two hundred screens are connected to each other to construct the grid. This is reminiscent of the metaphor of 'virtual networks', which draw people into contact with each other. Many overlapping synthetic voices and strong reverberating sounds represent a large space where such sounds can emerge and crowds of people can meet. A wide range of different verbal messages appear on the screens representing a sudden burst of communication all at once, as happens in large public places. In contrast to this animated virtual space, the artists use a rational design and 'cold' material to build the grid. The mechanical clicks of the relays in the background denaturalise the environment and have a machine-like effect. Hence this contrast between man and machine creates tension.

13.3.1 Scene 1: figures of being – how individuals construe personal identities

Scene 1 is dominated by representations of the individual. The meanings of the verbal messages, realised by the fonts and the synthetic voice, are foregrounded in this scene. Different people – all represented by the first person singular 'I' – are construing their personal identities through a taxonomy of classifications. The individual speaker is given a single voice, although the lexical items show that the text segments filtered are produced by people of different ages, coming from different places and having different jobs (e.g. *I am 18M, I'm 26, I am 14, I am 30, I am from latvian, I am in pennsylvania, I am an eastsider, I am from argentina, I am from rumania, I am a whitelighter, I am a student here, I am just a security guard*[2]). This 'individual voice' is a male voice realised in a friend-like social distance representing an online communication dominated by men. Table 13.1 shows the whole transcript of Scene 1, ordered according to functional processes.

As Table 13.1 indicates, the statements show people classifying themselves mainly by age, ethnicity, profession and place, as well as

Table 13.1: Functional processes

Figures of being focusing on entities	*Example*	*Example*
Existential	I am I am? I am	I am!! I am
Relational (describing identity in reference to qualities)	I'm bi I'm nice I am hot I am tired I am hot girl I am fully awake, Sir. I am comfortable with my assertions I am stumpy I am 18M	I am hungry I am still used to windows I am proud of not being british I'm not really I am good thanks I am not so god with english I am freezin I am stuck in oklahoma I am alive I am a student here
Relational (classifying identity by age, ethnicity, profession and place)	I'm 26 I am 14 I am 30 I am from latvian I am here I am in pennsylvania I am an eastsider I am a whitelighter I'm all yours I am a professional killer dear	I am from argentina I am an eastern canada grumpy I am in victoria right now I am from 1980 I am a colombian boy I am just a security guard I am from ontario I am at a train station I am from rumania
Figures of doing focusing on activity	*Example*	*Example*
Material	I am eating green pepper, I am going	I am giving you advice
Mental and verbal clauses focusing on sensing and saying/ or behaviour	*Example*	
Mental/behavioural	I am worried about that, lucky	
Verbal/behavioural	I am not repeating	

describing themselves in reference to several qualities (e.g. *nice, hot, tired, hungry, alive*). The existential clause 'am' appears five times in this scene – once with a question mark and once with an exclamation mark – expressing a 'heightened being', or pure existence in philosophical terms, that is sometimes questioned or emphasised. Processes of doing, sensing and saying do not seem to be important in the context of construing personal identities. The main participant in all clauses is realised in the first person singular pronoun 'I'. The personal pronoun allows strong identification between the 'virtual voice' and the audience. The informal language, expressed by contractions and lexical items (e.g. *I'm nice, I am worried about that, lucky, I'm all yours, I am good thanks*), realises social nearness. The verbal messages are visually represented in large fonts on the screens. These fonts are big enough to be read in a relaxed position at the back of the exhibition room (see the screenshot shown in Figure 13.2). The messages address the audience directly through their 'unnatural' size like the picture of a person, looking directly into their eyes. The verbal messages are displayed at a frontal and eye-level angle, which realises an equal relation between the audience and the installation and evokes both involvement and engagement.

Scene 1 is the only scene in which there is a melodic pattern. This musical pattern realised as ground (see van Leeuwen 1999:15-23 for a hierarchisation of sound into three groups – figure, ground and field) has

Figure 13.2: Big character mode.

a slow rhythm repeated in loops and two different melodic phrases which have the natural tone-quality of a piano. The first melodic phrase is at high pitch level, which stays at a relatively high level during the scene. This has the effect of continuity and open-endedness. In contrast to that, the second phrase has a falling pitch, which realises finality and closure. The melody has long intervals, which release more energy, give vent to strong feelings and thus involve the audience emotionally.

In contrast to the meanings of social nearness and involvement described above, social distance and isolation is realised by different semiotic resources of the very same modes. Verbally, no dialogue is in progress. All the messages are isolated personal statements. There is no reaction to them, or at least none is displayed on the screens, such as questions or answers that might illustrate some communication or exchange. The pitch range of the synthetic voice is small realising more inward looking music because less energy is released. Although the voice exhibits some accentuation and intonation, there is no variation in duration or in loudness. The voice is smooth and without the traces of human articulation which negates and restrains human emotions (see van Leeuwen 1999). The blue-green colour on the black background and the rational font style realise a cold machine-like effect, which emphasises the feeling of isolation and social distance. Instead of using different functional processes to express meaning (e.g. the algorithm could have looked for all clauses in which the personal pronoun 'I' is participant, instead of searching for all sentences that start with the phrase 'I am') or different voices distinguished by age and sex or different font styles to highlight the individuality of the different people speaking, the artists choose to use one realisation of being and a single voice and style for every verbal message. This realises unification in functional terms and sketches out a virtual environment in which people are disembodied. Hence they lack the resources to express their individuality.

Table 13.2 gives an overview of the main meanings and functions realised in Scene 1 and their key semiotic realisations in every mode.

13.3.2 Scene 2: representing a collective voice through the visual mode

In contrast to Scene 1, Scene 2 represents an experience of mass communication only, without the realisation of an individual voice speaking. This is mainly represented by the visual mode. A large number of verbal messages move in very quickly from the right side and spread over the grid (see Figure 13.3). All screens show the same text-segments displayed in small character mode. The messages flit dynamically over the

Table 13.2: Key semiotic realisations

Meaning or function	*Key semiotic realisation*		
	Language	*Sound*	*Image*
Social nearness and involvement	Personal pronoun 'I,' personal statements realised as relational clauses focusing on being, informal language	Male voice realised as if he is a friend, natural melodic pattern	Big fonts easy to read realised as close up directly addressing the audience, frontal and eye-level angle
Social distance and isolation	No dialog, no exchange realised	Small pitch range, non-emotional synthetic voice, denaturalised mechanical clicks	Rational font style, 'cold' colours
Unification	All clauses start with the phrase 'I am'	Same voice for all statements	Same font style for all statements

screens, and thus there is no chance to read them for their linguistic meaning. Then, all of a sudden, the screens stop and freeze for about three seconds (see Figure 13.4), all showing the same clause (*'do you speak english'*). After this short pause, the flittering begins again until all fonts disappear and the grid goes dark again.

There is no melody in the background and no synthetic voice. All that can be heard is the mechanical noise of the relays that evoke the rustle of leaves caused by a strong wind.

The unreadable messages and the flittering represent the communication between large numbers of people that is taking place in the virtual space of online communication.

13.3.3 Scene 3: how topical meaning is enacted through the mass of many voices

Scene 3 construes mass experience and represents 'world topics' by focusing on processes of doing and sensing, and on entities that are realised as single lexical items or noun-phrases. Most of the statements are material clauses of the type Actor + Goal or mental clauses of the type Senser + Phenomenon.

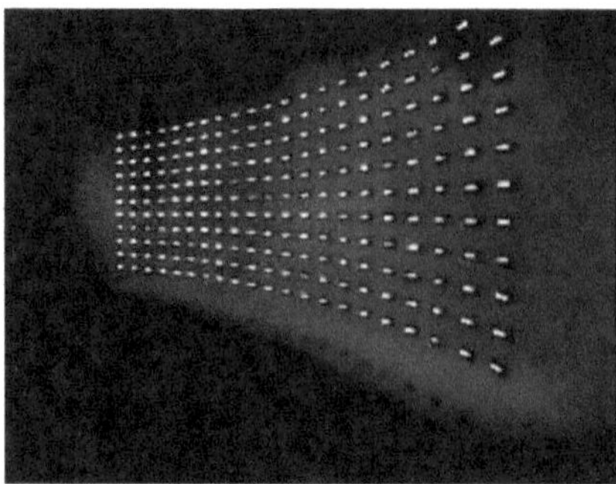

Figure 13.3: Flittering verbal messages

Figure 13.4: Screens stop and show a message

In many cases Actors and Sensers are realised as the personal pronouns 'I' and 'We', which appear in Theme position. The other participants are more generalised and abstract (e.g. they, people, communism). These lexicogrammatical resources realise what is going on in the English speaking chat community at a specific moment of time and what the people speaking think about it.

When I attended the exhibition in 2004, the main themes of Scene 3 were the 'US forces in Afghanistan' and the 'Enron-scandal', one of the biggest and most complex bankruptcy cases in US history (see Figure 13.5).

Figure 13.5: Topic Enron displayed in small character mode

The contrast between personal and general participants creates a tension between 'we' and 'they' in terms of social relation. There is a considerable amount of negativity in lexis and grammar (e.g. *destroyed, knocking down, stop, hurt, mistake, watch dogs, didn't even, can't*) because important topical news is rarely positive and this is reflected in public discourse. Unlike news items, the language is informal and there is not much distance between the writer and the reader in terms of mode.[3] The tenses used most frequently are past and present tense, and the clauses are realised in high modality. Table 13.3 is an extract from the verbal messages that are displayed on two different screens. Tables 13.4 and 13.5 are extracts from the text that can be heard through the synthetic voice. Table 13.4 gives examples of clauses or ellipses analysed in terms of their functional process. Table 13.5 gives examples of single nouns and noun-phrases.

In this scene the algorithm or agent searches for topics that match. Various individual but reverberating sounds are added each time a new topic match is made. The tone is a sampled bell or gong. Each topic that is placed on the screen is followed by another gong at a different pitch level. When the gong sound is added, a synthetic male voice reads out the text. It presents the text at different pitch levels with different degrees of

Table 13.3: Text displayed on screen

Process	*Example*
Material:	'$ 30,000 bad land deal... Enron **has destroyed** people to the tune of millions of dollars.'
Material:	'other day **run** right **into** an old couple, almost **knocking** the old man **down**... and'

Table 13.4:
Text read out by the synthetic voice

Process	*Example*
Material:	We **were** in Afghanistan **to stop** Communism
Verbal:	Next time I **suggest** you use your head first
Relational:	As a matter of fact they **have** more privileges
Mental:	I **know** the truth hurts
Mental:	I can't **figure out** why
Material:	**destroyed** people

Table 13.5:
Text read out by the synthetic voice

Nouns or noun-phrases
Every time the closing numbers
Bush
Contribution
Mistake
Watch dogs database
Pregnancy
Under those conditions
20 thousand dollars
Friday night
One thousand

reverberation. The installation ultimately features up to 40 different voices and gongs. The voices and gongs take on a polyrhythmic musical pattern, producing a polyphonic choir that takes on the quality of a chant or litany. In the middle of the sequence, when so many voices are added and overlapped that it is impossible to understand a single word or meaning, the gongs are foregrounded and the voices become back-grounded. What can then be heard is a musical pattern produced by the gongs realising the many voices of the mass of people who communicate with each other in the virtual space of online communication. The voices and gongs are at a low frequency and seem to come from all different directions simultaneously. This creates the effect that the listener is no longer part of a detached audience but is at the centre of the sound and immersed in the public virtual space.

The synthetic voices are steady and monotone. The male voice has a slightly rougher and more machine-like quality than the voice in Scene 1, with less stress and intonation and with reduced pitch and dynamic range. In functional terms, the voice realises a non-emotional, machine-like environment and an interpersonal relation of greater social distance.

The verbal messages in this scene are slowly displayed on the screens and disappear from the grid one by one in unpredictable order. The fonts are represented in small character mode and change every two seconds (see Figure 13.6). This scrolling evokes an experience of brief contact that lacks steadiness and is hard to capture. The text itself is hard to read. To catch the meaning it is necessary to move close to the grid and concentrate on a single screen. The fonts on the screens are displayed as a long shot and represent the offer of an image, which means that no contact is made between the represented participants and the viewer (Kress and van Leeuwen 1996: 119). At the end of Scene 3 about half of the screens are active (see Figure 13.7). After the last text message has been displayed, all the sentences disappear, one by one, until all the screens are dark again.

Figure 13.6:
Small character mode

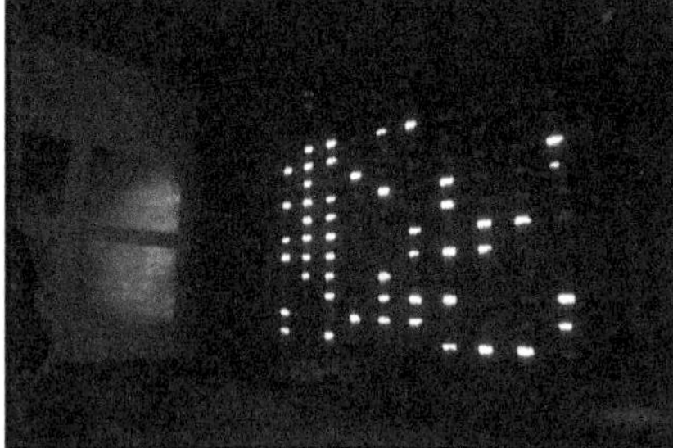

Figure 13.7:
Activated screens on the grid

Table 13.6 provides an overview of the main meanings and functions realised in Scene 3 and their key semiotic realisations in every mode.

13.3.4 Scene 4: representing a collective voice by visual and acoustic patterns

Like Scene 2, Scene 4 focuses on realising the mass of many voices. The installation turns into an organism of its own and the individual voice disappears. The sound environment is dominated by strong reverberating sounds at low frequency, which opens up a big acoustic virtual space. The meanings of the verbal messages are backgrounded while the visual and aural mode work together to realise a collective voice and social distance.

The fonts move in from the right side, producing a pattern that resembles a triangle on the grid (see Figure 13.8). When all the screens are filled with words, the fonts disappear slowly, one after another, until the grid turns dark again. This sequence is repeated several times. In this scene, the fonts are displayed in big character mode and appear all at once, moving too fast for any meaning to be caught (see Figure 13.9).

As the fonts move in, a strong reverberating tone at low frequency, resembling a gong, can be heard. In the background another low frequency sound fades in, reminiscent of an underwater environment. During the second loop, a new 'peep sound', similar to a heart rate machine, appears and increases in volume. In the third loop, a sub-aqueous sound at high

Table 13.6: Key semiotic realisations

Meanings or functions	*Key semiotic realisation*		
	Language	*Sound*	*Image*
Social distance	No dialog realised	Non-emotional, monotone, machine-like synthetic voice	Small character mode, rational font style, cold colours, long shot, text is hard to read
Involvement	Personal pronoun 'I' and 'we' in contrast to 'they' ('we are all in the same boat'), mental processes, informal language	Polyrhythmic sounds realised as wrap-around sound, audience in the centre of the sound.	—

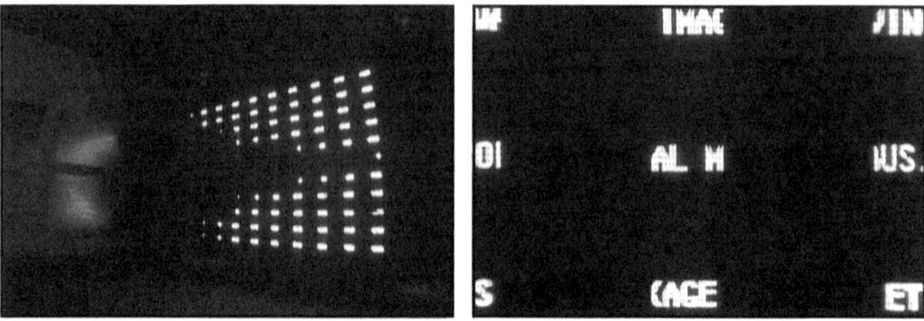

Figure 13.8: Pattern on the grid

Figure 13.9: Big mode

frequency can be heard. With the fourth loop, the synthetic male voice returns. This time, however, it sounds distorted and even more machine-like than in the other scenes. The voice is a strong reverberating sound and overlaps to the extent that it is impossible to understand anything. It turns into a low frequency murmuring sound realising a denaturalised machine-like environment.

The verbal messages in this scene do not seem to be as important as in the other scenes. Table 13.7 shows examples of clauses extracted from five different screens. They represent a list of topics, which do not build a coherent text. Most of them are material and relational clauses realising such speech acts as statements and demands. The last example indicates on-going communication where the writer is directly addressing the person he/she is reacting to (‘*sirmephisto*’).

13.3.5 Intermodal relations

Table 13.8 shows the intermodal relations of the three modes enacting representations of an individual voice and a mass voice in this work of art.

Table 13.7: Text displayed on screens

Process: Speech act	*Example*
Material: Statement	Bin Laden et al **made** the same mistake as the Japanese **did** with the attack of ...
Material: Demand	**reduce** each image **to make** it like 250k
Relational: Statement	being naked outside in the cold ... **can’t be** all too impressive ...
Material: Demand	too dangerous ... **eat** them first and **stuff** them later ...
Relational: Statement	my horses **aren’t** in stalls sirmephisto they **have** 5 acres to play in and ...

Table 13.8: Key semiotic realisations and intermodal relations

	Representations of individual		*Representations of mass*
Mode	**Key semiotic resource**		**Key semiotic resource**
Verbal	– Full clauses, personal	O	– Ellipses and noun-phrases, no
	pronoun 'I'	P	context
	– Focusing on being and sensing	P	– Focusing on "world" – topics
	REINFORCEMENT	O	**REINFORCEMENT**
Visual	– Big fonts realised as single	S	– Small fonts realised as visual
	statements	I	patterns
	– Slow motion	T	– Fast motion
	– Screens becoming active one	I	– Screens becoming active all
	by one	O	at once
	– Easy to read	**N**	– Hard or impossible to read
	REINFORCEMENT		**REINFORCEMENT**
Aural	– Single voice realised like a		– Murmuring of many voices
	friend		– Hard or impossible to
	– Easy to understand		understand
	– Natural sounds		– Machine-like sounds

Along the vertical line, the semiotic resources of the different modes reinforce each other to realise representations of individual and mass. Along the horizontal line, there is an intermodal relation of opposition between the semiotic resources of one mode and the semiotic resources of the different modes, which produce tension and visitor engagement.

In terms of interpersonal relations, functions of social nearness and social distance are opposed to each other, realising the dilemma of online communication, in which people are connected to each other in a virtual network and communicate, but are isolated and disembodied because they lack semiotic resources to express their individuality. This dilemma gives the installation a melancholic touch.

13.4 Conclusion

At first sight, the way *Listening Post* is designed relates to the genre of news texts that are presented on radio or TV. The physical appearance of the installation resembles a big screen and places the audience in a watching position. As in the news genre, most of the verbal messages that are displayed or read here are realised as statements giving information in high modality. Compared with news texts, however, the information given is strongly reduced in this artwork and is represented as a list of topics. Moreover, the information in *Listening Post* is not filtered by a reporter but by algorithms representing the topics that are most frequently discussed in the English-speaking online community. News reporters try to be objective. This is realised linguistically by several patterns: the use of formal language, no references to the writer, thematic prominence, frequent use of embedding, lexical density, sparse use of attitudinal loaded vocabulary and reference to "well known" and generalised participants and terms (see Eggins and Martin 1997 for a study of different genres and language use). In contrast to that, the language used in *Listening Post* is informal, makes frequent reference to the writer, who is grammatically the subject 'I', has a low level of nominalisation, is oriented to activity and sensing, and uses everyday vocabulary. Thus, the artwork in question resembles a reaction to the latest news and relates to the genre of personal letters and casual online conversation. The word 'Post' in the title also suggests this interpretation.

Listening Post is temporally organised by rhythm, such as loops in the musical patterns and repetition in visual motion (see Stillar (2005) for Loops as a Genre Resource). Regularly recurring semiotic resources, such as the dark screens and the short acoustic pause at the end of each scene, link the scenes of the installation together, with each new scene extending the others by simply adding new information. The verbal messages filtered by the algorithm are reorganised in this new context as in a montage. A dramatic effect is realised by opposing loud with low frequency sounds and visual appearance with disappearance.

In terms of composition and design, *Listening Post* is visually balanced. It construes a flat anarchical organisation and is presented at frontal and eye level angle, which realises an interpersonal meaning of involvement and a relationship of equals among the participants of the installation, the installation itself and the audience. On the one hand, the features of three-dimensionality, such as the physical appearance of the installation, the material and the light conditions, realise abstract truth and position the viewer in a setting of unreality similar to watching a movie. On the other hand, the audience of *Listening Post* is placed in a supernatural, omniscient position, watching and listening to the mass of online communication, extracted from real time data as if they were inside the virtual organism or space, immersed in the environment by wrap-around sounds and engaged in the social functions and meanings realised in the verbal, visual and aural modes of communication.

The analysis has revealed that *Listening Post* enacts representations of an individual and a collective voice in terms of experiential meaning and establishes social relationships of distance and nearness. The individual voice is realised in Scene 1 and this 'voice' basically provokes social nearness and involvement. In contrast, Scenes 2, 3 and 4 realise a mass voice that is mainly representing social distance in functional terms. The virtual space of online communication, where the individuals come into contact, is represented as a place where some sort of exchange is possible. But the individual as an isolated voice disappears in the large amount of communication that is going on among the masses. To realise the functional meanings mentioned above, *Listening Post* activates semiotic resources of the aural, the visual and the verbal modes of communication as well as features of three-dimensionality, such as physical appearance, light conditions and room arrangement. These modes work to produce an overall effect in two ways. On the one hand, they reinforce each other's meanings while, on the other hand, they stand in opposition to each other in order to produce tension and to engage the visitor.

Notes

1. All the figures in this chapter are images or screenshots taken from the website http://www.earstudio.com/projects/listeningpost.html with the artist's kind permission.
2. Spelling and other mistakes made by the people communicating with each other in the virtual space are represented here as in the original artwork.
3. Here the term mode refers to one of the context variables – field, tenor, mode – (for a detailed description see Eggins and Martin 1997: 242).

Source of data

http://www.earstudio.com/projects/listeningpost.html

References

Eggins, S. and Martin J. R. 1997. Genres and registers of discourse. In van Dijk, T. A. (ed.) *Discourse as Structure and Process. Discourse Studies: A Multidisciplinary Introduction, Vol. 1.* London: Sage, 230–256.

Halliday, M. A. K. 1978. *Language as Social Semiotic. The Social Interpretation of Language and Meaning.* London: Arnold.
Halliday, M. A. K. 1994. *An Introduction to Functional Grammar* (2nd edition). London: Arnold.
Kress, G. and van Leeuwen, T. 1996. *Reading Images: The Grammar of Visual Design.* London: Routledge.
Kress, G. and van Leeuwen, T. 2001. *Multimodal Discourse. The Modes and Media of Contemporary Communication.* London: Arnold.
Manovich, L. 2006. The poetics of augmented space. *Visual Communication,* 5/2: 219–240.
O'Toole, M. 1994. *The Language of Displayed Art.* London: Leicester University Press.
Rubin, M. and Hansen, B. 2001. Babble online: applying statistics and design to sonify the internet. Proceedings of ICAD. Espoo, 1–6.
Rubin, M. and Hansen, B. 2002. Listening post: giving voice to online communication. Proceedings of ICAD. Kyoto, 1–4.
Stillar, G. 2005. Loops as genre resources. *Folia Linguistica,* XXXIX/1–2: 197–212.
van Leeuwen, Theo 1999. *Speech, Music, Sound.* London: Palgrave Macmillan.
van Leeuwen, Theo 2005. *Introducing Social Semiotics.* London: Routledge.

14 Movies 'reloaded' into commercial reality: representational structures in *The Matrix* trilogy promotional posters

Arianna Maiorani

14.1 Introduction

When the first episode of *The Matrix* movie trilogy was released in 1999, it marked the beginning of a new trend in science fiction movies. It was the first film *about* the internet era made and released *in* the internet era, in a socio-cultural context where the possibility of accessing an alternative virtual reality is part of everyday life and where internet communities bring together people coming from different 'real' communities. Participants in these virtual communities, including occasional web-users, were already used to sharing the notion of 'virtual space', where they had a virtual identity and a virtual nickname. Internet users also shared an internet language and a certain knowledge of the web's ways and means (skills, tools, what was allowed, what was forbidden and by whom, etc.). The ability to use this particular code highlighted the difference between new users and 'masters' (not to mention hackers), establishing degrees of capacity to manage the web which were and still are comparable to social classes.

By addressing this very large, mixed public of internet users, *The Matrix* movie brought for the first time this virtual world on to the big screen, with an unexpected and very surprising story. While the classic science fiction movie plot develops from an 'anchorage' to the 'real world' and then gets away from it, *The Matrix* story turns things upside down. The beginning of the movie is set in what seems to be the present-day real world, which later becomes revealed to be a programme where people unconsciously live a virtual life. In the 'real world' human beings are kept in a state of perpetual sleep, and their bodies, plugged in enormous machines, provide energy to the artificial intelligences which created the Matrix itself. This is what made *The Matrix* trilogy mark a turning point. These movies erased the border between reality and 'virtuality', portraying the 'real' world as actually a 'fiction of science' rather than a science fiction vision of a future reality.

All these factors contributed to the particular social impact that this trilogy had on a worldwide audience, which was reached by a promotional campaign largely carried out by posters. This campaign developed over the years according to the audience's response to each movie as well as to each movie promotion.

This chapter investigates the multimodal interplay between visual and verbal semiotics of the particular discourse used in the campaign posters through addressing the following four points:

- how the poster campaign developed and why it changed progressively;
- the relation between these changes and the social impact of each single movie;
- how the posters campaign was progressively affected by marketing targets;
- how the market itself was affected by the development of the posters campaign.

In relations to these points, two general factors have to be kept in mind about movie advertising.

- Campaigns created for a single movie foreground salient features of the plot and the characters (i.e. special powers, characterising gadgets, look style, locations) which may also be useful for further campaigns. In fact, if a movie develops into a sequel or a trilogy, the potential public of fans will expect these elements to mark continuity;
- Campaigns created for sequels have to maintain continuity while singling out the novelty of a new product, so as to address fans as well as potential new audiences.

This chapter analyses the way the interplay between verbal and visual semiotics develops through a select corpus of posters[1] advertising *The Matrix* movie trilogy. After the theoretical introduction of Section 14.2, Section 14.3.1 analyses posters of *The Matrix* campaign (1999), focusing on the way the movie is presented. In Section 14.3.2, posters of *The Matrix*

Reloaded (2003) are analysed and differences with respect to the first movie campaign are highlighted. In Section 14.3.3 posters of *The Matrix Revolutions* (2003) are analysed and compared with the previous campaign. Conclusions on the whole trilogy campaign are drawn in Section 14.4.

14.2 Multimodal analysis: an approach to multi-semiotic communication

The method of analysis used in this chapter is based on the grammar of visual design developed by Kress and van Leeuwen (1996, 2006) and on the Hallidayan functional grammar (1985, 1994). The interplay between visual and verbal semiotics throughout the corpus of posters will be the subject of a socio-culturally oriented investigation. The aim is to show how the combination of different semiotic systems is used in advertising discourse in order to achieve three different goals at the same time:

- advertising each single movie of *The Matrix* trilogy;
- creating links between the movies of the trilogy;
- eliciting interaction from the audience in order to make them both watch the movies and buy by-products of the same trademark.

This analysis is based mainly (but not exclusively) on *representational structures* for visual semiotics, and on the *transitivity structure* for verbal semiotics. It will show how these structures, in combination with others, are used according to the *resource integration principle* (Bauldry and Thibault, 2006) as components of a semiotic resource system which is typical of advertising multimodal texts.[2]

As Kress and van Leeuwen's, and Halliday's, models are essentially based on Western modes of representation and on the English language, my corpus includes original posters exclusively released in the USA and the UK Kress and Van Leeuwen (1996: 2006) system, which is based on three main metafunctions introduced by Halliday (1985) and applied to visual semiotics: the Ideational metafunction activates representational meanings which are realised by representational structures (visual Processes and Circumstances). The Interpersonal metafunction activates interactive meanings like Perspective and expression of Power (horizontal and vertical angle), kind of Contact (demand or offer) and modality. The Textual metafunction activates compositional meanings through framing and salience of elements, and information values culturally attributed to the different areas of the visual space.

This investigation mainly focuses on *Narrative Processes* (designing social action), *Conceptual Processes* (designing social constructs), and *Circumstances* (those of Location, Accompaniment, and Means). It will be shown how the interplay between these visual structures and the transitivity structure of the slogans produces *integrated ideational meanings,* which basically rely on a central notion: the fuzzy border between the virtual and the real world,[3] a groundbreaking element of the plot in the whole movie trilogy and a key concept for marketing the by-products of the movies.

14.3 *The Matrix* trilogy and its posters

The plot developed in *The Matrix* movie trilogy is groundbreaking in the field of Science Fiction movies and movie technology. The story starts in what seems to be the real world, where a young hacker, Thomas Anderson, is approached by a group of people who look and act like outlaws. The group leader, Morpheus, gives the hacker a pill which makes him wake up in what is actually the real world: a destroyed planet where human beings are used as energy-providing bodies plugged into machines which support artificial intelligences. What keeps humans alive is a virtual existence, in which they unconsciously live, in a program created by the same artificial intelligences: the Matrix. Programs that create a human form are responsible for catching and eliminating hackers because these can find out the truth about the Matrix. There is also a community of human beings, Morpheus and his people, who were freed from the Matrix and who live in Zion, an underground hidden city, waiting for the leader who, according to a prophecy, will destroy the Matrix and free all men and women. Thomas will be revealed as this 'elect' leader, and will take the name of Neo. He will also find a companion, a young woman named Trinity. In the end, however, the fuzzy border between 'reality' and 'virtuality' becomes even fuzzier. In the third movie the final truth is revealed. Neo, as well as the whole community of Zion, are part of the Matrix program too. Neo's sacrifice and communion with supreme artificial intelligence will restore the balance between all beings living in the Matrix (human consciences, programs), but the uncertainty about what is the 'real reality' remains.

The plot combines many Western and Eastern cultural elements: a Christological myth of salvation, oriental martial arts, Zen meditation, Buddhist illumination, the ontological questions on what is real and what is not real, and on what is human and what is not human, the fight of the few against the many, and the new scenarios available after the 'advent' of the internet. These are only the main themes touched by these movies, whose global cultural impact on the twenty-first-century internet-oriented society has been very significant (Slevin 2000).

The three movies were advertised by three different poster campaigns, whose strategy aimed progressively at advertising not only the motion pictures but all the by-products and trademarks which were included in the *Matrix* market. The corpus of posters which has been used for this analysis comprises 11 posters:

- two from *The Matrix* campaign: the US theatrical poster (Fig. 14.1) and one international theatrical poster (Fig. 14.2);
- six from *The Matrix Reloaded*: two posters with characters (Figs. 14.3 and 14.4), one International Art poster (Fig. 14.5), two 'teaser posters' (Figs 14.6 and 14.7) and the Imax poster (Fig. 14.8);
- three from *The Matrix Revolutions*: one international poster (Fig. 14.9), the 'teaser poster' (Fig. 14.10), and the Imax poster (Fig. 14.11).

The posters belonging to each single movie campaign will be discussed in Sections 14.3.1, 14.3.2 and 14.3.3 in a chronological order.

14.3.1 *The Matrix* posters

When *The Matrix* posters began to appear in 1999, the film that was advertised was clearly an action movie, presumably a science fiction one. The campaign was not very different from those created for previous releases of action or science fiction movies. The two posters displayed in Figures 14.1 and 14.2 follow a standard format. They include the main characters, the title, a slogan and production features.

In both posters, representational structures realise Narrative Processes in the particular form of what here is defined as '*concealed*' reaction. In other words, these processes are determined by the action of looking and performed by represented participants. In the posters, all characters wear different models of very dark sunglasses: a salient, distinguishing feature for each represented participant. These conceal both the direction of characters' gazes and their eyes. Therefore the reaction can be both transactional – having a Phenomenon – or non-transactional. This '*concealed*' reaction also makes the interpersonal category of Contact very ambiguous, since it is impossible to tell if these posters realise a demand

Figure 14.1:
The Matrix: 'On April 2nd the Fight for the Future Begins'

Figure 14.2:
The Matrix: 'Believe the unbelievable'

(when represented participants 'demand' the viewer's attention by looking directly at them) or an offer (when represented participants do not look at the viewer) or both. Moreover, in the poster in Figure 14.1, slight action is realised both by the characters holding weapons and by the movement of the central character's coat, which suggests a protective act on Neo's part. In both posters, vertically aligned numbers and symbols in the background realise an unexpected, highly suggestive, Locative Circumstance. In the poster in Figure 14.2, these numbers and symbols even build a sort of frame around the three main characters. Both posters realise Analytical Conceptual Processes (since each character is the Carrier of his/her own Attributes), as well as a type of Classificational Process where all characters seem to be subordinate to Neo. A kind of 'trinity' is also spatially foregrounded: Neo as the Son, Morpheus as the Father, Trinity as the Holy Spirit. Accordingly, the fourth character in Figure 14.1, the 'Judas', is positioned on Neo's far right side. This kind of Participants' disposition in the visual space hints at the pseudo-Christological root of the plot the audience will recognise when watching the movie.

The slogan of the poster in Figure 14.1, 'On April 2nd the Fight for the Future Begins', is realised as a declarative clause; it implies a high degree of certainty on the part of the speaker/sender of the message. Here we find an inanimate, non-typical Actor, realising a kind of Process, which expresses the dynamicity of a Material Process and, at the same time, the immanence of an Existential Process. The fight is therefore foregrounded as inanimate Actor instead of visually represented fighters, while the date of the release of the movie is put in a marked thematic position.

The slogan in Figure 14.2, "Believe the Unbelievable", is realised as an imperative Mood clause, expressing a strong invitation. Here, grammatical parallelism focuses on oxymoron, thus foregrounding an important element of the plot.

Both the title and the slogan occupy the lower part of the visual space of the posters, which, as far as visual composition is concerned, is usually the area typically occupied by elements of the 'real'. Coding orientation (see Table 14.1), due to the values of modality markers, is naturalistic.

The main purpose of this kind of promotional campaign seems to be that of attracting the viewer's attention anticipating some elements of the plot and highlighting the date of release.

14.3.2 *The Matrix Reloaded* posters

When the second and third movies were released in 2003, within a few months, the 'Matrix community' of fans already existed. The movie was largely discussed in internet forums and blogs, and on websites, as well as through more' traditional' communication and information media. A wide range of issues was covered, from the most cryptic points of the Matrix

Table 14.1: Modality markers values of *The Matrix* posters (see Figures 14.1 and 14.2)

Modality marker	*Value*
Colour saturation	medium
Colour diversification	medium
Colour modulation	high
Brightness	medium
Illumination	medium/high
Depth	medium
Pictorial detail	high
Contextualisation	medium
Coding orientation	**NATURALISTIC**

philosophy to useful 'tips' for progressing in video games. The Matrix website was in full operation.

The poster campaign of *The Matrix Reloaded* differs from that of the first movie both in material and formal ways. The material difference is quantitative. For *Reloaded* four different types of posters were created, some of which were not exclusively devoted to advertise the movie. Here, samples from all series are analysed in different sections: in the first section, posters with *Reloaded* characters; in the next section, the International Art poster; then the 'teaser posters'; and in the last section, the Imax poster. The formal differences of each of these series with respect to the first movie posters will be pointed out in each of the above sections.

The character posters in *The Matrix Reloaded*

The poster in Figure 14.3 is an example of the Reloaded series, whose features are common to all other samples.

Several features differentiate these posters formally from *The Matrix* movie posters.

- There is only one represented participant/character (except in the case of the vampire twins, which in the movie are visualised as the double image of a single person).

Figure 14.3: *The Matrix Reloaded:* an example of the characters series

- There is no background.
- There is no slogan, only the title with the date of release and other similar details at the bottom of the poster.
- Each represented participant realises only the typical '*concealed*' non-transactional reaction against a blank background apart from one case (Morpheus's poster) where there is slight non-transactional action.
- Conceptual Processes are realised only in analytical form, being the Attributes of each participant/Carrier foregrounded by the effects of light and shade, and illumination.
- All these posters are static. The represented participants seem to be portrayed as dummies for fashion photographs rather than representations within the context of the movie.
- The coding orientation, according to the values of modality markers is mainly sensory as shown in Table 14.2.

The dummy-like aspect (and function) of the represented participants is even more enhanced in the next series, where the same characters are represented only in part. The poster in Figure 14.4 typifies these 'cuts'.

Here the non-exhaustive Analytical Process cuts off the most characterising part of each dummy-body, the face, along with the most characterising items, the sunglasses. For those who are unfamiliar with *The Matrix* movie, this could well be understood as a promotional campaign of a new fashion trademark. Furthermore, also in this series only the title of the movie is present, again at the bottom of the poster, along with the date of release and other similar details.

Table 14.2: Modality marker values of the *Reloaded* characters posters (see Figure 14.3)

Modality marker	*Value*
Colour saturation	high
Colour diversification	medium
Colour modulation	high
Brightness	high
Illumination	high
Depth	low
Pictorial detail	high
Contextualisation	low
Coding orientation	**SENSORY**

Figure 14.4: *The Matrix Reloaded*: an example of the 'cut characters' series.

In the absence of slogans, the effectiveness of the visual features of these posters is based on the interplay between verbal semiotics and the viewer's knowledge of internet language. In fact, the term *reloaded* in the title is a technical term, which is very well known to internet and computer users; a blank and white background is typically displayed on a computer screen when it is loading or reloading programs from the internet. According to the resource integration principle, here the posters exploit visual and verbal resources to create integrated ideational meanings aimed at eliciting interaction from the viewers, who are enticed to read the posters as web users and thus connect these new visual features to the plot of the first movie. In this way the posters may create continuity between the first and the second movie while also advertising new by-products like sunglasses.

The International Art poster in *The Matrix Reloaded*

The poster in Figure 14.5 is an example of the series of posters, that follow the character series.

Here, not even the whole head of a character is visible. Again, there is a blank background and the image clearly focuses on the sunglasses. Again, there is no slogan; only the title and production features are positioned in

Figure 14.5: *The Matrix Reloaded*: an example of the International Art posters

the lower part of each poster of this series. The movie seems to have become a sort of excuse for advertising the Matrix sunglasses as a fashion item. In fact, it is only in the 'embedded' scenes reflected on the sunglass lenses that features of the first movie campaign can be found: some action and reaction Processes, locative Circumstances, more than one participant.

In this particular series, then, two levels of advertisement coexist, delivering two different kinds of promotional message. The first level advertises sunglasses; the second 'embedded' level advertises the movie. Paradoxically, the Matrix movie campaign seems to be embedded in the 'Matrix look' campaign. This is due to the social impact of the first movie and its effect on the market of the movie by-products. After the release of *The Matrix*, the gadgets and clothes worn by characters were largely purchased by fans and others to be worn not only at fan conferences or similar occasions, but as items for everyday. Clothes, sunglasses, shoes, boots, trenches, etc. were part of a thriving market, whose clients were also people who had perhaps never watched the movies and certainly did not want to identify with any movie character. It is simply the case that the 'Matrix look' became fashionable in the real world.

The Matrix had highlighted and exploited the fuzzy border between fiction and reality foregrounding one of the major issues of the internet era: the problematic nature of reality and the difficulty to define it. The social behaviour elicited by the 'Matrix look' market enhanced this fuzziness and testified the social response to the movies as cultural events. Accordingly, dressing like the Matrix characters became trendy, and many prêt-à-porter trademarks started to produce clothes which imitated the movie characters' appearances. Fans consciously adopted the looks, clothes, and hair styles of those movie characters who enter the Matrix to distinguish themselves from the unconscious masses. Other people adopted this look simply because it had become fashionable through fashion magazines and shows.

The analysis performed so far shows that, with the second movie posters, the interest of the promotional campaign shifts from the movie itself to the commercial gadgets and fashion style it has introduced onto the market, almost turning the motion picture into a sort of 'big spot' for by-products. These by-products came either from the Warner Bros company itself or fashion firms, and even virtual shops, which sold them through the internet. For example, a Nepalese tailor shop, specialising in coats and jackets, sells Neo's coat (www.baronboutique.com/movie_replica.htm 15/06/2007). What becomes evident with the posters of the second movie campaign is that, in order to sell the whole range of the Matrix products, advertisers rely atypically and unexpectedly on the viewers' interaction with the multimodal messages[4] realised by the posters.

The 'teaser posters' in *The Matrix Reloaded*

For *The Matrix Reloaded* a series of 'teaser posters' was also created where no character appeared (Figs 14.6 and 14.7). This choice was most probably intended to separately foreground the slogans which, otherwise, would probably have drawn the viewers' attention away from the 'Matrix look'.

The first important feature to be noticed about these posters is that here, as in the first movie campaign, vertically aligned numbers and symbols function as Locative Circumstance. This construes a visual connection with *The Matrix* campaign as well as eliciting once more a 'web user reading' of the message. The poster in Figure 14.6, where the greenish 'matrix rain' of numbers and symbols is set against a black background, only displays the year of the movie release at the bottom. Not even a title is given but what is represented suggests a 'reloading' of some sort. The poster in Figure 14.7 foregrounds the specific date of release in central position, against the same 'matrix rain'. Here too there is no title but a slogan appears, though less salient than the large date numbers, in the

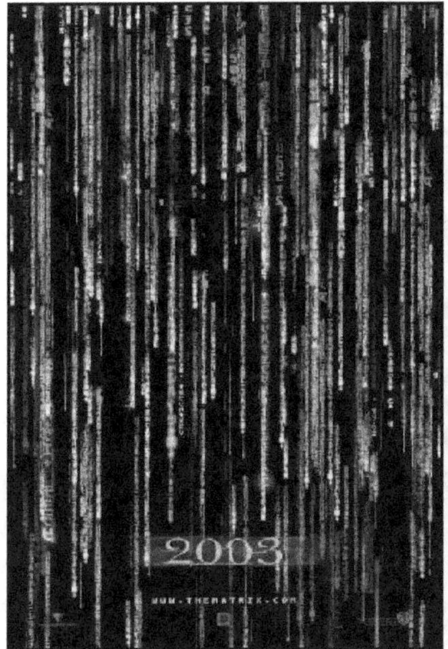

Figure 14.6: *The Matrix Reloaded*: teaser poster with year

Figure 14.7: *The Matrix Reloaded*: Manfrotto 055 tripod teaser poster with complete date

upper part of the poster: 'Free your mind.' This imperative clause explicitly invites the viewer to perform an action on him/herself in connection with the act of looking at the poster and its reloading 'matrix rain.' Both posters feature the Matrix website address. Also in both posters, visual and verbal semiotics contribute to the erasure of the border between reality and virtuality. By recognizing the poster as an advertisement for another Matrix movie, notwithstanding the absence of a title, the viewer implicitly 'enters' the world of the Matrix.

The Imax poster in *The Matrix Reloaded*

The Matrix Reloaded campaign was also characterised by an Imax poster, where the movie was advertised along with the technologically innovative chain of theatres where it was to be released (Fig. 14.8).

This poster is very similar to the 'teaser posters.' The 'matrix rain' is once more displayed against a black background but here the spatial composition is polarised by the title and the slogan.

The title is positioned in the area linked to the dimension of 'reality,' towards the bottom. The slogan is positioned near the top, in the area linked to the 'ideal' dimension, since the viewer is presumed not yet to

Figure 14.8: *The Matrix Reloaded*: the Imax poster

have seen the movie. The imperative clause inviting the viewer, 'Reload in Imax', realises a material Process strictly inherent in an activity involving the use of computers and internet, which the implied Actor 'you', the addressee of the message, is invited to perform. The slogan is also accompanied by a sub-slogan, "Think Big", which realises a Mental Process, whose 'bigness' is also related to the big screens in Imax theatres. The visual Locative Circumstance recalls computer screens displayed in the movie when characters enter the Matrix. According to the *resource integration principle*, therefore, this poster also uses resources from the visual and verbal systems to realise integrated ideational meanings in a message which elicits interaction. The viewer is actually invited to enter the Matrix as if he/she were a character within the movie: the 'door', the point of access, being the Imax theatre.

14.3.3 *The Matrix Revolutions* posters

The Imax theatre technology and all other novelties that characterised the release of *Reloaded* had lost their novelty when posters advertising the third movie of the trilogy, *The Matrix Revolutions*, started to appear all around the world. Furthermore, they were released just a few months after *Reloaded*, as was the movie.

The main focus of this third campaign seems to have shifted back to the movie as the main product advertised, since all the by-products had been 'launched' just a few months before. These posters can be considered as a 'synthesis' of the previous campaigns because they share characteristics of posters belonging to both the first and second campaigns. In this section, the sample posters are analysed according to which one of the three series they belong to. The next three sections focus respectively on, first, one international poster, then the 'teaser poster' and finally the Imax poster. A comparison with previous campaigns is included in each analysis.

The international poster in *The Matrix Revolutions*

Figure 14.9 shows a representative sample of the international posters released for *Revolutions.*

Though the majority of posters belonging to this series represent a single participant, this one has been chosen to show all the characteristics which this campaign shares with the previous campaigns.

- Represented participants realise both 'concealed' reaction and action as in the first campaign.

Figure 14.9: *The Matrix Revolution*: an example of international poster

- There are locative Circumstances as well as Circumstances of means as in the first campaign.
- Light and shade depict the design of the characters' clothes and weapons thus providing a type of 'aural' background characterised by the Matrix numbers and symbols as in the first campaign.
- Posters feature in most cases just one iconically[1] represented Participant as in the second campaign.
- When represented alone, participants almost only realise a Conceptual Analytical Process as in the second campaign.
- Movie locations are almost never represented as in the second campaign.
- Ambiguous contact is a constant interpersonal feature as in the first and second campaigns.

Coding orientation in these posters derives from a synthesis of different values too. As Table 14.3 shows, it is a hybrid of the natural and sensory values of modality markers.

This hybridity is the only new feature as far as visual semiotics is concerned. In this visual space, all verbal elements seem to rediscover their 'original' place. All samples have a slogan, which occupies the top area of the poster, while the title, as well as the date of release, occupy the bottom area.

Unlike the previous campaigns, the third one is characterised by a unique slogan, 'Everything that has a beginning has an end,' which precisely signals the end of the trilogy. The priority is in this case again that of

Table 14.3: Modality markers values of the *Revolutions* international posters (see Figure 14.9)

Modality Marker	*Value*
Colour saturation	high (sensory)
Colour diversification	low (sensory)
Colour modulation	medium/high (sensory)
Brightness	medium (natural)
Illumination	high (natural)
Depth	medium (natural)
Pictorial detail	high (natural)
Contextualisation	low (sensory)
Coding Orientation	**HYBRID: between natural and sensory**

advertising the movie as the main product and the final episode of a trilogy. The declarative clause here does not realise any invitation to the viewer, but simply implies a high degree of certainty about the fact that some kind of 'ending' is achieved in the movie. For the first time in all Matrix campaigns, a Relational Process of the possessive type is realised. Once more, interaction is elicited on the part of the viewer by integrated ideational meanings. Since a Relational possessive Process is also embedded in the Possessor, the viewer will have to interpret this reiterative slogan as addressing the whole trilogy, whose characters are represented as icons against the well known 'matrix rain'.

The 'teaser poster' in *The Matrix Revolutions*

The *Revolutions* campaign also adopts another characteristic of the *Reloaded* campaign: the 'teaser poster', in one poster which does not feature the title as shown in Figure 14.10.

As in the *Reloaded* teasers, discussed in Section above, this one too features the greenish 'matrix rain' against a black background. However, here it only occupies the upper part of the visual space as a reminder of the movie. The slogan is written in a vertical line which seems to drop from the 'matrix rain' and must be read from top to bottom. The final

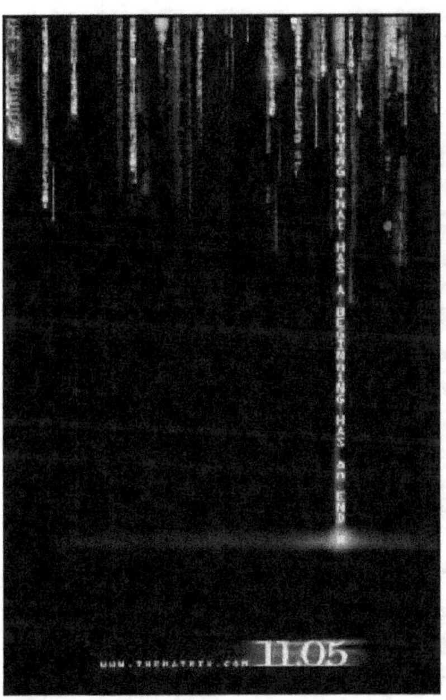

Figure 14.10: *The Matrix Revolutions*: the teaser poster

letter is actually a cursor, which follows the word 'end' and beams over the big numbers of the date of release, which come immediately after the website address. Both the slogan and the date are positioned near the bottom and towards the right side of the poster, the visual area typically containing the 'new' information. This poster has evidently been created according to the *resource integration principle* and in order to elicit interaction on the part of the viewer. Because the slogan is linked to the visually represented elements, the viewer will easily infer that this is a teaser poster for the final episode of the Matrix trilogy.

The Imax poster in *The Matrix Revolutions*

A specific advertisement for Imax theatres and technology was created also for *Revolutions*. This poster (Fig. 14.11) is almost identical to the teaser poster but, in addition, instead of beaming over the date of release, the slogan cursor beams over a slogan, 'The Imax Revolution.' Below it, the date of release and the website address follow.

Integrated ideational meanings elicit once more interaction from the viewer but here they work on two levels. On one level, the visual elements and the slogan remind the viewer of the trilogy and of its final episode. On another level, the Imax advertisement relies on its similarity to the

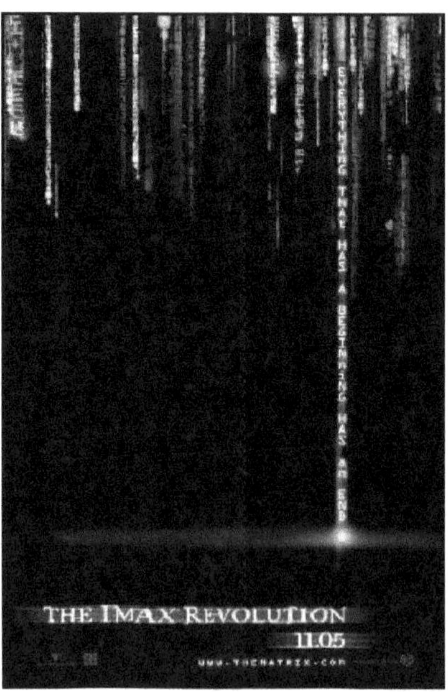

Figure 14.11: *The Matrix Revolutions*: the Imax poster

teaser poster to highlight for the viewer the connection between the movie title and the complementary slogan. The viewer's interaction is crucial to the success of the campaign.

14.4 Conclusion

The purpose of this multimodal analysis is to investigate how the poster campaign of one of the most successful movie trilogies released at the turn of the twentieth/twenty-first centuries has developed in relation to two social phenomena:

1. the birth, growth and consolidation of the 'Matrix community' with its 'Matrix culture', made up of fans, who collect items, communicate on dedicated web forums and blogs, and create their own Matrix virtual identity.
2. the creation of a 'Matrix market' of by-products and correlated trademarks, which addressed not only fans but all buyers who were attracted by the 'Matrix look'.

The analysis of the whole trilogy campaign has shown that a progressively increasing demand for viewer interaction was developed through integrated ideational meanings. This demand was based on a fundamental factor which characterises the whole trilogy plot: the ambiguous, unidentifiable border between fiction and everyday life, between virtuality and reality, which are all social issues generated by contemporary internet culture.

The use of the *resource integration principle* in the posters of the second and third movie campaigns marks a break away from the more 'traditional' posters of the first movie campaign. Material as well as formal differences of posters used to advertise *Reloaded* and *Revolutions* have been highlighted. These differences are due to the social impact of *The Matrix* and to the creation and marketing of Matrix by-products. The interplay between visual and verbal semiotics as it develops in the whole corpus of posters testifies of the Matrix social phenomenon.

This kind of research shows how a multimodal analysis[5] of multisemiotic texts can be an effective method for studying how society elaborates cultural elements in time, modifying and exploiting them according to social and commercial phenomena. It also shows that multimodal discourse analysis is a significant step towards understanding contemporary ways of communication. In examining texts through the integration of different semiotic systems, multimodal discourse analysis turns transdisciplinarity into multidisciplinarity.[6] This perspective offers researchers an effective analytic tool for developing investigations in several fields of study: cultural studies, semiotics, communications, media, humanities as well as linguistics.[7] It also offers a systematic way of examining the new semiotic environment offered by the internet in order to gain a deeper understanding of our internet-oriented world.

The Matrix movies are a science fiction trilogy where our reality is seen as a fictional world. The 'Matrix community' and the 'Matrix market' are the social and commercial outcomes of the impact these works of fiction have had on our culture. The multimodal analysis employed here has revealed how the multimodal discourse realised by the posters advertising the trilogy can be regarded as building a semiotic bridge between fiction and reality, revealing the new, mystifying nature of the internet and its hyper-semiotic space.

Notes

1. Original posters do not appear in this chapter. Computer screen shots are used to show descriptions of original materials. Fair Law for reproduction of copyrighted material in works for academic and educational purposes applies to these.
2. The *'resource integration principle'* 'views a semiotic resource as something used for the purposes of making meaning ... Semiotic modalities. such as language, gesture, depiction, gaze and so on, can be formalised and described as *resource systems* in this sense. A *semiotic resource system* is thus a system of semiotic forms that we can *use* for the purposes of making texts. The forms have particular *functions* in the texts in which they are used. The notion of resource therefore captures these two aspects – *use* and *function* – of the relevance of semiotic systems to the texts which these systems make possible. ... Multimodal texts integrate selections of different semiotic resources to their principles of organisation ... A *semiotic resource system* is thus a system of possible meanings and forms typically used to make meanings in particular contexts.' (Baldry, A. and P. Thibault, 2006: 18).
3. 'For some time now, there has been, in Western culture, a distinct preference for monomodality [...] More recently this situation has begun to reverse [...] The desire for crossing boundaries inspired twentieth-century semiotics. The main schools of semiotics all sought to develop a theoretical framework applicable to all semiotic modes [...] We move away from the idea that different modes in multimodal texts have strictly bounded and framed specialist tasks [...] Instead we move towards a view of multimodality in

which common semiotic principles operate in and across different modes [...]' (Kress and van Leeuwen, 2001: 1–2).

4. 'Advertising is a prominent discourse type in virtually all contemporary societies [...] Because of this prominence, advertising can tell us a good deal about our own society and our own psychology' (Cook, 1992: 5).
5. For the latest developments of multimodal analysis application see in particular O'Halloran 2004 and Ventola *et al.* 2004.
6. 'Social semiotics is not "pure" theory, not a self-contained field. It only comes into its own when it is applied to specific instances and specific problems, and it always requires immersing oneself not just in semiotic concepts and methods as such but also in some other field' (van Leeuwen, 2005: xiii).
7. 'Meaning resides so strongly and pervasively in other systems of meaning, in a multiplicity of visual, aural, behavioural, and other codes, that a concentration on words alone is not enough [...] So, a theory of verbal language has to be seen in the context of a theory of all sign systems as socially constituted, and treated as social practices' (Hodge and Kress, 1988: vii).

Sources of poster data

www.warnerbros.com
www.whatisthematrix.warnerbros.com
www.allposters.com

References

Baldry, A. and Thibault, P. 2006. *Multimodal Transcription and Text Analysis.* London: Equinox.

Beasley, R. and Danesi, M. 2002. *Persuasive Signs. The Semiotics of Advertising.* Berlin and New York: Mouton de Gruyter.

Chatman, S. 1978. *Story and Discourse: Narrative Structure in Fiction and Film.* Ithaca and London: Cornell University Press.

Cook, G. 1992. *The Discourse of Advertising.* London: Routledge.

Gordon, D. 2003. 'The Matrix Look', *Newsweek Web Exclusive,* 26 April. Retrieved April 2005 from www.newsweek.com.

Halliday, M. A. K and Hasan, R. 1989. *Language, Context and Text.* Oxford: Oxford University Press.

Halliday, M. A. K. and Matthiessen, C. M. I. M. 2004. *An Introduction to Functional Grammar* (3rd edition). London: Arnold.

Hodge, R. and Kress, G. 1988. *Social Semiotics*. Cambridge: Polity Press.
Kress, G. and van Leeuwen, T. 2006. *Reading Images* (2nd edition). London: Routledge.
Kress, G. and van Leeuwen, T. 2001. *Multimodal Discourse: The Modes and Media of Contemporary Communication*. London: Arnold.
La Ferla, R. 2003. 'Allure of the Trench Coat: That "Matrix" look', *New York Times* on line edition, Section 9: 1, 4 May. Retrieved April 2005 from www.newyorktimes.com.
O'Halloran, K. (ed.). 2004. *Multimodal Discourse Analysis*. London and New York: Continuum.
Slevin, J. 2000. *The Internet and Society*. Cambridge: Polity Press.
Tulloch, J. and Jenkins, H. 1995. *Science Fiction Audiences: Watching Dr. Who and Star Trek*. London: Routledge.
van Leeuwen, T. 2005. *Introducing Social Semiotics*. London: Routledge.
Ventola, E., Charles, C. and Kaltenbacher, M. (eds). 2004. *Perspectives on Multimodality*. Amsterdam and Philadelphia, PA: Benjamins.

15 Representing Experience: the co-articulation of verbiage and image in multimodal text

Dai Fei Yang

15.1 Introduction

Multimodal texts enhance communication by using different semiotic resources in meaning-making and in the realisation of social goals and purposes (Martin and Rose 2003; Thibault 2004; Unsworth 2001). In contemporary newspapers, texts are becoming increasingly multimodal and complex in the construction of social values and beliefs (Iedema *et al.* 1994; White 1998). The key contribution of this chapter lies in its eclectic three level approach, which provides a unique, in-depth understanding of highly complex multimodal media texts. It aims to complement the theoretical framework of systemic functional linguistics (SFL) as a mode of presenting temporal and social experience (Halliday, 1994; Hasan, 1996; Martin, 1995, 2001).

This chapter first demonstrates how Bakhtin's concept of time and space in literature studies (1981) can be used to account for the rhetorical connections between the 11 September 2001 attacks (referred to as 'the 9/11 event') and the consequent development of 'war on terror' and the Iraq war. The chapter also applies Bakhtin's concept of metamorphosis (transformation) to explain how children's social experiences, particularly during a catastrophic event, can bring about internal transformations and transmute their concepts of an object or idea into new forms. This argument is further supported in Thibault's work (2004) on how children use their symbolic resources to construct their social experience by reflecting on their immediate environment.

The second part of the chapter applies three levels of analysis: Barthes' (1977) concept of levels of meaning; Bateman and Delin's (2001) five levels of structure; and Kress and van Leeuwen's (1996) grammar of images.

These are used to account for three perspectives: viz the rhetorical significance of images: the structural juxtapositioning of adult verbiage and children's drawings; and the grammar of images in the modelling of ideational meanings.

The chapter concludes with the argument that the distinctive features in the children's drawings were the epitome (Thibault 2004) of success for ensuring greater emotional connections with the readers. The deployment of children's work appears to have helped the editors achieve their social agenda and maximise the sensational nature of the news.

15.2 Social context

On 16 September 2001, the following extract appeared in an editorial in the *Sun Herald*:

> As Australia watched its TV screens in numbed disbelief, it was hard not to think of the children who, in times to come, will find this year defined by the awesome horror of a few short hours and a few mad men in their school history books. (*The Sun Herald*, 16 September 2001: 18).

The article, written five days after the 9/11 event, reported on attempts to deal with concerns about how that event might have impacted on school

THE SUN-HERALD September 16, 2001 AMERICA AT WAR 17

Our children speak out

Schools encourage drawing as an emotional release

LINES OF FIRE: A Lakemba student's drawing.

By MIRANDA WOOD
EDUCATION REPORTER

SCHOOL students across NSW have been encouraged to express their shock and grief at the attacks on the United States, with some pupils drawing graphic pictures of the disaster.

Schools also organised condolence books and prayer sessions last week and held moments of silence to allow students to reflect.

St Therese's School, Lakemba, cancelled morning assembly on Wednesday to pray for those who died.

Principal Steve Conlan said the students were also free to express themselves through words or pictures.

"They were confused," Mr Conlan said. "These were ways to express themselves."

Year 1 student Stephane Leveque drew a picture of people jumping out of the World Trade Center as a plane slammed into it.

"I was sad," he said.

"At first I thought it was a little bit like a movie."

Other younger students drew similar pictures to Stephane's while older students wrote prayers.

Mr Conlan said students wanted to discuss the events in the US.

"We're a multicultural school and we've got kids that have families in the Middle East.

"It must be hard for them as well."

Teachers were asked to monitor students last week and organise counselling if required.

NSW Department of Education school counselling director Eleanor Davidson said NSW schools were prepared for crises including floods, fire or plane crashes. "We have to reinforce normal routines to make sure young children feel safe," Ms Davidson said.

She said schools which had American exchange students had been affected greatly last week.

"They were a group who were very distressed but our counsellors are trained to work with students and support them."

Mr Conlan said it was difficult for parents to shelter their children from the horrific images in New York and Washington.

"It's in the newspaper, on the internet and on television."

The Education Department recommended parents help children deal with the tragedy by monitoring their viewing or turning off the television.

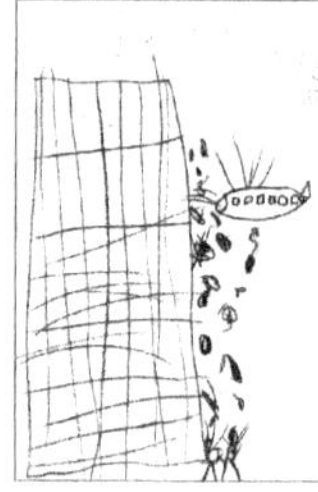

SAD: Stephane Leveque's art.

Figure 15.1: The article: 'Our children speak out'. (*The Sun Herald* (16 September 2001: 17)

children in the state of New South Wales, Australia. It offered advice and strategies on how to help children cope with their distress and grief. The sensational 9/11 event evoked worldwide reaction. In Australia, the sense of shock and anger coupled with some fear was probably not much less than that in America itself. Newspapers, radio and TV programmes carried continuous detailed images of the tragedy and the aftermath. TV stations suspended normal programming to cover developments in New York.

15.3 Traversal of time and space

In his studies on novels, Bakhtin (1981) defined time and space (place) as the two key prerequisites of event-development which together constitute what he called the *temporal chronotope* (1981: 84). In the case of the 9/11 event, the time, 11 September 2001, and the place, the Twin Towers in New York City, were the prerequisites which gave rise to the global anti-terrorism campaign.

Bakhtin further argued that the elements of time and space construe the most essential staging points of any significant event in history and literature and that the intersection of such time and space was often termed as the 'marker' of these events. Reflecting back, the 9/11 event impacted on the world in many ways and on people from all walks of life. In the United States in 2002 and 2003, fear of terrorism resulted in great financial difficulties for numerous international and domestic airlines since people did not feel safe on passenger aircraft and either opted for other means of transport or simply stayed at home. Moreover, life was never the same again for the thousands of families who had lost their loved ones in the tragedy. It was evident that the 9/11 event also led the American government into a long and never-ending campaign of retaliation, wide-ranging anti-terrorism measures and ultimately, if this did not actually cause the war in Iraq, it certainly greatly speeded up its onset. Such a sequence of events forms what Bakhtin (1981) called the *traversal of time*, which includes the time at which the event took place and the times at which the many events followed. In his studies of novels he asserted that the traversal of time usually ended when a conclusion was reached. However, it remains an open question as to whether the traversal of time begun by the 9/11 event has reached a conclusion. Have many families resolved their sadness and been able to start a new life? Has the USA reached its ultimate resolution of the 9/11 event through the Iraq war? The answers to these questions are probably 'no', as, at the time of writing, both the on-going violence in Iraq and terrorist attacks worldwide continued (Glasser, 2005). As reported in a *Washington Post* article 'The number of terrorist attacks worldwide increased nearly fourfold in 2005 to 11,111, with strikes in Iraq accounting for 30 percent of the total, according to statistics released by US counterterrorism officials yesterday' (De Young, 2006).

The connection of time and space of the 9/11 event formed the starting point of the worldwide spatial expansion of the crisis. As already remarked, their distance from the tragedy did not lessen its impact on Australians. On the contrary, its extension in time and space dramatically increased its extraordinary social impact and historical significance. Although millions of Australians demonstrated against the Iraq war, nonetheless, Australian troops were sent to the Iraq war and the anti-terrorism movement is no less than anywhere else in the world. In fact, it might not be too much to claim that the 9/11 event had the same historical significance as Pearl Harbor did in 1941 for Australia.

Bakhtin's theory of traversal of time and space as crucial motifs of event development has been amplified by communications technologies, of which he would have had no knowledge at the time he was developing his concepts. The social impact of these events has been greatly speeded up by communications technology and thus their effects have become much greater than those described in his literature studies.

15.4 Social impact and rhetorical significance

This chapter draws on Bakhtin's (1981: 111) concept of *metamorphosis* (transformation) to explain how children construct new knowledge through their social experience. It provides a new insight into the transformation of the children's concepts of the world induced by the 9/11 event. This adds a parallel perspective to the social construction of ideational meanings in line with SFL theory (Halliday 1994; Hasan 1996; Martin 1995, 2001; Martin and Rose 2003).

In his analysis of Apuleius's classic 'The Golden Ass' (written in 160 CE), Bakhtin (1981) identifies the three fundamental stages of the hero Lucius's life by using three key images: the image before his life crisis (being transformed into an ass due to his sins), the time of the crisis (during which he lived as an ass) and the image of him after he was re-transformed into a man (his rebirth). Bakhtin refers to these three transformations as *metamorphosis*.

> Metamorphosis is concerned with transformation of identity. It forms the basis for a method of portraying the whole of an individual's life in its more important moments of crisis. (1981: 114)

Bakhtin's analysis of metamorphosis in Lucius's life is too deep and complex to be examined in detail here. However, his concept of the distinctive temporal sequence of the metamorphoses is used to analyse the psychological impact on the community and on the school children.

The three fundamental temporal stages mentioned in Bakhtin's work are evident in the 9/11 event and its aftermath. The first stage, the time prior to 9/11, was characterised by the normality of daily life in New York City and business activity in the Twin Towers. The second stage was that dominated by the violence and death caused by the terrorist attacks and their immediate aftermath, while the third stage encompasses that time during which the social impacts of the attacks, the effects of the 'war on terror' and the Iraq conflict made themselves felt. However, since the *Sun Herald* article was published after the 9/11 event, it does not include the first stage: only the second and third stages.

The children's drawings discussed here represent the second stage, while the verbal text is concerned with the third stage. The children's drawings in narrative form (Kress and van Leeuwen 1996) depict the exact moment of crisis and the story of what had happened and how it happened. In Figure 15.1, the drawing on the left shows one of the Twin Towers was in flames while an aircraft was flying directly towards it. The drawing on the right depicts people jumping out of the windows of one of the towers to their deaths. Here, too, an aircraft is about to crash into the building, promising a fiery holocaust and more death.

Based on the children's drawings depicting the second stage, the verbal text addresses the third stage: the time after the crisis and the way in which it impacted on children. It urges school teachers, counsellors and parents to give guidance to their school-going children and stresses the importance of monitoring children's TV viewing of an event like 9/11. Here it is argued that the second stage leads to the third stage and orientates readers to the issues addressed in the verbal text. The temporal sequence of 9/11 represented by verbal and visual elements is summarised in Table 15.1.

What is clear is that the defining moment of the 9/11 tragedy, the important moment of crisis, transformed the children's perception of the world. In reflecting the distress and shock caused by the horrific event, the drawings demonstrate that the children had internalised the sequence and details of the tragedy. Their internal transformation of the event is denoted by their ability to produce detailed drawings that mirror the photographic

Table 15.1: Temporal sequence of 9/11

Temporal sequence of crucial time	*Motif of time*	*Multimodal elements in the article*	*Functions and articulation of meanings*	*Social significance*
Stage 1				
The time prior to 9/11	Prior to event	This stage is omitted in the article.		
Stage 2				
The event of 9/11 in New York City	During the event	Children's drawings.	Depicting how and what happened in the 9/11 incident. Orientating readers to the social context of the article.	The psychological impact on children's knowledge about terrorism.
Stage 3				
Aftermath: social issues arising from the event	After the event	Verbal text.	Addressing adults' concerns about the social impact on our children. Offering advice on how to help our children deal with critical events.	Adults' responsibility and the importance in dealing with children's psychological issues in the aftermath of terrorism.

and electronic images presented by the media. In their drawings they made use of the semiotic resources and visual representations available to them to express their views. As Kress and van Leeuwen (1996) state, children express what they have in mind and what they know; for example, they draw circles as wheels and wheels denote cars. We may suggest here that the children's knowledge of peace prior to the attacks has been transformed into an image of terror. For many young children, a passenger aircraft is a symbol of enjoyment – holidays or family trips – denoting a means of going to somewhere like Disneyland, while the airport is seen as a place for meeting friends, relatives or mum and dad coming home from overseas. However, in the drawings, planes are depicted as weapons of destruction, indicating that their concept of a plane has been transformed.

It is in this particular context that Bakhtin's concept of metamorphosis is relevant because it helps to explain how a particular historical event can bring about internal transformation of concepts, objects or ideas. My personal experience is worth mentioning here. In July 2002, nine months after the 9/11 event, I was organising a family trip from Sydney to Melbourne. My husband and I had great trouble convincing our nine-year-old son that it was safe to travel on an aircraft as he worried that it would blow up in mid-air, killing us like the people in the 9/11 tragedy. I was shocked to realise how much the 9/11 event had impacted on my young son. Similarly, the incidents of the Madrid train terrorist attack in March 2004 and the London Underground bombings in July 2005 were likely to have reinforced such fears in children as well as their knowledge-formation and experiences of the world. In the demonstrations after the Madrid event, anti-terrorism signs and images were carried by young children, articulating the same theme of war and terror. Similarly, the detailed narratives in the children's drawings in the *Sun Herald* article articulate the fear of terrorism in the children's minds and their formation of the new images of an unsafe world.

15.5 The interplay of images and verbal text

When Barthes (1977) presented images from Ivan the Terrible he proposed three distinctive levels of meaning: the *informational* level, the *symbolic* level and the level of the *obtuse meaning* (that which could not be named). He defined the information level as 'everything I can learn from the setting, the costumes, the characters, their relations, their insertion in an anecdote with which I am (even if vaguely) familiar' (1977: 52). This level is that of communication. The symbolic level, which he also referred to as signification, has the referential symbolism of an 'imperial ritual of baptism by gold ... theme of gold, of wealth' (p. 52). Baptism is normally carried out either in or with water. However, the image of molten gold pouring over the head symbolised the ritual of baptism. Barthes (1977) had difficulties in naming the third level but later he referred to it as a level of significance (obtuse) which he described as 'evident, erratic and obstinate' (p. 54). This level is indifferent to the narrative and outside language. It is not situated structurally; yet it is a 'passage from language to significance' (p. 65) in order to achieve our social and political agenda.

Applying Barthes' concept of levels of meaning, we may identify the *informational* level and *symbolic* level in the children's drawings. However, the third level of significance, that of the *obtuse meaning*, is not as evident as the other two levels. The *informational* and *symbolic* levels of the drawings form a distinctive semantic and rhetorical structure in the multimodal text while the *obtuse meaning* helps to endorse its effective engagement and support from the readers.

On the *informational* level, the images tell the story of the 9/11 event in a narrative process structure (Kress and van Leeuwen 1996). (A detailed discussion on narrative structure is provided in Section 15.7.) The drawings provide detailed information on how it happened, where it took place and who was involved in the tragedy. At the *symbolic* level, the images articulated the children's knowledge about the world and their awareness of what was happening around them. Their detailed illustrations of the terrorist acts raise adults' concerns about the social impact of terrorism on children. These images were designed to evoke the readers' engagement with the emotional needs of the children which in turn led readers to the text with the focus on strategies for counselling children in a tragic or crisis situation.

On the level of *significance*, the children deployed their limited multimodal resources by focusing on the participants and processes in the narrative. They drew square boxes as windows, a few lines on the plane to signify an explosion and, by means of black smudges, depicted people jumping out of the windows. These distinctive features of the children's work denoted the innocence and honesty of their thinking and what they had in their minds at the time. In Thibault's terms (2004), the children were using their symbolic resources to construct their social experience and reflect on the immediate environment for the enactment of social relationships. The emergence of this meta-level enabled and enables them to formulate their actions in response to events around them. The compilers of the *Sun Herald* article, both writers and layout artists, were doubtless aware that these distinctive features in the children's drawings would achieve optimal success in inducing greater emotional connections with the readers. This would have particularly been the case after the newspaper staff had exhausted their image and language resources to endorse the truthfulness and wholeness of the article in order to maximise the temporal social significance of the event. The levels of meaning of the children's drawings are presented in Table 15.2.

As shown in Table 15.2, the adult text and the children's drawings play a complementary role in reinforcing one another through their semantic and rhetorical relationship. The drawings expressed the children's social experience and effectively shared with the reader their pre-knowledge and experience in order to evoke interest in the verbiage. This supports Kress and van Leeuwen's (1996, 2001) claim that two major functions are fulfilled

Table 15.2: Levels of meaning in the children's drawings

Levels of meaning	*Representation*	*Image/verbal text inter-relationship*	*Functionality*
Informational level	Images as narrative of events to inform readers of how, who, where and what happened.	Orientation to the social context of the text: context-dependent relationship.	Communication of information.
Symbolic level	Symbolic messages of children's knowledge about the world.	Foundation of forming the theme and topic of the text.	Evoke concerns and attention from the society and community.
Significance (Obtuse) level	Represent children's multimodal skills and the distinctive traits of their work.	Tenuous relationship with both verbiage and images, as it is outside language, yet a passage from language to significance: innocence and honesty in the children's work reflecting its truthfulness.	Endorse its truthfulness and wholeness of the article in order to maximize its temporal social significance of the event.

by semiotic modes: the function of representing the world around and inside us, and an interpersonal function of interaction and social relations.

15.6 Multimodal text composition

The deployment of different semiotic resources in multimodal text is presenting ever-greater challenges to the configuration of textual organisation. The intermeshing of textual and graphic information in the design of digital multimodal text layout is the central focus of Bateman and Delin's work (2001). They identify five levels of information structure on a multimodal text page. These are the content structure, rhetorical structure, layout structure, linguistic structure and navigation structure (for digital texts). Their model can be used to analyse the structural co-presentation of the textual and graphical information in the *Sun Herald* article, although due to the scope of this chapter, such analysis will necessarily be brief.

Being a printed text, the *Sun Herald* lacks any navigation structure. Analysis in terms of the other four structures shows the following:

Content structure: The content structure consists of both the drawings and the verbiage. They both construe the ideational meanings in representing the children's experience and adult concerns over the need for psychological support for children on the part of parents and school teachers. This structure is parallel to Barthes' information level as discussed in Section 15.5.

Rhetorical structure: The rhetorical relationship between the verbiage and its accompanying drawings creates a distinctive link between adults and the children's work. Here the children's drawings effectively established the social context in which the article was written. Such contextualisation maximised the emotional engagement in the topic of concern. Again, this structure is parallel to Barthes' symbolic level.

Layout structure: The positioning and organisation of multimodal elements on the page is structured in columns with frames which separate the verbiage and images. This is similar to Kress van Leeuwen's concepts of information value, salience and framing (1996). This is discussed in detail later in Section 15.7 of reading images.

Linguistic structure: Language is structured to realise the layout element of the verbiage in the article.

The application of Bateman and Delin's structural framework provides a new approach which can be used to complement both Barthes' levels of images and Kress and van Leeuwen's reading images. These are discussed in Section 15.7.

15.7 Reading images: a narrative structure of the children's drawings in the article

The analysis of the visual composition of the children's drawings is guided by Kress and van Leeuwen's (1996) work in reading images and their proposed visual structure of narrative. In both drawings, the narrative structure is presented by the essential elements of the *participants* (people or objects) and the *processes* (1996). There are two kinds of processes. If the process has a target, the terms *actor* and *goal* are used. The actor is the person or object that carries out the action while the goal is the target of the action (here, not in the sense of the direction of the action). If the action has a goal (a target) such action is termed as *unidirectional transactional action*. Otherwise it is referred to as *non-transactional action*. Figures 15.2 and 15.3 illustrate how these elements have been used to deconstruct the children's drawings.

To further illustrate the children's drawings of narrative structure, Table 15.3 presents each component in detail.

Children drawing 1

Unidirectional transactional action (Kress and van Leeuwen, 1996, p. 74)

←

Building (Goal/Object)

Plane (Participant) (Actor)

Vector

Non-transactional action
Smoke is coming out of the building.

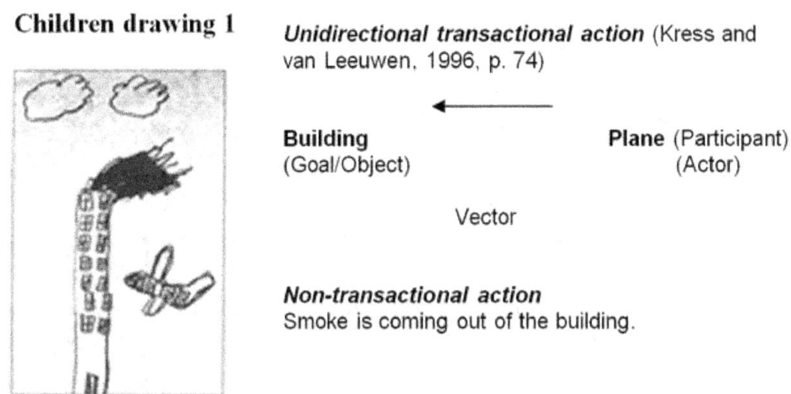

Lines of fire: a Lakemba student's drawing.

Figure 15.2: Narrative Structure of Children's Drawing 1.

Children drawing 2

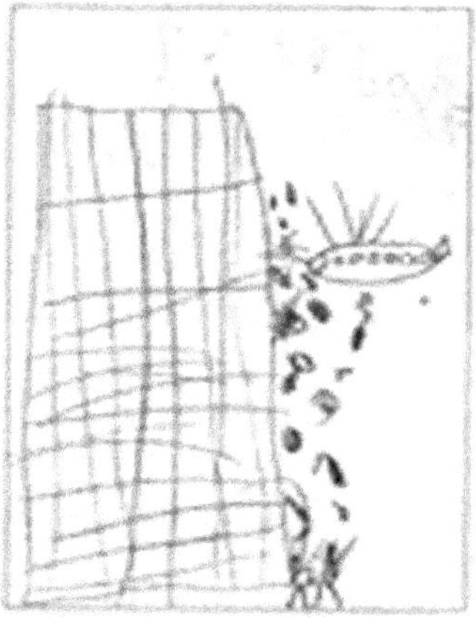

Unidirectional transactional action

Building (Goal/Object)

Plane (Participant) (Actor)

Vector

←

Non-transactional action
People are jumping out of the windows.

SAD: Stephane Levque's art.

Figure 15.3: Narrative Structure of Children's Drawing 2.

Table 15.3: Narrative structure of the children's drawings

Image	*Participant*	*Process*	*Actor*	*Goal*
Drawing 1	Building, aircraft and smoke	Aircraft flying towards the building, smoke billowing from the building.	Aircraft	Building
Drawing 2	Building, aircraft and people	Aircraft crashing into the building and people leaping out of windows.	Aircraft	Building

As shown in Table 15.3 the *participants* in Drawings 1 and 2 include the aircraft, the buildings, the smoke and the people affected. The *process* consists of the actions of the doomed aircraft flying towards the buildings and people leaping out of the windows. The flight path of the aircraft towards the buildings creates a vector (the transaction between participant and process). The two drawings have both unidirectional transactional action and non-transactional action. The unidirectional transactional action depicts the aircraft (actor) flying towards the tower (target) and the anticipated fiery impact. The non-transactional action depicts the smoke billowing from the building, shown in Figure 15.2, and the action of people leaping from the windows, shown in Figure 15.3. These actions do not have a goal and do not point to any other participants/targets.

It is not sufficient simply to analyse the structural composition of the children's drawings. Therefore an analysis of the multimodal text as a whole is presented in the next section.

15.8 Information value, salience and framing

According to Kress and van Leeuwen (1996: 183), multimodal text composition is based on three principles. These are information value, salience and framing. *Information value* is concerned with page layout and how multimodal elements are positioned on the page, such as left and right, top and bottom, centre and margin. *Salience* addresses how multimodal elements attract the viewer's attention by using colour, size, and methods of foregrounding or back grounding. *Framing* indicates the connection between the text and images, signifying the semantic relationship between them. What follows is an in-depth analysis to explain and scaffold the distinguished multimodal structure display in the article.

Salience: the large and bold font foregrounds the topic and significance of the social concern

Our children speak out

Schools encourage drawing as an emotional release

Framing: Separating children's work from adult's text

Signals the independent structure of meaning of different semiotic modes

Informational value: Adult's text takes central position of the page

Figure 15.4: Information value, salience and framing of Our Children Speak Out

From Figure 15.4, we can see that the three compositional principles, of information value, salience and framing, are equally relevant to the multimodal composition of the article. The verbal text is placed in the central position with the images on either side. The information value is loaded in the text. The salience is the large, and bold font used for the headline, as it dramatically foregrounds the topic and significance of the social concern signalling the explosive emotional release in the drawings. This 'megaphone' headline effectively reflects the words Speak Out. Such co-deployment of salience in font size and wording is common in newspaper articles dealing with emotional social issues and events.

Framing is used for both drawings. The border separates the adult's verbal text from the children's drawings and signals the independent structure of meaning of different semiotic modes, such as text and images (Kress and van Leeuwen 1996: 183). These two modes of presentation are combined to reinforce each other, fulfilling a complementary role. The images are well integrated into the page layout, as each shares the same amount of space as the text columns. Kress and van Leeuwen define this code of integration as a 'code of spatial composition' (p. 183). Table 15.4 highlights the information value, salience and framing approach in the article.

In summary, this section has presented a complete framework of analysing multimodal text composition which illustrates Kress and van Leeuwen's model of multimodal text analysis. This complements the previous two models by providing the grammar for unfolding and describing the structural composition of different semiotic resources. Also, it complements the textual meanings in SFL.

Table 15.4: Multimodal text composition of Our Children Speak Out

	Informational value	*Salience*	*Frame*	*Code of spatial composition*
Verbiage	Centre position.	Large bold heading Body text in the central position.	No frame.	Text takes up three columns out of five.
Images	Two images: one is on the left of the text and the other is on the right.	Small images and positioned on both sides of the text.	Both images are framed.	Each image takes up one column.

15.9 An eclectic approach to multimodal text analysis

In this chapter, an eclectic approach to multimodal text analysis has been used to complement the ideational meanings proposed by SFL. I have first applied Bakhtin's concept of time and space as markers for critical event development to contextualise the impact of the 9/11 event. This is further complemented by using Bakhtin's concept of metamorphosis to show how children transform their social experience into new knowledge.

In addition, the chapter has drawn on the works of Barthes, Bateman and Delin, and Kress and van Leeuwen as follows. In Barthes' work (1977), the dependent relationship between verbiage and images is fulfilled by an image illustrating the text or the text defining the meaning of the image. But, in the *Our Children Speak Out* article, the interdependent relationship of the verbal text and images lies in their semantic relationship by the images contextualising the verbal text. This is complemented by using Bateman and Delin's (2001) rhetorical structure in media texts. Using the concept of Kress and van Leeuwen's (1996) social functions of semiotic modes, the chapter has revealed the two social functions fulfilled by the children's drawings. These first express the children's experiences of the 9/11 event, and second effectively engage readers in sharing those experiences with them.

I would argue that only by using an eclectic approach is it possible to make a complex and in-depth analysis of the interplay of verbiage and images displayed in the article because no single method would cover the complexity of the social impact of an event such as that of 9/11 upon children. I argue further that, in relation to SFL, the eclectic approach used in this chapter adds richness to the modelling of multimodal text analysis.

15.10 Conclusion

The 9/11 event of 2001 constitutes a significant temporal marker in world history. The subsequent USA-led 'war on terror' and the Iraq war extended the trajectory of the intersection of time and space of these terrorist attacks. This sequence of events makes Bakhtin's (1981) concept of the traversal of time and space particularly relevant to the theme of this chapter in the contextualisation of the 9/11 event and its historical significance.

Drawing on different aspects of the work on multimodal texts by Barthes (1977), Bateman and Delin (2001) and Kress and van Leeuwen (1996), this chapter has attempted to provide a useful framework for analysing the nature of contemporary media texts, which, as pointed out, are increasingly complex. We can conclude that, in contemporary media, different semiotic modes are selected, organised and integrated in the editing process to suit particular communication situations in order to maximise their meaning-making potential and effects. The *Sun Herald* used the children's drawings to evoke stronger emotional reactions than were likely to be accomplished by the use of photographic images or of written text, particularly when the media have exhausted their photographic image resources.

Acknowledgement

The author would like to thank the *Sun Herald* and Miranda Wood, the author Our Children Speak Out, for permission to use the article and also Stephane Leveque for the permission to use the children's drawing in Figure 15.2. However, extensive efforts to contact the owner of the children's drawing in Figure 15.1 for copyright permission, met with no success. The owner is welcome to contact the author of the chapter or the publisher at any time.

Source of Data

Wood, M. (2001) September 16. Our Children Speak Out. *The Sun-Herald*, 18.

References

Bakhtin, M. (1981) *The Dialogic Imagination* (translated by Emerson, C. and Holquist, M.) Austin, TX: University of Texas Press.

Barthes, R. (1977) *Image, Music, Text* (translated by Stephen, H.). New York: Hill and Wang.

Bateman, J. and Delin, J. (2001). From genre to text critiquing in multimodal documents. Paper presented at the MAD 2001: The 4th International Workshop on Multidisciplinary Approaches to Discourse: Improving Text: From Text Structure to Text Types. Yttre, Belgium.

De Young, K. (2006) US Figures Show Sharp Global Rise In Terrorism in 2005. Washington Post website. Retrieved 20 March 2006, from: http://www.washingtonpost.com/wpdyn/content/article/2006/04/28/AR2006042802181_pf.html

Halliday, M. A. K. (1994) *An Introduction to Functional Grammar* (2nd edition). London: Arnold.

Hasan, R. (1996) Speech genre, semiotic mediation and the developement of higher mental functions. In Cloran, D. Butt, D. and Williams, G. (eds) *Ways of Saying: Ways of Meaning: Selected Papers of Ruquiya Hasan*. London: Cassell.

Glasser, S. (2005) US Figures Show Sharp Global Rise In Terrorism. Washington Post website. Retrieved June 10 2005, from: http://www.washingtonpost.com/wpdyn/content/article/2005/04/26/AR2005042601623.html

Iedema, R., Feez, S. and White, P. (1994) *Right It Write: Media Literacy*. Sydney: NSW Department of School Education. Available for download at http://www.grammatics.com/appraisal

Kress, G. and van Leeuwen, T. (1996) *Reading Images: The Grammar of Visual Design*. London: Routledge.

Kress, G. and van Leeuwen, T. (2001) *Multimodal Discourse: The Modes and Media of Contemporary Communication*. London: Arnold.

Martin, J. R. (1995) Interpersonal meaning, persuasion and public discourse: packing semiotic punch. *Australian Journal of Linguistics*, 15/1: 33–67.

Martin, J. R. (2001) Language, register and genre. In Burns, A. and Coffin, C. (eds). *Analysing English in a Global Context*. London: Routledge.

Martin, J. R. and Rose, D. (2003) *Working with Discourse: Meaning Beyond the Clause*. London: Continuum.

Thibault, P. J. (2004) *Agency and Consciousness in Discourse: Self – other Dynamics as a Complex System*. London: Continuum.

Unsworth, L. (2001) *Teaching Multiliteracies across the Curriculum*. Buckingham: Open University Press.

White, P. (1998) Telling media tales: the news story as rhetoric. Unpublished Ph dissertation. Sydney: University of Sydney. Available for download at http://www.grammatics.com/appraisal/whiteprr_phd.html

16 Decoding meaning in political cartoons

Maria J. Pinar Sanz

16.1 Introduction

During the British election campaign of 2001, *The Guardian* published three cartoons by Steve Bell that were based on thematically similar political billboards displayed by either the Labour or the Conservative Party during the same period. This chapter focuses on decoding the meanings transmitted in the cartoons. It aims to show how representational meanings can be encoded in various semiotic modes, in this case the verbal and the visual, and how the representational meanings in the cartoons are interrelated with the representational meanings encoded in the billboards that appeared during the campaign. It will be argued that the decoding of the cartoons relies, among other aspects, on knowledge of the meaning encoded in the corresponding billboard.

Attention will primarily be given to the Ideational metafunction, which is concerned with the clause as representation of patterns of experience. Systemic Functional Grammar (henceforth SFG) has traditionally mainly dealt with the study of the linguistic aspects of representation in context. According to Halliday (1994: 106), 'Language enables human beings to build a mental picture of reality and to make sense of what goes on around them as well as inside them.' This suggests that SFG can be extended to other modes; it can, for example, also be applied to the visual mode, the further realisational mode in cartoons alongside language. Various scholars, in fact, have shown that other semiotic modes – the visual among them – can also be assigned representational meanings (see e.g. Kress and van Leeuwen 2006; O'Toole 1994, 1999; Hofinger and Ventola 2004). Lemke (1998) argues that the representational metafunction in visual depiction presents a scene, the elements of which can easily be recognised. Similar to language representation (see e.g. Downing and Locke 2006: 122), images can represent processes, participants involved in those processes, attributes ascribed to them and circumstances of place, time and manner.

New ways of capturing representation, realised by other modes, have made cartoons popular subjects of study in multisemiotic discourse analysis. Cartoons use two semiotic modes, the visual and the verbal, which are embedded in a complementary relationship within a specific socio-cultural domain (Kress and van Leeuwen 2001: 20). The meaning potential of multisemiotic texts is greatly expanded in comparison to texts with a single semiotic code. In fact, Lemke (1998) refers to 'the multiplication of meaning,' which takes place in multimodal texts, because the same meaning can be expressed in different modes thus transmitting additional details or nuances. Lemke (1998) also maintains that the meaning of the linguistic text is the product of subtle, conventional and creative interplay of the meaning-making aspects of the three macrofunctions of language. The same is true for visual texts. In line with Lemke (1998) and O'Toole (1994), the assumption in this chapter is that an image makes meaning not just through the selection it makes in a system but through its place in a larger organisation and its intertextual relation to other (visual) texts. In addition, the relation between the verbal and visual elements in the cartoons will be another important issue in this chapter. When decoding the meanings transmitted through both the verbal and visual elements of cartoons, a number of issues arise, which include, among others, semiotic spanning (Ventola 1999) and visual metaphor (Kaplan 2005, El Refaie 2003). Knowledge of the contemporary social and political circumstances underlies the understanding of these issues.

The chapter is organised as follows. Section 16.2 sets out the theoretical underpinning with a number of questions targeting the issues mentioned above. Section 16.3 introduces the data to be analysed. Section 16.4 examines each question proposed in Section 16.2 through the data analysis. Section 16.5 discusses the issues drawn from the analysis. The chapter ends with some conclusions and reflections for further investigation.

16.2 The theoretical issues

In order to examine the cartoons by Steve Bell and the political billboards on which they are based, four questions will be addressed:

1. What are the main generic characteristics of cartoons?
2. What are the cognitive mechanisms involved in the creation and interpretation of the three political cartoons presented in this chapter?

3. What is the role of the relation between verbal and visual elements in these cartoons?
4. To what extent are these cartoons likely to be influenced by the social and political circumstances at the time?

The aim is to work with these questions and cartoons in order to inform the decoding of meanings transmitted in political cartoons in general. It must be noted that there are no clearcut boundaries separating the scope of each question and sometimes the answers to one question have to be understood in relation to the others, as the following sections will show.

16.2.1 What are the main generic characteristics of cartoons?

The main generic characteristics of cartoons are approached from three different perspectives. First of all, as political cartoons typically contain a political or social image, it could be said that they exhibit the features of a narrative, in that they consist of characters, setting and plot (Edwards 1997). In the context of SFG, the characters are the participants involved in the narrative; the setting is associated with the circumstances of time, place, manner, etc. and the plot with the processes. Second, according to Seymour-Ure (2001: 333), political cartoons share three characteristics: (a) they are graphic in a largely verbal medium, (b) they exaggerate and distort in a type of publication that values accuracy and objectivity, and (c) they offer meanings open to interpretation. Finally, political cartoons tend to be located as a subcategory of political humour or satire. This chapter, however, aims to examine whether it is political criticism and debate on relevant points in the campaigns, or rather the humorous component that is the predominant criterion for characterising the genre.

These issues, especially the fact that political cartoons offer meanings open to interpretation, lead us to investigating the cognitive mechanisms involved in the creation and interpretation of cartoons.

16.2.2 What are the cognitive mechanisms involved in the creation and interpretation of the cartoons presented here?

The three basic meaning-making features employed in cartoons mentioned in the above section – participants, circumstances and processes – are enlivened by several inventional means which include two cognitive mechanisms: visual metaphor (Kaplan 2005; El Refaie 2003) and semiotic spanning (Ventola 1999). Further key aspects pursued in the analysis will be the degree of cognitive effort involved in the interpretation of the cartoons and the degree of participant distinctiveness and identifiability of the target depicted (Marín Arrese 2005).

Even though the cartoons analysed in this chapter contain verbal metaphors, attention will be focused on visual metaphors, as their effect seems to be more striking and because, traditionally, they have been neglected. Visual metaphors are essential in the creation of cartoons, as they tend to consist of simplified processes, participants or circumstances designed to stand for more complex issues (Werner 2004). It seems that, rather than making a literal statement about an issue, the artist likens the issue to something else, and thus invites interpretation. Therefore, cartoons offer meanings open to interpretation. In order to decode analogies and metaphors, intertextuality and the broader concept of semiotic spanning are two cognitive aspects that need to be studied. According to Werner (2004), 'intertextuality refers to the act of appropriating or quoting prior visual or written texts, and the reader's interpretation of the cartoon in the light of those other texts.' Other authors, however, use this notion to describe the relationship only between written texts. To avoid such a limitation, Ventola (1999: 113) proposes the term *semiotic spanning*, which takes place between various kinds of texts independent of their generic qualities and their realisation modalities. In fact, the cartoons analysed here are based on the billboards published by the political parties, which in turn may be based on other images. Readers are able to interpret them according to the nature and extent of their own background knowledge. For example, some readers may have seen the billboard but not heard about the piece of news that typically accompanies it, in which case it will be more difficult to decode. In political cartoons, there is semiotic spanning to at least three different genres: political billboards, newspaper articles and the broader one, which would include the social and political circumstances at the time (cfr. Section 16.2.4).

16.2.3 What is the role of the relation between verbal and visual elements in the cartoons?

The interrelation between the verbal and the visual elements in the cartoons is a fundamental aspect to be considered, as cartoons cannot be adequately understood in terms of any one semiotic modality only, be it verbal or visual. In fact, the decoding of visual metaphors relies heavily on the interrelation between these two modes. However, although it is widely recognised that both the linguistic and visual modalities should share an equal status (O'Halloran 2000; Kress and van Leeuwen 2001; Baldry and Thibault 2006), what is not clear is how the verbal and the visual actually complement each other. As Kaindl points out:

> Non-verbal elements [...] not only perform the function of illustrating the linguistic part of the text but also play an integral role in the constitution of meaning, whether through interaction with the linguistic elements or as an independent semiotic system. (Kaindl 2004: 176)

Conversely, the linguistic items may also help to decode the meanings transmitted in the visual part.

16.2.4 To what extent are the cartoons likely to be influenced by the social and political circumstances at the time?

This question is proposed as a separate item but it is clearly connected with the other three. El Refaie (2003: 76) suggests that 'the extent to which metaphors are connected to the way people think cannot be described universally, or even for a whole linguistic community, but must instead be explored in specific socio-political contexts'. This is especially true in the case of metaphors in political cartoons, as each reader will have a specific ideology and specific contextual knowledge. According to El Refaie (2003: 76), 'every individual reader or viewer is likely to bring his or her own experiences and assumptions to the interpretation process'. The decoding of the range of possible interpretations in some of the cartoons will depend on individual attitude towards, and level of knowledge of, the sociopolitical context. This accounts for the fact, as Moya (2005: 201) points out, that in cognitive approaches the general meaning of a text is not always considered to be intrinsically present but is instead assigned to that text by its readers. Therefore, the issues relating to this question will also feature in the discussion relating to the other three questions already addressed in Sections 16.2.1, 16.2.2 and 16.2.3.

16.3 The cartoons under analysis.

This section presents the cartoons to be analysed and the billboards on which the cartoons are based.

16.3.1 Not all parties are the same

The first cartoon to be discussed, Figure 16.1, was published after the Tories sparked a furious row by using their first general election broadcast on television and radio to blame Labour for a wave of crimes, including two rapes carried out by prisoners released under a government scheme. The scheme had been introduced in 1999 to allow prisoners serving sentences of under four years to be released up to two months earlier than originally stipulated. The television broadcast, which depicted a group of prisoners gloating as they walked out of jail, announced: 'Labour have let out 35,000 convicted criminals under their early release scheme'. After scenes of criminals carrying out a burglary and selling drugs to youngsters, the screen listed a series of crimes, adding finally: '...and two rapes'.

Figure 16.1 cartoon depicts one of the scenes in the TV broadcast. The slogan makes reference to a series of billboards published by the Conservative Party in which the left hand side represents what the situation was like with the Labour Party in power and the right hand side what the situation would be like with the Conservative Party in power. Thus the slogan of Figure 16.1 cartoon is the same as the slogan in the billboard (Figure 16.2)

Figure 16.1: Not all parties are the same (cartoon).

Figure 16.2: Not all parties are the same (billboard).

and the broadcast, *Not all parties are the same*, which, together with the caption, *Labour wants to kill your granny and eat your children*, gives us a clear indication for decoding the cartoon.

16.3.2 Who are you calling a bubblehead?

The next cartoon, Figure 16.3, is based on another billboard, Figure 16.4, launched by the Conservative Party, which features a grinning Mr Blair inside a bubble about to be burst by a pin and the slogan: *Go on, burst his bubble*. According to the Conservative Party, New Labour was living in a bubble, out of touch with reality. As the slogan points out, this billboard campaign urged voters to burst Tony Blair's bubble by voting Conservative and thus deprive him of a landslide victory. In addition, Figure 16.3 cartoon makes reference to the new postal voting system. In previous elections, voters were expected to turn up in person and could only have postal or proxy votes if they were disabled, in hospital or working away from home. In this election, however, any voter was entitled to have a postal vote which provoked controversy about the possibility of vote rigging.

16.3.3 Urgent reminder (2001)

Figure 16.5 cartoon is a humorous and critical reinterpretation of Figure 16.6 billboard, which was published by the Labour Party during the final week of the campaign, just before polling day. In the billboard (Figure

Figure 16.3: Who are you calling a bubblehead? (cartoon)

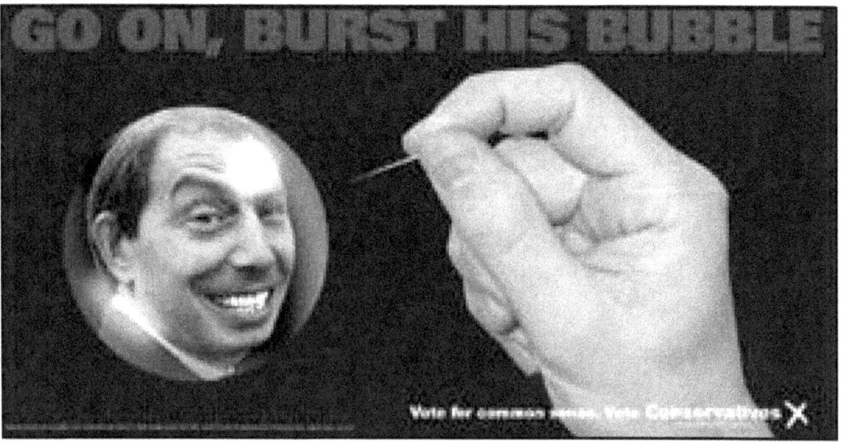

Figure 16.4: Who are you calling a bubblehead? (billboard)

16.6) the message is: *Urgent reminder. Vote for schools and hospitals tomorrow,* handwritten on a 'post-it' note. This slogan emphasises the party's determination to keep debate away from the Euro, which was much discussed at the time, in order to maintain focus on those issues that voters were saying concerned them most. However, Figure 16.5 cartoon seems to focus on a wide range of totally irrelevant topics, such as feeding the dog or collecting a suit.

Figure 16.5: Urgent reminder (cartoon)

16.4 Data analysis

Here these cartoons are analysed in detail, in terms of the four questions proposed in Section 16.2. The topic of each question is addressed in turn: first the main generic characteristics of cartoons; second the cognitive mechanisms involved in the creation and interpretation of cartoons; third the role of the relation between the verbal and visual elements in the cartoons; and finally the extent to which the cartoons are likely to be influenced by the social and political circumstances at the time. In each

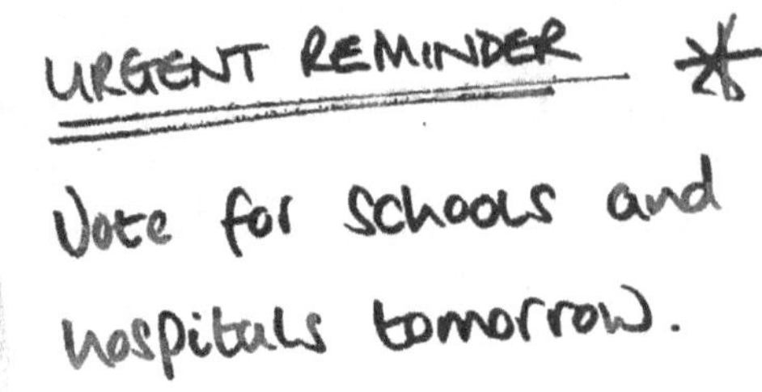

Figure 16.6: Urgent reminder (billboard)

case, reference will be made to the three cartoons and the associated billboards.

16.4.1 The main generic characteristics of cartoons

In this section, the generic structure of cartoons is discussed with reference to the three cartoons and their billboards presented in Section 16.3. In

Figure 16.1 cartoon, the participants are Tony Blair (then leader of the Labour Party and Prime Minister), William Hague (then leader of the Conservative Party) and Margaret Thatcher (past leader of the Conservative Party). They are all represented through visual metaphors in the form of caricatures, as well as verbally. Tony Blair is depicted as a criminal, wearing clothes typically associated with burglars and which are similar to the clothes worn by the mugger in the television broadcast mentioned in Section 16.3.1. He is given characteristic features used by the cartoonist, Steve Bell: big ears and teeth. Margaret Thatcher and William Hague represent ordinary citizens, who might be in danger of being mugged, thus closely resembling the participants in the same broadcast. The processes and circumstances associated with this narrative, *Kill your granny and eat your children,* are complemented by Margaret Thatcher holding hands with William Hague. Since Hague is Thatcher's second successor after John Major, we could regard him as her grandson, particularly by taking into account Hague's youthfulness.

There are two narratives in Figure 16.3 cartoon. On the one hand, there is the caricature shown in Figure 16.4 billboard, published by the Labour Party, and on the other, there is the letterbox with the verbal component, *Save the weirdo. Vote early and often.* The main participant in both narratives is William Hague, who is also caricatured. In the first narrative, he is depicted resembling Blair inside a bubble. The hand and the pin, which are next to Blair in the billboard, represent the other participants present in Figure 16.3 cartoon. There is an important difference, though, between this cartoon and Figure 16.4 billboard. The hand and the pin in the cartoon could be interpreted as belonging to Hague. However, the hand and the pin in the billboard are clearly not Blair's, but those of potential Conservative voters who are going to burst Blair's bubble. The visual process of bursting Hague's *bubblehead* has to be understood in relation to the slogan in Figure 16.4 billboard, *Go on, burst his bubble.* The second narrative in Figure 16.3 cartoon concerns the letterbox, the centre of which has an interesting message about the controversy created by postal voting, *Save the weirdo. Vote early and often,* which are the two main processes in this narrative. This was about the possibility of rigging votes under the new postal voting regime. The implication is that Hague could only win the election through fraud.

As in Figure 16.3 there are also two narratives in Figure 16.5 cartoon, which complement each other. The first narrative deals with the three 'post-it' messages representing the message in the billboard (Figure 16.6). The second one is the representation of the two participants who will carry out the 'post-it' messages: Blair, depicted with big teeth and ears as Bell usually represents him, and John Prescott, who was deputy leader of the Labour party at the time. The central point of the three 'post-it' messages in the first narrative is Blair's big idea, *Urgent reminder.*

The first message is placed on the top left-hand side of the billboard depicted in the cartoon. It refers to Labour's slogan for the last week of the campaign, *Vote for schools and hospitals.* This slogan, however, is followed by *but mainly Banks this Thurs.,* which strongly implies that schools and hospitals are not as important as money. It could also refer to the controversy about changing to the Euro currency.

The second 'post-it' message underneath contains a list of four items which can be grouped under two categories: on the one hand *five loaves* and *two fishes* and on the other hand *collect suit* and *smooth rumpled crotch. Five loaves* and *two fishes* could be considered as ambitious promises. They make reference to the biblical story about a miracle that Jesus performed in order to feed 5,000 people. His disciples were able to find only five loaves of bread and two fishes. But by blessing the food, dividing it and giving it to his disciples to distribute, Jesus was able to feed all 5,000 with plenty left over. *Collect suit* and *smooth rumpled crotch* are at the other extreme to the point of suggesting banality and degradation. Hence, these latter two items make a mockery of the first two, which cannot be taken seriously either. In this way, the cartoon is highly ironic and criticises the sometimes semi-religious language that characterised Blair's comments on the need for public service improvement (Ward 2001).

The third message to the right, taking account of its prominent position on the page, could be considered as the most salient: *feed dog,* which can be assumed to be John Prescott, and *do something about green hair problem.* The original colour cartoon makes reference to a problem that arose when Blair was making a campaign speech from a soapbox. There was a reflection, which gave Blair's lectern a gentle shade of green and made his hair seem green. It is depicted in the original cartoon by a shade of green both in the lectern and in Blair's hair and by a bright green colour strip along the bottom of the cartoon below the board. The synthetic effect of the green colour strengthens the insinuation that Blair cannot be believed.

There is another important issue in relation to the three 'post-it' messages. There is an inversely proportional relationship between the extent of the urgency signalled by the heading: *urgent reminder, more urgent reminder, even more urgent reminder,* and the importance of the issues to be dealt with as signalled by the set of items underneath. The more urgent they are, the more Blair is portrayed as focusing on what is really important for him: not schools and hospitals or even the voters but himself and the 'cupboard love' he needs to show to John Prescott.

16.4.2 Cognitive aspects involved in the decoding of cartoons

The two key mechanisms that reveal the cognitive aspects of the cartoons are visual metaphor (Kaplan 2005, El Refaie 2003) and semiotic spanning (Ventola 1999). There are two visual metaphors in Figure 16.1 cartoon: TONY BLAIR IS A CRIMINAL; MARGARET THATCHER AND WILLIAM HAGUE ARE GRANDMOTHER AND GRANDSON. The idea being transmitted is that the Labour Party is a criminal entity that is going to kill the values established by the Conservative Party and also threaten public security. Tony Blair represents the state while Thatcher and Hague represent the citizens harassed by the government. In this cartoon there is semiotic spanning to the billboard, the broadcast, the controversy created by the broadcast and the whole socio-political context of the time. Meaning cannot be fully grasped if access to all those genres is not available.

From the above it becomes clear that the cognitive effort needed is important, especially if the reader is unfamiliar with the culture in which it was published or if s/he is not particularly interested in politics or in the development of election campaigns. Even though the three participants in Figure 16.1 cartoon (Blair, Thatcher and Hague) are easily recognisable, the underlying ideas they represent are not.

The visual metaphor associated with the first narrative shown in Figure 16.3 cartoon is WILLIAM HAGUE IS A BALLOON. The decoding of this metaphor relies on the verbal component: *Vote Conservative or the balloon gets it. Balloon* is one of the terms used to label Hague because it makes a reference to his bald head. The slang meaning of *gets it* ('receive a scolding or punishment', according to the Merriam Webster Dictionary Online) gives us another clue for interpreting the visual metaphor in this cartoon. The second narrative may have a number of visual metaphors associated such as WILLIAM HAGUE IS A HAMBURGER, A LETTERBOX OR A LIGHTBULB. I consider that the most plausible one is WILLIAM HAGUE IS A LETTERBOX. The decoding of this metaphor relies on another verbal component: *save the weirdo. Vote early and often. Weirdo* is the term used to describe Hague, who, due to his youth and lack of experience as a party leader, was not very popular during that election campaign and received a wide variety of insults and criticisms. *Vote early and often* refers to the controversy about the new postal voting system. In addition, the juxtaposition of the two narratives may yield other interpretations. Even though the letterbox is in the foreground, it is dark and seems to be under the influence of the big, light coloured balloon behind it. In fact, both the head and the eyes in the first narrative could be perceived as an exaggeration of the top of the letterbox in the second narrative. The irony lies in the fact that both the visual and the verbal elements contribute to the interpretation of the balloon as something empty or ephemeral and therefore unlikely to influence voters. The implication might be that it is Hague and not Blair who is living in a bubble out of touch with reality.

There is no doubt that the cognitive effort required for the decoding of Figure 16.3 cartoon is considerable. The meaning as a whole can only be fully decoded through the application of semiotic spanning of the cartoon to the associated billboard (Figure 16.4), through the news concerning postal voting and the current political situation.

The two metaphors which can be deduced in Figure 16.5 cartoon are: BLAIR IS A MISGUIDED MESSIAH and JOHN PRESCOTT IS A DOG. The first one is a reference to the story of Jesus feeding the crowd with only five loaves and two fishes, suggesting not only that can Blair perform miracles, but also that he makes banal and insincere promises. The second one refers to the relationship between Blair and his deputy, John Prescott, who is caricatured as a dog, thus symbolising Blair's faithful companion throughout the campaign. It is the verbal component, *feed dog,* that allows for the interpretation of the metaphor, JOHN PRESCOTT IS A DOG, which transmits all the values associated with friendship and faithfulness. In spite of the inclusion of the metaphors and the presence of semiotic spanning, the cognitive effort required to decode Figure 16.5 cartoon is less demanding than for Figure 16.3 cartoon, given the explicitness of its analogies, references and context. However, there is one exception. It concerns the green hair problem, which may have been unfamiliar to some readers.

16.4.3. Verbal/visual relationship

The verbal/visual relationship is essential when it comes to decoding the meaning of Figure 16.1 cartoon. The slogan, *Not all parties are the same,* gives us the clue as to which billboard and broadcast the cartoon is referring to. The caption underneath, *Labour wants to kill your granny and eat your children,* can only be properly understood in relation to the images represented in the cartoon. The verbal component puts into words the meanings transmitted in the visual mode. In addition, it can be deduced that examining the nature of the semiotic spanning allows access to the verbal/visual relationship and how that is influenced by the social and political circumstances at the time.

Figure 16.3 cartoon shows that the multiplication of meanings (Lemke 1998) through the use of verbal and visual modes is considerable. *A bubblehead* stands for an empty headed or stupid person. Hague has traditionally been represented by the Labour Party as a stupid person. This idea is reinforced by the depiction of his big head, whose size is augmented by its complete baldness. In this cartoon, Steve Bell is reversing the situation presented in the original billboard (Figure 16.4) by caricaturing Hague instead of Blair. *Weirdo* is an offensive term and applies to somebody who behaves in a way regarded as strange or unconventional, especially somebody whose sexual tastes or habits are regarded as unusual. A second definition of *weirdo* is 'somebody who is regarded as prone to dangerous behaviour because of a psychiatric disorder' (Encarta World English Dictionary). The reference of *weirdo* and *bubblehead* to Hague in the cartoon becomes clear through the visual depiction of Hague's head as a balloon taken from the associated billboard, while the verbal reference to the new postal voting system, *Vote early and often,* is clear. Thus it is essential to decode both parts of Figure 16.3 cartoon – Hague's resembling Blair in a bubble and the verbal component associated – for the verbal/visual relation and for the visual metaphors, which reinforces the idea proposed in the introduction that the different components of analysis complement one another.

Even though Figure 16.5 cartoon resembles the billboard (Figure 16.6), the meanings that are transmitted have been multiplied (Lemke 1998), since many other elements, both visual and verbal, have been included. Taking into account the visual/verbal complementariness, the meaning of two metaphors, BLAIR IS A MISGUIDED MESSIAH and JOHN PRESCOTT IS A DOG, can be deduced. In both metaphors, the visual element helps to anchor the context in which the verbal elements have to be understood. On the one hand, Blair is presented as a Messiah who is able to 'feed' the voters with those things they need. On the other hand he is presented as a distasteful and repugnant individual, who has no respect for the voters. In this way an exaggerated contradiction of two extremes is displayed, which provides the point of criticism for the cartoon. The other metaphor, JOHN PRESCOTT IS A DOG, refers to the reputation that John Prescott had at that time. He was considered to be Blair's faithful sidekick. Loyalty is one of the main characteristics associated with dogs, and this is mapped on to Prescott, the target of this metaphor. In addition, the verbal component *even more urgent reminder-feed dog* allows for the interpretation of the metaphor, thus suggesting a particular relationship between Blair and Prescott.

16.4.4 Influence of the social and political circumstances at the time

Sections 16.4.1 to 16.4.3 have shown that the cartoons are clearly influenced by the sociopolitical context and that knowledge of the contemporary political situation on the part of the reader is essential in order to decode the meanings transmitted. The narrative transmitted in the cartoons, the visual metaphors and the verbal/visual relation can be understood thanks to these issues. However, the interpretation of the sociopolitical circumstances will vary according to the readers' ideology and level of knowledge.

Figure 16.1 cartoon, for example, clearly refers to the controversy created by the Conservative Party during their first general election broadcast where they blamed Labour for a wave of crimes. As a result, the cartoon is a direct criticism of Hague because he was considered to be under the influence of Margaret Thatcher. It also implies that Margaret Thatcher should retire from the political scene, as she was getting too much media attention during the election campaign period.

The two narratives in Figure 16.3 cartoon imply knowledge of two complex issues: first knowledge of the billboard (Figure 16.4), which urged the electorate to vote for the Conservative Party to spoil Blair's day, and second knowledge of the controversy created by the new postal voting system. The cartoon implies that Hague will have to resign or that he will be punished if the Conservative Party does not win the election.

The two narratives in Figure 16.5 are also clearly influenced by the sociopolitical situation. Because they have little to do with the key issues in the campaign, they can be interpreted as a criticism of the campaign, in which each party focuses on the issues concerning it most, irrespective of the voters' opinions. In particular they can be interpreted as a criticism of the efforts made by the Labour Party to detract attention away from the Euro at a time when scepticism about the European single currency was one of the main controversies for both political parties.

16.5 Discussion

The analysis of the three cartoons confirms that they exhibit the features of a narrative in terms of participants, processes and circumstances. The participants tend to be the political leaders, whereas the processes and circumstances are related to key issues in the campaign. In addition, the purpose of election campaigns, which is to persuade the public to vote for one party, favours the use of these kinds of processes. The fact that more than one narrative tends to be developed in cartoons accounts for the complexity of the socio-political context within which cartoons are situated.

The three characteristics shared by political cartoons generally (Seymour-Ure 2001), mentioned in Section 16.2.1, are present in all three cartoons here. First, the cartoons present graphic caricatures of the participants. Tony Blair, William Hague and Margaret Thatcher are caricatured in Figure 16.1. William Hague's caricatures dominate Figure 16.3 whereas Tony Blair and John Prescott are caricatured in Figure 16.5. Second, the cartoons distort reality. The narratives in all three political cartoons do not represent the actual facts with which they are related. Third, they are open to interpretation because they depend on the ideology and sociopolitical contextual knowledge of the individual reader. The different interpretations will depend on (i) the way the reader decodes the visual metaphors, (ii) the verbal/visual relationship and (iii) on how far and in which way the reader applies semiotic spanning to what s/he sees in the cartoon with other semiotic sources such as the associated billboards and the sociopolitical context. This confirms that, even though a humorous component is present in all three cartoons, it is the criticism of political issues that seems to be the main characteristic in them. The humorous component serves to reveal the political issues being dealt with: e.g. health, education, postal voting or the outcome of the election.

The analysis of the cartoons highlights the importance of visual metaphors. Up until now, little attention has been given to the representation of visual metaphor in spite of the fact that the view of metaphor as a cognitive phenomenon, applied mainly to verbal modes, started gaining attention in the early 1980s (Lakoff and Johnson 1980). The metaphors found in these three cartoons serve to prove that metaphors are indeed perceived as a cognitive, rather than merely a linguistic phenomenon, which can be expressed in any form of communication (Forceville 2004a; El Refaie 2003), including the visual. The way the metaphors are linked to the representational metafunction has also been shown. Metaphors are basic interpretive frameworks for organising information about the world – election campaigns in this case – and making sense of experience through the different issues that are addressed (Kaplan 2005:170). They shape how people come to understand new ideas and political issues (Gozzi 1999). Such use of metaphor is valuable to the cartoonist, who is thus permitted to express ideas that could otherwise, if written, bear too great a risk of controversy. Certain metaphors, it may be argued, are acceptable only within this genre, where their potential to offend is minimised. An example of this can be found in Figure 16.3 cartoon, where the depiction of Hague as a hamburger, a lightbulb or even a penis would not be acceptable in another context. The important fact here is that the way people understand the issues dealt with in the campaign do not necessarily coincide with the intended message on the part of the different political parties, or the cartoonist. Visual metaphors consist of simplified processes, participants or circumstances designed to stand for more complex issues, which in this specific context are related to key points in the election campaign. In Figure 16.1 cartoon, for example, the issue dealt with is crime and the way it has been approached by the Labour Party. The metaphors TONY BLAIR IS A CRIMINAL and MARGARET THATCHER AND WILLIAM HAGUE ARE GRANDMOTHER AND GRANDSON allow for simplification of the issue in a humorous way and represent one of many possible interpretations. In Figure 16.3 cartoon, the visual metaphors, WILLIAM HAGUE IS A BALLOON and WILLIAM HAGUE IS A LETTERBOX also stand for more complex issues by criticising the effort made by the Conservative Party to minimise Labour's possible landslide. The same is true for the visual metaphors in Figure 16.5 cartoon: BLAIR IS A MISGUIDED MESSIAH and JOHN PRESCOTT IS A DOG. Through these metaphors, Bell is criticising the last days of the campaign for focusing on seemingly unimportant issues for the electorate. But as it has been mentioned elsewhere, these are only some of the possible interpretations.

It has also been shown that the application of semiotic spanning (Ventola 1999) among the cartoons, the associated billboards and the sociopolitical context are all important. The reader is able to interpret any one cartoon to the extent permitted by background knowledge: for example, the degree of knowledge about the associated billboard and news item. Knowledge of the controversy created by an election broadcast used by the Conservatives or of the controversy created by the new postal voting system is essential in order to decode Figures 16.1 and 16.3 cartoons as well as knowledge of the associated billboards. As the analysis has shown, cartoons assume an ideal reader who is able to establish this semiotic spanning. In fact, the cartoons are meaningful only to those who understand the larger discourse within which they are constructed and read.

The analysis of these cartoons has confirmed Lemke's point about the multiplication of meaning (1998). Cartoons cannot be fully understood if the verbal/visual relationship is not taken into account and, in most cases, unless references to other modes can be accessed. The full meanings of the verbal element in the cartoons analysed in this chapter are understood only in relation to the visual elements in the cartoons and to the visual components in the associated billboards. Hence, Lemke's (1998) and O'Toole's (1994) assumption that images make meaning not just through the selection they make in a system but through their place in a larger organisation and their intertextual relation to other (visual) texts is also confirmed. For example, in Figure 16.1 cartoon, the meaning of the caption *Labour wants to kill your granny and eat your children* is fully decoded by taking into account all the associated visual elements. In addition, the visual elements acquire their full meaning when they are related to the associated billboard and broadcast. Thus, Kaindl's (2004: 176) assertion that non-verbal elements in cartoons perform the function of illustrating the linguistic part of the text is also confirmed. This is clearly seen in Figure 16.3, where non-verbal elements help to decode the verbal component. It is through the visual that the referent *bubblehead,* for example, becomes clear. Nevertheless, visual metaphors and images are, in general, only fully understood when their relationship with the verbal component is explained. In fact, one area of investigation in multimodal studies nowadays is to see how the verbal contributes semiotically to the visual (Renkema 2004). In addition, cartoons and the metaphors embedded in them are influenced by the contemporary social and political circumstances and by the personal knowledge of the members of the culture within which they are situated. In order to appreciate their full meaning, various types of background knowledge must be activated, as has previously been demonstrated (Forceville 2005).

16.6 Conclusion and further research

To summarise, it can be concluded that the decoding of political cartoons in the context of election campaigns relies on knowledge not only of the meaning encoded in the corresponding billboard but also on knowledge of the whole sociopolitical context including, specifically, the key issues of the election campaign. This meaning can be decoded if (i) the different elements of the cartoon as a narrative may be accessed and the generic characteristic of cartoons can be established; (ii) the reader is able to interpret the visual metaphors and the semiotic spanning established; (iii) the verbal/visual relation is taken into account and (iv) the reader is able to see to what extent the cartoon is influenced by the sociopolitical context.

This view can be complemented if other aspects are taken into account. For example, the analysis shows that the target of the metaphor in the cartoons tends to be a political leader, who can be assigned a variety of characteristics from the source domain, from a criminal, as in Figure 16.1, to a Messiah, as in Figure 16.3. It would therefore be interesting to carry out a further investigation on possible target and source domains in visual metaphors in political cartoons, as different source domains account for different structures in the target domain. Each source domain 'highlights' certain features in the target domain and 'hides' others (Lakoff and Johnson 1980). In this way, the resulting metaphors may amount to ideological frameworks for individuals or for communities (Forceville 2004b). Forceville (2004b) suggests that source domains may have very different salient connotations from one (sub)culture to another. This implies that different individuals may interpret the same metaphor in completely different ways, depending on the ideology of the newspaper where it is published or the reader's own ideology. Furthermore, metaphors can be understood differently from how they were intended by their makers (Forceville 2004b).

This chapter has addressed the complexity of meanings encoded in political cartoons by highlighting some relevant issues and tools which can be used for decoding meaning, as well as the intricacies of political cartoons. These reflections may serve as a starting point for analysing cartoons as multisemiotic texts that cannot be fully understood until we have looked at how both modes – the verbal and the visual – make meaning together.

Acknowledgements

My sincere gratitude to Charles Forceville and Elisabeth El Refaie for their valuable comments on previous versions of this chapter, also to Carys Jones and Eija Ventola for their time and their useful comments and suggestions. All responsibility for the omissions that may still remain is mine alone. I am further indebted to Steve Bell for granting permission to reproduce the cartoons and to the Labour and Conservative parties for granting permission to reproduce the billboards.

References

Baldry, A. and Thibault, P.(2006) *Multimodal Transcription and Text Analysis. A Multimodal Toolkit and Coursebook.* London: Equinox.

Downing, A. and Locke, P. (2006) *English Grammar. A University Course.* 2nd Edition. London and New York: Routledge.

Edwards, J. L. (1997) *Political Cartoons in the 1988 Presidential Campaign: Image, Metaphor and Narrative.* New York: Garland.

El Refaie, E. (2003) Understanding visual metaphor: the example of newspaper cartoons. *Visual Communication,* 2/1: 75–95.

Forceville, C. (2004a) Visual representations of the idealized cognitive model of *anger* in the Asterix album *La Zizanie*. *Journal of Pragmatics,* 37: 69–88.

Forceville, C. (2004b) A course in pictorial and multimodal metaphor. Retrieved on 8 October 2007 from http://www.chass.utoronto.ca/epc/srb/cyber/cforcevilleout.html

Forceville, C. (2005). Adressing an audience: time, place and genre in Peter van Straaten's calendar cartoons. *Humour,* 18/3: 247–78.

Gozzi, R. (1999) The power of metaphor: in the age of electronic media. *ECT: A Review of General Semantics, 56*: 380–9.

Halliday, M. A. K. (1994) *An Introduction to Functional Grammar.* London: Arnold.

Hofinger, A. and Ventola, E. (2004) Multimodality in operation: language and picture in a museum. In Ventola, E. *et al.* (eds) *Perspectives on Multimodality.* Amsterdam: Benjamins, 193–209.

Kaindl, K. (2004) Multimodality in the translation of humour in comics. In Ventola, E. *et al.* (eds) *Perspectives on Multimodality.* Amsterdam: Benjamins, 173–92.

Kaplan, S. (2005) Visual metaphors in print advertisements for fashion products. In Smith, K. (ed.) *Handbook of Visual Communication Research: Theory, Methods, and Media.* LEA's communication series. Mahwah, NJ: Erlbaum, 167–77.

Kress, G. and van Leeuwen, T. (2006 [1996]) *Reading Images. The Grammar of Visual Design.* London: Routledge.

Kress, G. and van Leeuwen, T. (2001) *Multimodal Discourse. The Modes and Media of Contemporary Communication.* London: Arnold.

Lakoff, G. and Johnson, M. (1980) *Metaphors We Live By.* Chicago, IL: University of Chicago Press.

Lemke, J. (1998) Multiplying meaning: visual and verbal semiotics in scientific text. Last retrieved on 4 December 2007 from http://www.personal.umich.edu/~jaylemke/papers/mxm-syd.htm

Marín Arrese, J. (2005) Humour as subversion in political cartooning. In Labarta Postigo, M. (ed.) *Approaches to Critical Discourse Analysis.* Valencia: Universitat de València, Servei de Publicacions, 1–22.

Moya, A. J. (2005) The assignment of topical status in FDG: a textual analysis. In Mackenzie, J. L. and Gómez-González, M. A. (eds) *Studies in Functional Discourse Grammar.* Bern: Peter Lang.

O'Halloran, K. (2000) Classroom discourse in mathematics: a multisemiotic analysis. *Linguistics and Education,* 10/3, 359–88.

O'Toole, M. (1994) *The Language of Displayed Art.* London: Leicester University Press.

O'Toole, M. (1999) *Engaging with Art. A New Way of Looking at Paintings.* Perth: Murdoch University.

Renkema, J. (2004) *Introduction to Discourse Studies.* Amsterdam: Benjamins.

Seymour-Ure, C. (2001). What future for the British Political Cartoon? *Journalism Studies* 2/3: 333–55.

Ventola, E. (1999) Semiotic spanning at conferences; cohesion and coherence in and across conference papers and their discussions. In Bublizt, W., Lenk,

U. and Ventola, E. (eds) *Coherence in Spoken and Written Discourse. How to Create It and How to Transcribe It.* Amsterdam: Benjamins, 101–25.

Ventola, E., Charles, C. and Kaltenbacher, M. (2004) *Perspectives on Multimodality.* Amsterdam: Benjamins.

Ward, L. (2001. War of words. Labour unveils new slogan. *The Guardian,* 1 June 2001.

Werner, W. (2004). On political cartoons and social studies textbooks: visual analogies, intertextuality and cultural memory. *Canadian Social Studies,* 38/ 2. Retrieved on 10 October 2005 from www.quasar.ualberta.ca/css*Perspectives on Multimodality.* Amsterdam: Benjamins.

Index of names

Index of subjects

www.ingramcontent.com/pod-product-compliance
Lightning Source LLC
LaVergne TN
LVHW010443080826
844660LV00026B/1204

* 9 7 8 1 8 4 5 5 3 9 1 1 5 *